Baby Blues® **11** Scrapbook

If I'm a Stay-At-Home Mom, Why Am I Always in the Car?

By
Rick Kirkman & Jerry Scott

Other Baby Blues® books from Andrews McMeel Publishing

Guess Who Didn't Take a Nap?
I Thought Labor Ended When the Baby Was Born
We Are Experiencing Parental Difficulties. . . Please Stand By
Night of the Living Dad
I Saw Elvis in My Ultrasound
One More and We're Outnumbered!
Check, Please. . .
threats, bribes & videotape

Treasury

The Super-Absorbent Biodegradable Family-Size Baby Blues®

Baby Blues® 11 Scrapbook

If I'm a Stay-At-Home Mom, Why Am I Always in the Car?

By
Rick Kirkman & Jerry Scott

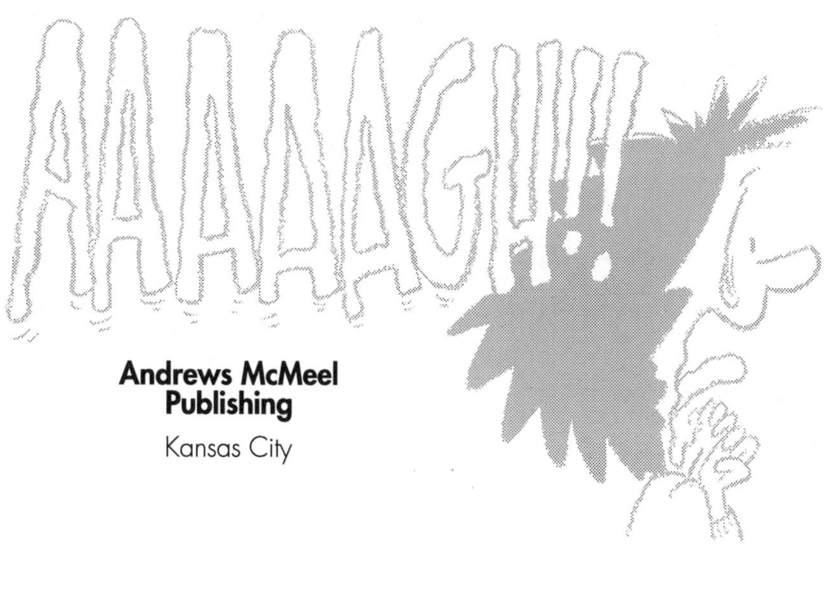
AAAAGH!!

Andrews McMeel
Publishing

Kansas City

Baby Blues is syndicated internationally by King Features Syndicate, Inc. For information, write King Features Syndicate, Inc., 216 East 45th Street, New York, New York 10017.

www.andrewsmcmeel.com

99 00 01 02 03 BAH 10 9 8 7 6 5 4 3 2 1

ISBN: 0-8362-7845-3

Library of Congress Catalog Card Number: 98-88672

ATTENTION: SCHOOLS AND BUSINESSES

Andrews McMeel books are available at quantity discounts with bulk purchase for educational, business, or sales promotional use. For information, please write to: Special Sales Department, Andrews McMeel Publishing, 4520 Main Street, Kansas City, Missouri 64111.

To Kim with high-octane, no-lead love.

—J.S.

To Sukey: Mere thanks are not enough for your decision to stay at home—uh, in the van—er, on the road—with our children. Maybe a medal, a statue, a taxi license . . .

P.S. To all those parents out there (and you know who you are): *Buckle up those children!*

—R.K.

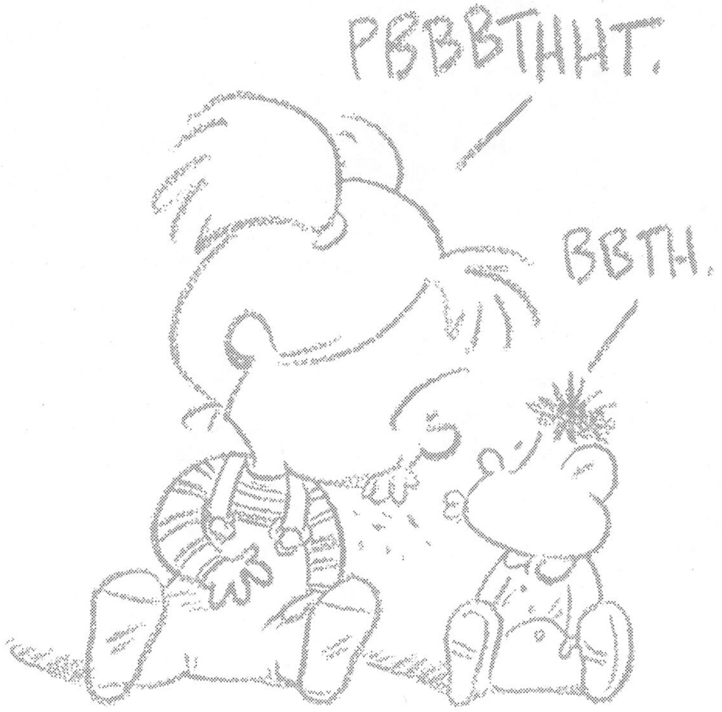
PBBBTHHT.
BBTH.

BABY BLUES®
BY
RICK KIRKMAN / JERRY SCOTT

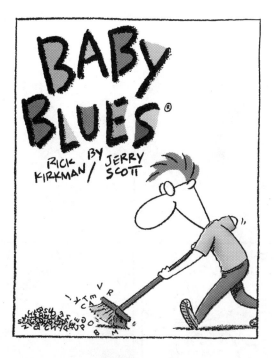

UMMMM... ALWAYS SAY "PLEASE" AND "THANK YOU"...
...WASH YOUR HANDS AFTER USING THE BATHROOM... LOOK BOTH WAYS BEFORE YOU CROSS... LISTEN TO THE TEACHER...
...BE NICE TO EVERY-ONE... NO ELBOWS ON THE TABLE... BRUSH YOUR TEETH AFTER EVERY MEAL... DON'T SPIT... KEEP YOUR HANDS TO YOURSELF... WAIT YOUR TURN... DON'T TALK WITH YOUR MOUTH FULL... KEEP YOUR FINGERS OUT OF YOUR NOSE...
I GUESS THAT'S ABOUT IT.
THAT'S NICE, SWEETHEART...
...BUT "WHADDA YA' KNOW?" IS MORE OF A GREETING THAN A REAL QUESTION.
OH.
KIRKMAN & SCOTT

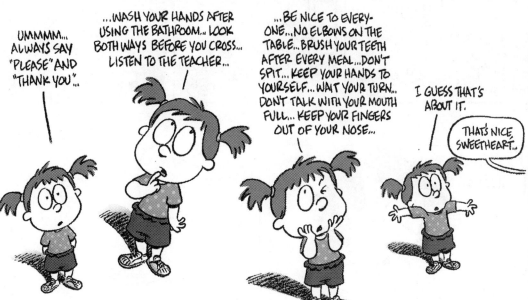

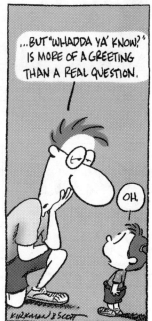

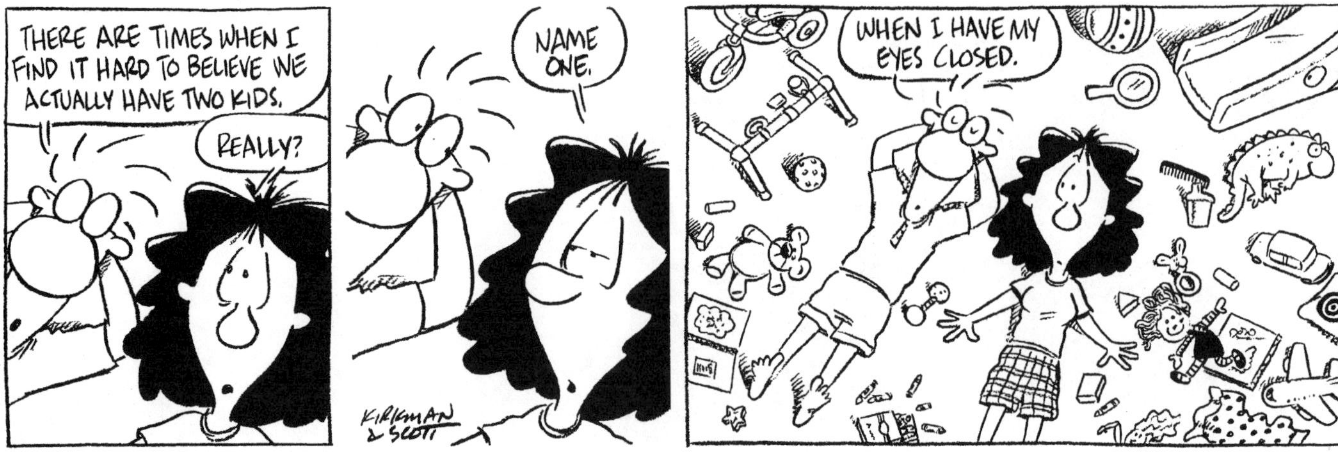
THERE ARE TIMES WHEN I FIND IT HARD TO BELIEVE WE ACTUALLY HAVE TWO KIDS.
REALLY?
NAME ONE.
KIRKMAN & SCOTT
WHEN I HAVE MY EYES CLOSED.

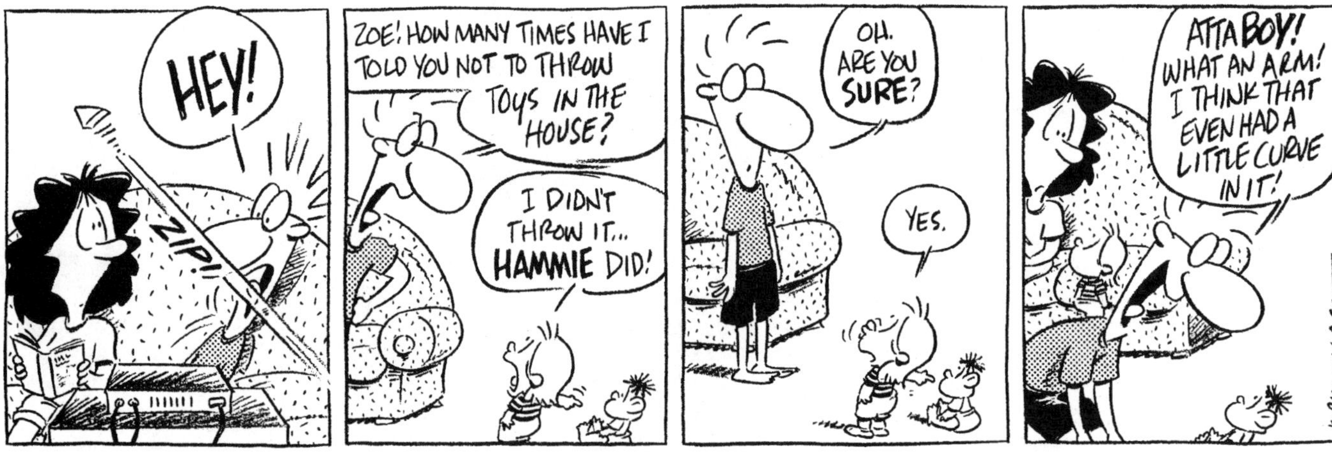
HEY!
ZIP!
ZOE! HOW MANY TIMES HAVE I TOLD YOU NOT TO THROW
TOYS IN THE HOUSE?
I DIDN'T THROW IT... HAMMIE DID!
OH. ARE YOU SURE?
YES.
ATTA BOY! WHAT AN ARM! I THINK THAT EVEN HAD A LITTLE CURVE IN IT!
KIRKMAN & SCOTT

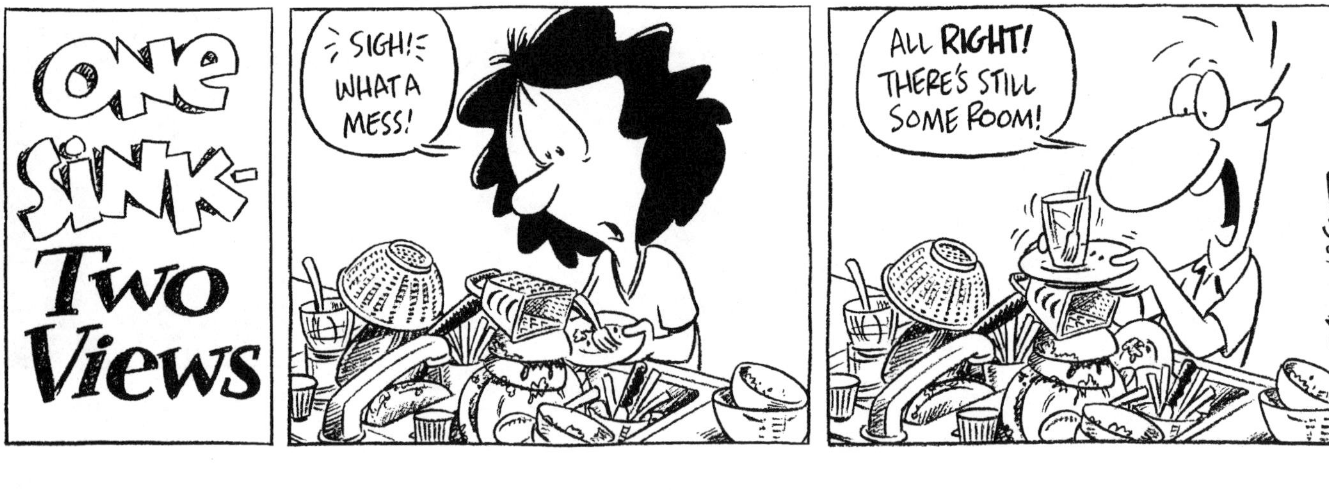
ONE SINK-TWO VIEWS
SIGH! WHAT A MESS!
ALL RIGHT! THERE'S STILL SOME ROOM!
KIRKMAN & SCOTT

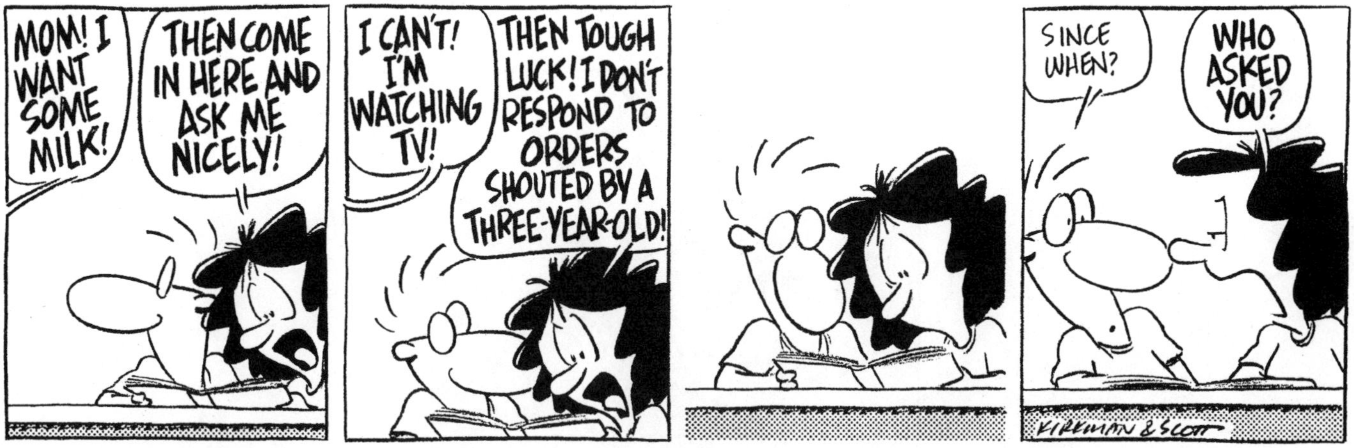
MOM! I WANT SOME MILK!
THEN COME IN HERE AND ASK ME NICELY!
I CAN'T! I'M WATCHING TV!
THEN TOUGH LUCK! I DON'T RESPOND TO ORDERS SHOUTED BY A THREE-YEAR-OLD!
SINCE WHEN?
WHO ASKED YOU?
KIRKMAN & SCOTT

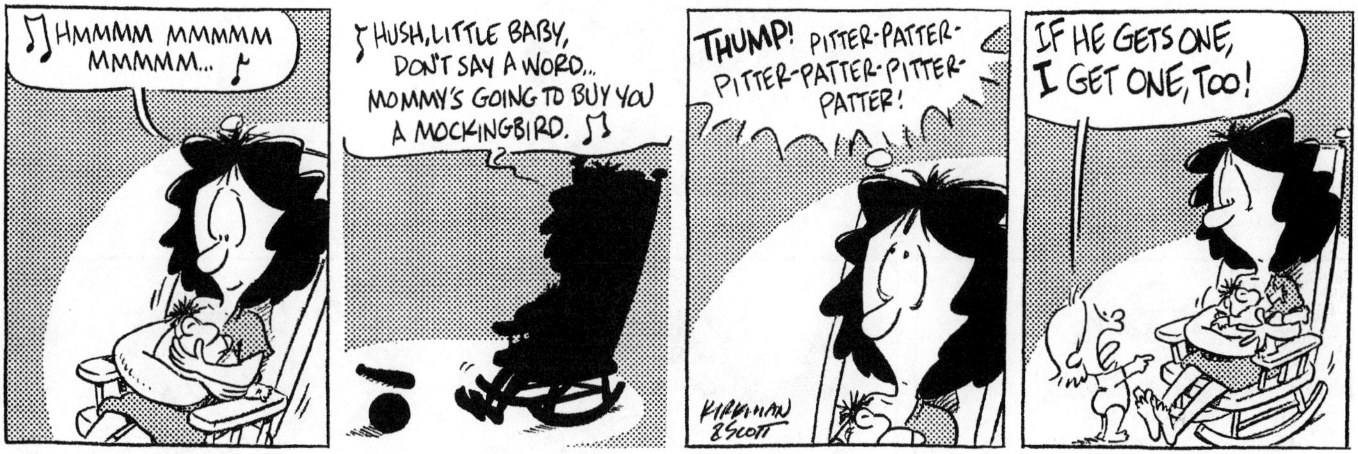
HMMMM MMMMM MMMMM...
HUSH, LITTLE BABY, DON'T SAY A WORD... MOMMY'S GOING TO BUY YOU A MOCKINGBIRD.
THUMP! PITTER-PATTER-PITTER-PATTER-PITTER-PATTER!
KIRKMAN & SCOTT
IF HE GETS ONE, I GET ONE, TOO!

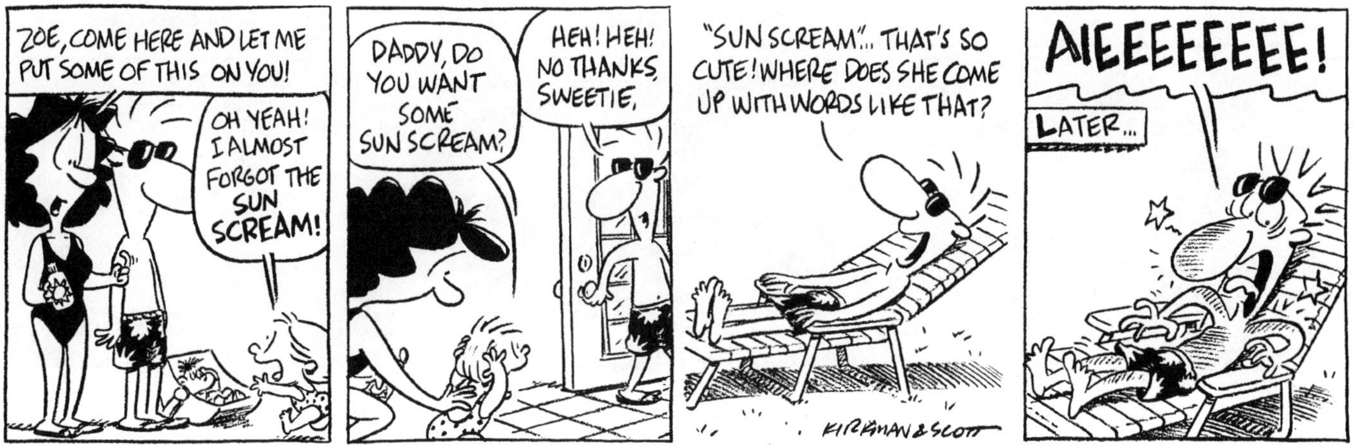
ZOE, COME HERE AND LET ME PUT SOME OF THIS ON YOU!
OH YEAH! I ALMOST FORGOT THE SUN SCREAM!
DADDY, DO YOU WANT SOME SUN SCREAM?
HEH! HEH! NO THANKS, SWEETIE.
"SUN SCREAM"... THAT'S SO CUTE! WHERE DOES SHE COME UP WITH WORDS LIKE THAT?
KIRKMAN & SCOTT
AIEEEEEEEE!
LATER...

BABY BLUES®
BY RICK KIRKMAN / JERRY SCOTT

IN YOU GO, LITTLE BUDDY!
HEY...
...CUT IT OUT! BEND!
GRUNT! YOU LITTLE OOF! DICKENS!
RELAX YOUR MUSCLES SO I CAN UNNH!
GET YOU IN THE HIGH-CHAIR!
KIRKMAN & SCOTT
THERE! THAT'S B—
NOT THAT RELAXED!!!
Y'KNOW, SOME PEOPLE HAVE TO EAT DINNER WITHOUT ENTERTAINMENT LIKE THIS.
TOO BAD.

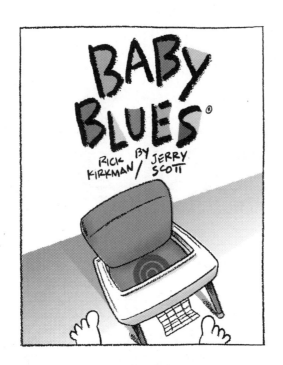

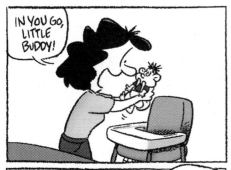

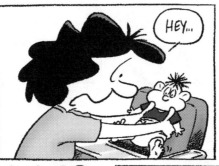

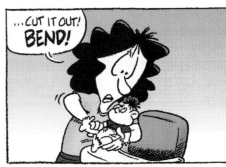

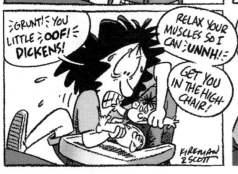

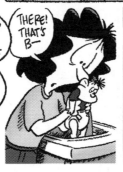

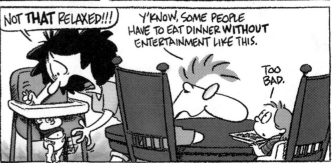

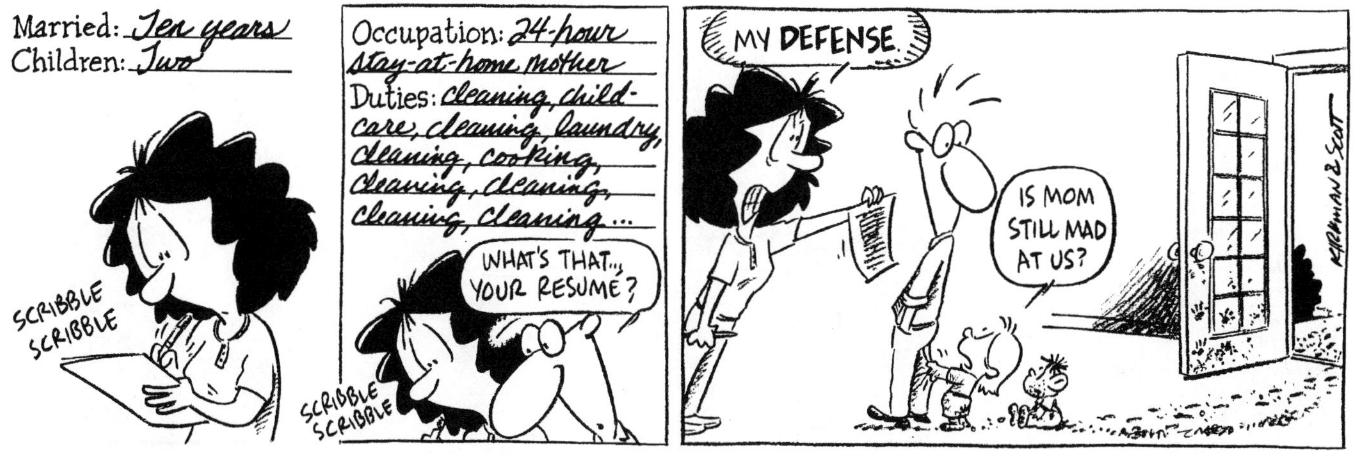

Married: Ten years
Children: Two
SCRIBBLE SCRIBBLE
Occupation: 24-hour stay-at-home mother
Duties: cleaning, child-care, cleaning, laundry, cleaning, cooking, cleaning, cleaning, cleaning, cleaning...
WHAT'S THAT..., YOUR RESUME?
SCRIBBLE SCRIBBLE
MY DEFENSE.
IS MOM STILL MAD AT US?
KIRKMAN & SCOTT

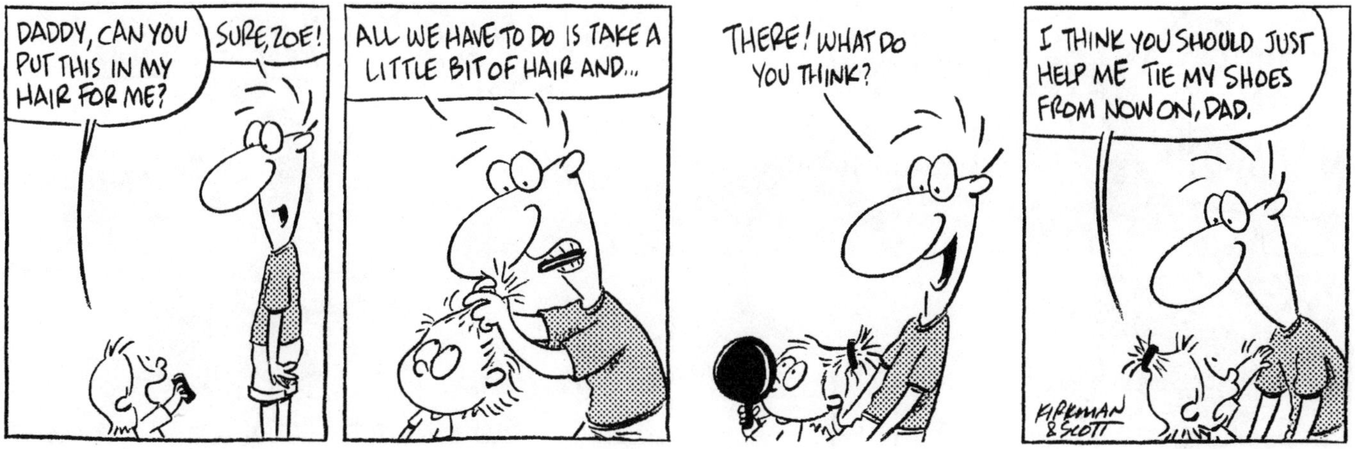

DADDY, CAN YOU PUT THIS IN MY HAIR FOR ME?
SURE, ZOE!
ALL WE HAVE TO DO IS TAKE A LITTLE BIT OF HAIR AND...
THERE! WHAT DO YOU THINK?
I THINK YOU SHOULD JUST HELP ME TIE MY SHOES FROM NOW ON, DAD.
KIRKMAN & SCOTT

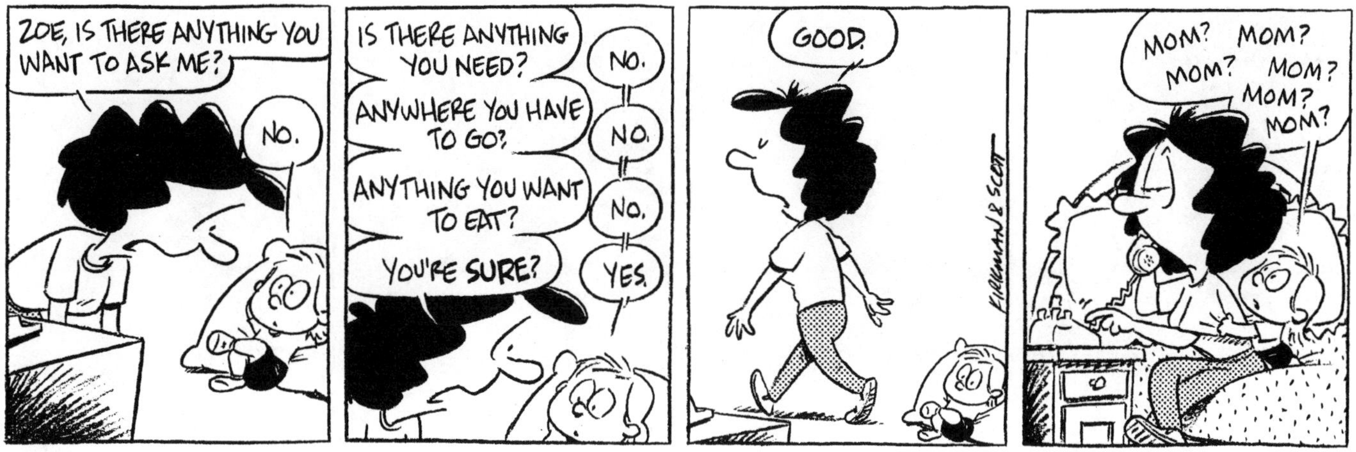

ZOE, IS THERE ANYTHING YOU WANT TO ASK ME?
NO.
IS THERE ANYTHING YOU NEED?
NO.
ANYWHERE YOU HAVE TO GO?
NO.
ANYTHING YOU WANT TO EAT?
NO.
YOU'RE SURE?
YES.
GOOD.
KIRKMAN & SCOTT
MOM? MOM? MOM? MOM? MOM? MOM?

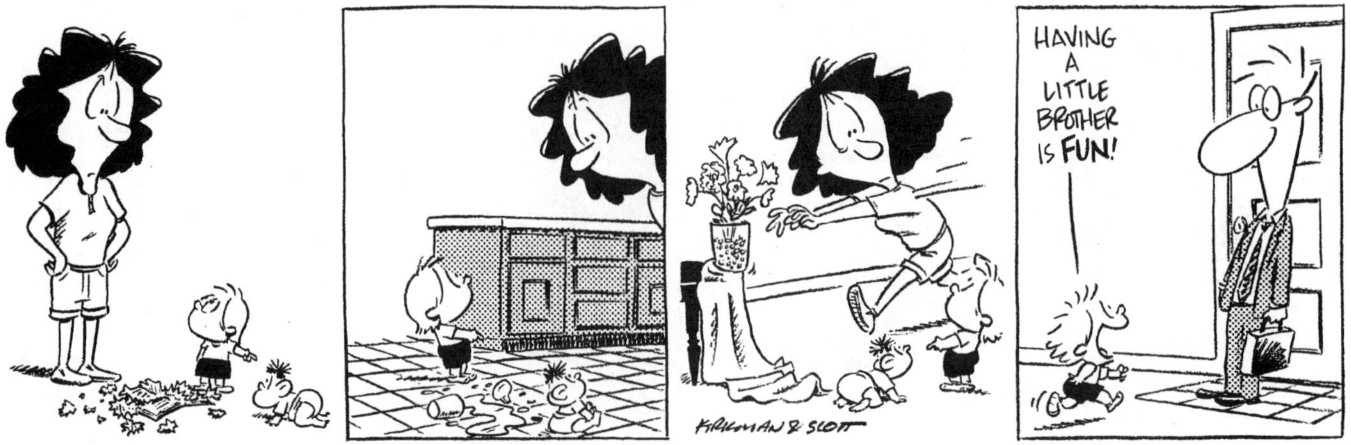
HAVING A LITTLE BROTHER IS FUN!
KIRKMAN & SCOTT

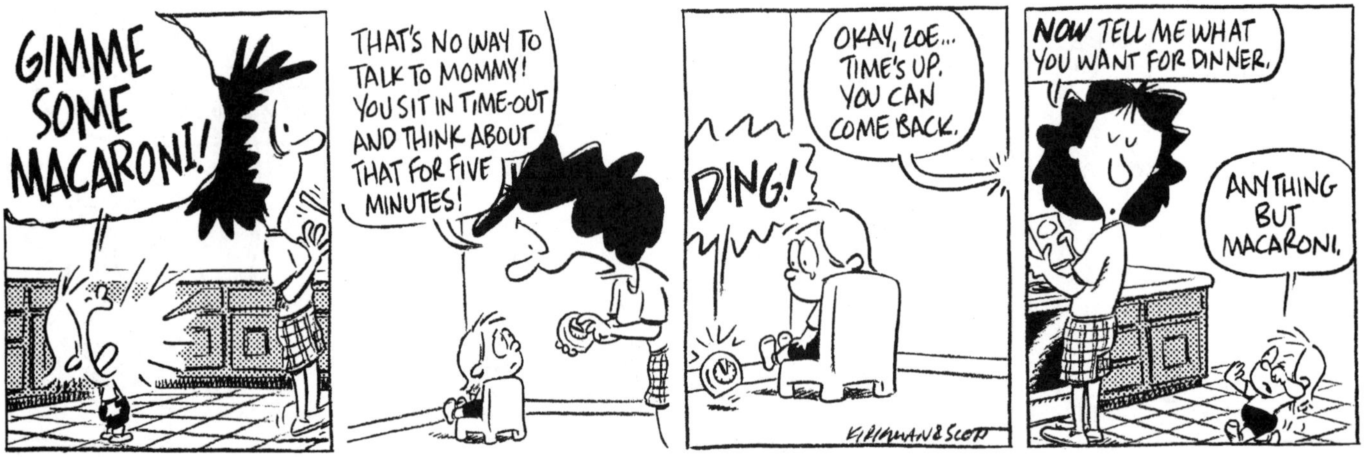
GIMME SOME MACARONI!
THAT'S NO WAY TO TALK TO MOMMY! YOU SIT IN TIME-OUT AND THINK ABOUT THAT FOR FIVE MINUTES!
DING!
OKAY, ZOE... TIME'S UP. YOU CAN COME BACK.
NOW TELL ME WHAT YOU WANT FOR DINNER.
ANYTHING BUT MACARONI.
KIRKMAN & SCOTT

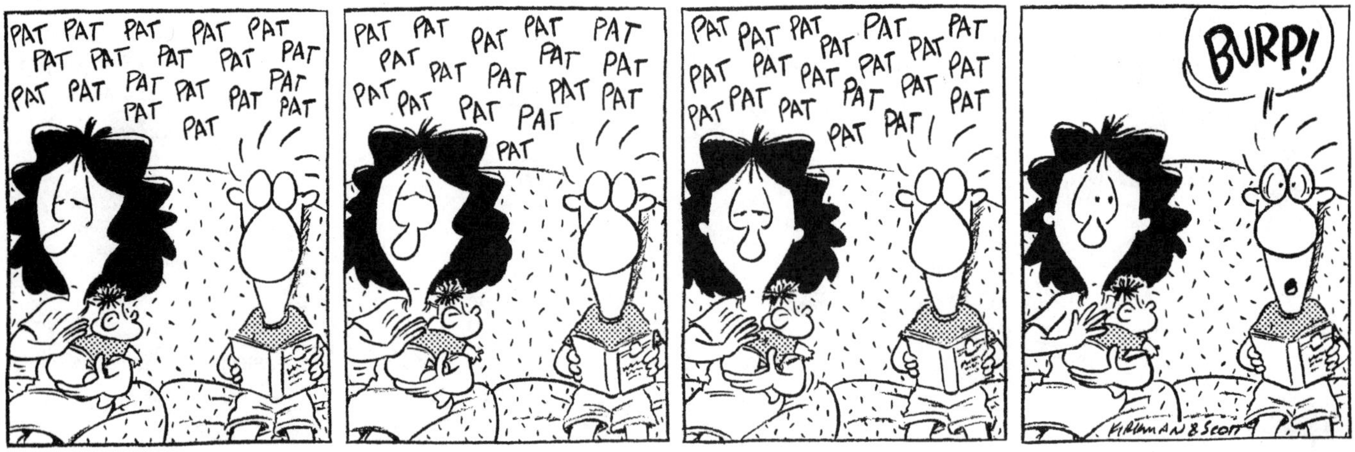
PAT PAT PAT PAT PAT PAT PAT PAT PAT PAT PAT PAT PAT PAT PAT PAT PAT PAT PAT PAT PAT
PAT PAT PAT PAT PAT PAT PAT PAT PAT PAT PAT PAT PAT PAT PAT PAT PAT
PAT PAT PAT PAT PAT PAT PAT PAT PAT PAT PAT PAT PAT PAT PAT PAT PAT PAT PAT PAT PAT PAT PAT PAT
BURP!
KIRKMAN & SCOTT

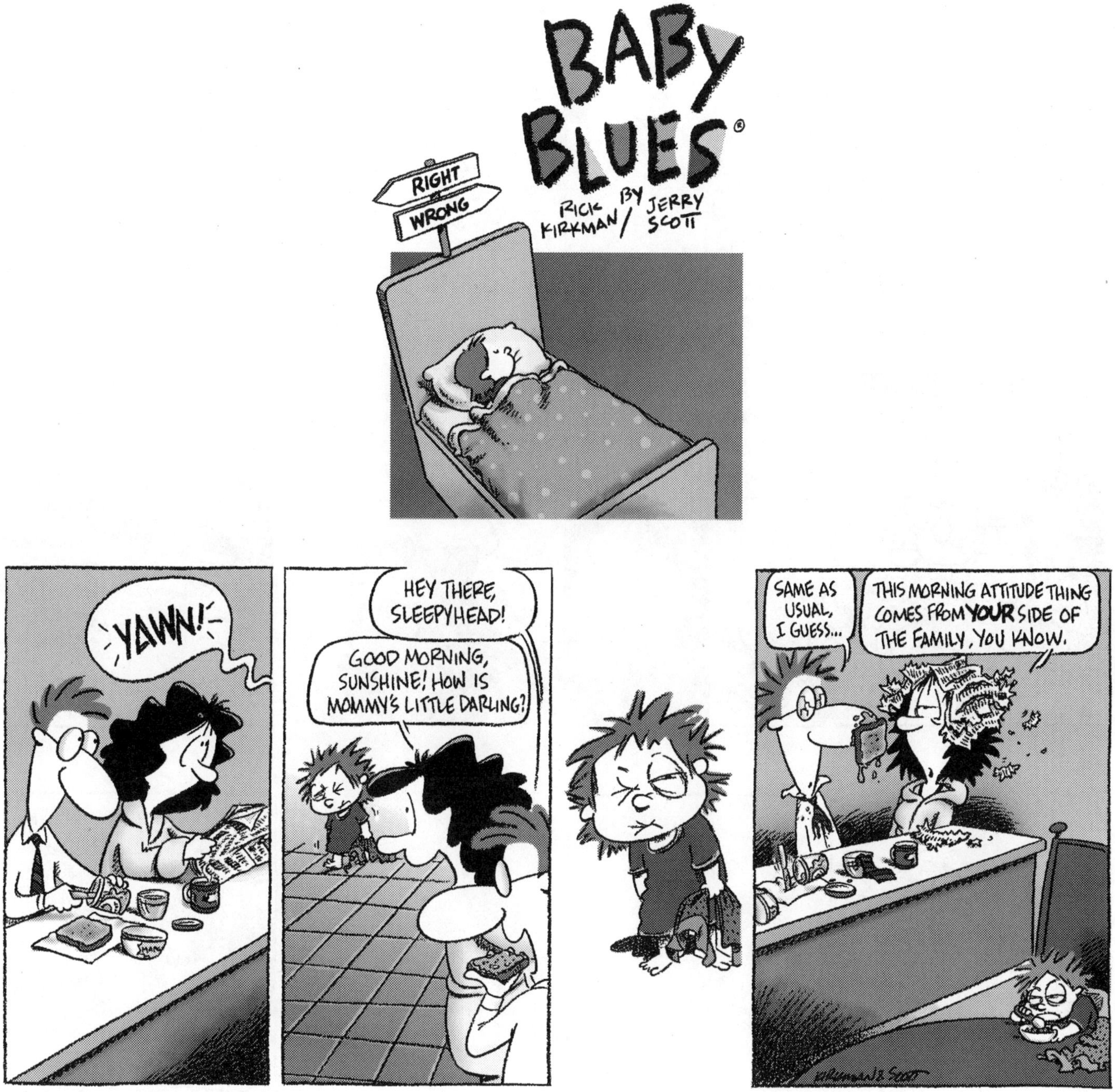
BABY BLUES®
RIGHT
WRONG
BY RICK KIRKMAN / JERRY SCOTT
YAWN!
HEY THERE, SLEEPYHEAD!
GOOD MORNING, SUNSHINE! HOW IS MOMMY'S LITTLE DARLING?
SAME AS USUAL, I GUESS...
THIS MORNING ATTITUDE THING COMES FROM **YOUR** SIDE OF THE FAMILY, YOU KNOW.
KIRKMAN & SCOTT

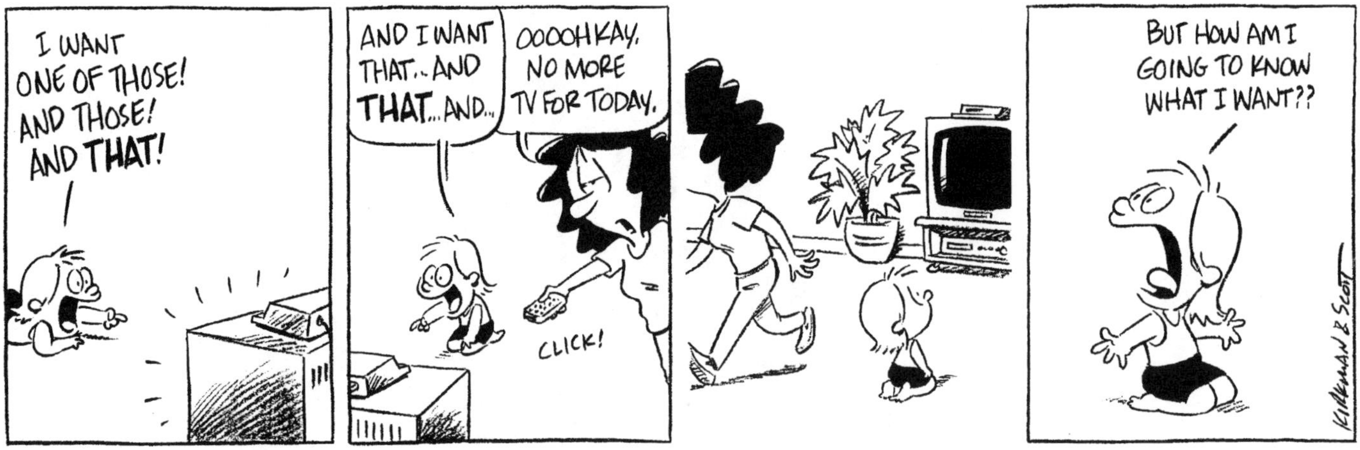
I WANT ONE OF THOSE! AND THOSE! AND THAT!
AND I WANT THAT... AND THAT... AND...
OOOOHKAY. NO MORE TV FOR TODAY.
CLICK!
BUT HOW AM I GOING TO KNOW WHAT I WANT??
KIRKMAN & SCOTT

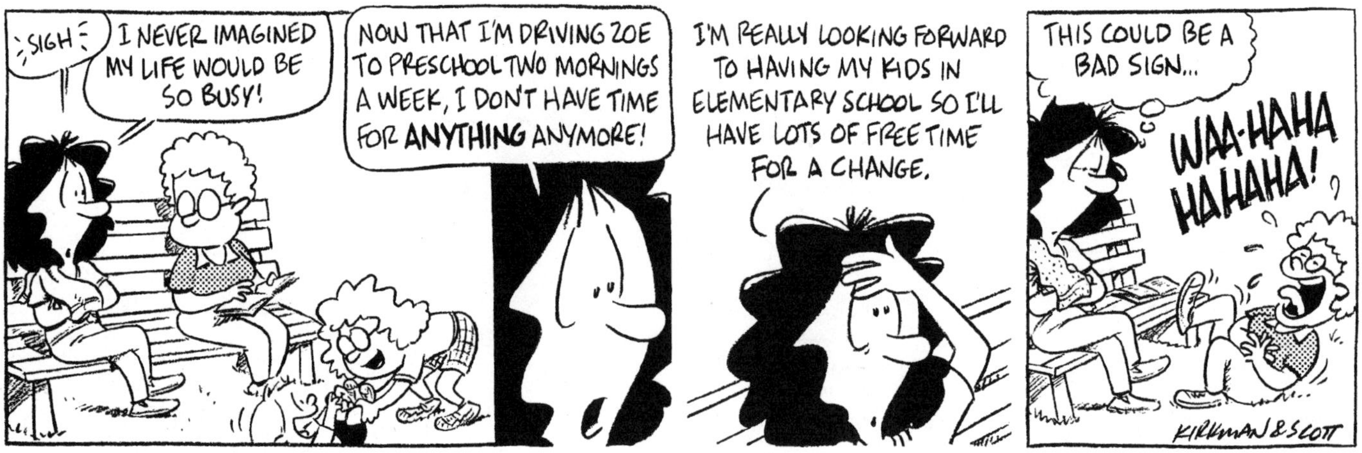
SIGH
I NEVER IMAGINED MY LIFE WOULD BE SO BUSY!
NOW THAT I'M DRIVING ZOE TO PRESCHOOL TWO MORNINGS A WEEK, I DON'T HAVE TIME FOR ANYTHING ANYMORE!
I'M REALLY LOOKING FORWARD TO HAVING MY KIDS IN ELEMENTARY SCHOOL SO I'LL HAVE LOTS OF FREE TIME FOR A CHANGE.
THIS COULD BE A BAD SIGN...
WAA-HAHA HAHAHA!
KIRKMAN & SCOTT

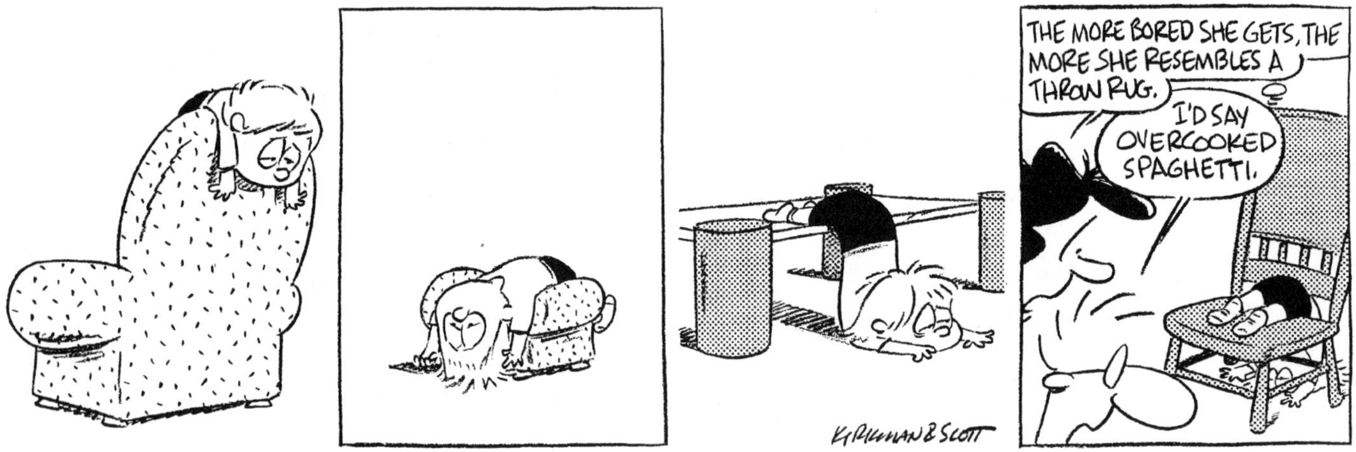
KIRKMAN & SCOTT
THE MORE BORED SHE GETS, THE MORE SHE RESEMBLES A THROW RUG.
I'D SAY OVERCOOKED SPAGHETTI.

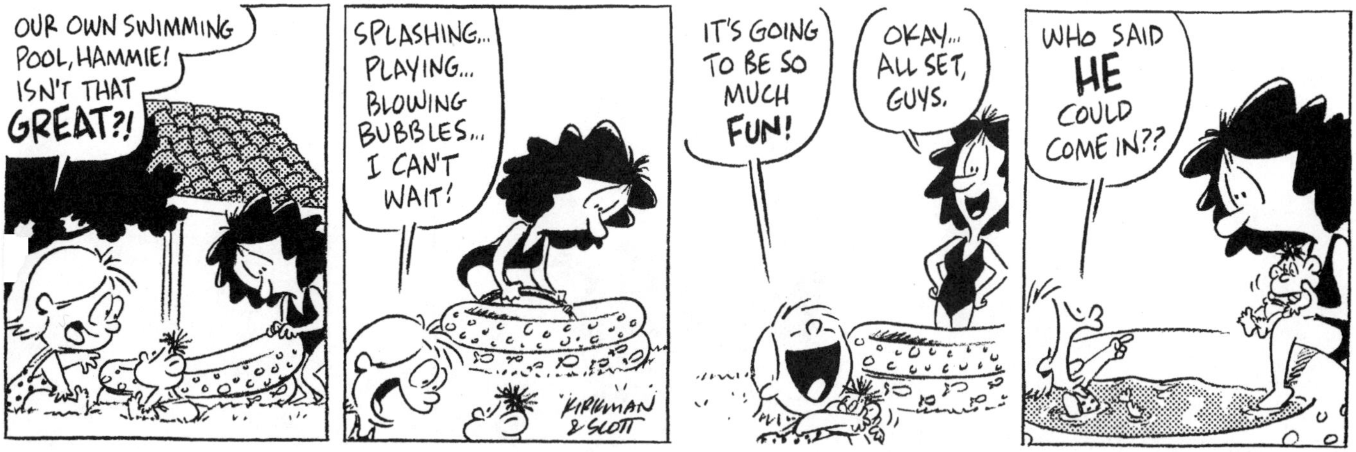
OUR OWN SWIMMING POOL, HAMMIE! ISN'T THAT GREAT?!
SPLASHING... PLAYING... BLOWING BUBBLES... I CAN'T WAIT!
KIRKMAN & SCOTT
IT'S GOING TO BE SO MUCH FUN!
OKAY... ALL SET, GUYS.
WHO SAID HE COULD COME IN??

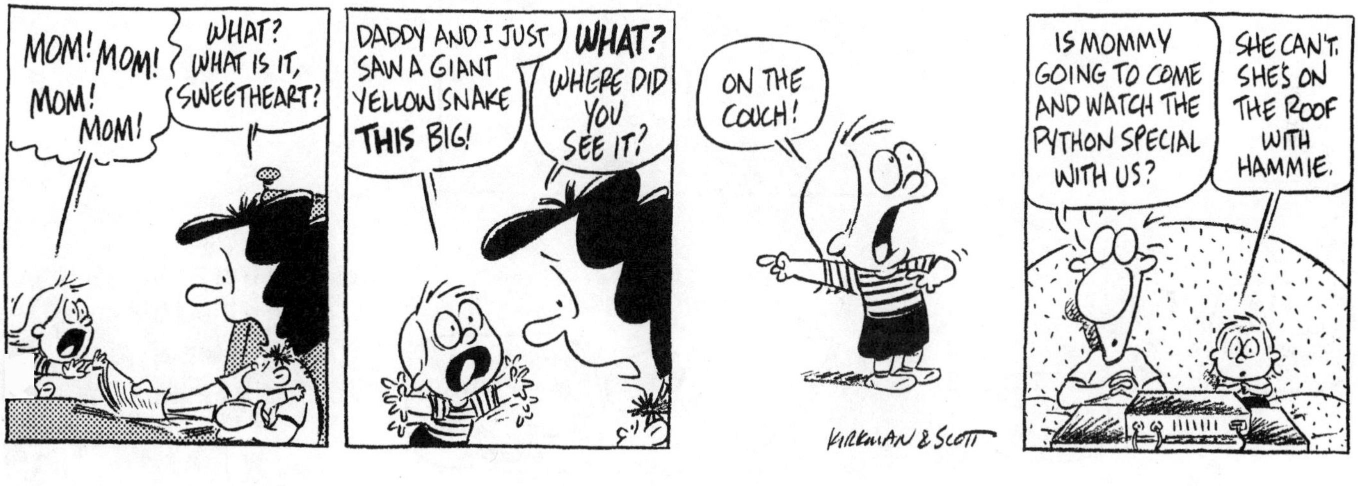
MOM! MOM! MOM! MOM!
WHAT? WHAT IS IT, SWEETHEART?
DADDY AND I JUST SAW A GIANT YELLOW SNAKE THIS BIG!
WHAT? WHERE DID YOU SEE IT?
ON THE COUCH!
KIRKMAN & SCOTT
IS MOMMY GOING TO COME AND WATCH THE PYTHON SPECIAL WITH US?
SHE CAN'T. SHE'S ON THE ROOF WITH HAMMIE.

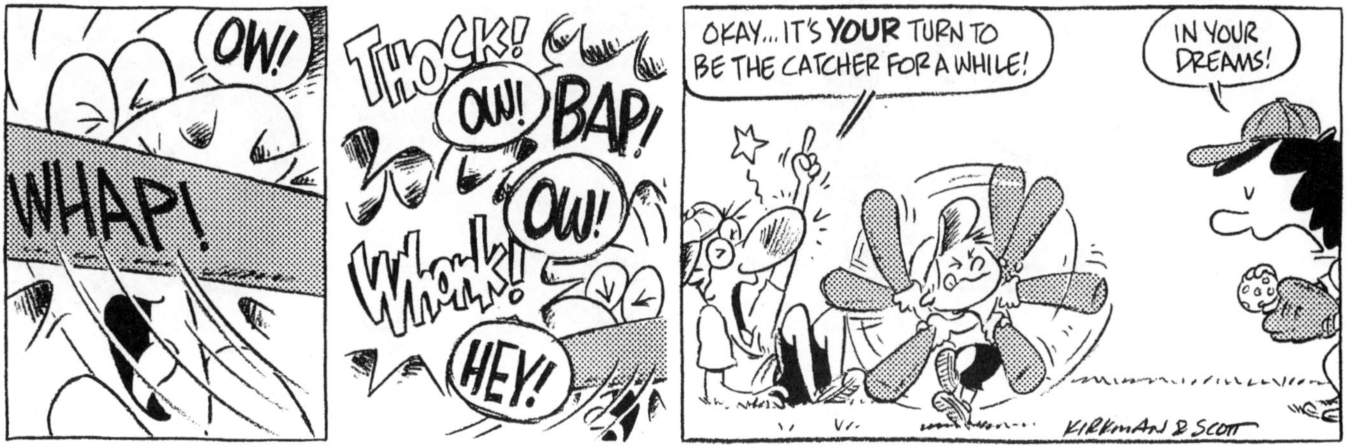
OW!
WHAP!
THOCK!
OW!
BAP!
OW!
Whork!
HEY!
OKAY... IT'S YOUR TURN TO BE THE CATCHER FOR A WHILE!
IN YOUR DREAMS!
KIRKMAN & SCOTT

BABY BLUES®
BY RICK KIRKMAN / JERRY SCOTT

OKAY, I'M GOING TO WASH HAMMIE'S HAIR FIRST.
HE'S GOING TO CRY.
YEP! BETTER GET READY! HE'S GOING TO START HOLLERING ANY MINUTE.
OOOH! THIS IS THE WORST PART! WATCH OUT... HERE HE GOES, THE **BIG BABY**!
THERE YOU GO! ALL DONE! NOW IT'S ZOE'S TURN.
WAAAA AAAAAA!
KIRKMAN & SCOTT

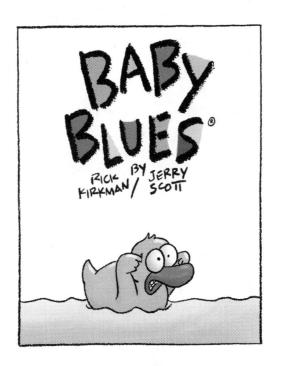

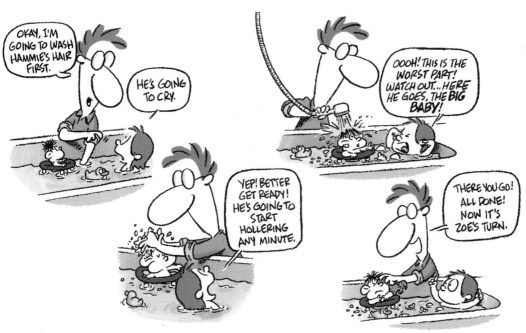

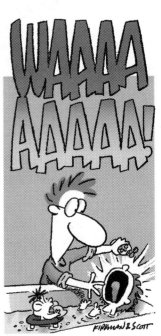

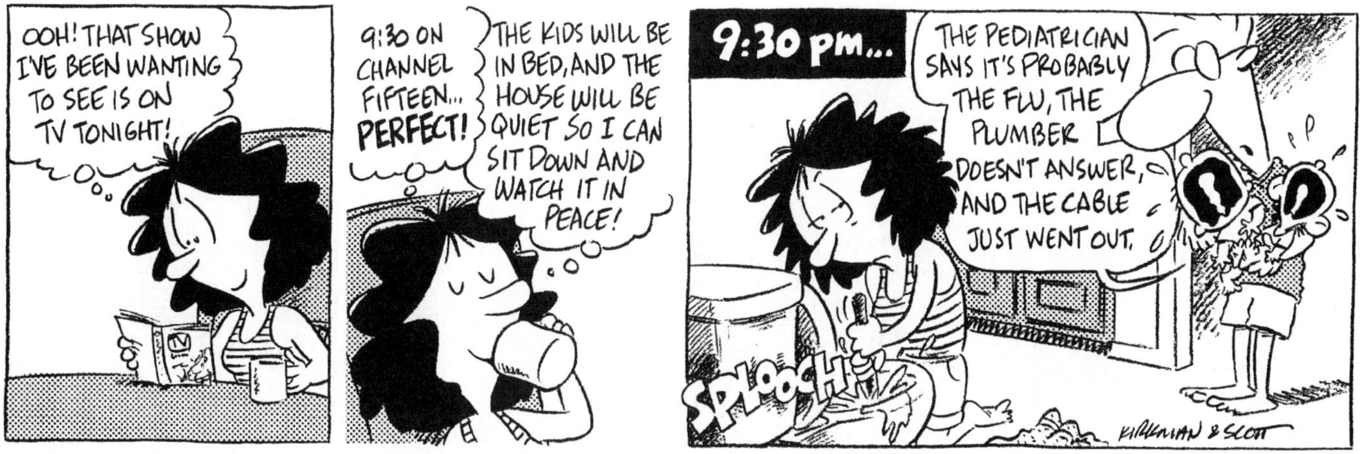
OOH! THAT SHOW I'VE BEEN WANTING TO SEE IS ON TV TONIGHT!
9:30 ON CHANNEL FIFTEEN... PERFECT!
THE KIDS WILL BE IN BED, AND THE HOUSE WILL BE QUIET SO I CAN SIT DOWN AND WATCH IT IN PEACE!
9:30 pm...
THE PEDIATRICIAN SAYS IT'S PROBABLY THE FLU, THE PLUMBER DOESN'T ANSWER, AND THE CABLE JUST WENT OUT.
SPLOOCH
KIRKMAN & SCOTT

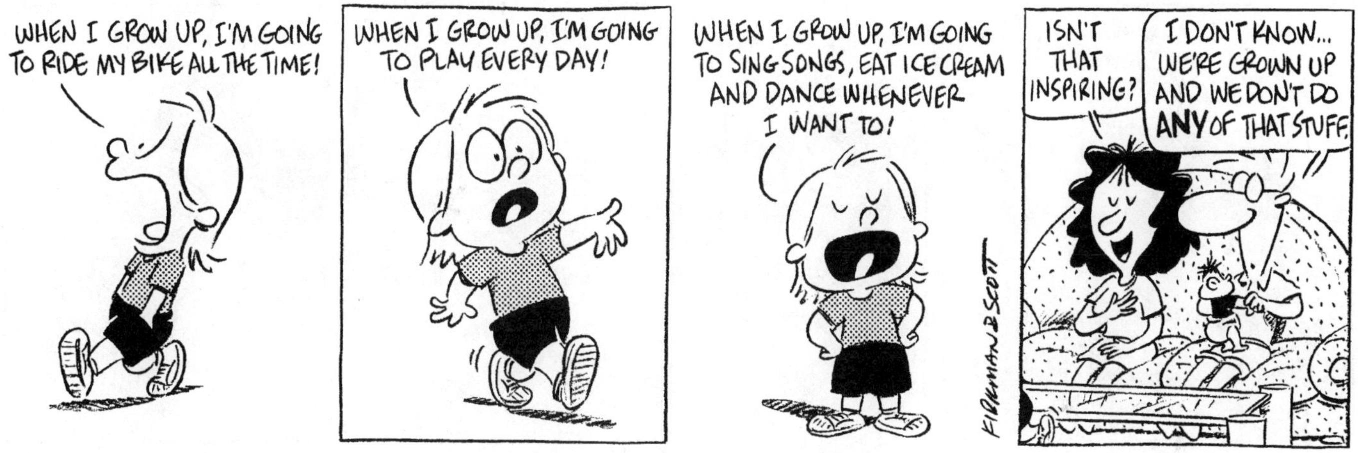
WHEN I GROW UP, I'M GOING TO RIDE MY BIKE ALL THE TIME!
WHEN I GROW UP, I'M GOING TO PLAY EVERY DAY!
WHEN I GROW UP, I'M GOING TO SING SONGS, EAT ICE CREAM AND DANCE WHENEVER I WANT TO!
KIRKMAN & SCOTT
ISN'T THAT INSPIRING?
I DON'T KNOW... WE'RE GROWN UP AND WE DON'T DO ANY OF THAT STUFF.

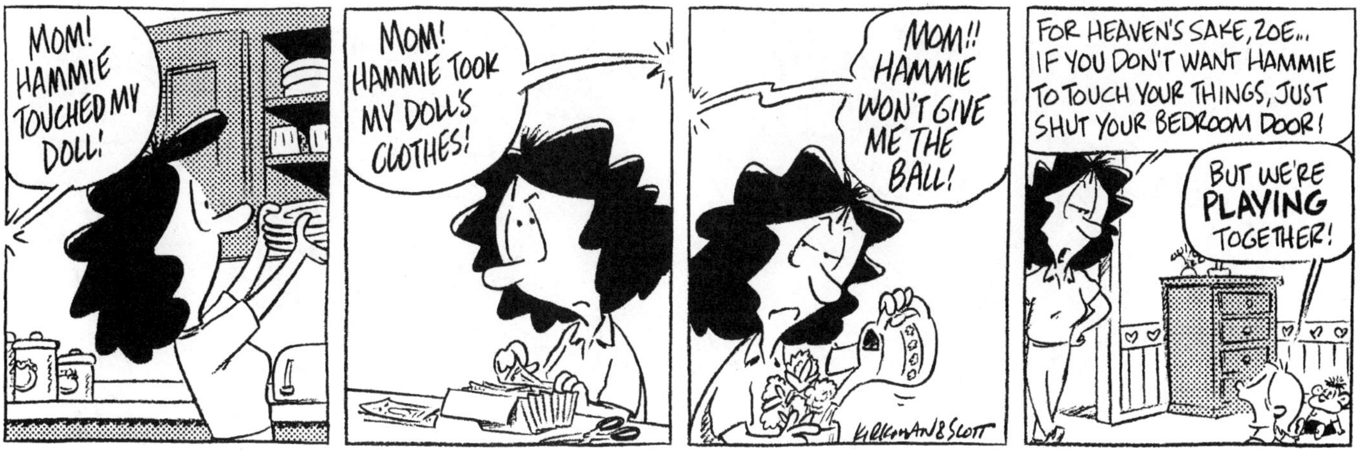
MOM! HAMMIE TOUCHED MY DOLL!
MOM! HAMMIE TOOK MY DOLL'S CLOTHES!
MOM!! HAMMIE WON'T GIVE ME THE BALL!
KIRKMAN & SCOTT
FOR HEAVEN'S SAKE, ZOE... IF YOU DON'T WANT HAMMIE TO TOUCH YOUR THINGS, JUST SHUT YOUR BEDROOM DOOR!
BUT WE'RE PLAYING TOGETHER!

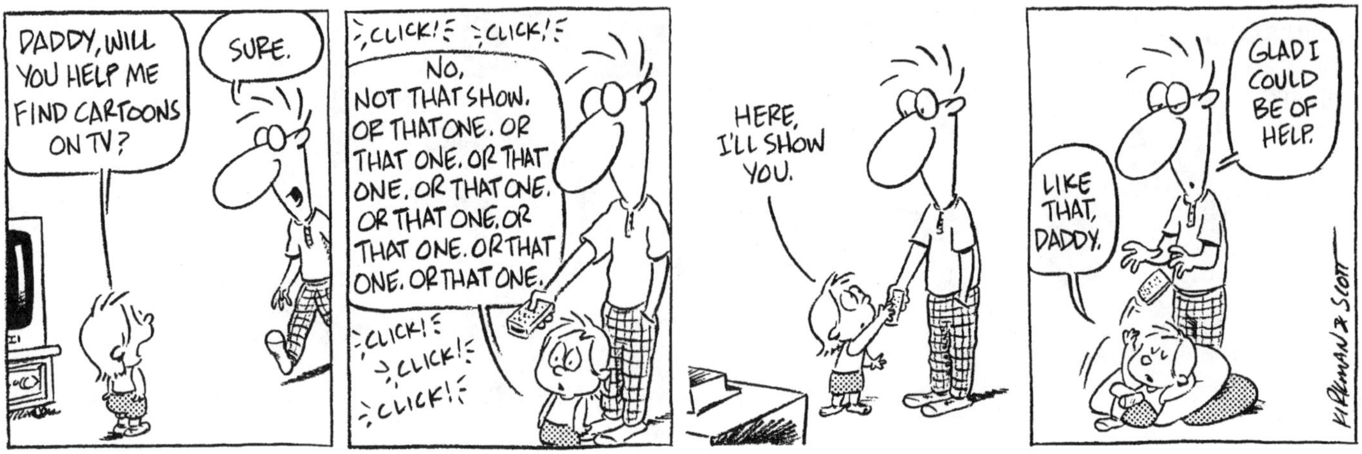
DADDY, WILL YOU HELP ME FIND CARTOONS ON TV?
SURE.
CLICK! CLICK!
NO, NOT THAT SHOW. OR THAT ONE. OR THAT ONE. OR THAT ONE. OR THAT ONE. OR THAT ONE. OR THAT ONE. OR THAT ONE. OR THAT ONE.
CLICK! CLICK! CLICK!
HERE, I'LL SHOW YOU.
GLAD I COULD BE OF HELP.
LIKE THAT, DADDY.
KIRKMAN & SCOTT

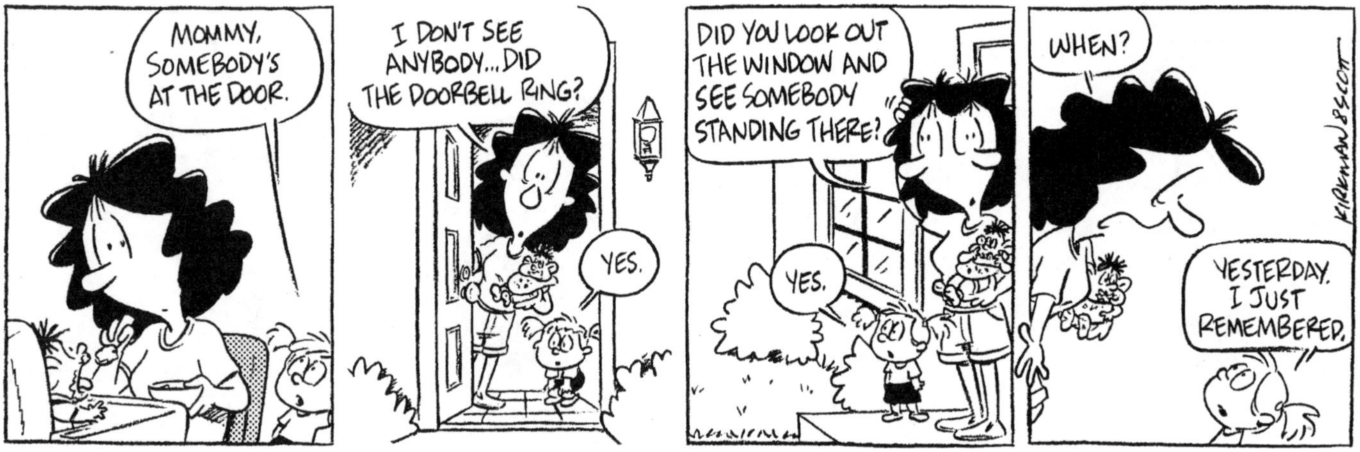
MOMMY, SOMEBODY'S AT THE DOOR.
I DON'T SEE ANYBODY... DID THE DOORBELL RING?
YES.
DID YOU LOOK OUT THE WINDOW AND SEE SOMEBODY STANDING THERE?
YES.
WHEN?
YESTERDAY. I JUST REMEMBERED.
KIRKMAN & SCOTT

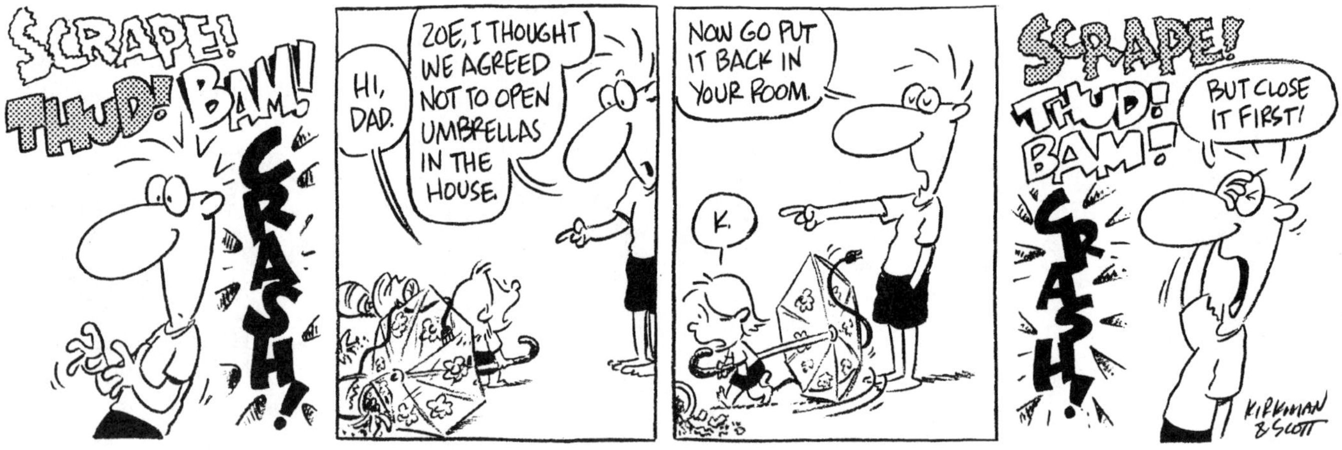
SCRAPE!
THUD!
BAM!
CRASH!
HI, DAD.
ZOE, I THOUGHT WE AGREED NOT TO OPEN UMBRELLAS IN THE HOUSE.
NOW GO PUT IT BACK IN YOUR ROOM.
K.
SCRAPE!
THUD!
BAM!
CRASH!
BUT CLOSE IT FIRST!
KIRKMAN & SCOTT

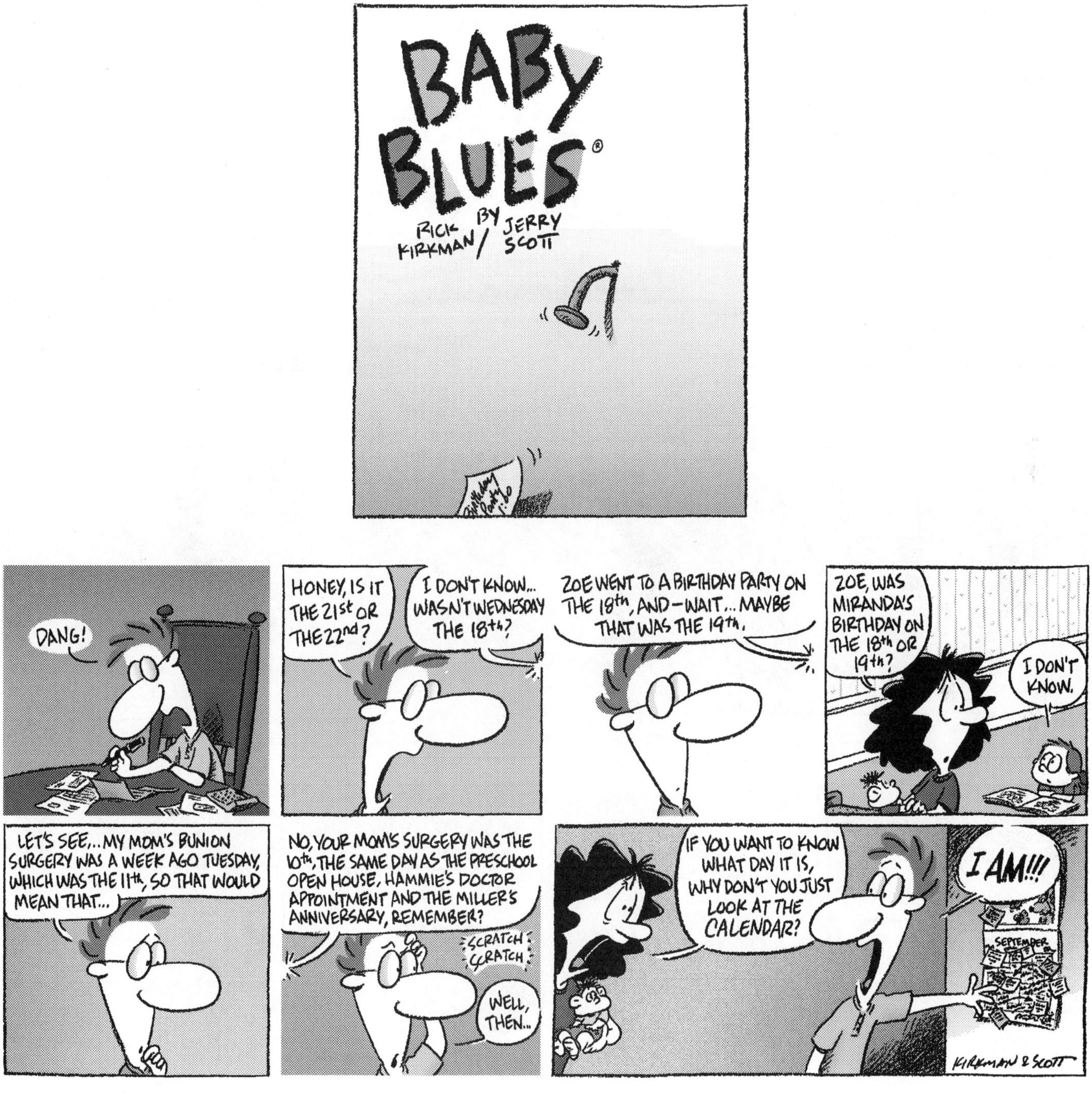
BABY BLUES®
BY RICK KIRKMAN / JERRY SCOTT
DANG!
HONEY, IS IT THE 21st OR THE 22nd?
I DON'T KNOW... WASN'T WEDNESDAY THE 18th?
ZOE WENT TO A BIRTHDAY PARTY ON THE 18th, AND—WAIT... MAYBE THAT WAS THE 19th.
ZOE, WAS MIRANDA'S BIRTHDAY ON THE 18th OR 19th?
I DON'T KNOW.
LET'S SEE,.. MY MOM'S BUNION SURGERY WAS A WEEK AGO TUESDAY, WHICH WAS THE 11th, SO THAT WOULD MEAN THAT...
NO, YOUR MOM'S SURGERY WAS THE 10th, THE SAME DAY AS THE PRESCHOOL OPEN HOUSE, HAMMIE'S DOCTOR APPOINTMENT AND THE MILLER'S ANNIVERSARY, REMEMBER?
SCRATCH SCRATCH
WELL, THEN...
IF YOU WANT TO KNOW WHAT DAY IT IS, WHY DON'T YOU JUST LOOK AT THE CALENDAR?
I AM!!!
SEPTEMBER
KIRKMAN & SCOTT

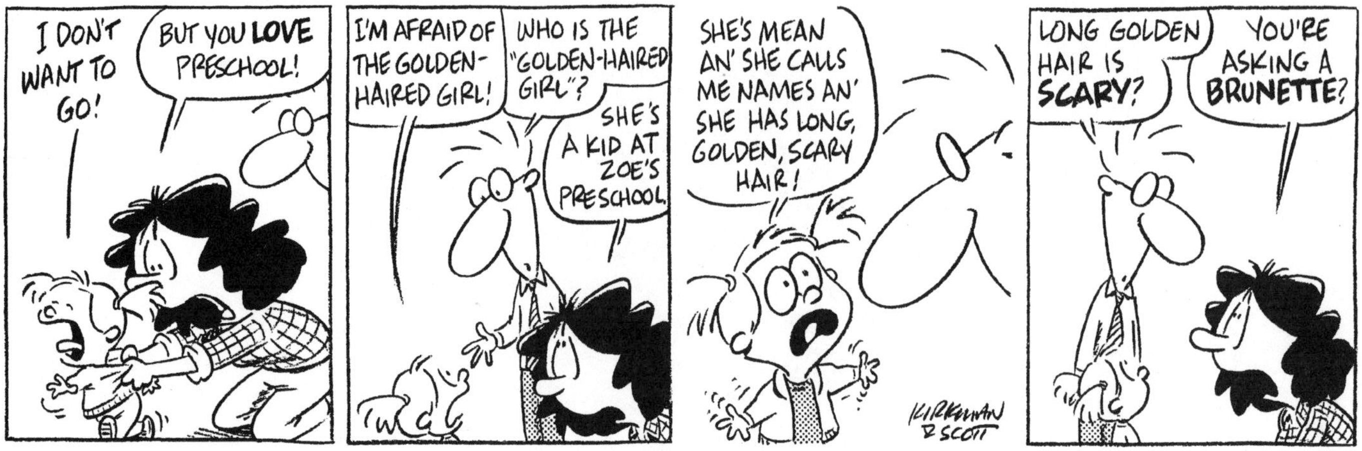
I DON'T WANT TO GO!
BUT YOU LOVE PRESCHOOL!
I'M AFRAID OF THE GOLDEN-HAIRED GIRL!
WHO IS THE "GOLDEN-HAIRED GIRL"?
SHE'S A KID AT ZOE'S PRESCHOOL.
SHE'S MEAN AN' SHE CALLS ME NAMES AN' SHE HAS LONG, GOLDEN, SCARY HAIR!
KIRKMAN & SCOTT
LONG GOLDEN HAIR IS SCARY?
YOU'RE ASKING A BRUNETTE?

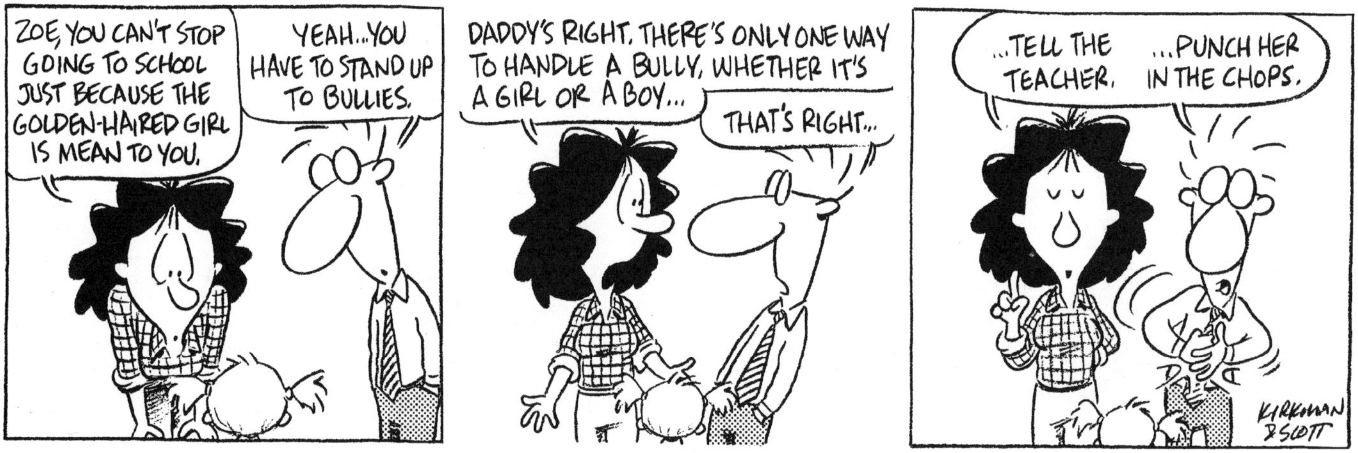
ZOE, YOU CAN'T STOP GOING TO SCHOOL JUST BECAUSE THE GOLDEN-HAIRED GIRL IS MEAN TO YOU.
YEAH...YOU HAVE TO STAND UP TO BULLIES.
DADDY'S RIGHT. THERE'S ONLY ONE WAY TO HANDLE A BULLY, WHETHER IT'S A GIRL OR A BOY...
THAT'S RIGHT...
...TELL THE TEACHER.
...PUNCH HER IN THE CHOPS.
KIRKMAN & SCOTT

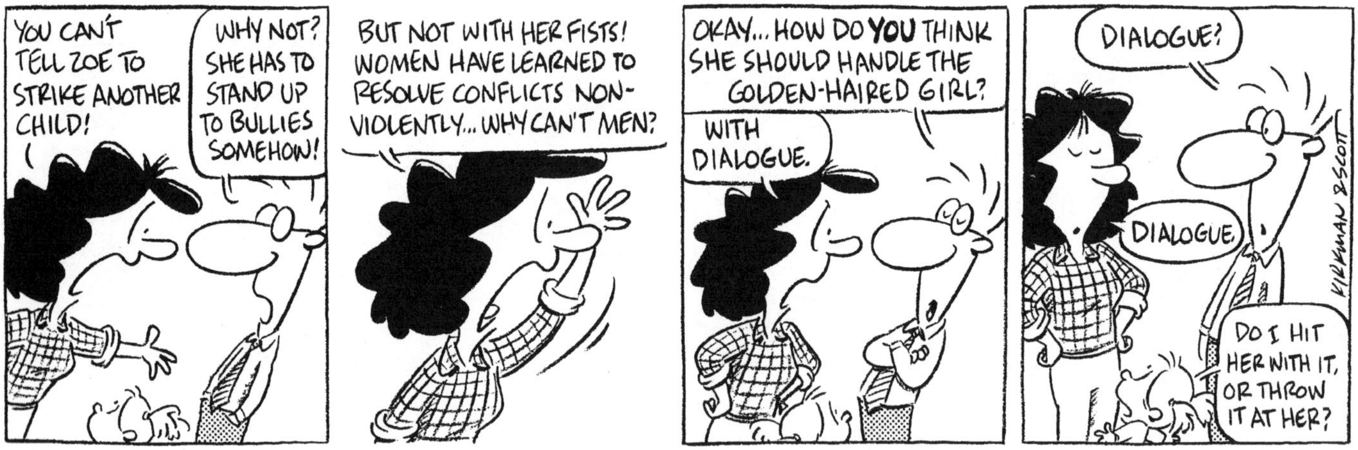
YOU CAN'T TELL ZOE TO STRIKE ANOTHER CHILD!
WHY NOT? SHE HAS TO STAND UP TO BULLIES SOMEHOW!
BUT NOT WITH HER FISTS! WOMEN HAVE LEARNED TO RESOLVE CONFLICTS NON-VIOLENTLY... WHY CAN'T MEN?
OKAY... HOW DO YOU THINK SHE SHOULD HANDLE THE GOLDEN-HAIRED GIRL?
WITH DIALOGUE.
DIALOGUE?
DIALOGUE.
KIRKMAN & SCOTT
DO I HIT HER WITH IT, OR THROW IT AT HER?

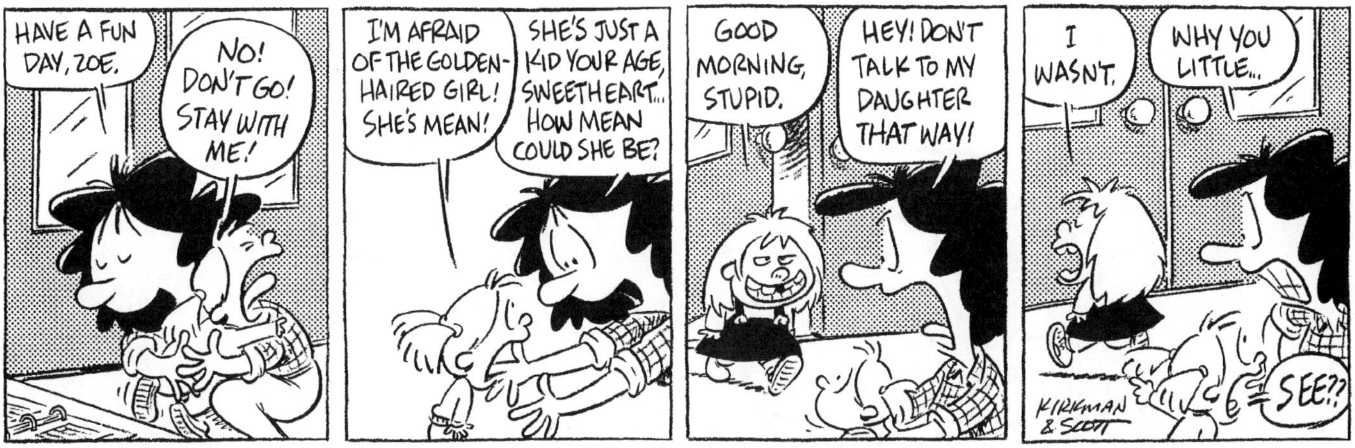
HAVE A FUN DAY, ZOE.
NO! DON'T GO! STAY WITH ME!
I'M AFRAID OF THE GOLDEN-HAIRED GIRL! SHE'S MEAN!
SHE'S JUST A KID YOUR AGE, SWEETHEART... HOW MEAN COULD SHE BE?
GOOD MORNING, STUPID.
HEY! DON'T TALK TO MY DAUGHTER THAT WAY!
I WASN'T.
WHY YOU LITTLE...
SEE??
KIRKMAN & SCOTT

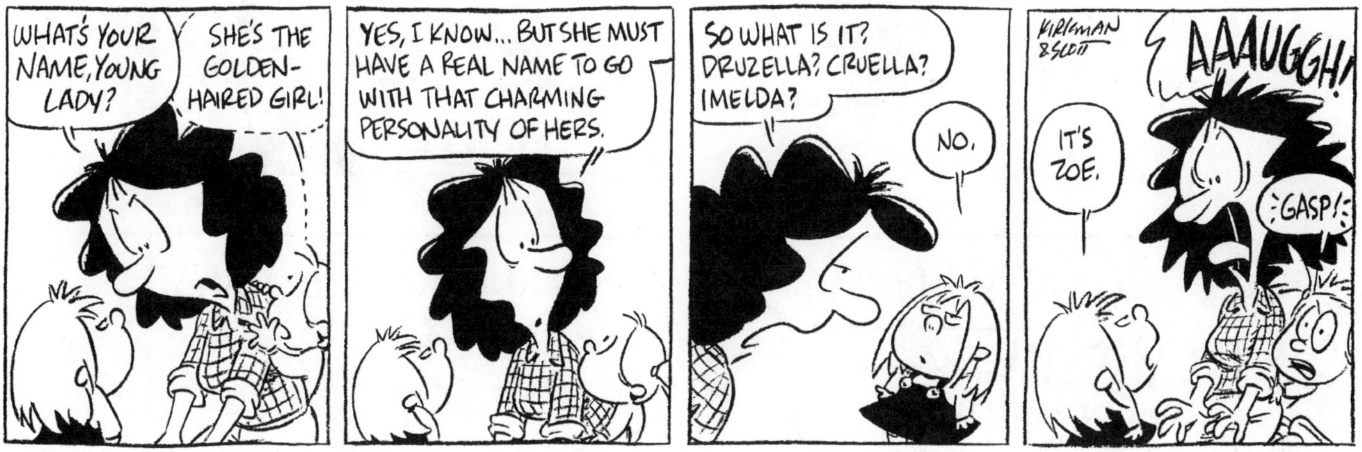
WHAT'S YOUR NAME, YOUNG LADY?
SHE'S THE GOLDEN-HAIRED GIRL!
YES, I KNOW... BUT SHE MUST HAVE A REAL NAME TO GO WITH THAT CHARMING PERSONALITY OF HERS.
SO WHAT IS IT? DRUZELLA? CRUELLA? IMELDA?
NO.
KIRKMAN & SCOTT
AAAUGGH!
IT'S ZOE.
GASP!

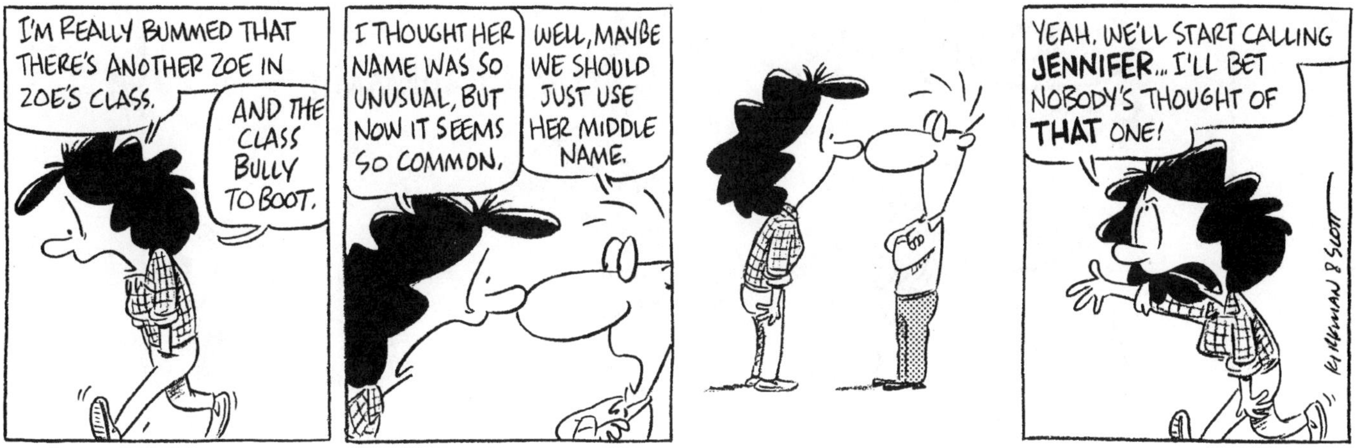
I'M REALLY BUMMED THAT THERE'S ANOTHER ZOE IN ZOE'S CLASS.
AND THE CLASS BULLY TO BOOT.
I THOUGHT HER NAME WAS SO UNUSUAL, BUT NOW IT SEEMS SO COMMON.
WELL, MAYBE WE SHOULD JUST USE HER MIDDLE NAME.
YEAH. WE'LL START CALLING JENNIFER... I'LL BET NOBODY'S THOUGHT OF THAT ONE!
KIRKMAN & SCOTT

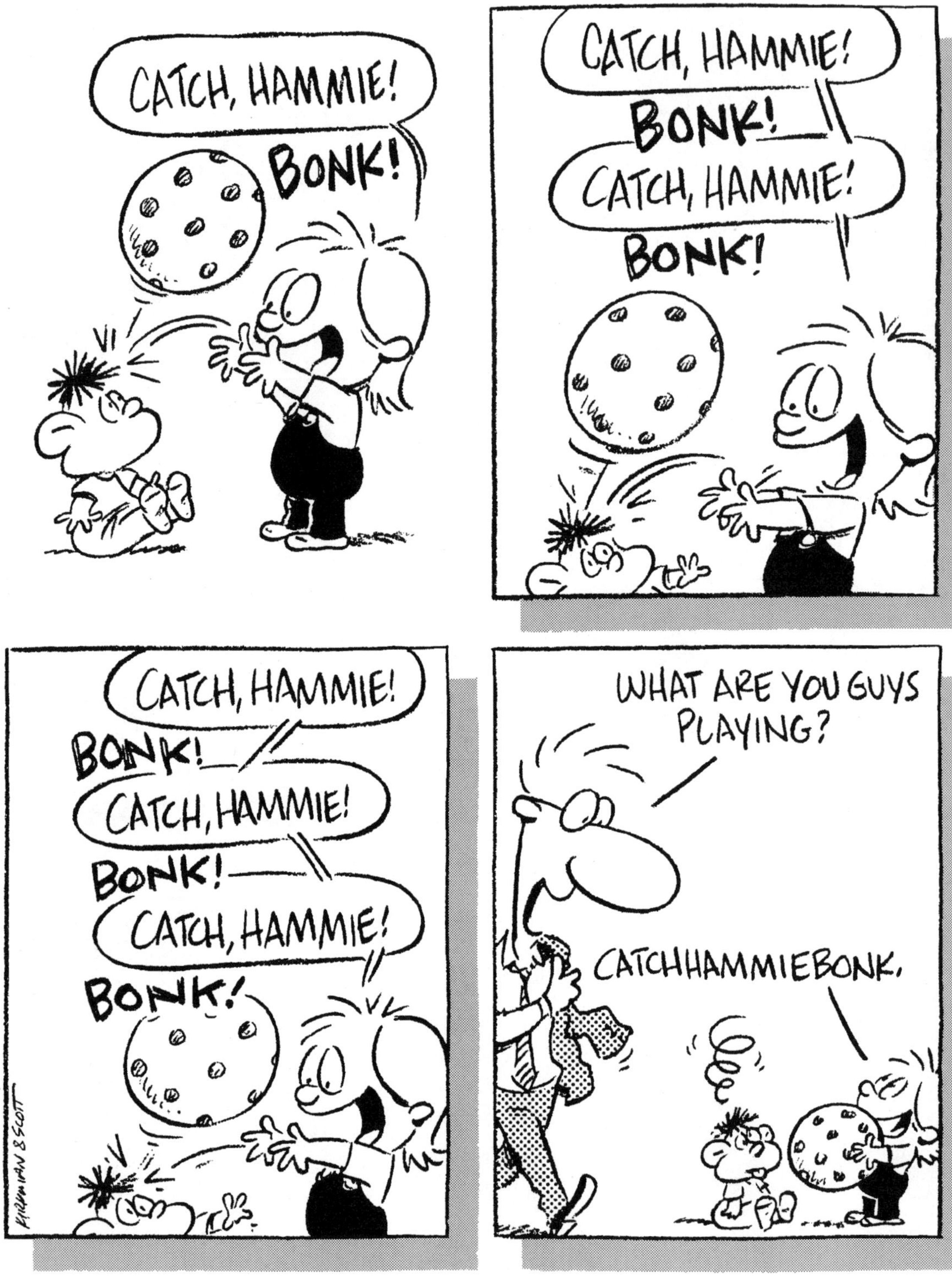
CATCH, HAMMIE!
BONK!
CATCH, HAMMIE!
BONK!
CATCH, HAMMIE!
BONK!
CATCH, HAMMIE!
BONK!
CATCH, HAMMIE!
BONK!
CATCH, HAMMIE!
BONK!
KIRKMAN & SCOTT
WHAT ARE YOU GUYS PLAYING?
CATCHHAMMIEBONK.

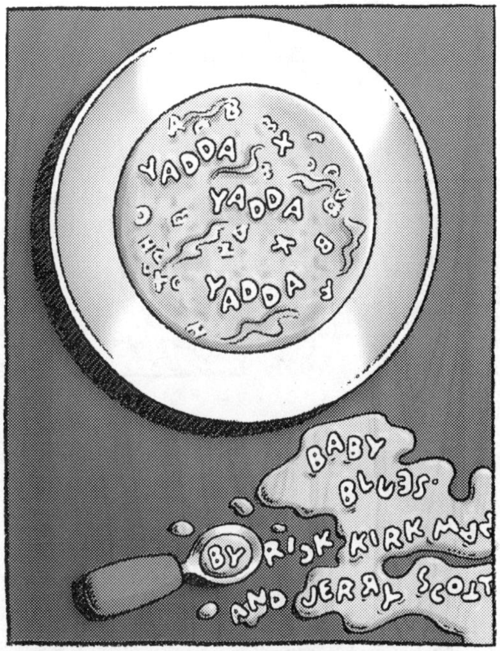
YADDA
YADDA
YADDA
BABY BLUES
BY RICK KIRKMAN AND JERRY SCOTT

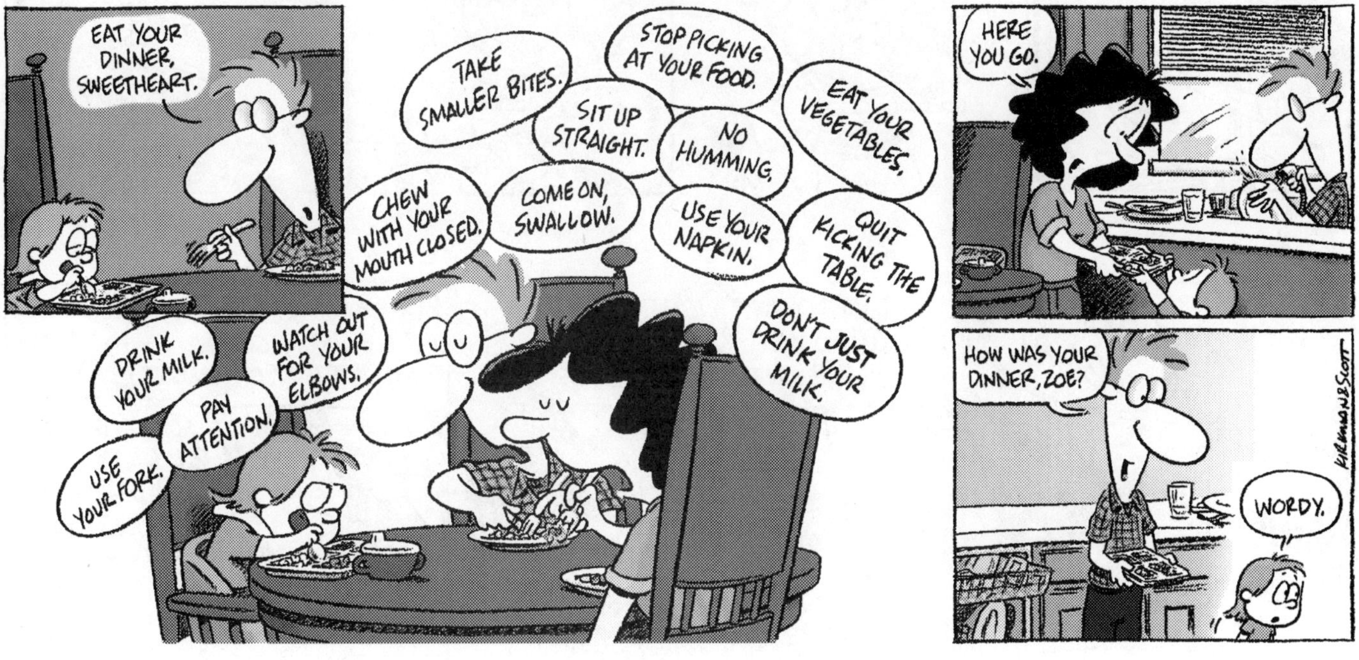
EAT YOUR DINNER, SWEETHEART.
TAKE SMALLER BITES.
STOP PICKING AT YOUR FOOD.
EAT YOUR VEGETABLES.
SIT UP STRAIGHT.
NO HUMMING.
CHEW WITH YOUR MOUTH CLOSED.
COME ON, SWALLOW.
USE YOUR NAPKIN.
QUIT KICKING THE TABLE.
DON'T JUST DRINK YOUR MILK.
DRINK YOUR MILK.
WATCH OUT FOR YOUR ELBOWS.
PAY ATTENTION.
USE YOUR FORK.
HERE YOU GO.
HOW WAS YOUR DINNER, ZOE?
WORDY.
KIRKMAN & SCOTT

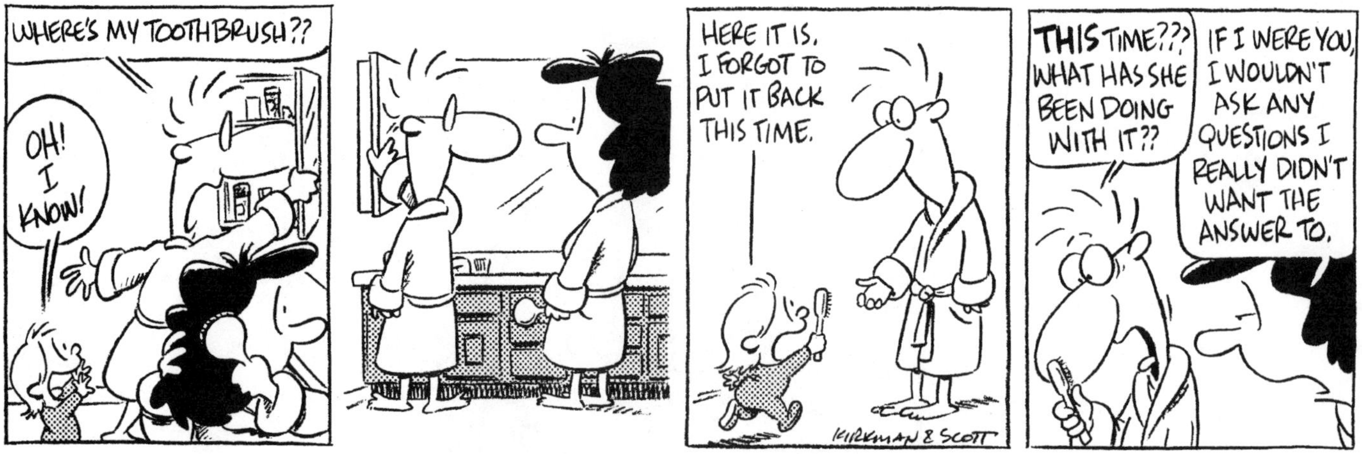
WHERE'S MY TOOTHBRUSH??
OH! I KNOW!
HERE IT IS. I FORGOT TO PUT IT BACK THIS TIME.
KIRKMAN & SCOTT
THIS TIME??? WHAT HAS SHE BEEN DOING WITH IT??
IF I WERE YOU, I WOULDN'T ASK ANY QUESTIONS I REALLY DIDN'T WANT THE ANSWER TO.

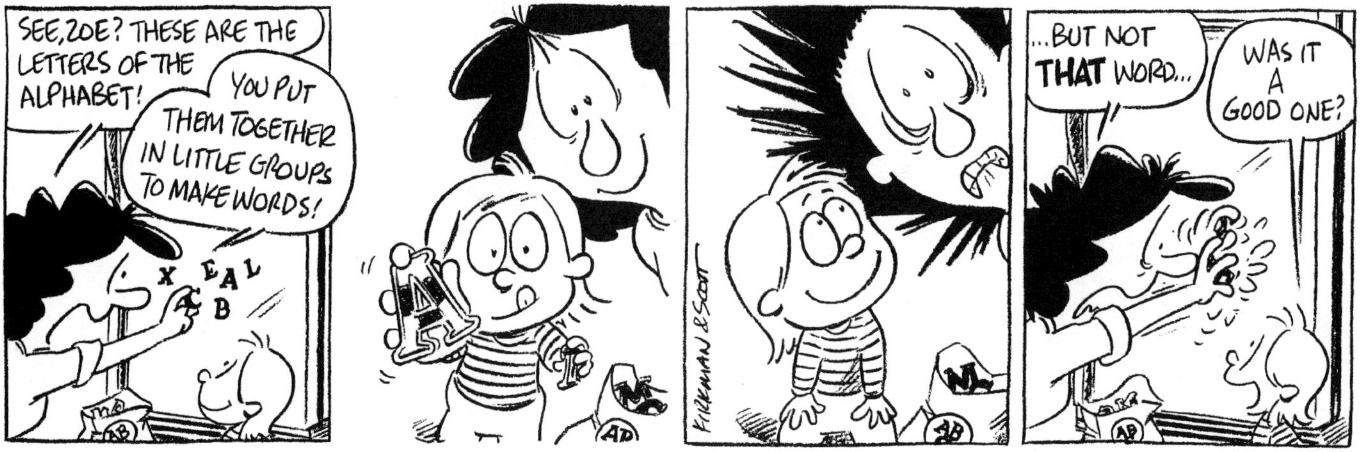
SEE, ZOE? THESE ARE THE LETTERS OF THE ALPHABET!
YOU PUT THEM TOGETHER IN LITTLE GROUPS TO MAKE WORDS!
X E A L
B
KIRKMAN & SCOTT
...BUT NOT THAT WORD...
WAS IT A GOOD ONE?

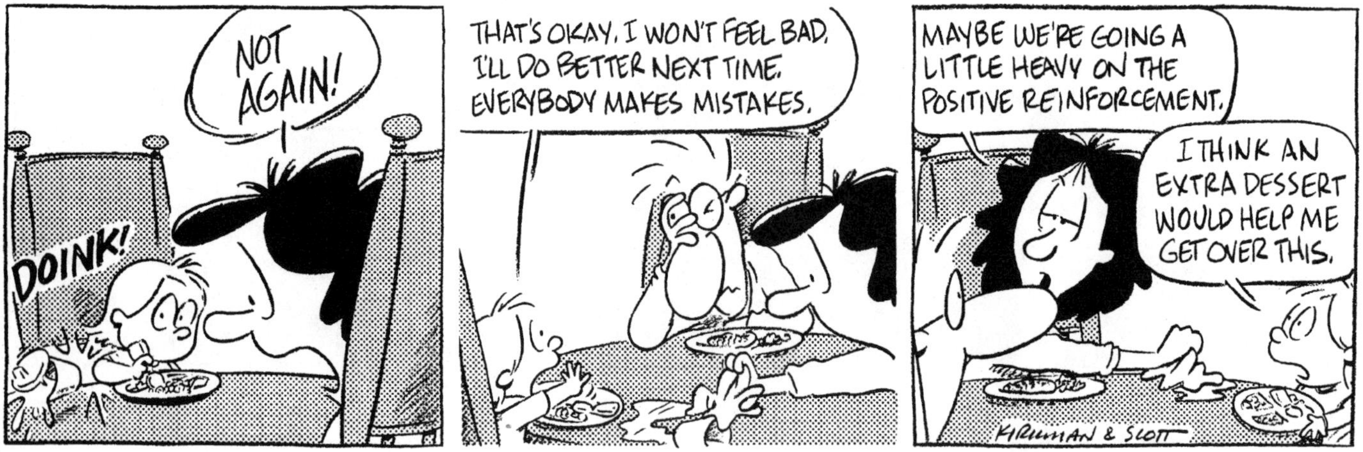
NOT AGAIN!
DOINK!
THAT'S OKAY. I WON'T FEEL BAD. I'LL DO BETTER NEXT TIME. EVERYBODY MAKES MISTAKES.
MAYBE WE'RE GOING A LITTLE HEAVY ON THE POSITIVE REINFORCEMENT.
I THINK AN EXTRA DESSERT WOULD HELP ME GET OVER THIS.
KIRKMAN & SCOTT

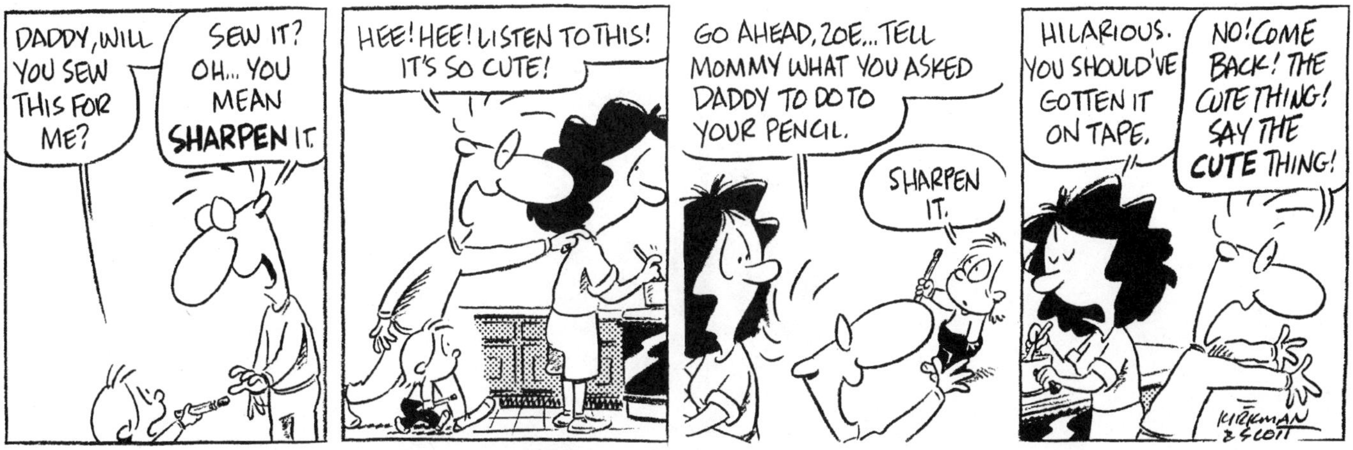
DADDY, WILL YOU SEW THIS FOR ME?
SEW IT? OH... YOU MEAN SHARPEN IT.
HEE! HEE! LISTEN TO THIS! IT'S SO CUTE!
GO AHEAD, ZOE... TELL MOMMY WHAT YOU ASKED DADDY TO DO TO YOUR PENCIL.
SHARPEN IT.
HILARIOUS. YOU SHOULD'VE GOTTEN IT ON TAPE.
NO! COME BACK! THE CUTE THING! SAY THE CUTE THING!
KIRKMAN & SCOTT

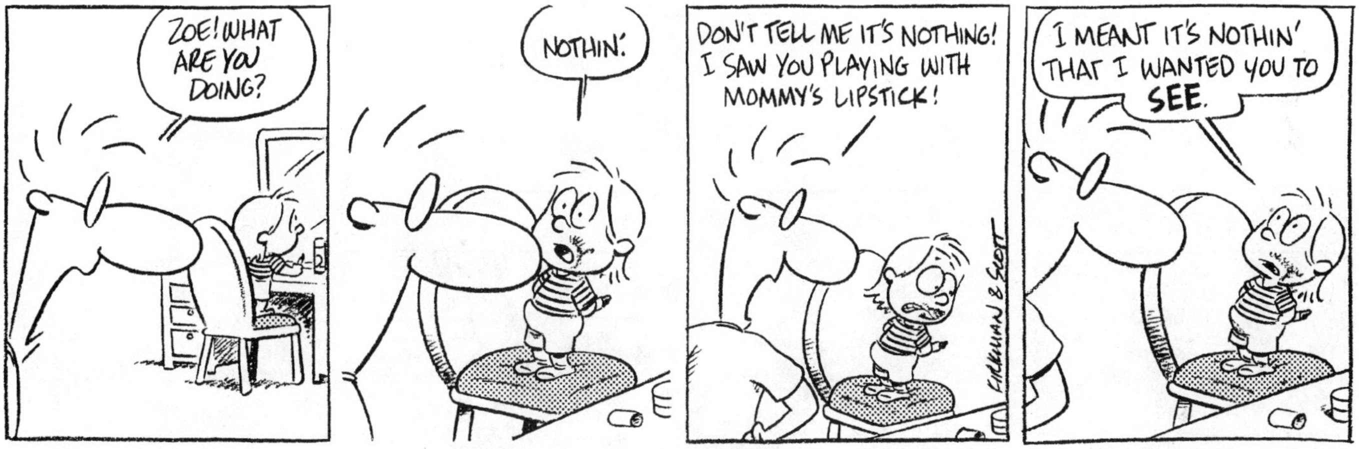
ZOE! WHAT ARE YOU DOING?
NOTHIN'.
DON'T TELL ME IT'S NOTHING! I SAW YOU PLAYING WITH MOMMY'S LIPSTICK!
KIRKMAN & SCOTT
I MEANT IT'S NOTHIN' THAT I WANTED YOU TO SEE.

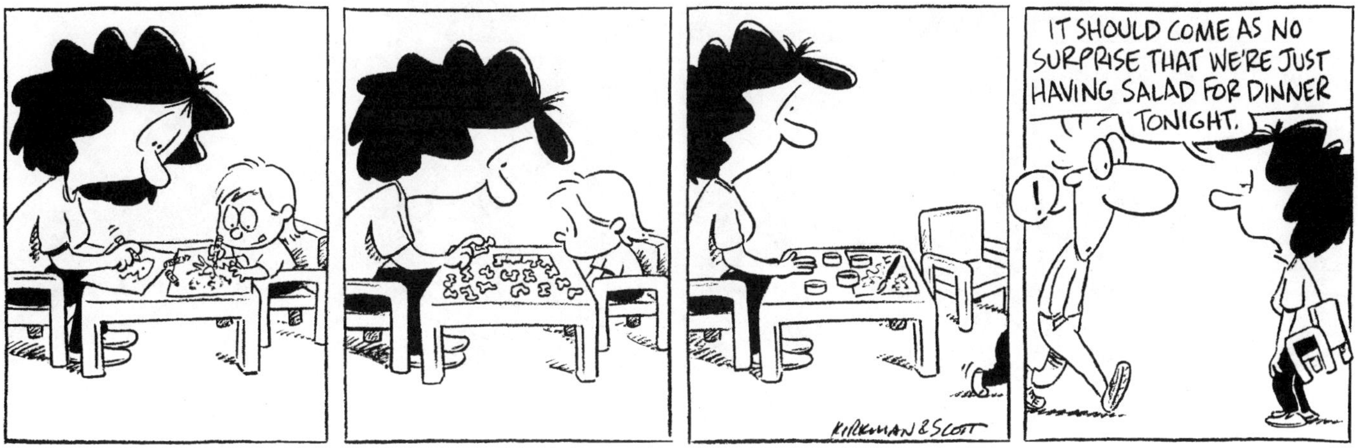
KIRKMAN & SCOTT
IT SHOULD COME AS NO SURPRISE THAT WE'RE JUST HAVING SALAD FOR DINNER TONIGHT.
!

BABY BLUES®
BY
RICK KIRKMAN / JERRY SCOTT

OUR OWN BASKETBALL HOOP! THIS IS GOING TO BE SO COOL!
I CAN TEACH ZOE HOW TO DRIBBLE, HOW TO REBOUND... AND WHEN HAMMIE GETS BIG ENOUGH, WE CAN–
I THINK IT'S TOO HIGH.
BUT TEN FEET IS REGULATION.
HOW IS ZOE GOING TO BE ABLE TO GET THE BALL UP THERE?
OKAY, SO THE IDEA IS TO TOSS THE BALL THROUGH THE HOOP...
HMMM... OKAY... HOW'S THIS?
LOWER.
HERE?
MORE.
BUT...
MORE.
BUT...
RIGHT THERE! PERFECT! NOW IT'S FAIR!
WAY UP THERE??
KIRKMAN & SCOTT

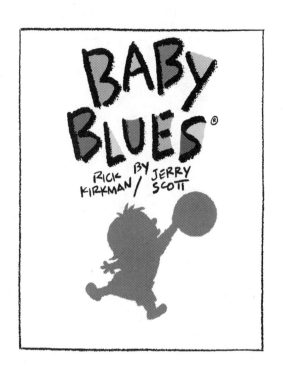

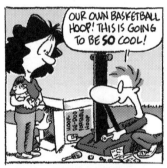

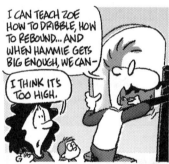

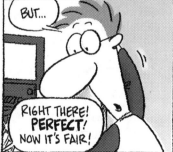

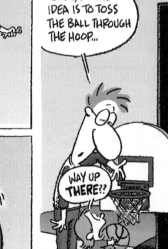

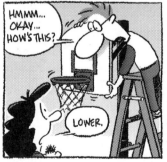

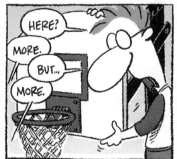

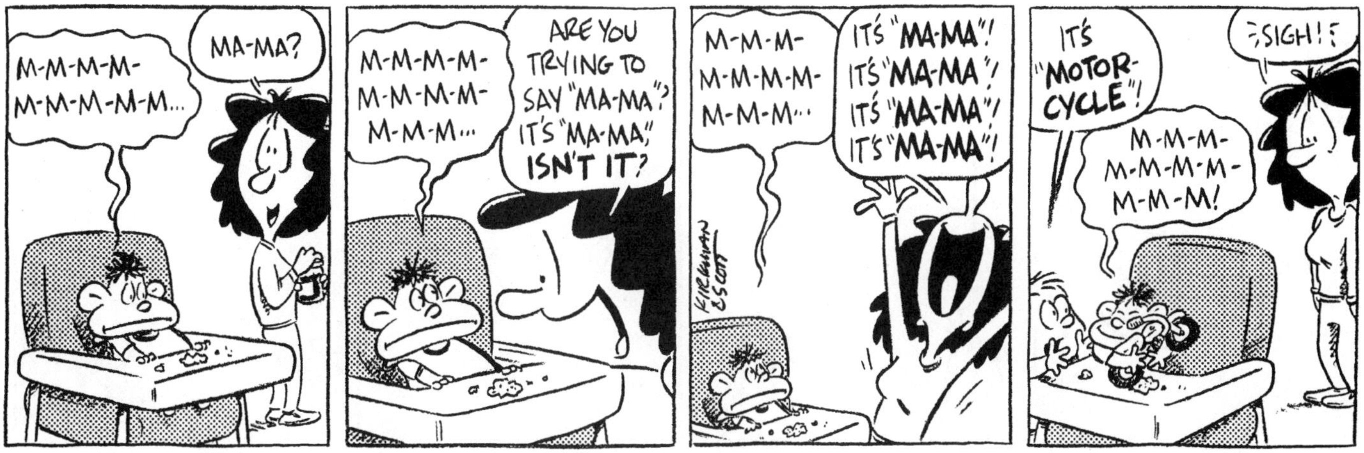
M-M-M-M-
M-M-M-M-M...
MA-MA?
M-M-M-M-
M-M-M-M-
M-M-M...
ARE YOU TRYING TO SAY "MA-MA"? IT'S "MA-MA," ISN'T IT?
M-M-M-
M-M-M-M-
M-M-M...
IT'S "MA-MA"! IT'S "MA-MA"! IT'S "MA-MA"! IT'S "MA-MA"!
KIRKMAN & SCOTT
IT'S "MOTOR-CYCLE"!
SIGH!
M-M-M-
M-M-M-M-
M-M-M!

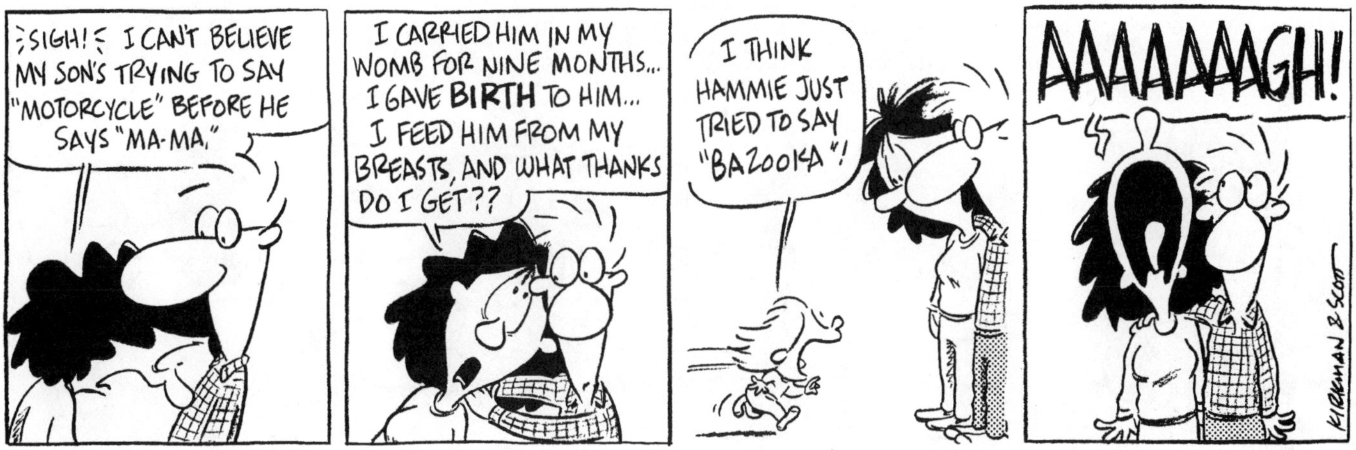
SIGH! I CAN'T BELIEVE MY SON'S TRYING TO SAY "MOTORCYCLE" BEFORE HE SAYS "MA-MA."
I CARRIED HIM IN MY WOMB FOR NINE MONTHS... I GAVE BIRTH TO HIM... I FEED HIM FROM MY BREASTS, AND WHAT THANKS DO I GET??
I THINK HAMMIE JUST TRIED TO SAY "BAZOOKA"!
AAAAAAAGH!
KIRKMAN & SCOTT

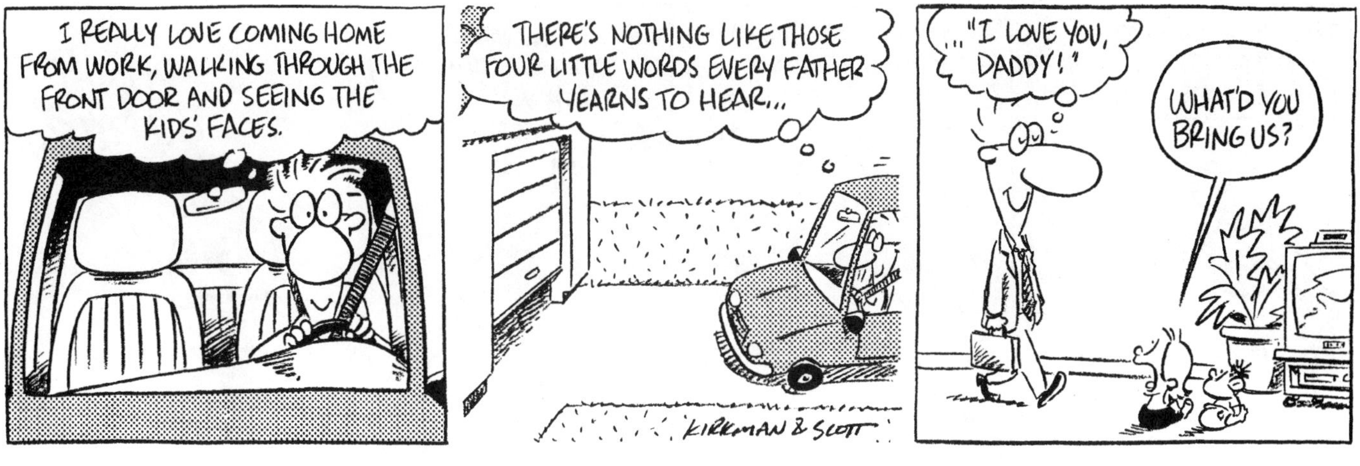
I REALLY LOVE COMING HOME FROM WORK, WALKING THROUGH THE FRONT DOOR AND SEEING THE KIDS' FACES.
THERE'S NOTHING LIKE THOSE FOUR LITTLE WORDS EVERY FATHER YEARNS TO HEAR...
KIRKMAN & SCOTT
..."I LOVE YOU, DADDY!"
WHAT'D YOU BRING US?

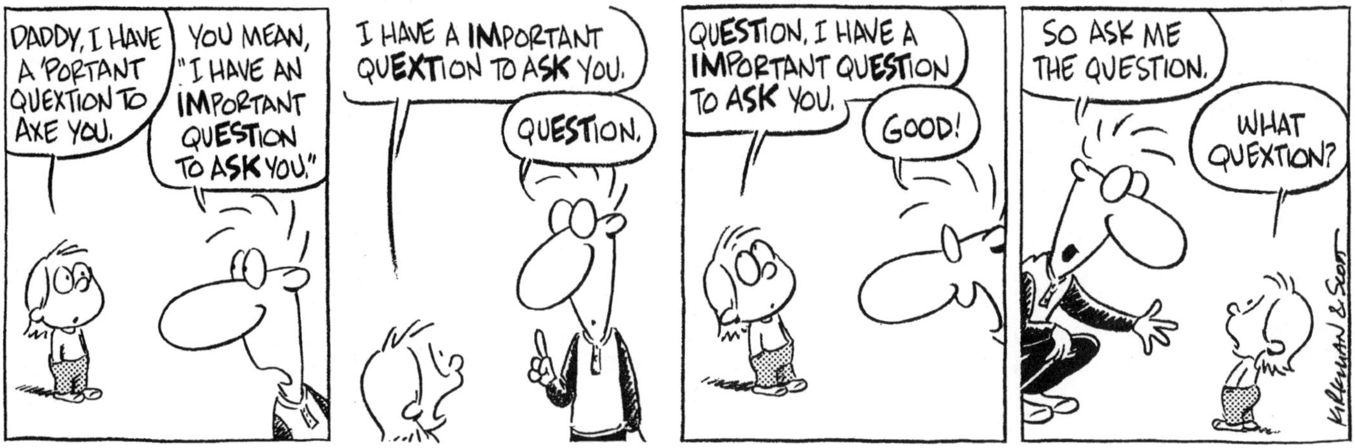
DADDY, I HAVE A 'PORTANT QUEXTION TO AXE YOU.
YOU MEAN, "I HAVE AN IMPORTANT QUESTION TO ASK YOU."
I HAVE A IMPORTANT QUEXTION TO ASK YOU.
QUESTION.
QUESTION. I HAVE A IMPORTANT QUESTION TO ASK YOU.
GOOD!
SO ASK ME THE QUESTION.
WHAT QUEXTION?
KIRKMAN & SCOTT

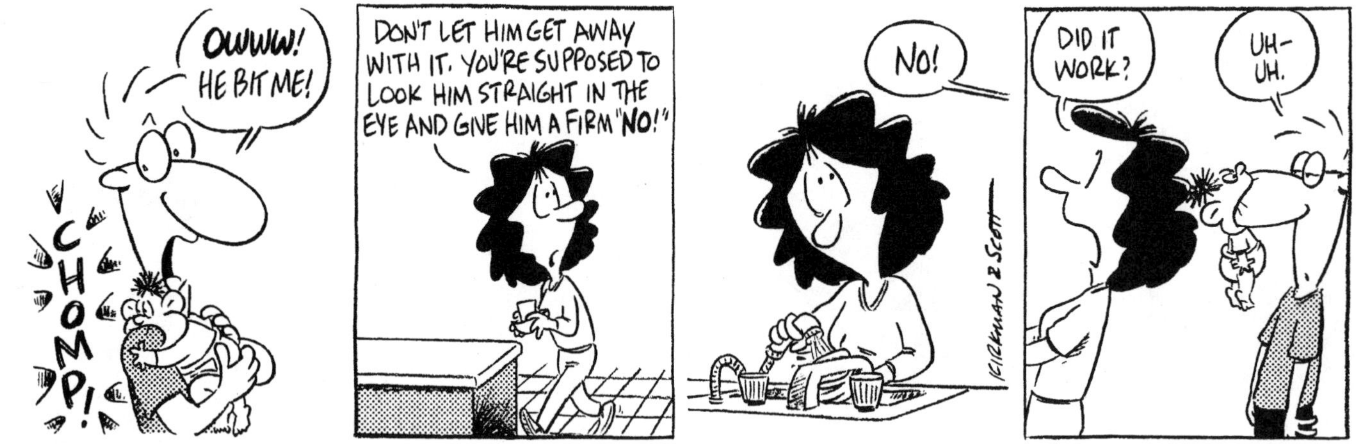
OWWW! HE BIT ME!
CHOMP!
DON'T LET HIM GET AWAY WITH IT. YOU'RE SUPPOSED TO LOOK HIM STRAIGHT IN THE EYE AND GIVE HIM A FIRM "NO!"
NO!
KIRKMAN & SCOTT
DID IT WORK?
UH-UH.

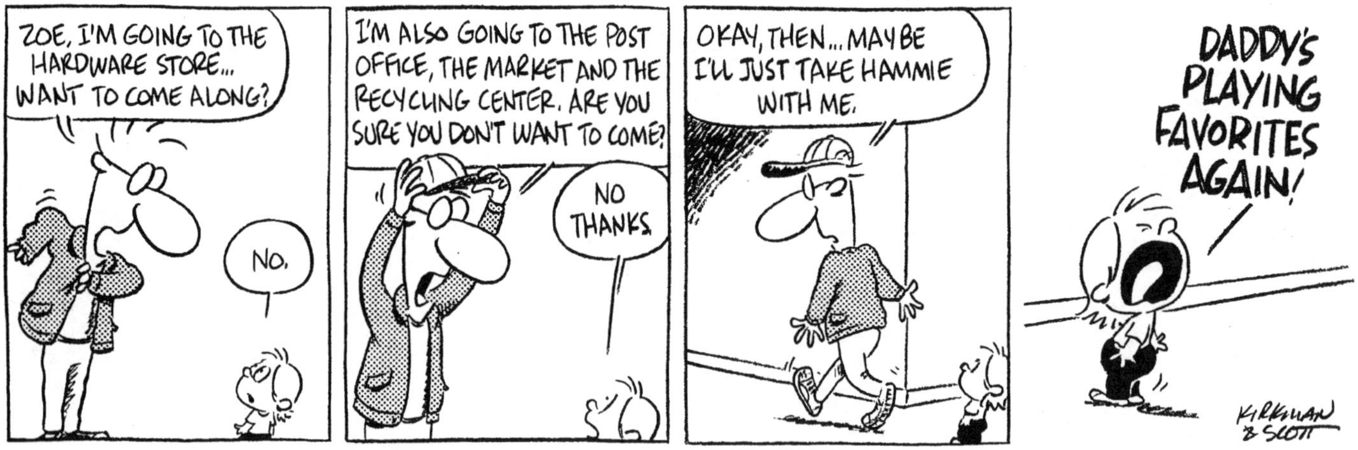
ZOE, I'M GOING TO THE HARDWARE STORE... WANT TO COME ALONG?
NO.
I'M ALSO GOING TO THE POST OFFICE, THE MARKET AND THE RECYCLING CENTER. ARE YOU SURE YOU DON'T WANT TO COME?
NO THANKS.
OKAY, THEN... MAYBE I'LL JUST TAKE HAMMIE WITH ME.
DADDY'S PLAYING FAVORITES AGAIN!
KIRKMAN & SCOTT

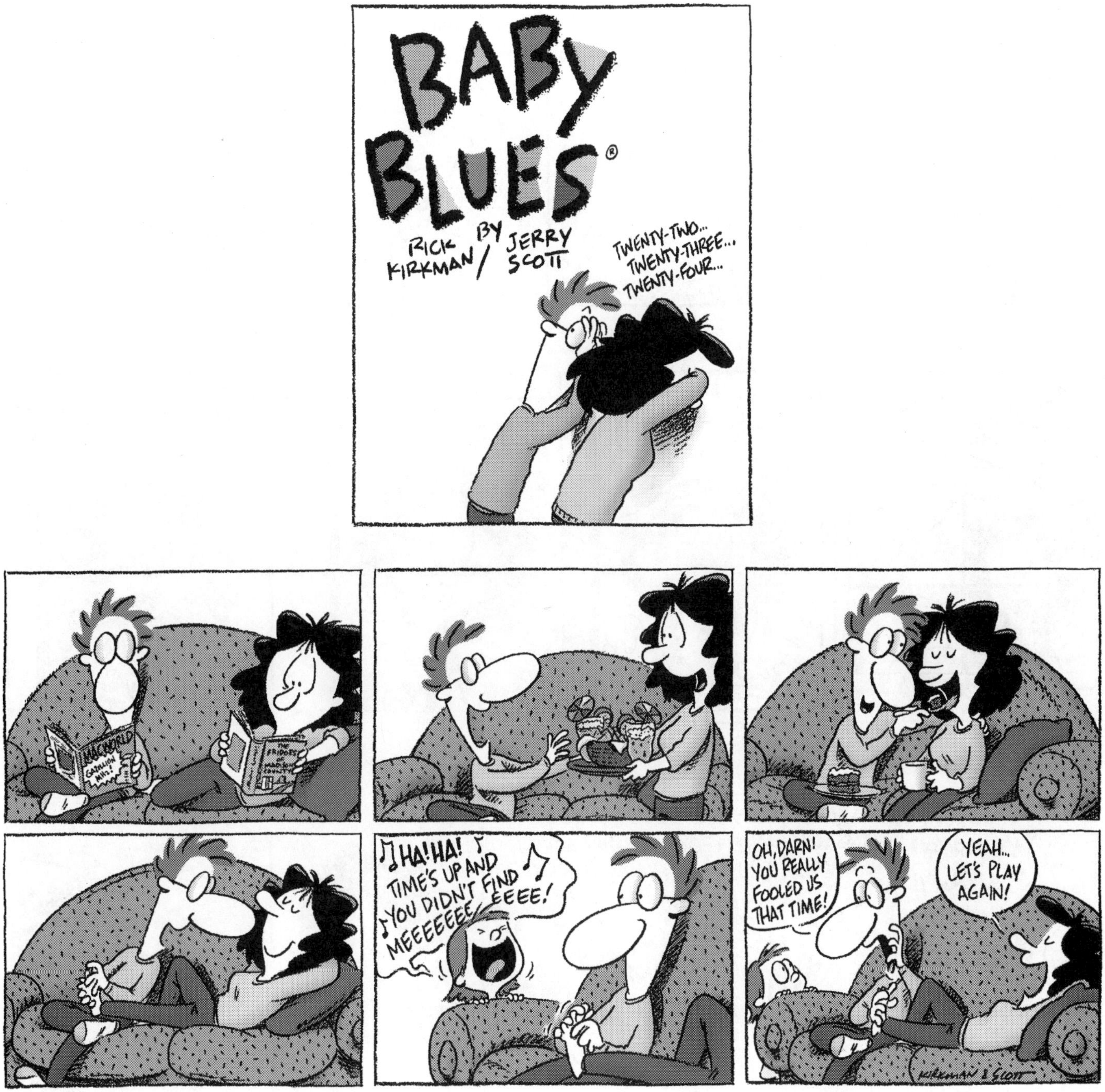
BABY BLUES®
BY RICK KIRKMAN / JERRY SCOTT
TWENTY-TWO... TWENTY-THREE... TWENTY-FOUR...
MACWORLD
HA! HA! TIME'S UP AND YOU DIDN'T FIND MEEEEEEE EEEE!
OH, DARN! YOU REALLY FOOLED US THAT TIME!
YEAH... LET'S PLAY AGAIN!
KIRKMAN & SCOTT

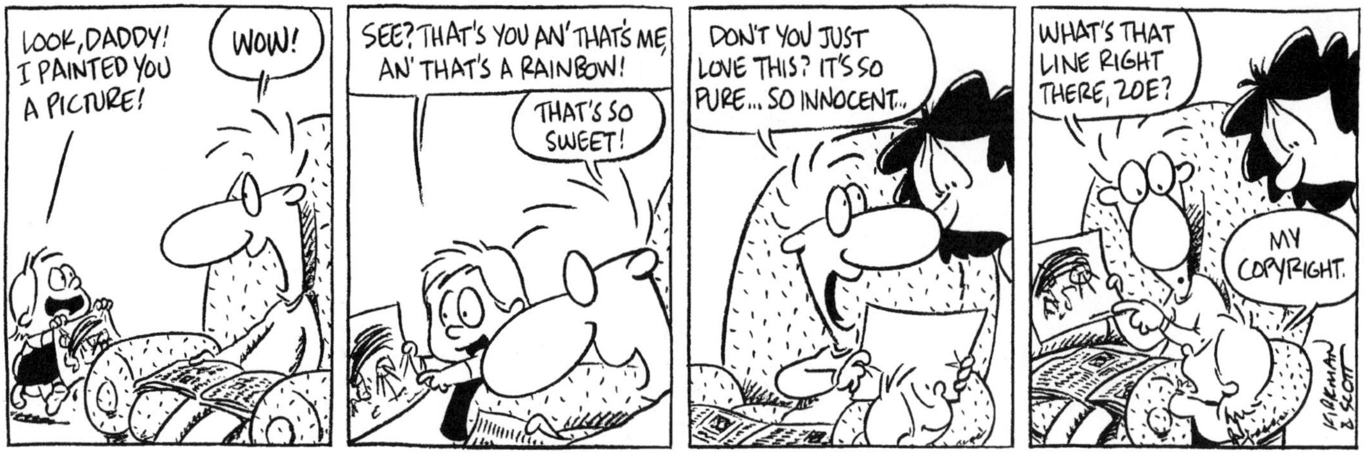
LOOK, DADDY! I PAINTED YOU A PICTURE!
WOW!
SEE? THAT'S YOU AN' THAT'S ME, AN' THAT'S A RAINBOW!
THAT'S SO SWEET!
DON'T YOU JUST LOVE THIS? IT'S SO PURE... SO INNOCENT...
WHAT'S THAT LINE RIGHT THERE, ZOE?
MY COPYRIGHT.
KIRKMAN & SCOTT

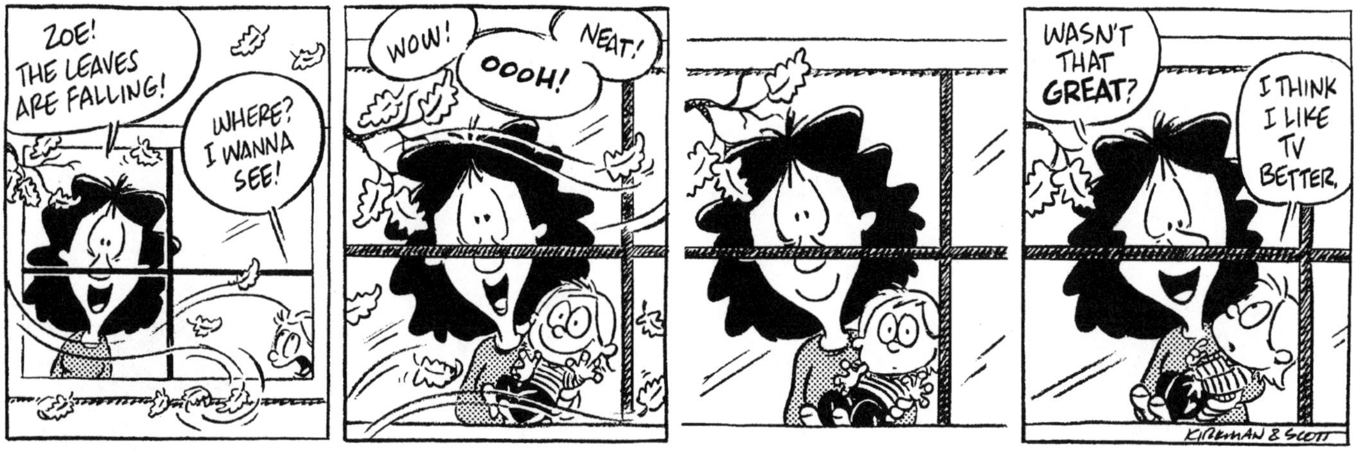
ZOE! THE LEAVES ARE FALLING!
WHERE? I WANNA SEE!
WOW!
OOOH!
NEAT!
WASN'T THAT **GREAT**?
I THINK I LIKE TV BETTER.
KIRKMAN & SCOTT

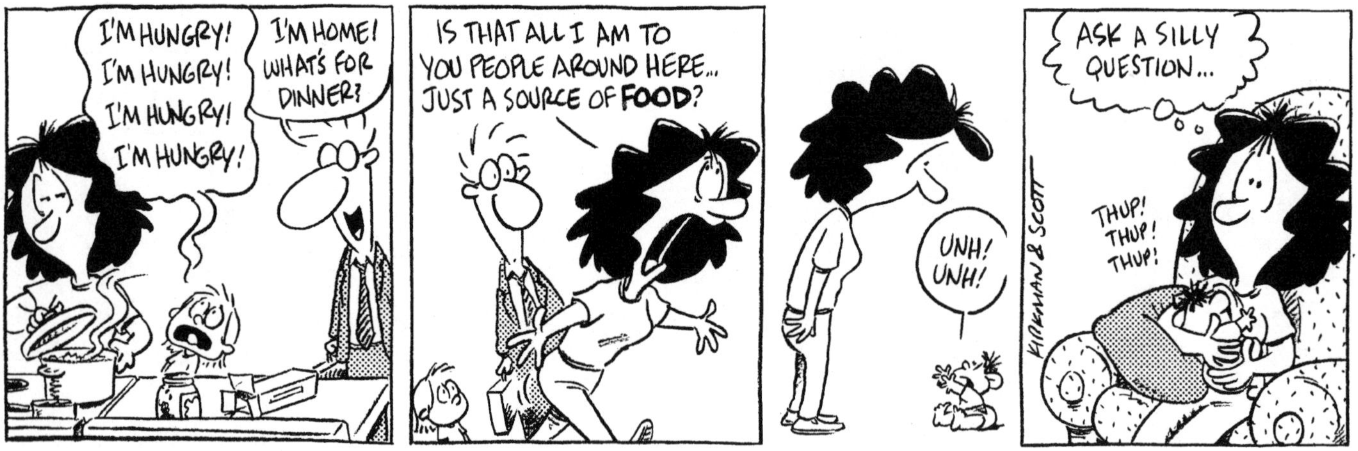
I'M HUNGRY! I'M HUNGRY! I'M HUNGRY! I'M HUNGRY!
I'M HOME! WHAT'S FOR DINNER?
IS THAT ALL I AM TO YOU PEOPLE AROUND HERE... JUST A SOURCE OF **FOOD**?
UNH! UNH!
KIRKMAN & SCOTT
ASK A SILLY QUESTION...
THUP! THUP! THUP!

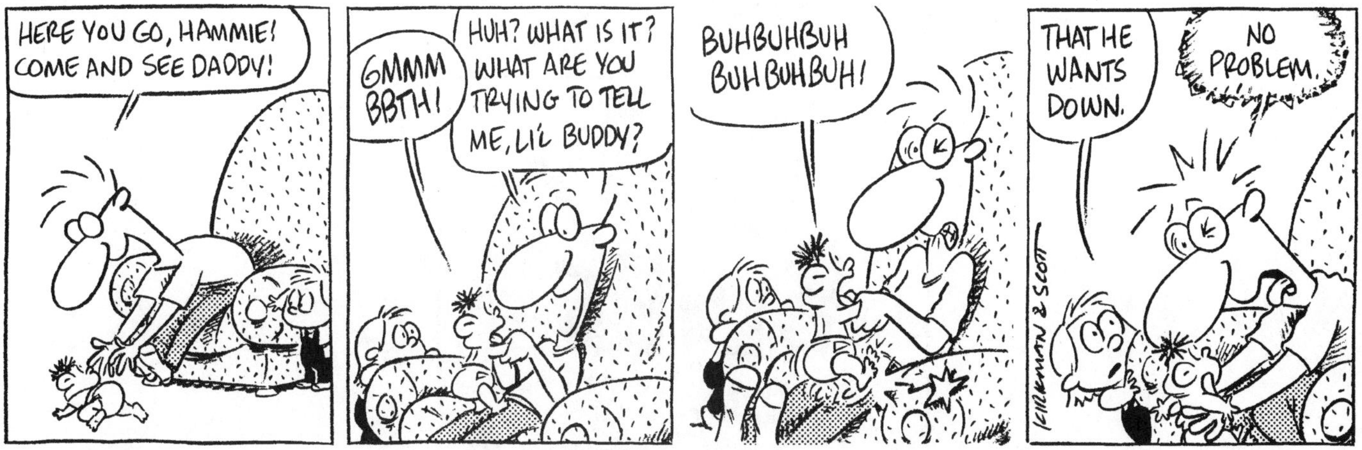
HERE YOU GO, HAMMIE! COME AND SEE DADDY!
GMMM BBTH!
HUH? WHAT IS IT? WHAT ARE YOU TRYING TO TELL ME, LI'L BUDDY?
BUHBUHBUH BUHBUHBUH!
THAT HE WANTS DOWN.
NO PROBLEM.
KIRKMAN & SCOTT

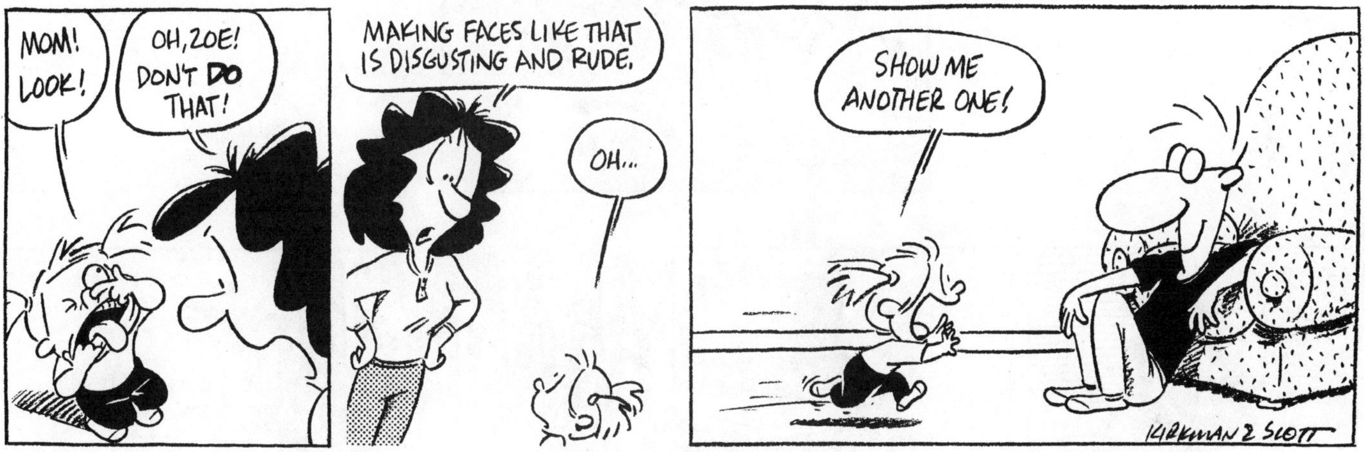
MOM! LOOK!
OH, ZOE! DON'T **DO** THAT!
MAKING FACES LIKE THAT IS DISGUSTING AND RUDE.
OH...
SHOW ME ANOTHER ONE!
KIRKMAN & SCOTT

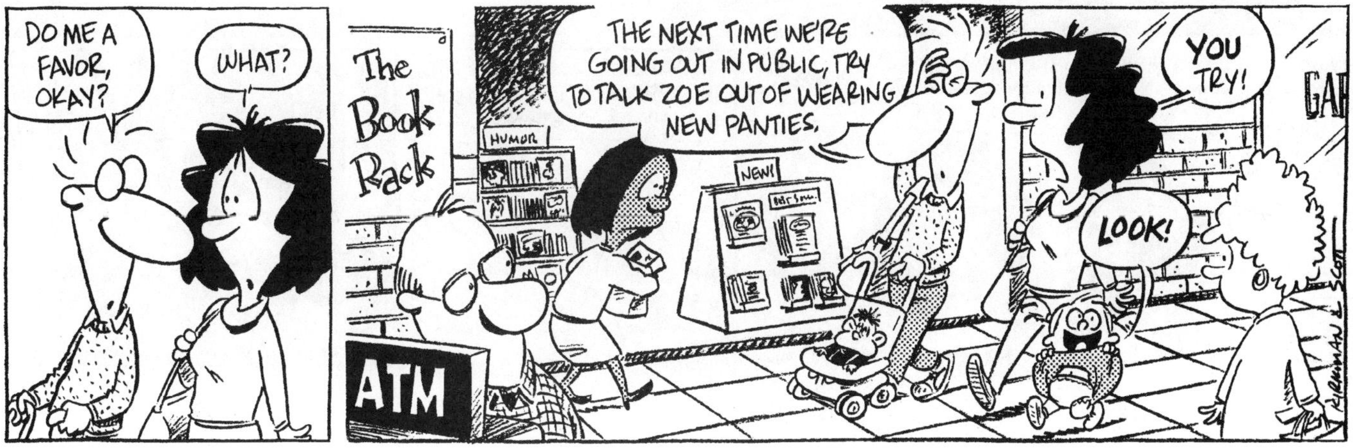
DO ME A FAVOR, OKAY?
WHAT?
The Book Rack
HUMOR
NEW!
ATM
THE NEXT TIME WE'RE GOING OUT IN PUBLIC, TRY TO TALK ZOE OUT OF WEARING NEW PANTIES.
YOU TRY!
LOOK!
KIRKMAN & SCOTT

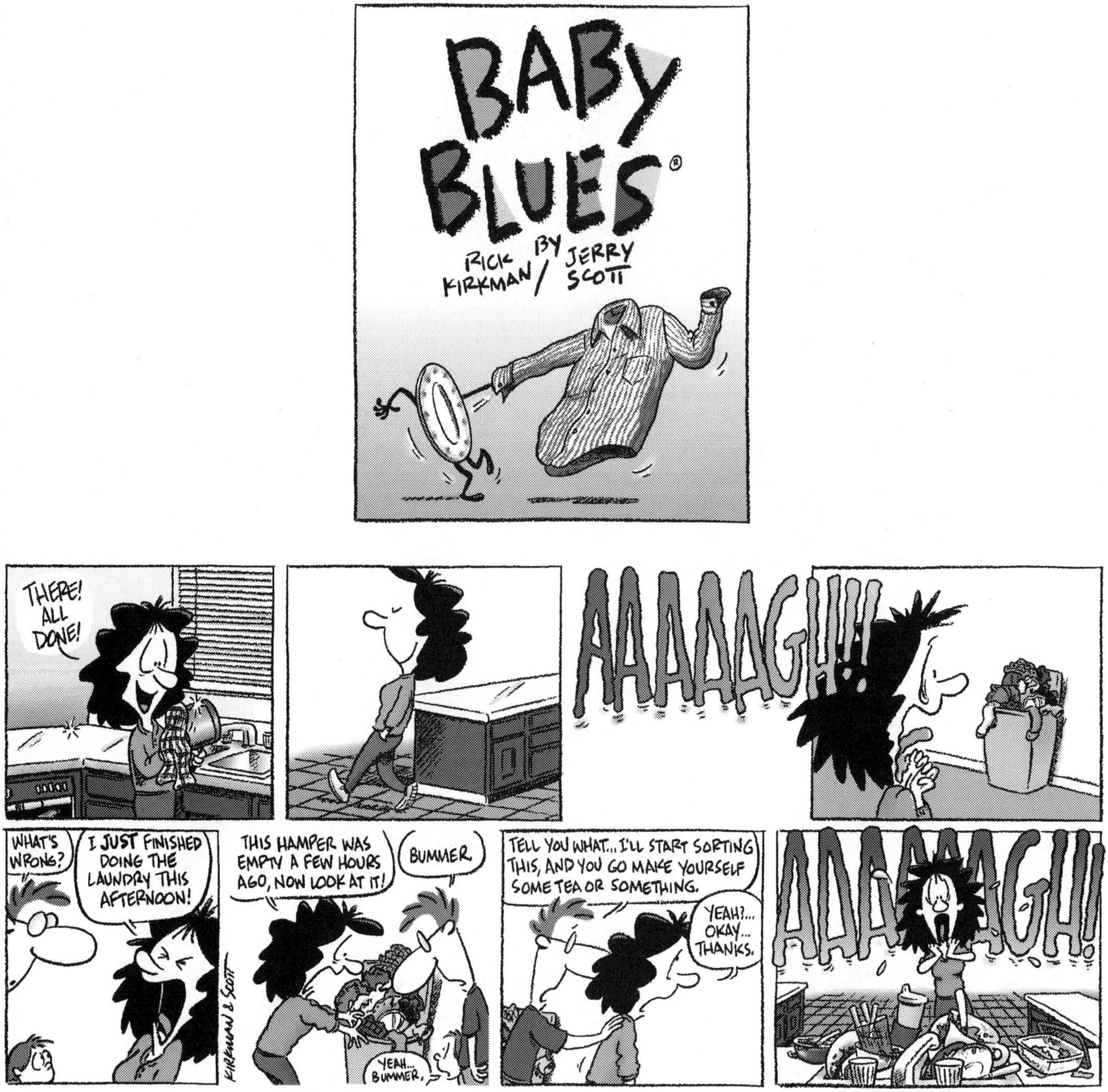
BABY BLUES®
BY RICK KIRKMAN / JERRY SCOTT
THERE! ALL DONE!
AAAAAGH!!
WHAT'S WRONG?
I JUST FINISHED DOING THE LAUNDRY THIS AFTERNOON!
KIRKMAN & SCOTT
THIS HAMPER WAS EMPTY A FEW HOURS AGO, NOW LOOK AT IT!
BUMMER.
YEAH... BUMMER.
TELL YOU WHAT... I'LL START SORTING THIS, AND YOU GO MAKE YOURSELF SOME TEA OR SOMETHING.
YEAH?... OKAY... THANKS.
AAAAAAGH!

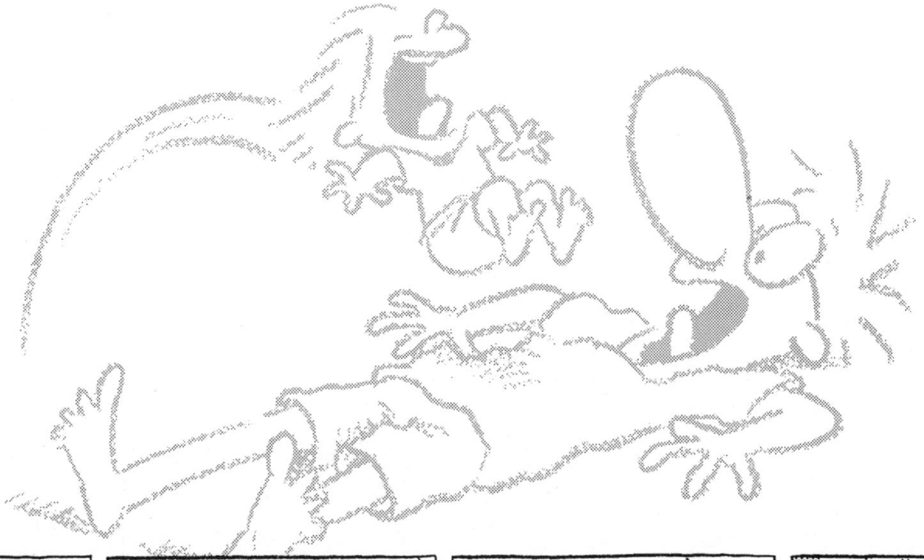

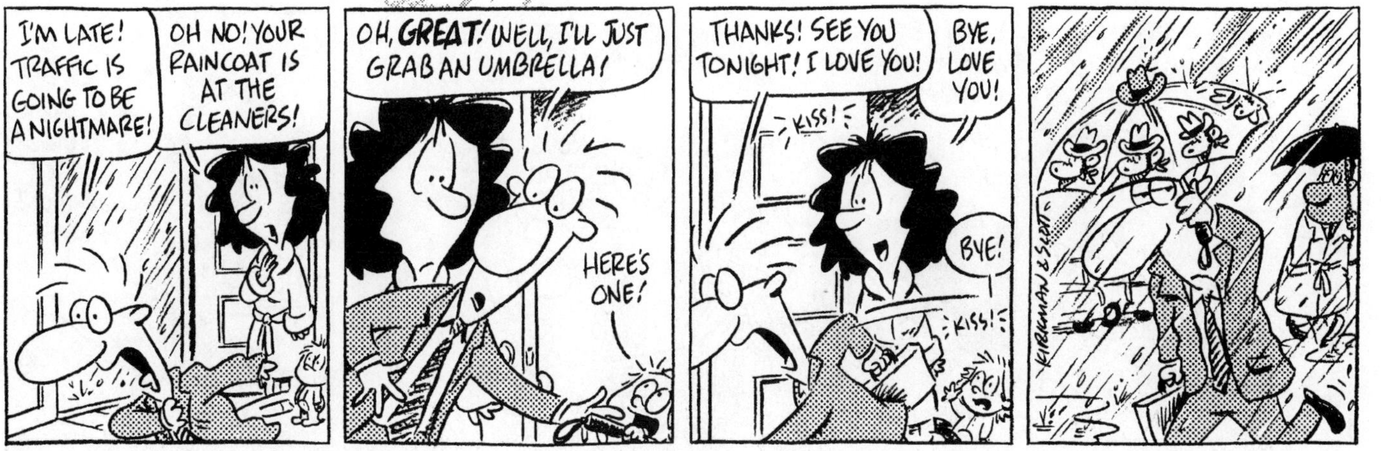
I'M LATE! TRAFFIC IS GOING TO BE A NIGHTMARE!
OH NO! YOUR RAINCOAT IS AT THE CLEANERS!
OH, GREAT! WELL, I'LL JUST GRAB AN UMBRELLA!
HERE'S ONE!
THANKS! SEE YOU TONIGHT! I LOVE YOU!
BYE, LOVE YOU!
KISS!
BYE!
KISS!
KIRKMAN & SCOTT

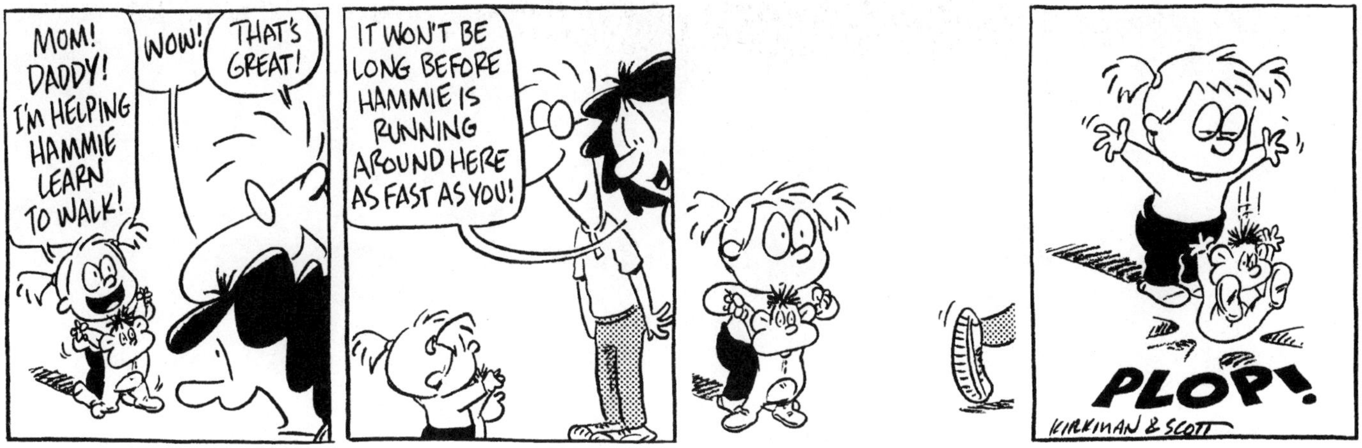
MOM! DADDY! I'M HELPING HAMMIE LEARN TO WALK!
WOW!
THAT'S GREAT!
IT WON'T BE LONG BEFORE HAMMIE IS RUNNING AROUND HERE AS FAST AS YOU!
!!
PLOP!
KIRKMAN & SCOTT

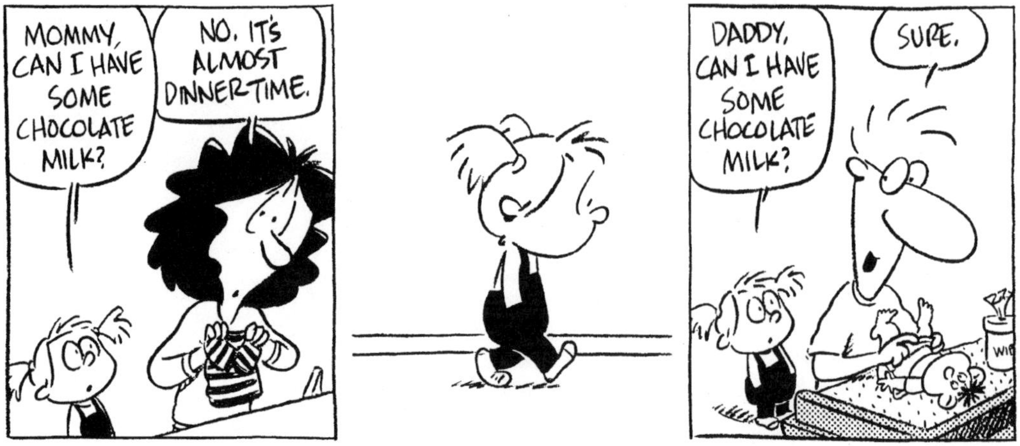
MOMMY, CAN I HAVE SOME CHOCOLATE MILK?
NO. IT'S ALMOST DINNERTIME.
DADDY, CAN I HAVE SOME CHOCOLATE MILK?
SURE.
I WANT DADDY TO BE THE MOMMY FROM NOW ON.
KIRKMAN & SCOTT

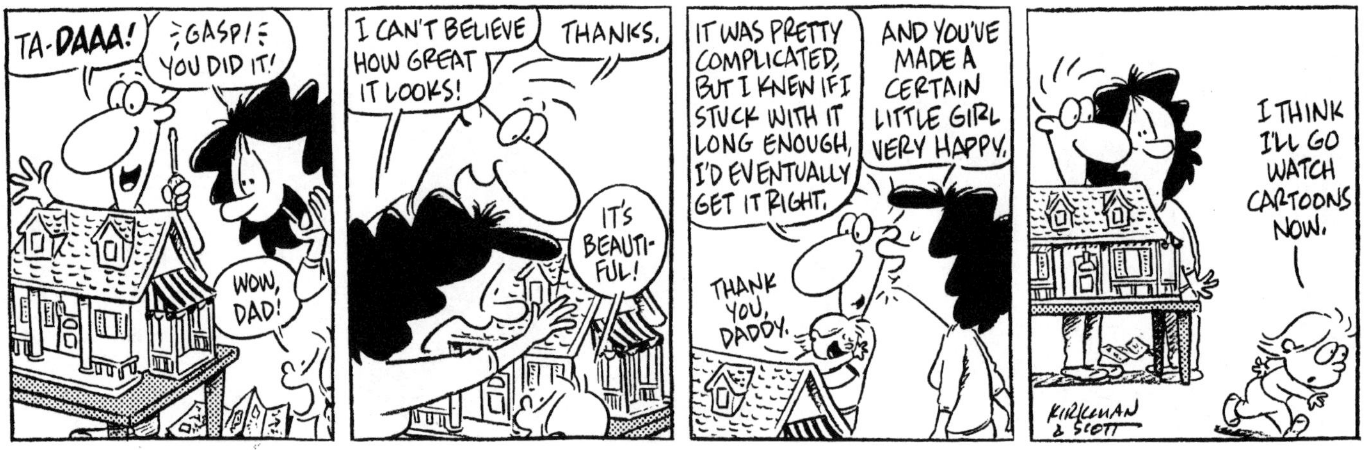
TA-DAAA!
GASP! YOU DID IT!
WOW, DAD!
I CAN'T BELIEVE HOW GREAT IT LOOKS!
THANKS.
IT'S BEAUTIFUL!
IT WAS PRETTY COMPLICATED, BUT I KNEW IF I STUCK WITH IT LONG ENOUGH, I'D EVENTUALLY GET IT RIGHT.
AND YOU'VE MADE A CERTAIN LITTLE GIRL VERY HAPPY.
THANK YOU, DADDY.
I THINK I'LL GO WATCH CARTOONS NOW.
KIRKMAN & SCOTT

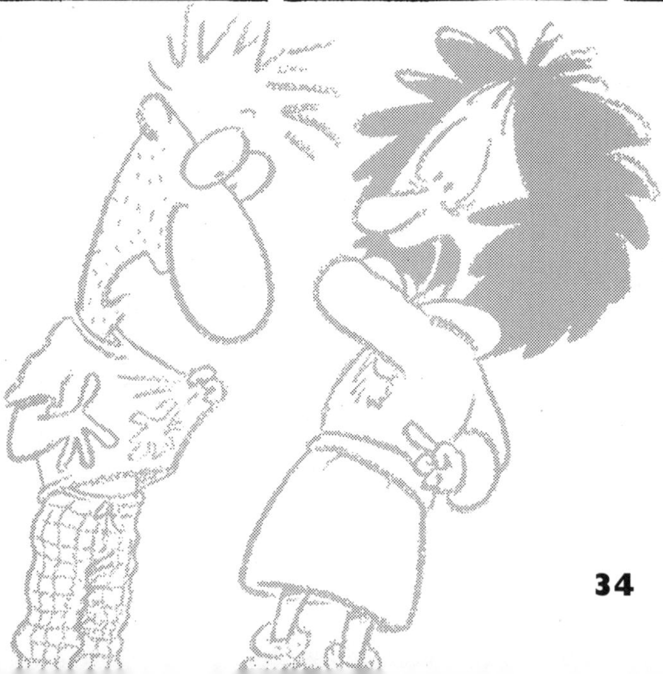

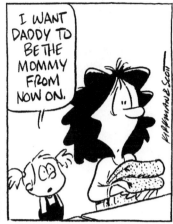

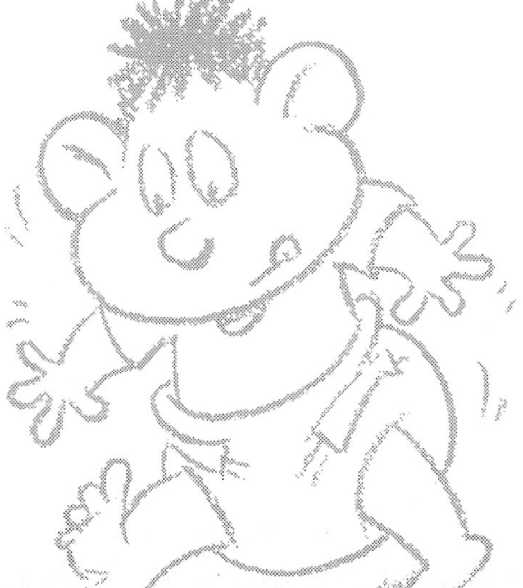

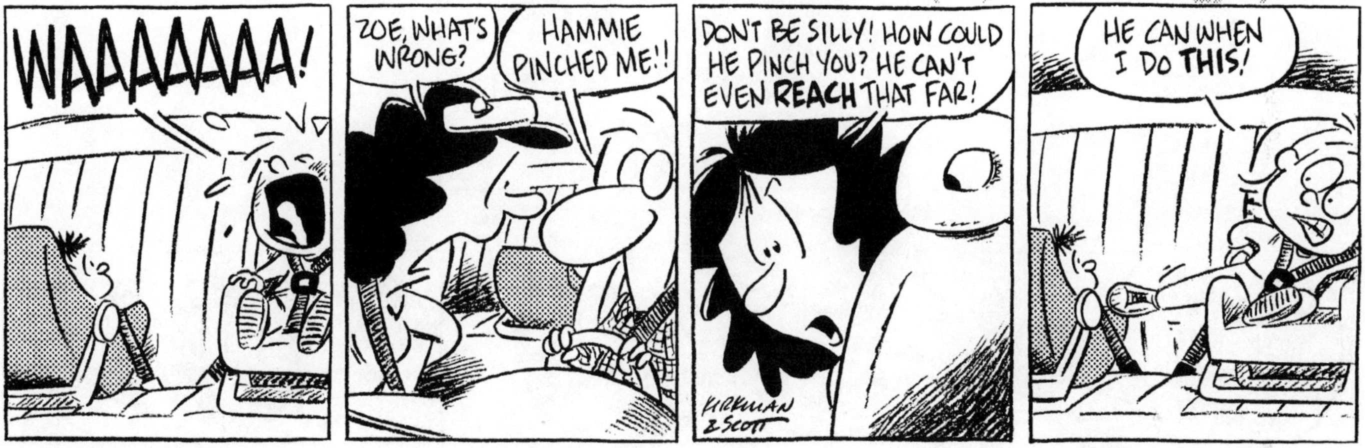
WAAAAAAA!
ZOE, WHAT'S WRONG?
HAMMIE PINCHED ME!!
DON'T BE SILLY! HOW COULD HE PINCH YOU? HE CAN'T EVEN **REACH** THAT FAR!
KIRKMAN & SCOTT
HE CAN WHEN I DO **THIS**!

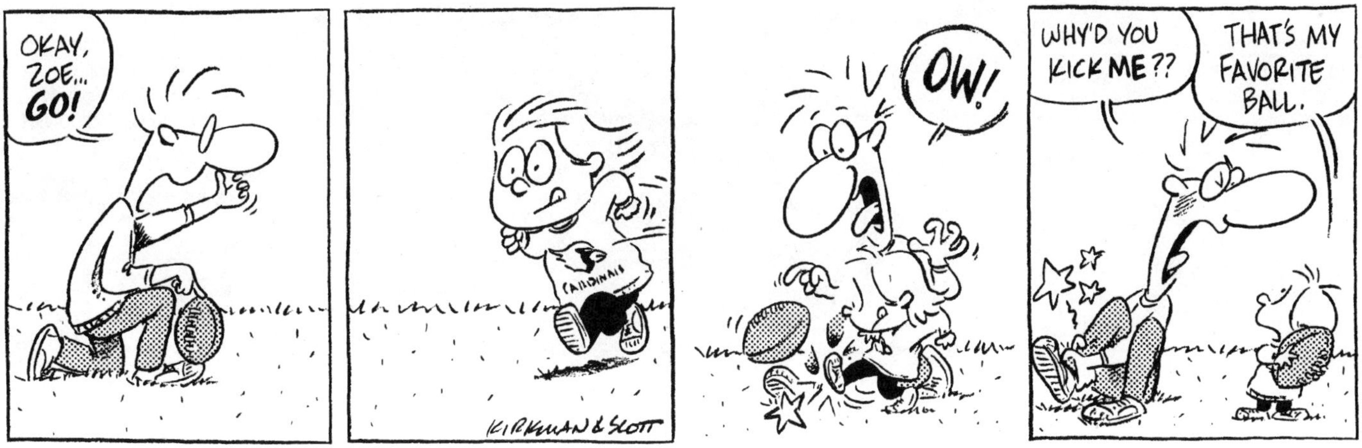
OKAY, ZOE... **GO!**
KIRKMAN & SCOTT
CARDINALS
OW!
WHY'D YOU KICK **ME**??
THAT'S MY FAVORITE BALL.

BABY BLUES®
BY RICK KIRKMAN / JERRY SCOTT

GAAAAAA! THESE STUPID PANTS ARE DRIVING ME NUTS!
WHAT'S WRONG WITH THEM?
ACTUALLY, NOTHING. IT'S ME. SOMEHOW I'VE GAINED FIVE POUNDS.
I CAN'T FIGURE IT OUT. NONE OF MY DIET OR EXERCISE HABITS HAVE CHANGED.
IN FACT, THE ONLY THING IN MY LIFE THAT'S DIFFERENT IS THAT ZOE IS GOING TO PRESCHOOL A COUPLE OF DAYS A WEEK!
I SEE...
SO ZOE'S BEEN GOING TO PRESCHOOL FOR ABOUT FIVE MONTHS, RIGHT?
YEAH. SO?
TWO DAYS A WEEK TIMES FOUR WEEKS IS EIGHT DAYS A MONTH, TIMES FIVE MONTHS IS 40 DAYS, RIGHT? SO IF ZOE TAKES ONE SANDWICH A DAY THAT AVERAGES FIVE OUNCES EACH, AND YOU...
WHAT? WHAT ARE YOU DOING?
KIRKMAN & SCOTT
ACCORDING TO MY FIGURES, YOU'RE WEARING FIVE POUNDS OF PEANUT BUTTER AND JELLY SANDWICH CRUSTS ON YOUR HIPS.
ET TU, SKIPPY?

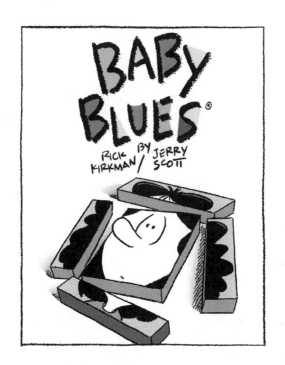

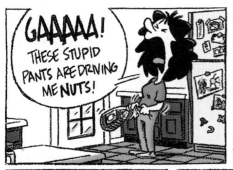

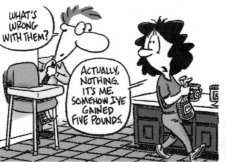

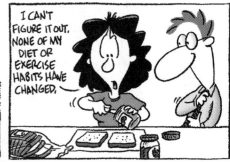

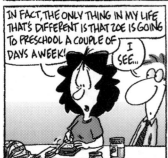

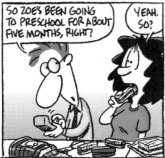

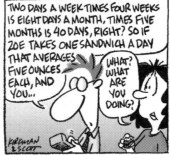

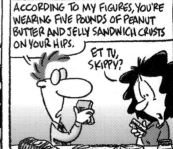

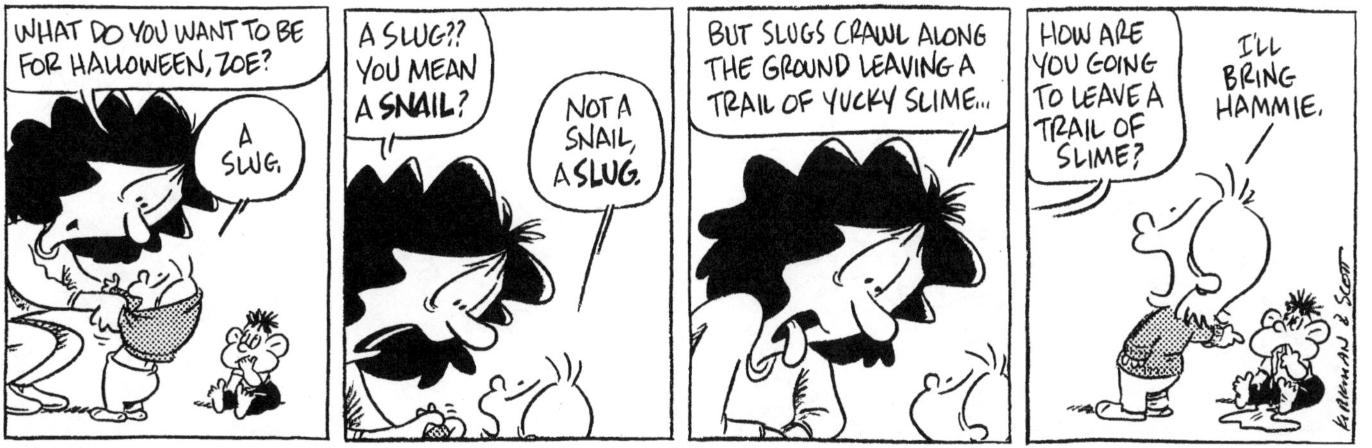
WHAT DO YOU WANT TO BE FOR HALLOWEEN, ZOE?
A SLUG.
A SLUG?? YOU MEAN A **SNAIL**?
NOT A SNAIL, A **SLUG**.
BUT SLUGS CRAWL ALONG THE GROUND LEAVING A TRAIL OF YUCKY SLIME...
HOW ARE YOU GOING TO LEAVE A TRAIL OF SLIME?
I'LL BRING HAMMIE.
KIRKMAN & SCOTT

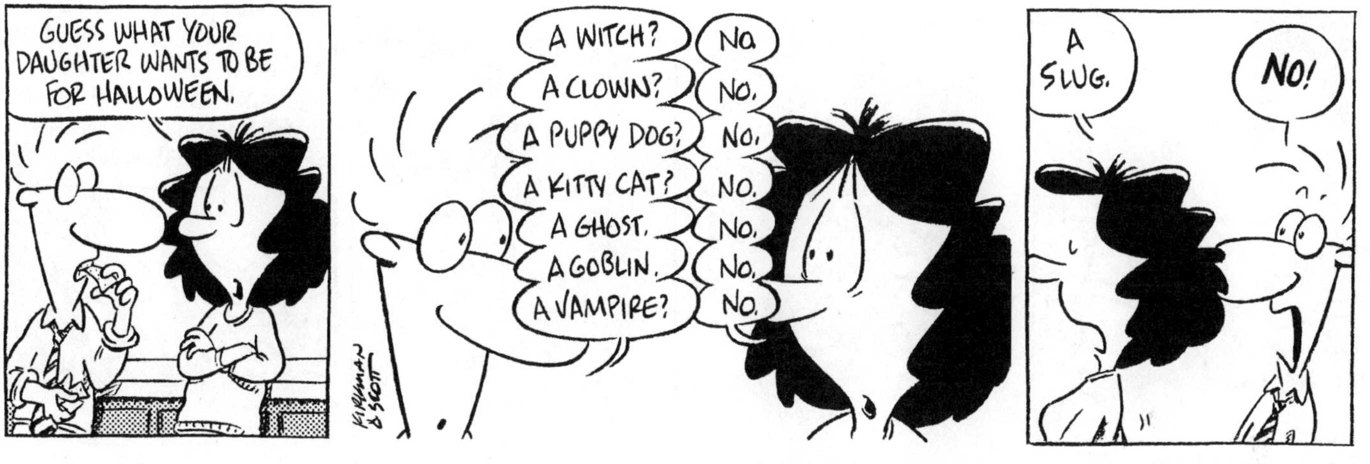
GUESS WHAT YOUR DAUGHTER WANTS TO BE FOR HALLOWEEN.
KIRKMAN & SCOTT
A WITCH?
NO.
A CLOWN?
NO.
A PUPPY DOG?
NO.
A KITTY CAT?
NO.
A GHOST.
NO.
A GOBLIN.
NO.
A VAMPIRE?
NO.
A SLUG.
NO!

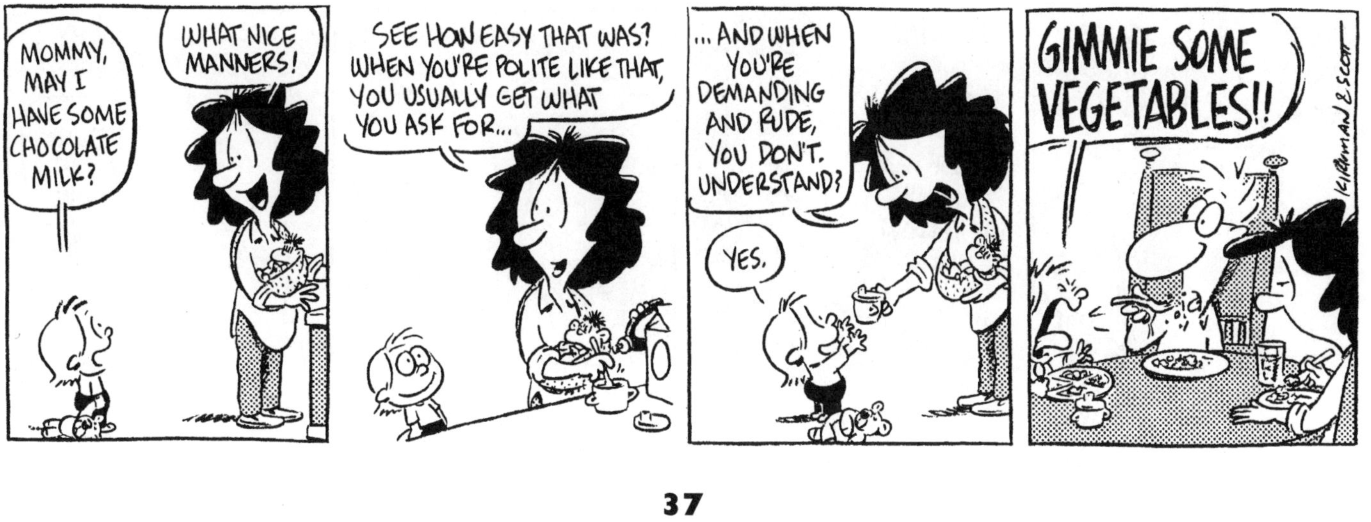
MOMMY, MAY I HAVE SOME CHOCOLATE MILK?
WHAT NICE MANNERS!
SEE HOW EASY THAT WAS? WHEN YOU'RE POLITE LIKE THAT, YOU USUALLY GET WHAT YOU ASK FOR...
... AND WHEN YOU'RE DEMANDING AND RUDE, YOU DON'T. UNDERSTAND?
YES.
GIMMIE SOME VEGETABLES!!
KIRKMAN & SCOTT

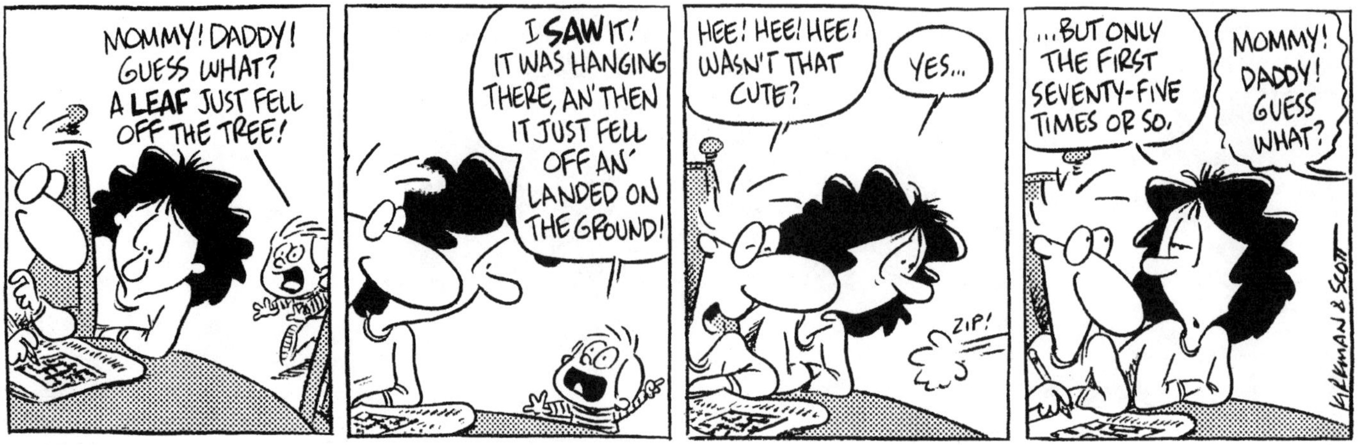
MOMMY! DADDY! GUESS WHAT? A LEAF JUST FELL OFF THE TREE!
I SAW IT! IT WAS HANGING THERE, AN' THEN IT JUST FELL OFF AN' LANDED ON THE GROUND!
HEE! HEE! HEE! WASN'T THAT CUTE?
YES...
ZIP!
...BUT ONLY THE FIRST SEVENTY-FIVE TIMES OR SO.
MOMMY! DADDY! GUESS WHAT?
KIRKMAN & SCOTT

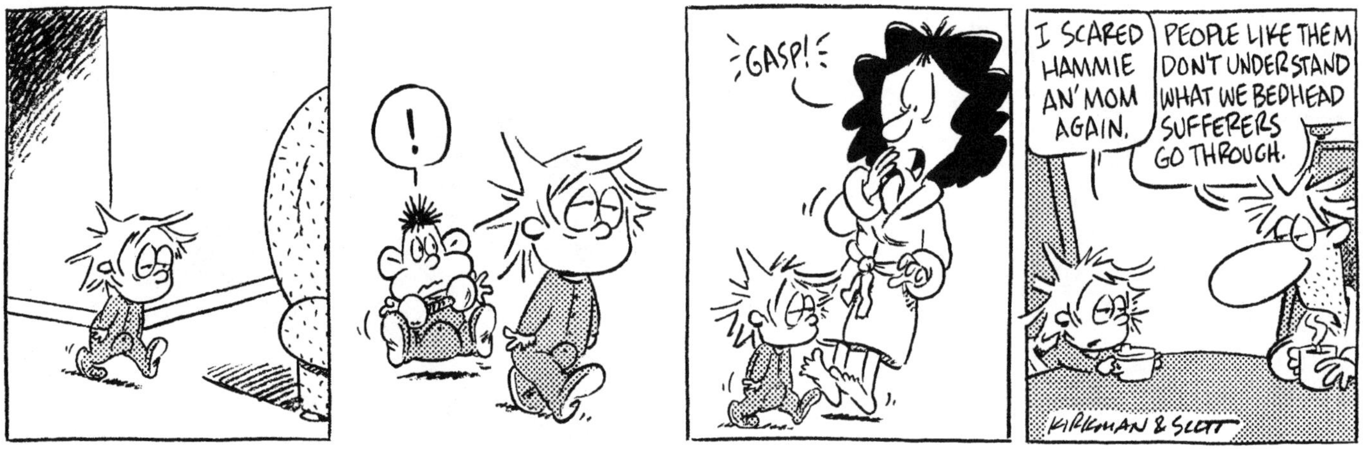
!
GASP!
I SCARED HAMMIE AN' MOM AGAIN.
PEOPLE LIKE THEM DON'T UNDERSTAND WHAT WE BEDHEAD SUFFERERS GO THROUGH.
KIRKMAN & SCOTT

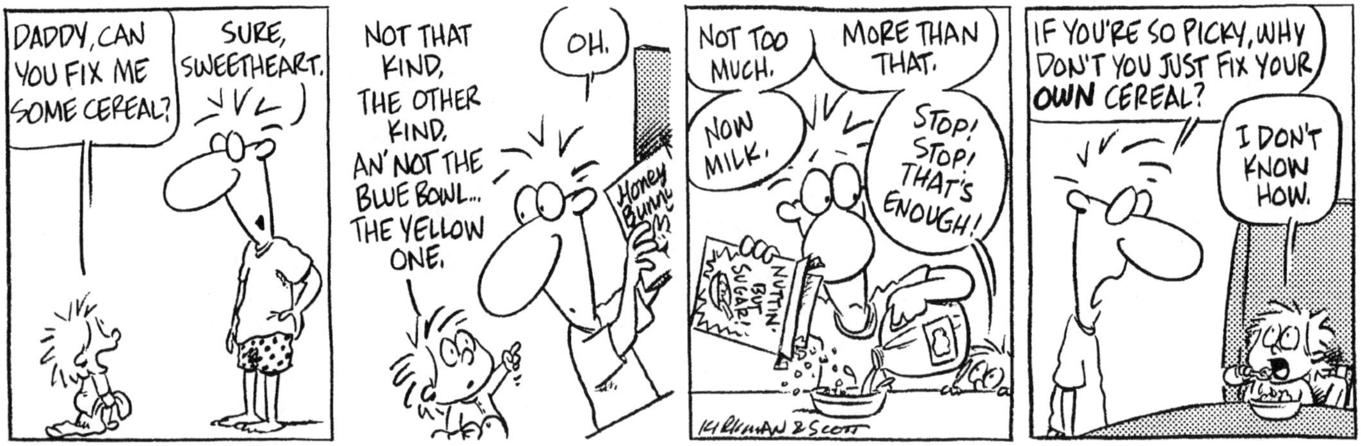
DADDY, CAN YOU FIX ME SOME CEREAL?
SURE, SWEETHEART.
NOT THAT KIND, THE OTHER KIND. AN' NOT THE BLUE BOWL... THE YELLOW ONE.
OH.
Honey Bunny
NOT TOO MUCH.
MORE THAN THAT.
NOW MILK.
STOP! STOP! THAT'S ENOUGH!
NUTTIN' BUT SUGAR!
KIRKMAN & SCOTT
IF YOU'RE SO PICKY, WHY DON'T YOU JUST FIX YOUR OWN CEREAL?
I DON'T KNOW HOW.

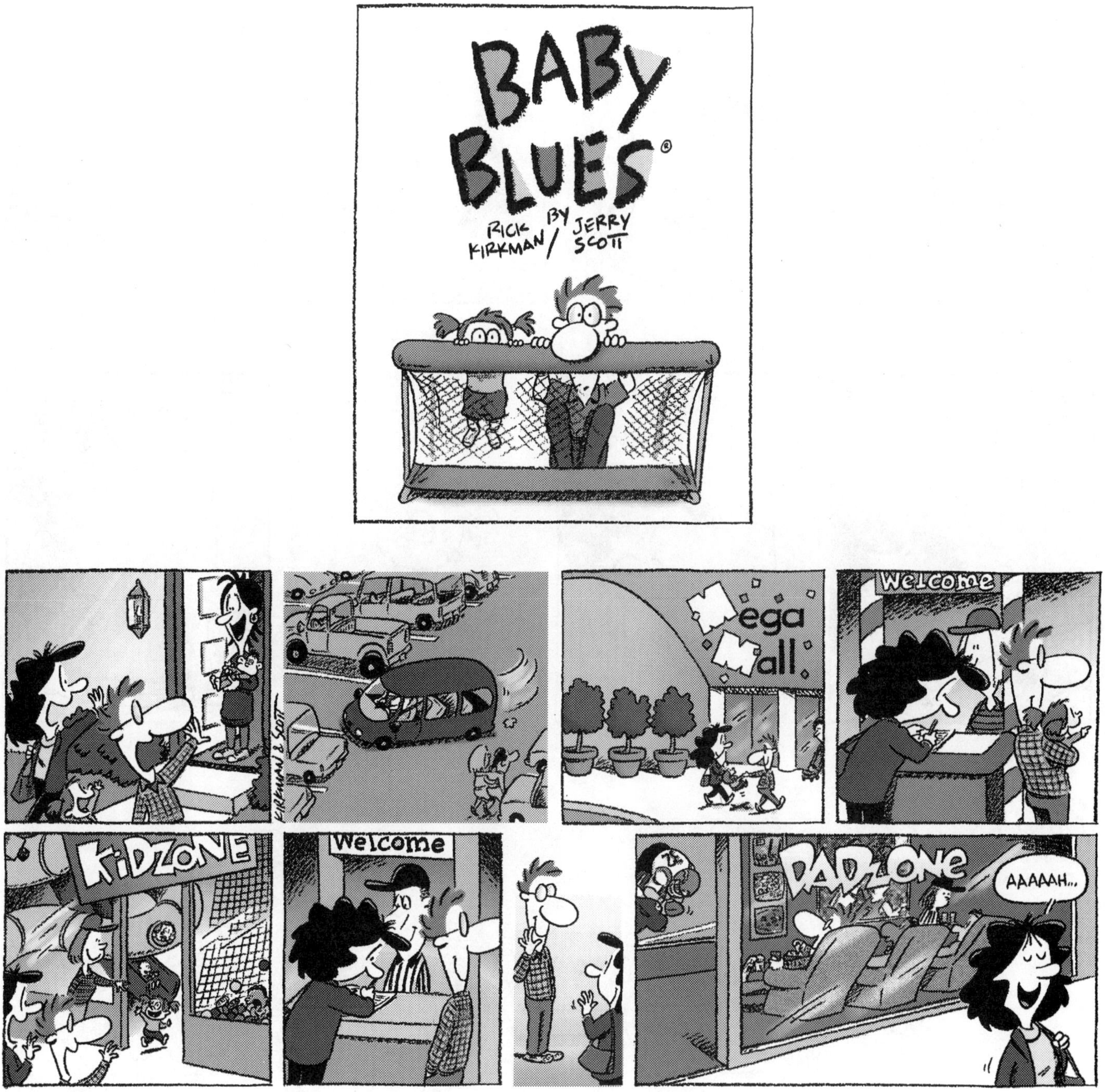
BABY BLUES®
BY RICK KIRKMAN / JERRY SCOTT
KIRKMAN & SCOTT
Mega Mall
Welcome
KIDZONE
Welcome
DADZONE
AAAAAH...

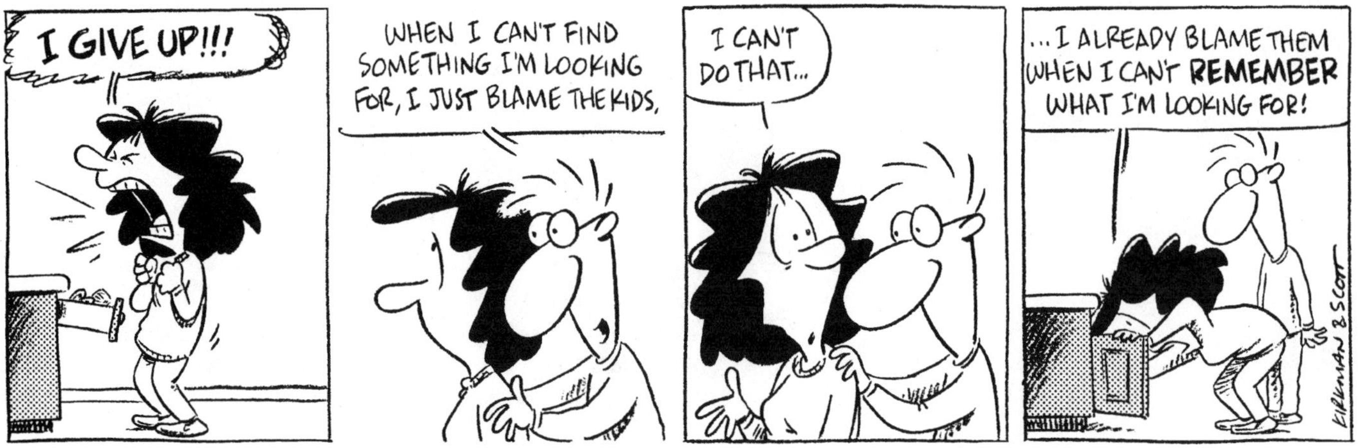
I GIVE UP!!!
WHEN I CAN'T FIND SOMETHING I'M LOOKING FOR, I JUST BLAME THE KIDS.
I CAN'T DO THAT...
...I ALREADY BLAME THEM WHEN I CAN'T **REMEMBER** WHAT I'M LOOKING FOR!
KIRKMAN & SCOTT

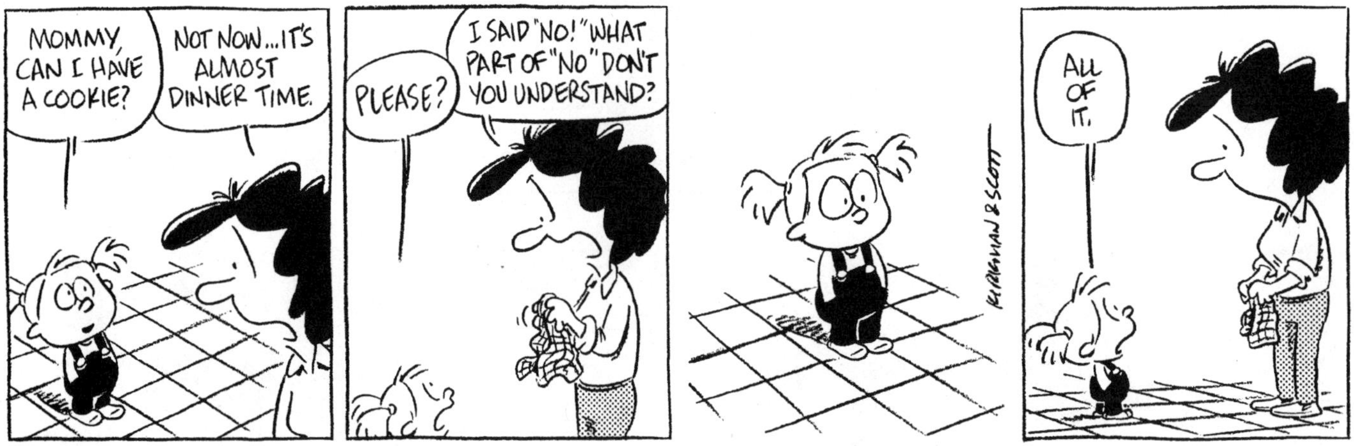
MOMMY, CAN I HAVE A COOKIE?
NOT NOW...IT'S ALMOST DINNER TIME.
PLEASE?
I SAID "NO!" WHAT PART OF "NO" DON'T YOU UNDERSTAND?
KIRKMAN & SCOTT
ALL OF IT.

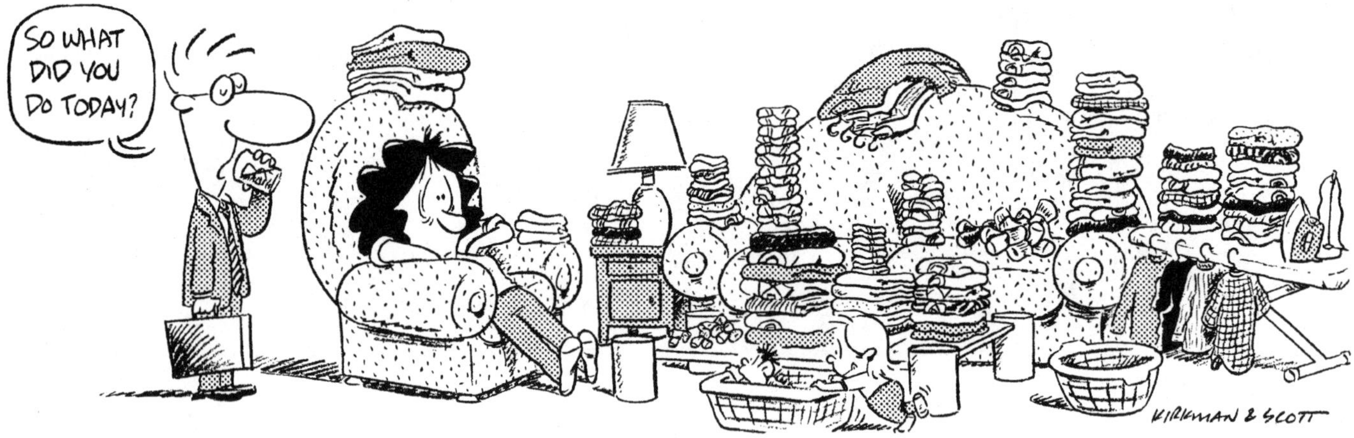
SO WHAT DID YOU DO TODAY?
KIRKMAN & SCOTT

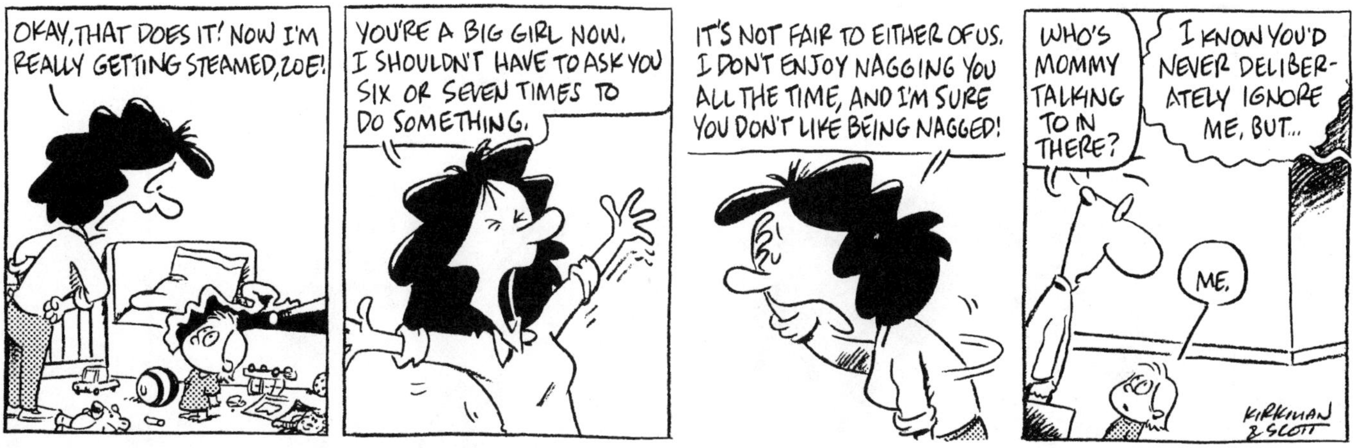
OKAY, THAT DOES IT! NOW I'M REALLY GETTING STEAMED, ZOE!
YOU'RE A BIG GIRL NOW. I SHOULDN'T HAVE TO ASK YOU SIX OR SEVEN TIMES TO DO SOMETHING.
IT'S NOT FAIR TO EITHER OF US. I DON'T ENJOY NAGGING YOU ALL THE TIME, AND I'M SURE YOU DON'T LIKE BEING NAGGED!
WHO'S MOMMY TALKING TO IN THERE?
I KNOW YOU'D NEVER DELIBERATELY IGNORE ME, BUT...
ME.
KIRKMAN & SCOTT

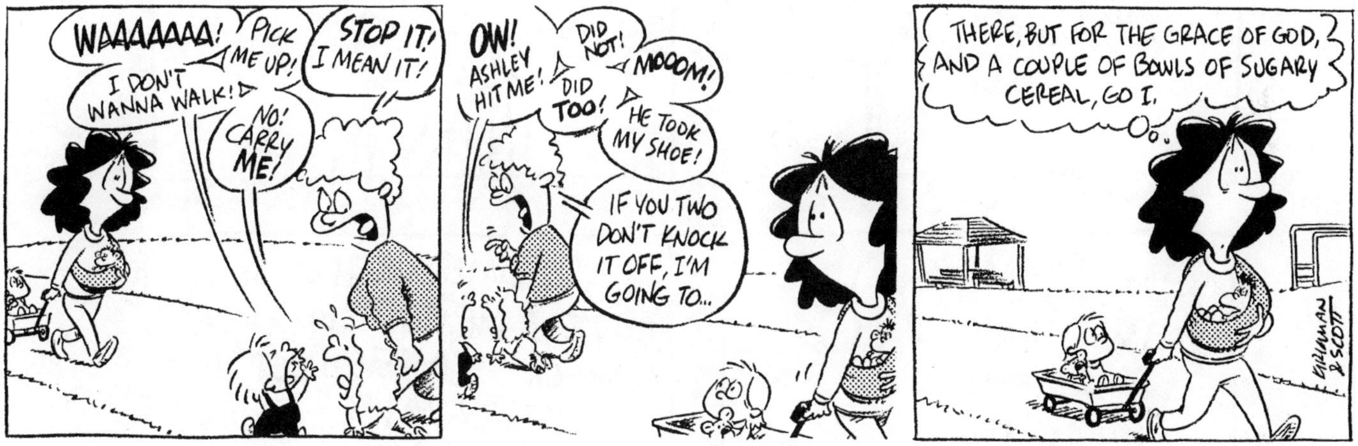
WAAAAAAA!
PICK ME UP!
I DON'T WANNA WALK!
NO! CARRY ME!
STOP IT! I MEAN IT!
OW! ASHLEY HIT ME!
DID NOT!
DID TOO!
MOOOM!
HE TOOK MY SHOE!
IF YOU TWO DON'T KNOCK IT OFF, I'M GOING TO...
THERE, BUT FOR THE GRACE OF GOD, AND A COUPLE OF BOWLS OF SUGARY CEREAL, GO I.
KIRKMAN & SCOTT

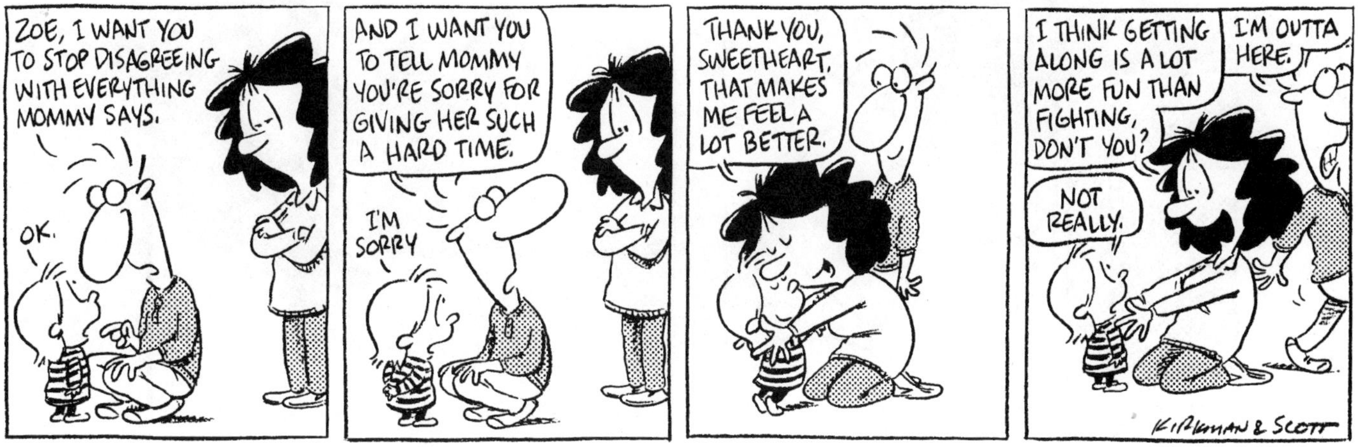
ZOE, I WANT YOU TO STOP DISAGREEING WITH EVERYTHING MOMMY SAYS.
OK.
AND I WANT YOU TO TELL MOMMY YOU'RE SORRY FOR GIVING HER SUCH A HARD TIME.
I'M SORRY
THANK YOU, SWEETHEART. THAT MAKES ME FEEL A LOT BETTER.
I THINK GETTING ALONG IS A LOT MORE FUN THAN FIGHTING, DON'T YOU?
I'M OUTTA HERE.
NOT REALLY.
KIRKMAN & SCOTT

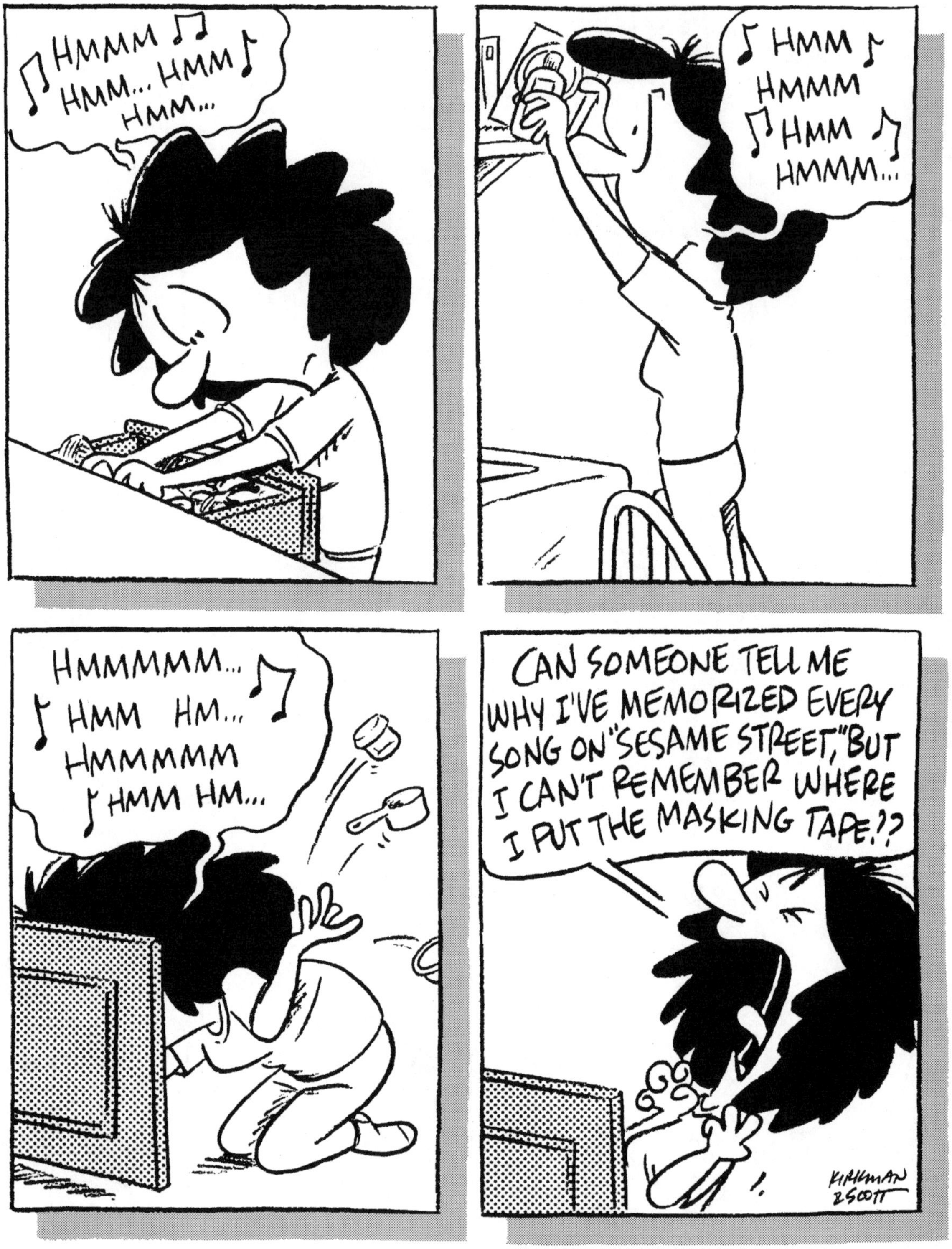
HMMM
HMM... HMM
HMM...
HMM
HMMM
HMM
HMMM...
HMMMMM...
HMM HM...
HMMMMM
HMM HM...
CAN SOMEONE TELL ME WHY I'VE MEMORIZED EVERY SONG ON "SESAME STREET," BUT I CAN'T REMEMBER WHERE I PUT THE MASKING TAPE?!
KIRKMAN & SCOTT

BABY BLUES®
BY
RICK KIRKMAN / JERRY SCOTT

PBBBTHHT.
PBBBTHHT.
PBBBTHHT.
PTH.
PBBBTHHT.
BBTH.
PBBBTHHT.
PBBTH.
PBBBTHHT?
PBBBTHHT!
MOM! HAMMIE WON'T STOP COPYING ME!!!
PBBBTHHT.
KIRKMAN & SCOTT

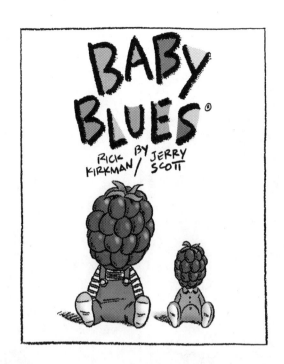

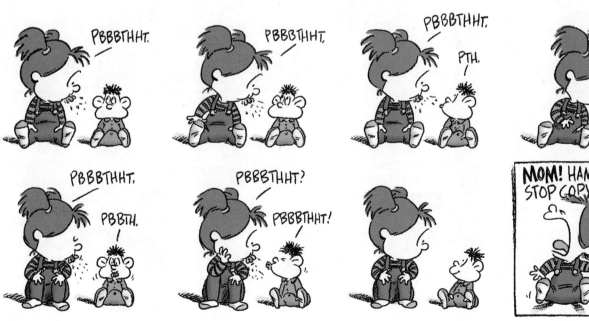

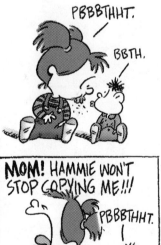

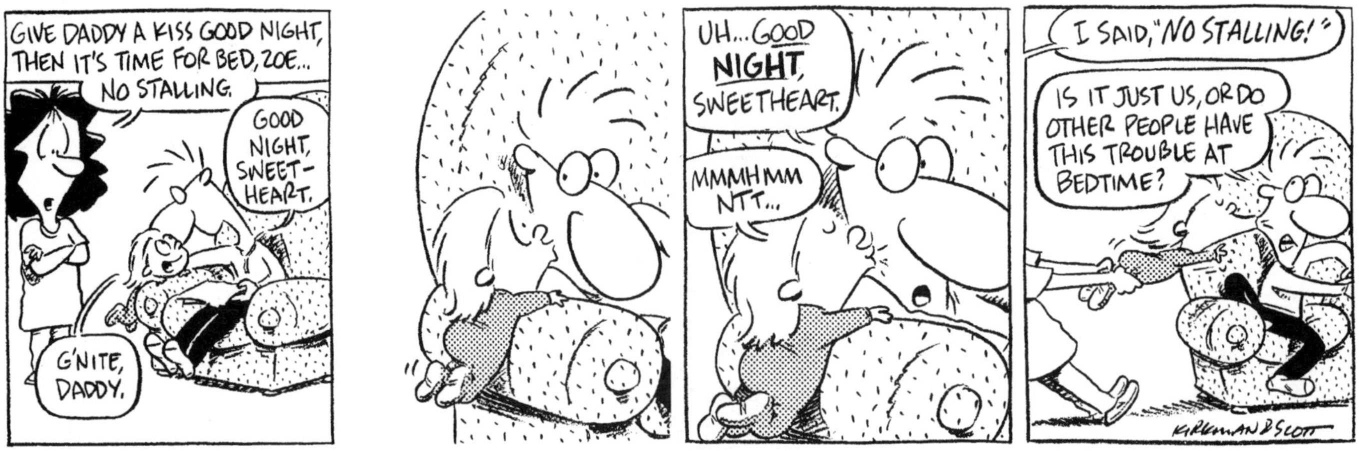
GIVE DADDY A KISS GOOD NIGHT, THEN IT'S TIME FOR BED, ZOE... NO STALLING.
GOOD NIGHT, SWEET-HEART.
G'NITE, DADDY.
UH...GOOD NIGHT, SWEETHEART.
MMMHMM NTT...
I SAID, "NO STALLING!"
IS IT JUST US, OR DO OTHER PEOPLE HAVE THIS TROUBLE AT BEDTIME?
KIRKMAN & SCOTT

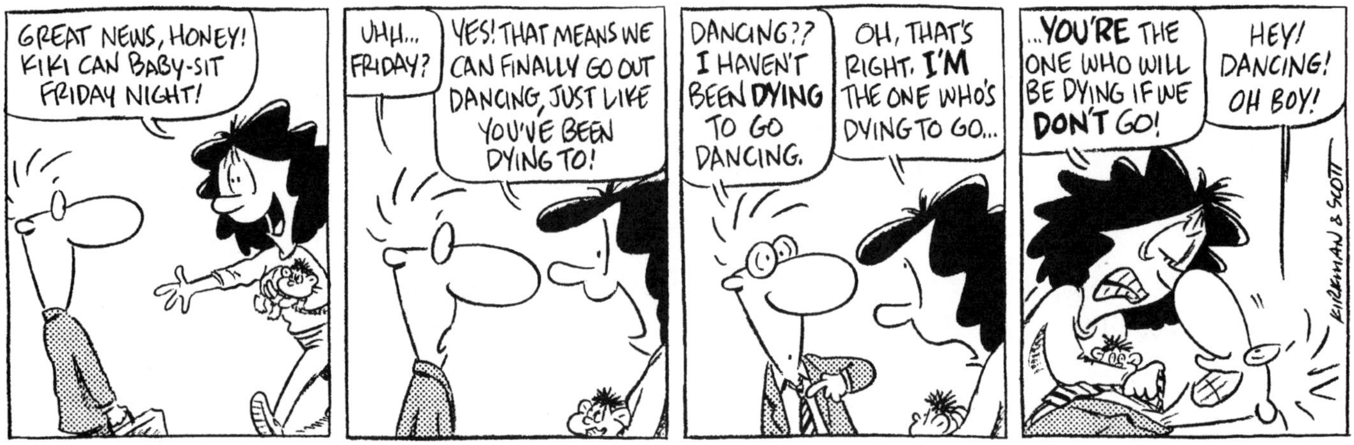
GREAT NEWS, HONEY! KIKI CAN BABY-SIT FRIDAY NIGHT!
UHH... FRIDAY?
YES! THAT MEANS WE CAN FINALLY GO OUT DANCING, JUST LIKE YOU'VE BEEN DYING TO!
DANCING?? I HAVEN'T BEEN DYING TO GO DANCING.
OH, THAT'S RIGHT. I'M THE ONE WHO'S DYING TO GO...
...YOU'RE THE ONE WHO WILL BE DYING IF WE DON'T GO!
HEY! DANCING! OH BOY!
KIRKMAN & SCOTT

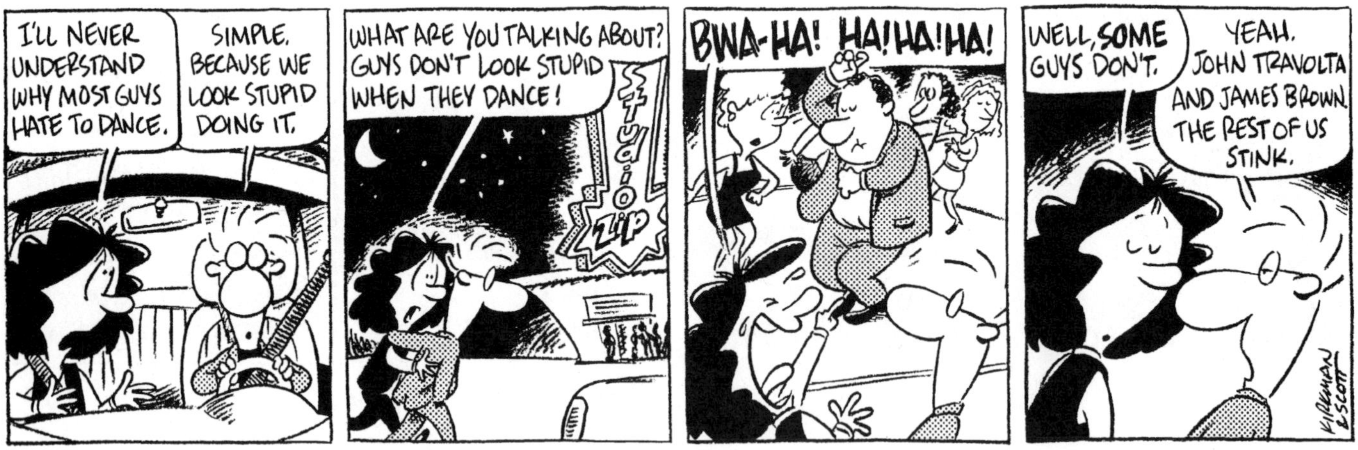
I'LL NEVER UNDERSTAND WHY MOST GUYS HATE TO DANCE.
SIMPLE. BECAUSE WE LOOK STUPID DOING IT.
WHAT ARE YOU TALKING ABOUT? GUYS DON'T LOOK STUPID WHEN THEY DANCE!
Studio Zip
BWA-HA! HA! HA! HA!
WELL, SOME GUYS DON'T.
YEAH. JOHN TRAVOLTA AND JAMES BROWN. THE REST OF US STINK.
KIRKMAN & SCOTT

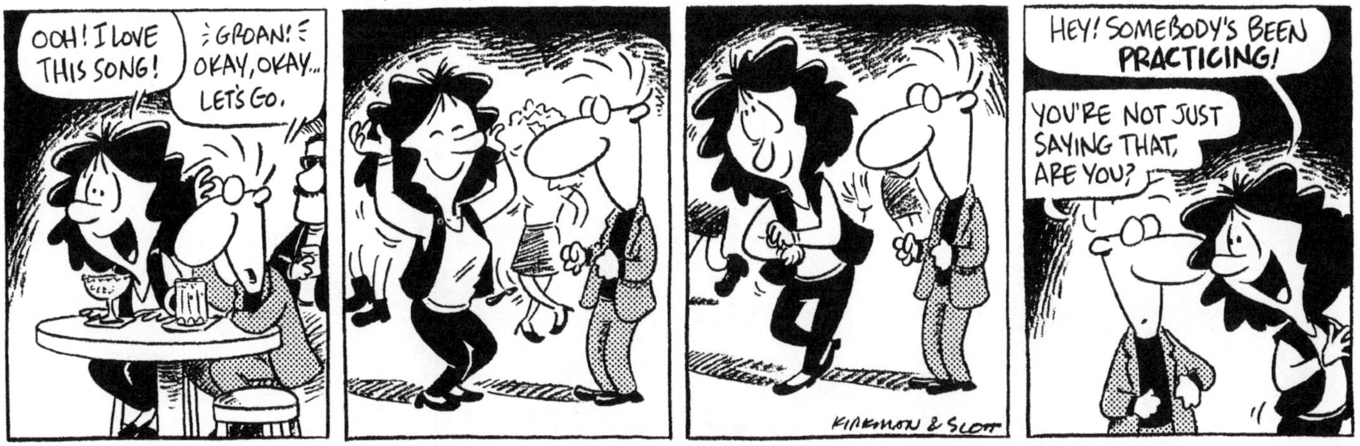
OOH! I LOVE THIS SONG!
GROAN! OKAY, OKAY... LET'S GO.
HEY! SOMEBODY'S BEEN PRACTICING!
YOU'RE NOT JUST SAYING THAT, ARE YOU?
KIRKMAN & SCOTT

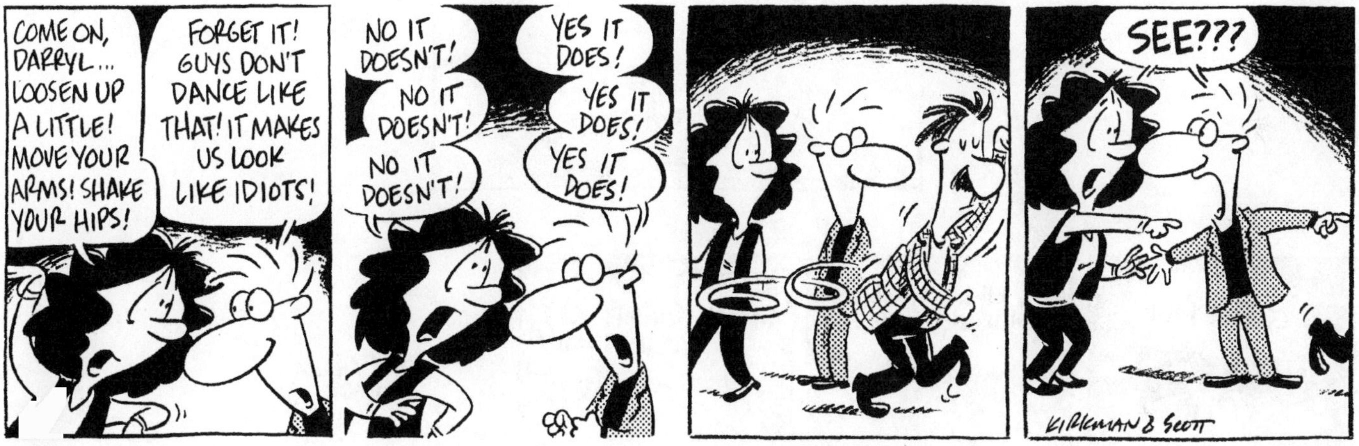
COME ON, DARRYL... LOOSEN UP A LITTLE! MOVE YOUR ARMS! SHAKE YOUR HIPS!
FORGET IT! GUYS DON'T DANCE LIKE THAT! IT MAKES US LOOK LIKE IDIOTS!
NO IT DOESN'T!
YES IT DOES!
NO IT DOESN'T!
YES IT DOES!
NO IT DOESN'T!
YES IT DOES!
SEE???
KIRKMAN & SCOTT

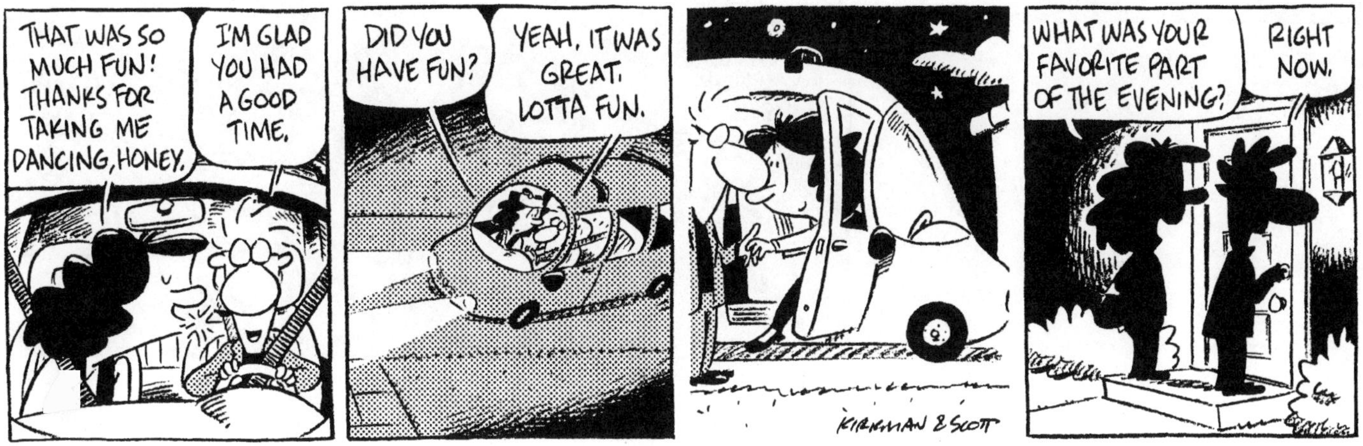
THAT WAS SO MUCH FUN! THANKS FOR TAKING ME DANCING, HONEY.
I'M GLAD YOU HAD A GOOD TIME.
DID YOU HAVE FUN?
YEAH, IT WAS GREAT. LOTTA FUN.
WHAT WAS YOUR FAVORITE PART OF THE EVENING?
RIGHT NOW.
KIRKMAN & SCOTT

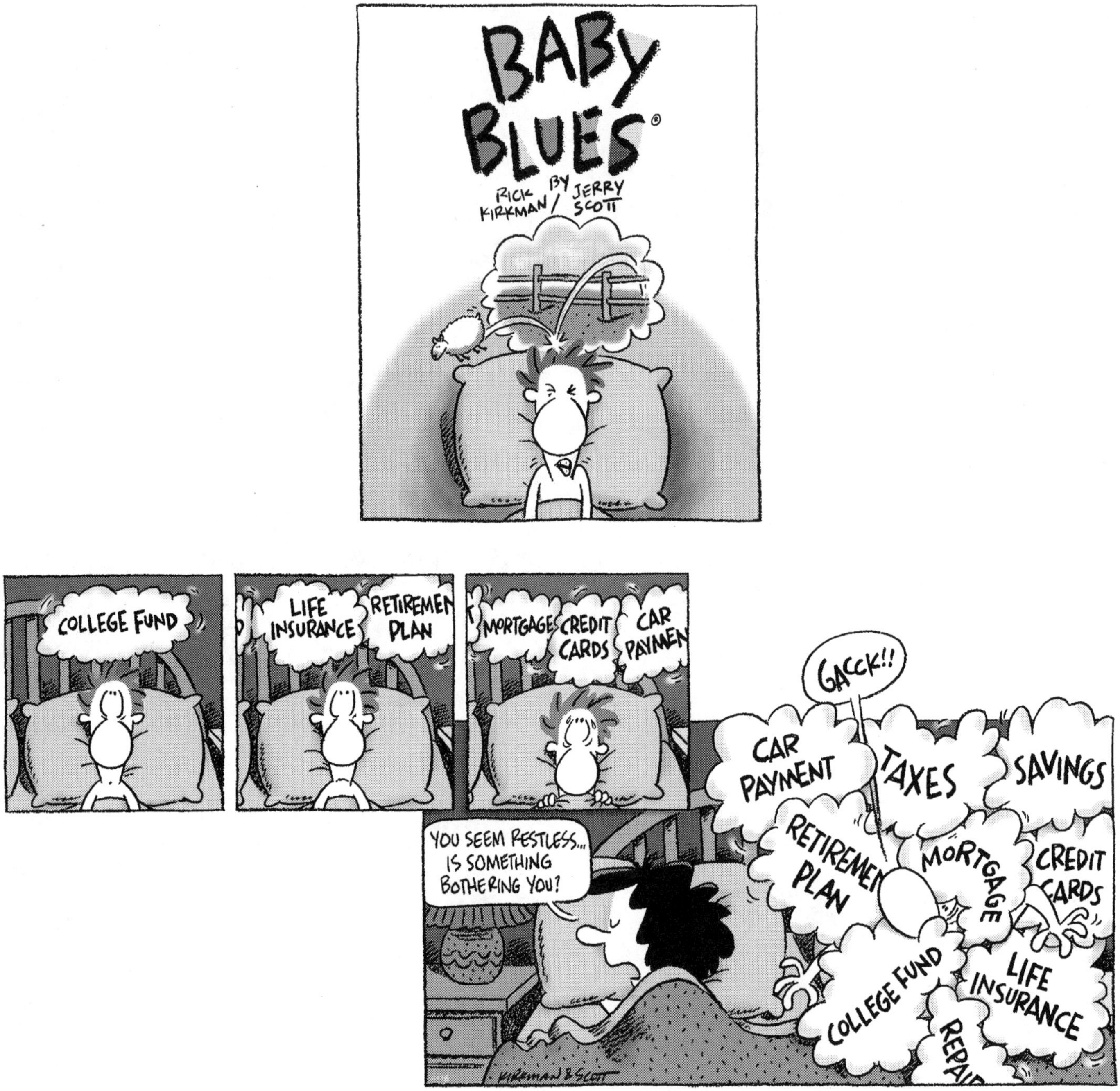
BABY BLUES®
BY RICK KIRKMAN / JERRY SCOTT
COLLEGE FUND
LIFE INSURANCE
RETIREMEN PLAN
MORTGAGE
CREDIT CARDS
CAR PAYMEN
YOU SEEM RESTLESS... IS SOMETHING BOTHERING YOU?
GACCK!!
CAR PAYMENT
TAXES
SAVINGS
RETIREMEN PLAN
MORTGAGE
CREDIT CARDS
COLLEGE FUND
LIFE INSURANCE
REPAI
KIRKMAN & SCOTT

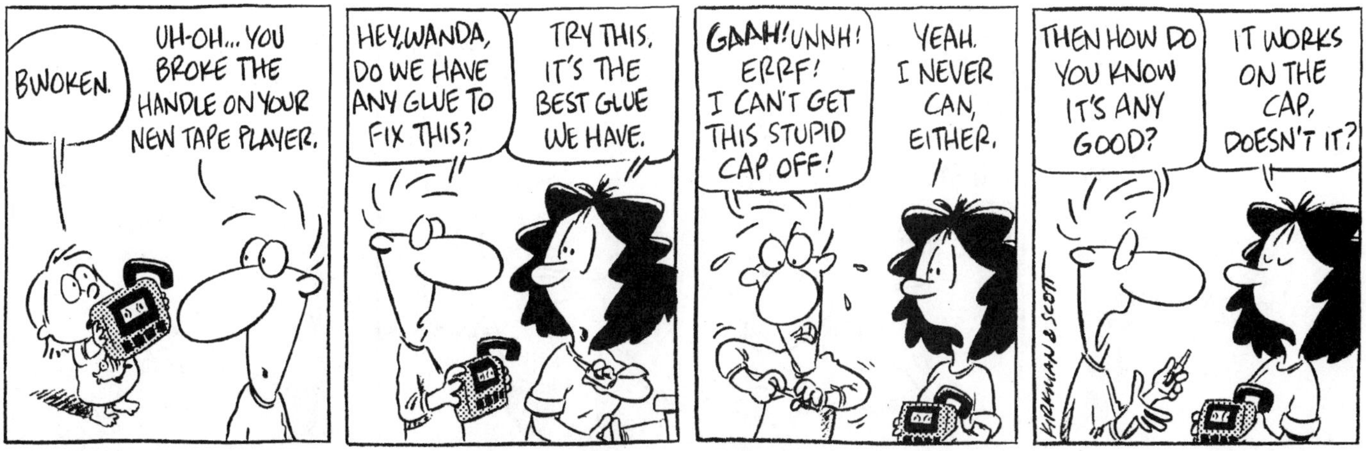
BWOKEN.
UH-OH... YOU BROKE THE HANDLE ON YOUR NEW TAPE PLAYER.
HEY, WANDA, DO WE HAVE ANY GLUE TO FIX THIS?
TRY THIS. IT'S THE BEST GLUE WE HAVE.
GAAH! UNNH! ERRF! I CAN'T GET THIS STUPID CAP OFF!
YEAH. I NEVER CAN, EITHER.
THEN HOW DO YOU KNOW IT'S ANY GOOD?
IT WORKS ON THE CAP, DOESN'T IT?
KIRKMAN & SCOTT

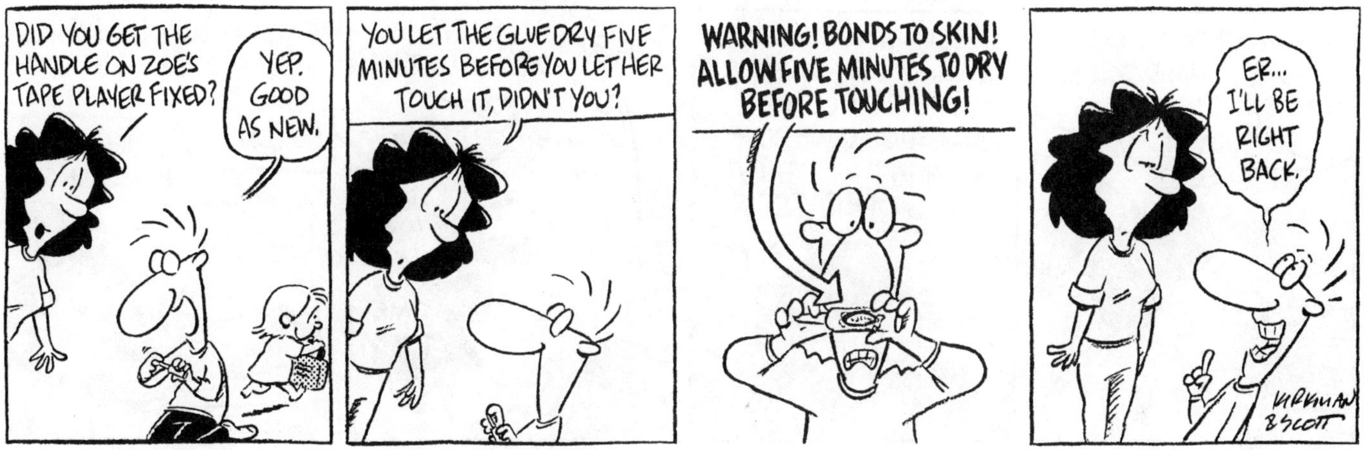
DID YOU GET THE HANDLE ON ZOE'S TAPE PLAYER FIXED?
YEP. GOOD AS NEW.
YOU LET THE GLUE DRY FIVE MINUTES BEFORE YOU LET HER TOUCH IT, DIDN'T YOU?
WARNING! BONDS TO SKIN! ALLOW FIVE MINUTES TO DRY BEFORE TOUCHING!
ER... I'LL BE RIGHT BACK.
KIRKMAN & SCOTT

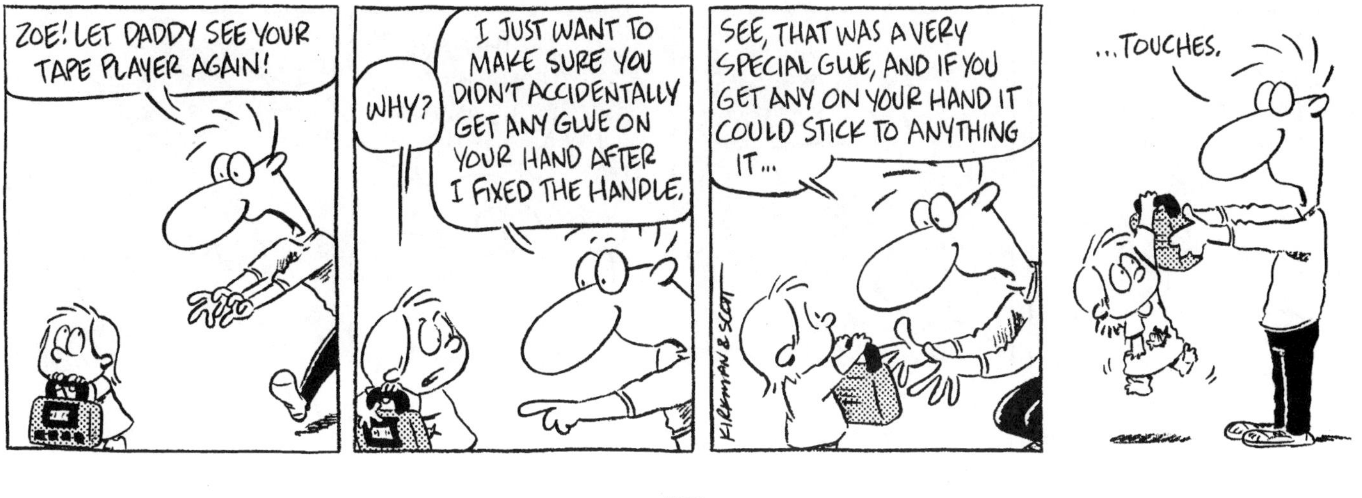
ZOE! LET DADDY SEE YOUR TAPE PLAYER AGAIN!
WHY?
I JUST WANT TO MAKE SURE YOU DIDN'T ACCIDENTALLY GET ANY GLUE ON YOUR HAND AFTER I FIXED THE HANDLE.
SEE, THAT WAS A VERY SPECIAL GLUE, AND IF YOU GET ANY ON YOUR HAND IT COULD STICK TO ANYTHING IT...
KIRKMAN & SCOTT
...TOUCHES.

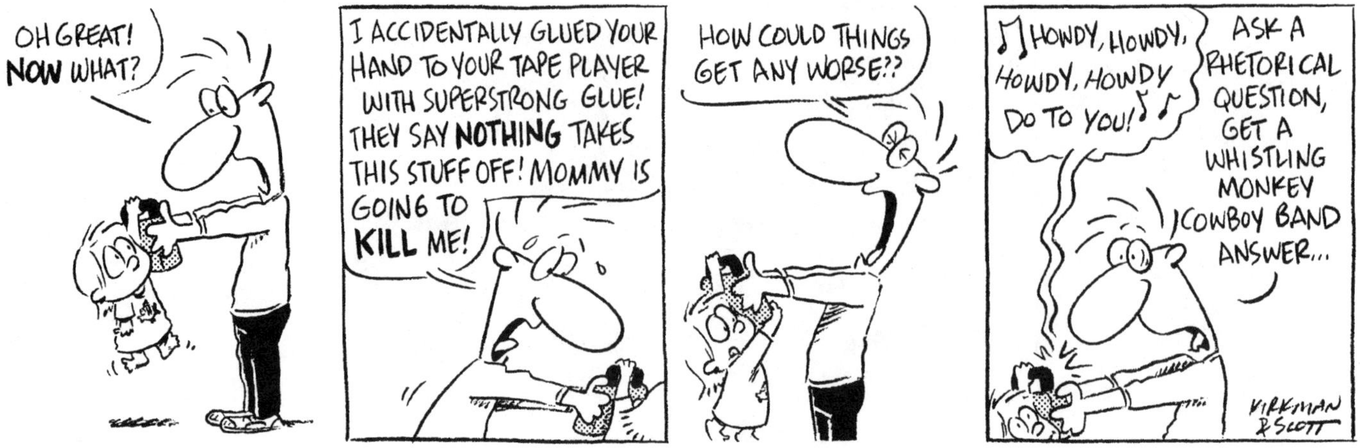
OH GREAT! NOW WHAT?
I ACCIDENTALLY GLUED YOUR HAND TO YOUR TAPE PLAYER WITH SUPERSTRONG GLUE! THEY SAY NOTHING TAKES THIS STUFF OFF! MOMMY IS GOING TO KILL ME!
HOW COULD THINGS GET ANY WORSE??
HOWDY, HOWDY, HOWDY, HOWDY DO TO YOU!
ASK A RHETORICAL QUESTION, GET A WHISTLING MONKEY COWBOY BAND ANSWER...
KIRKMAN & SCOTT

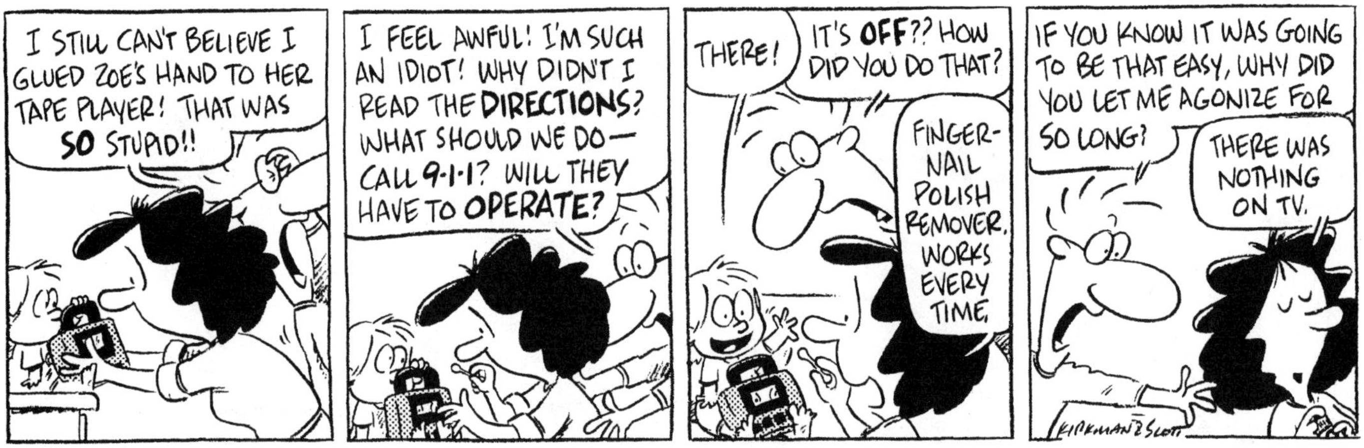
I STILL CAN'T BELIEVE I GLUED ZOE'S HAND TO HER TAPE PLAYER! THAT WAS SO STUPID!!
I FEEL AWFUL! I'M SUCH AN IDIOT! WHY DIDN'T I READ THE DIRECTIONS? WHAT SHOULD WE DO— CALL 9-1-1? WILL THEY HAVE TO OPERATE?
THERE!
IT'S OFF?? HOW DID YOU DO THAT?
FINGER-NAIL POLISH REMOVER. WORKS EVERY TIME.
IF YOU KNOW IT WAS GOING TO BE THAT EASY, WHY DID YOU LET ME AGONIZE FOR SO LONG?
THERE WAS NOTHING ON TV.
KIRKMAN & SCOTT

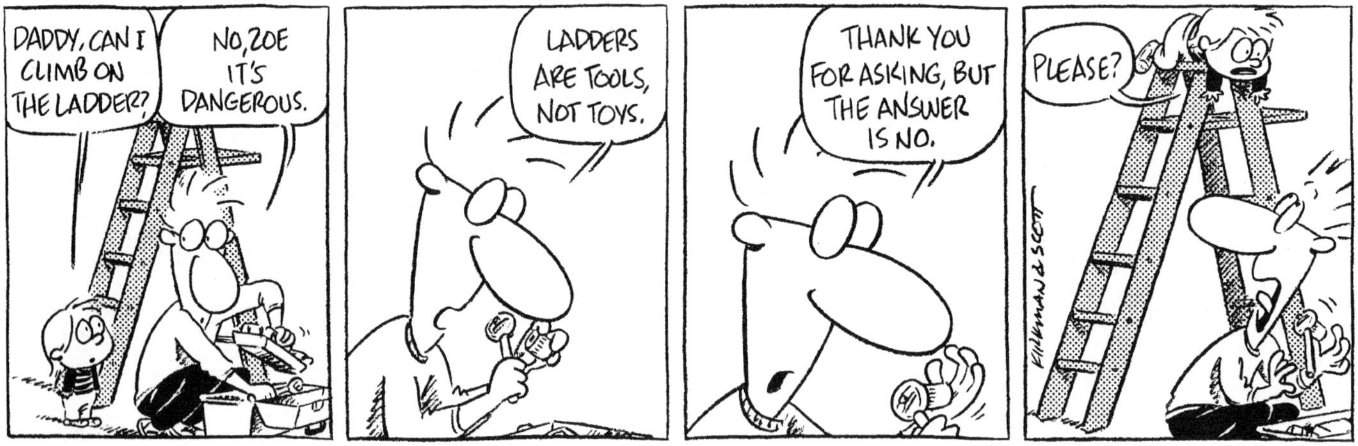
DADDY, CAN I CLIMB ON THE LADDER?
NO, ZOE IT'S DANGEROUS.
LADDERS ARE TOOLS, NOT TOYS.
THANK YOU FOR ASKING, BUT THE ANSWER IS NO.
PLEASE?
KIRKMAN & SCOTT

BABY BLUES®
BY
RICK KIRKMAN / JERRY SCOTT

CLICK!
HAPPY HANDS
PRESCHOOL
ZOE SEEMS A BIT SLUGGISH THIS MORNING...
TELL ME ABOUT IT.
SIGN IN
YAWN!
KIRKMAN & SCOTT

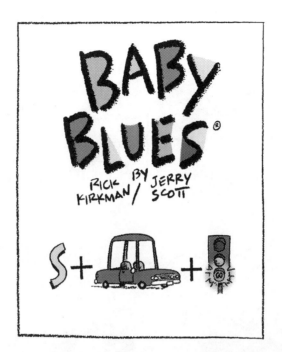

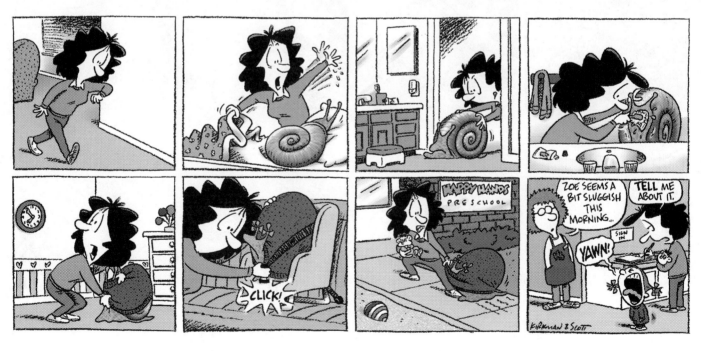

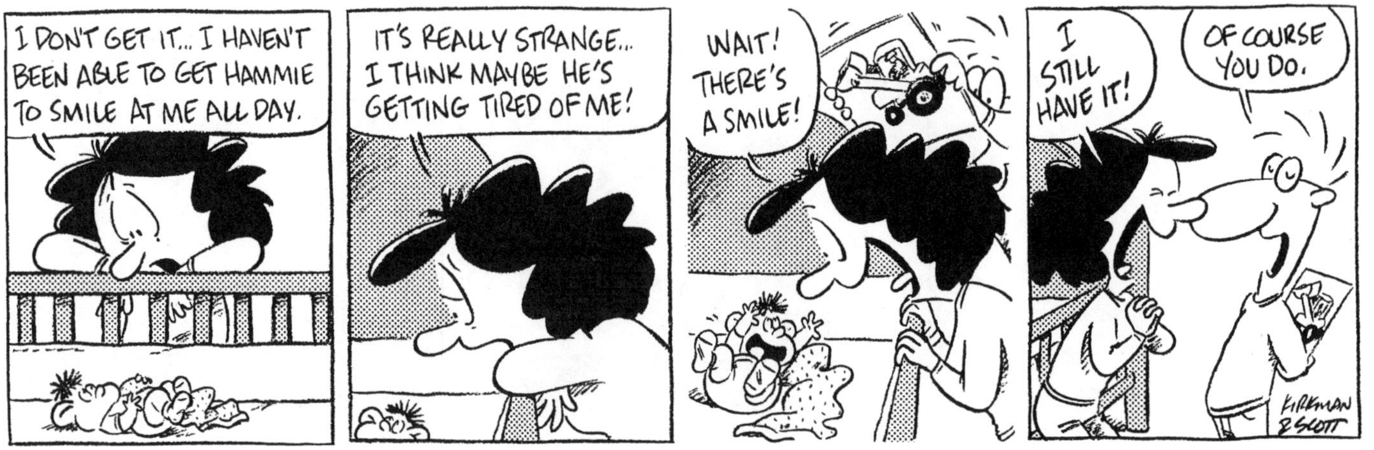
I DON'T GET IT... I HAVEN'T BEEN ABLE TO GET HAMMIE TO SMILE AT ME ALL DAY.
IT'S REALLY STRANGE... I THINK MAYBE HE'S GETTING TIRED OF ME!
WAIT! THERE'S A SMILE!
I STILL HAVE IT!
OF COURSE YOU DO.
KIRKMAN & SCOTT

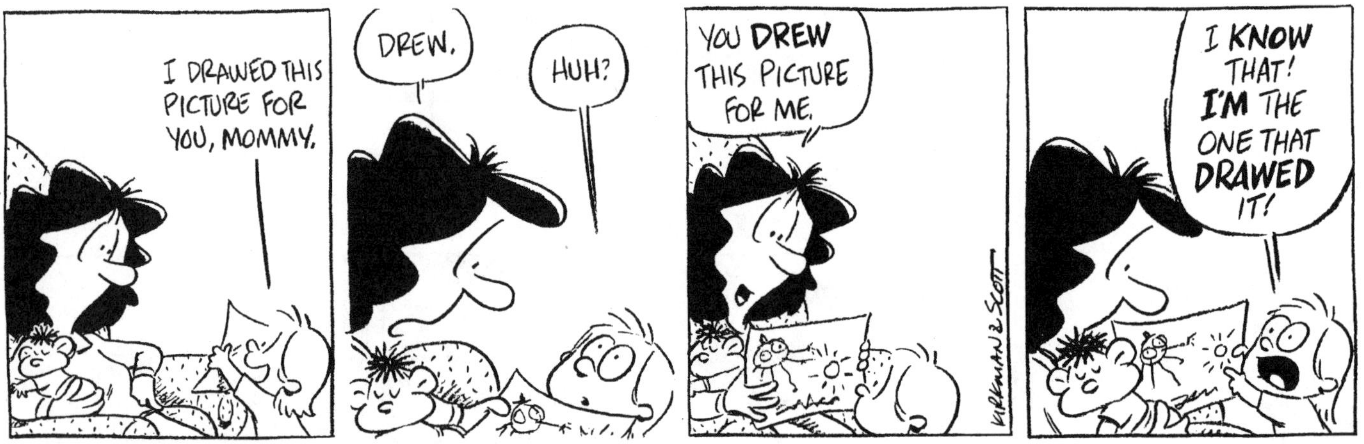
I DRAWED THIS PICTURE FOR YOU, MOMMY.
DREW.
HUH?
YOU **DREW** THIS PICTURE FOR ME.
KIRKMAN & SCOTT
I **KNOW** THAT! **I'M** THE ONE THAT **DRAWED** IT!

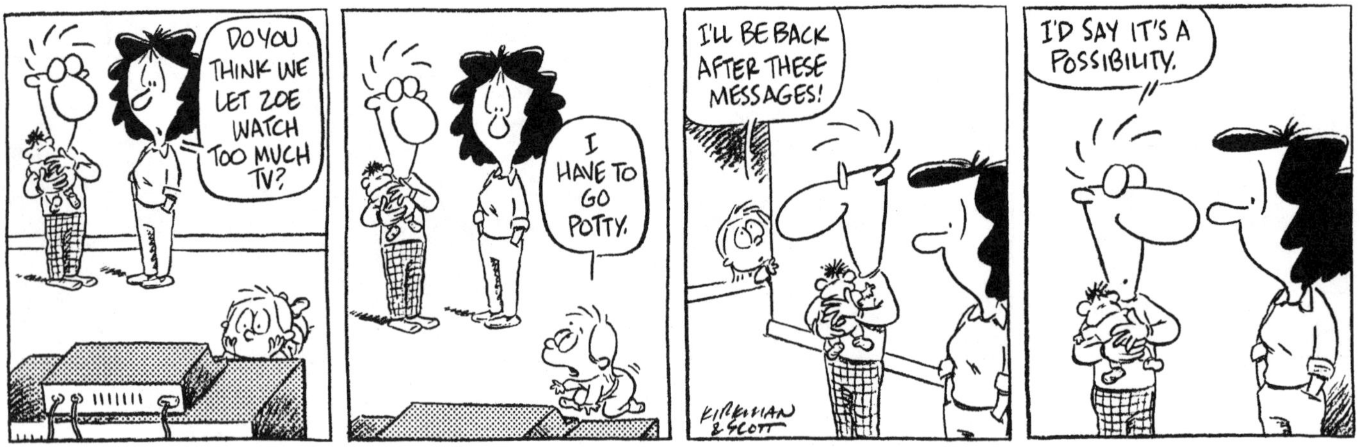
DO YOU THINK WE LET ZOE WATCH TOO MUCH TV?
I HAVE TO GO POTTY.
I'LL BE BACK AFTER THESE MESSAGES!
KIRKMAN & SCOTT
I'D SAY IT'S A POSSIBILITY.

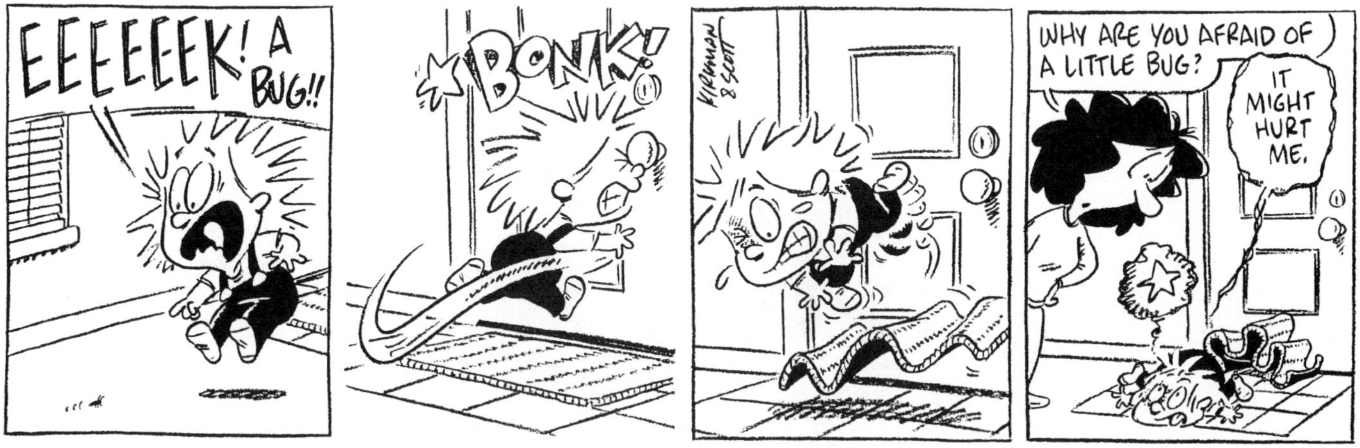
EEEEEEK! A BUG!!
BONK!
KIRKMAN & SCOTT
WHY ARE YOU AFRAID OF A LITTLE BUG?
IT MIGHT HURT ME.

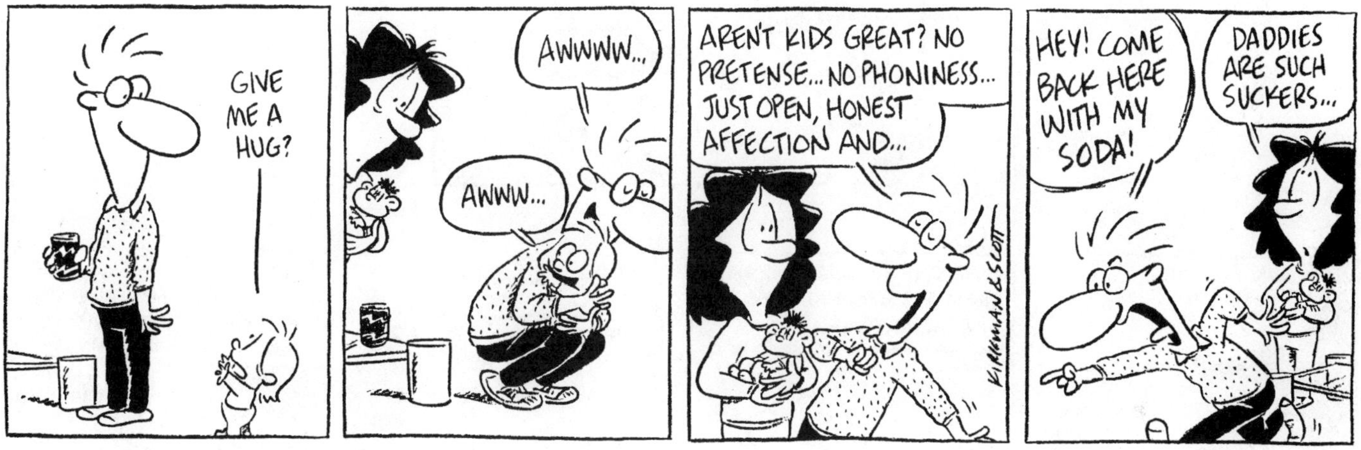
GIVE ME A HUG?
AWWWW...
AWWW...
AREN'T KIDS GREAT? NO PRETENSE... NO PHONINESS... JUST OPEN, HONEST AFFECTION AND...
KIRKMAN & SCOTT
HEY! COME BACK HERE WITH MY SODA!
DADDIES ARE SUCH SUCKERS...

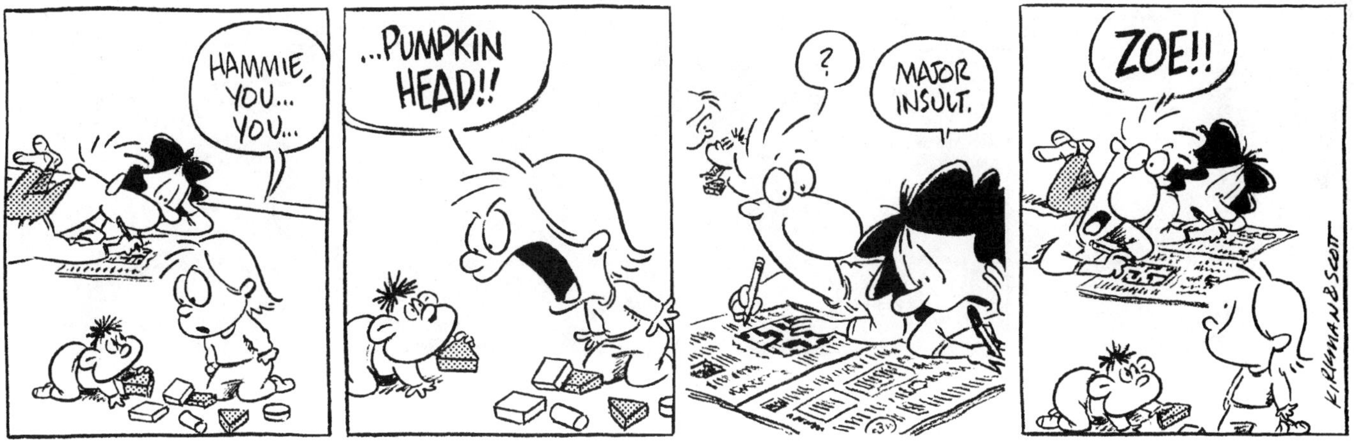
HAMMIE, YOU... YOU...
...PUMPKIN HEAD!!
?
MAJOR INSULT.
ZOE!!
KIRKMAN & SCOTT

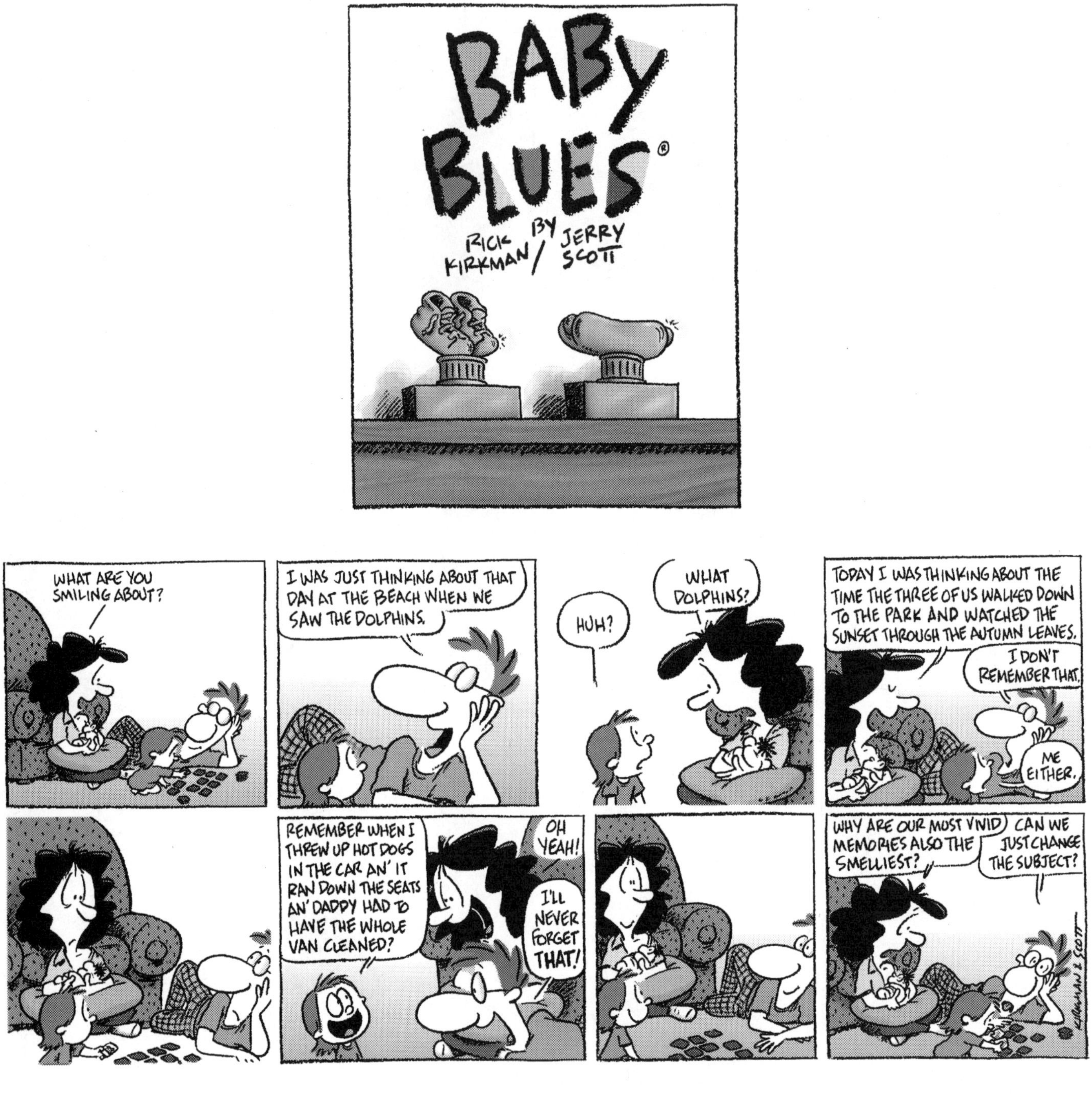
BABY BLUES®
BY RICK KIRKMAN / JERRY SCOTT
WHAT ARE YOU SMILING ABOUT?
I WAS JUST THINKING ABOUT THAT DAY AT THE BEACH WHEN WE SAW THE DOLPHINS.
HUH?
WHAT DOLPHINS?
TODAY I WAS THINKING ABOUT THE TIME THE THREE OF US WALKED DOWN TO THE PARK AND WATCHED THE SUNSET THROUGH THE AUTUMN LEAVES.
I DON'T REMEMBER THAT.
ME EITHER.
REMEMBER WHEN I THREW UP HOT DOGS IN THE CAR AN' IT RAN DOWN THE SEATS AN' DADDY HAD TO HAVE THE WHOLE VAN CLEANED?
OH YEAH!
I'LL NEVER FORGET THAT!
WHY ARE OUR MOST VIVID MEMORIES ALSO THE SMELLIEST?
CAN WE JUST CHANGE THE SUBJECT?
KIRKMAN & SCOTT

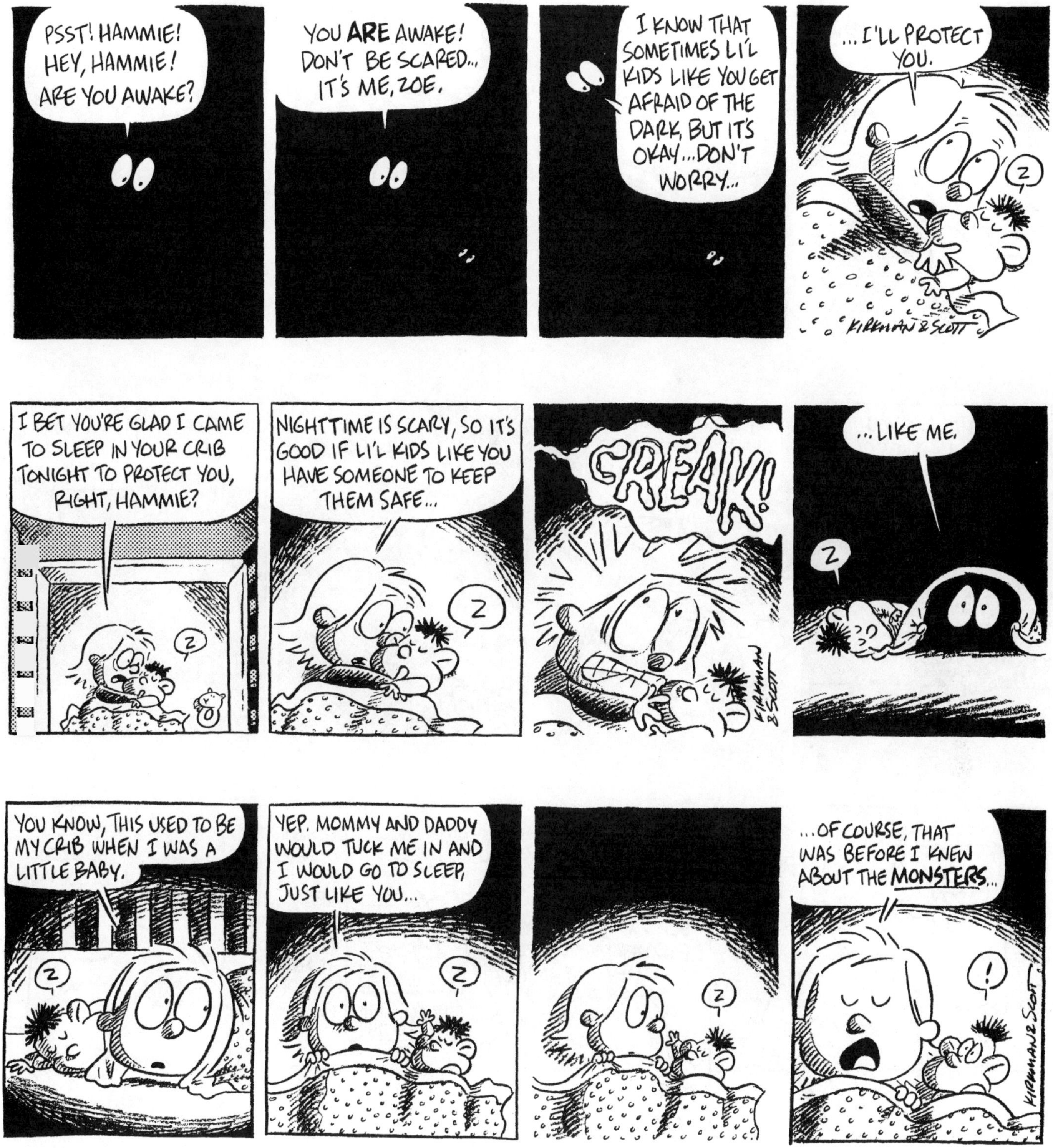
PSST! HAMMIE! HEY, HAMMIE! ARE YOU AWAKE?
YOU ARE AWAKE! DON'T BE SCARED... IT'S ME, ZOE.
I KNOW THAT SOMETIMES LI'L KIDS LIKE YOU GET AFRAID OF THE DARK, BUT IT'S OKAY... DON'T WORRY...
...I'LL PROTECT YOU.
Z
KIRKMAN & SCOTT
I BET YOU'RE GLAD I CAME TO SLEEP IN YOUR CRIB TONIGHT TO PROTECT YOU, RIGHT, HAMMIE?
Z
NIGHTTIME IS SCARY, SO IT'S GOOD IF LI'L KIDS LIKE YOU HAVE SOMEONE TO KEEP THEM SAFE...
Z
CREAK!
KIRKMAN & SCOTT
...LIKE ME.
Z
YOU KNOW, THIS USED TO BE MY CRIB WHEN I WAS A LITTLE BABY.
Z
YEP. MOMMY AND DADDY WOULD TUCK ME IN AND I WOULD GO TO SLEEP, JUST LIKE YOU...
Z
Z
...OF COURSE, THAT WAS BEFORE I KNEW ABOUT THE MONSTERS...
!
KIRKMAN & SCOTT

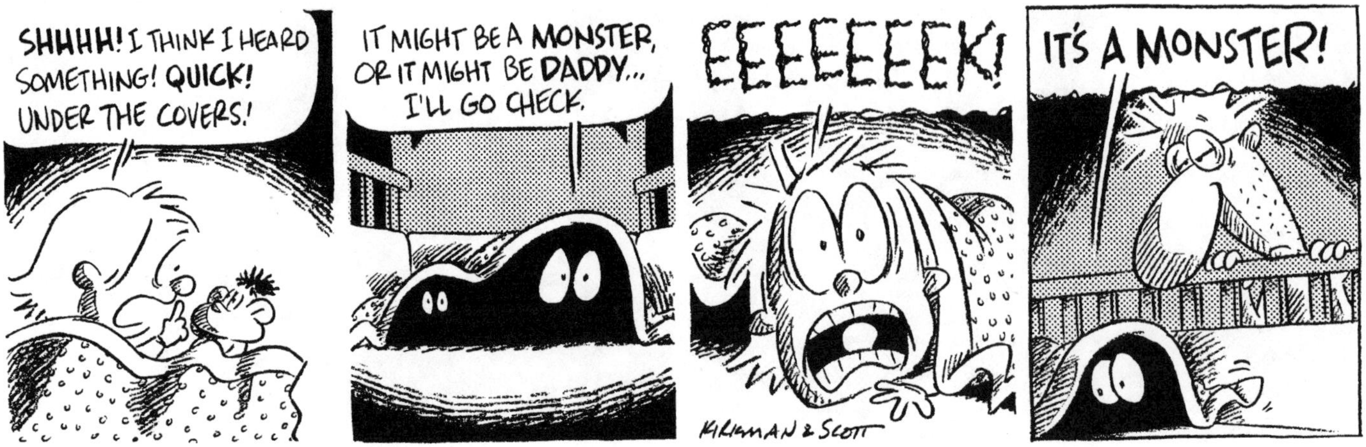
SHHHH! I THINK I HEARD SOMETHING! QUICK! UNDER THE COVERS!
IT MIGHT BE A MONSTER, OR IT MIGHT BE DADDY... I'LL GO CHECK.
EEEEEEEK!
IT'S A MONSTER!
KIRKMAN & SCOTT

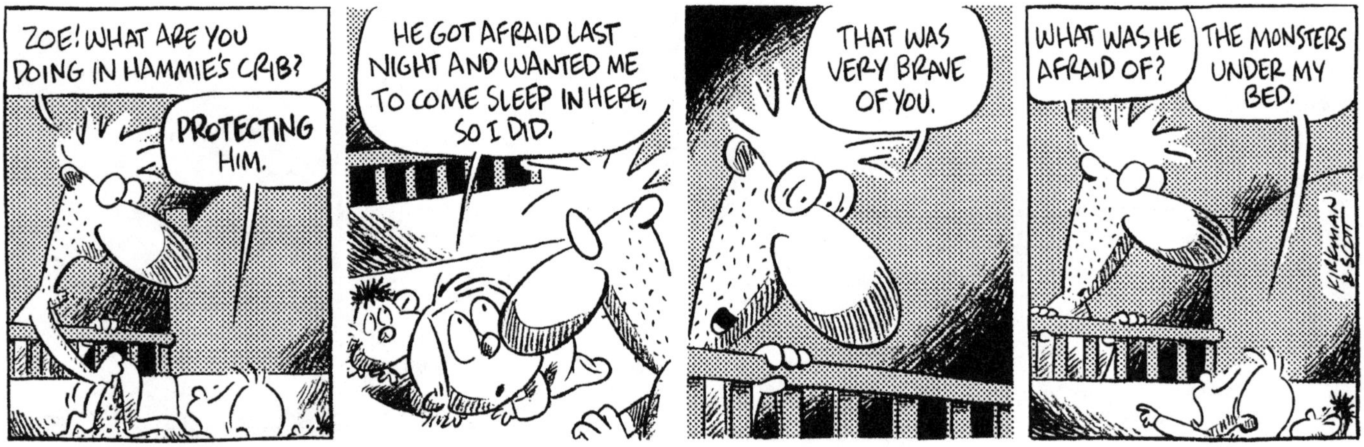
ZOE! WHAT ARE YOU DOING IN HAMMIE'S CRIB?
PROTECTING HIM.
HE GOT AFRAID LAST NIGHT AND WANTED ME TO COME SLEEP IN HERE, SO I DID.
THAT WAS VERY BRAVE OF YOU.
WHAT WAS HE AFRAID OF?
THE MONSTERS UNDER MY BED.
KIRKMAN & SCOTT

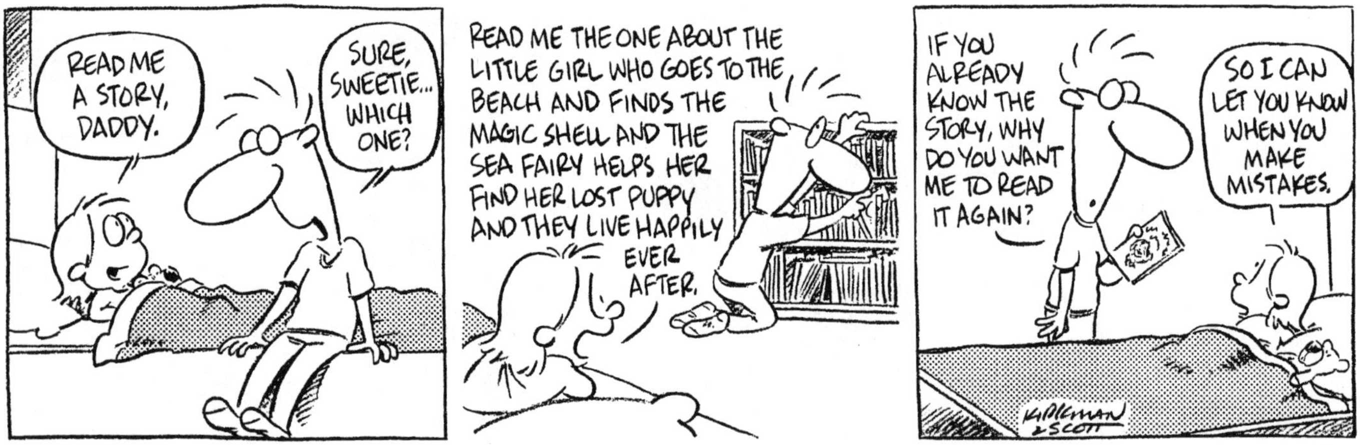
READ ME A STORY, DADDY.
SURE, SWEETIE... WHICH ONE?
READ ME THE ONE ABOUT THE LITTLE GIRL WHO GOES TO THE BEACH AND FINDS THE MAGIC SHELL AND THE SEA FAIRY HELPS HER FIND HER LOST PUPPY AND THEY LIVE HAPPILY EVER AFTER.
IF YOU ALREADY KNOW THE STORY, WHY DO YOU WANT ME TO READ IT AGAIN?
SO I CAN LET YOU KNOW WHEN YOU MAKE MISTAKES.
KIRKMAN & SCOTT

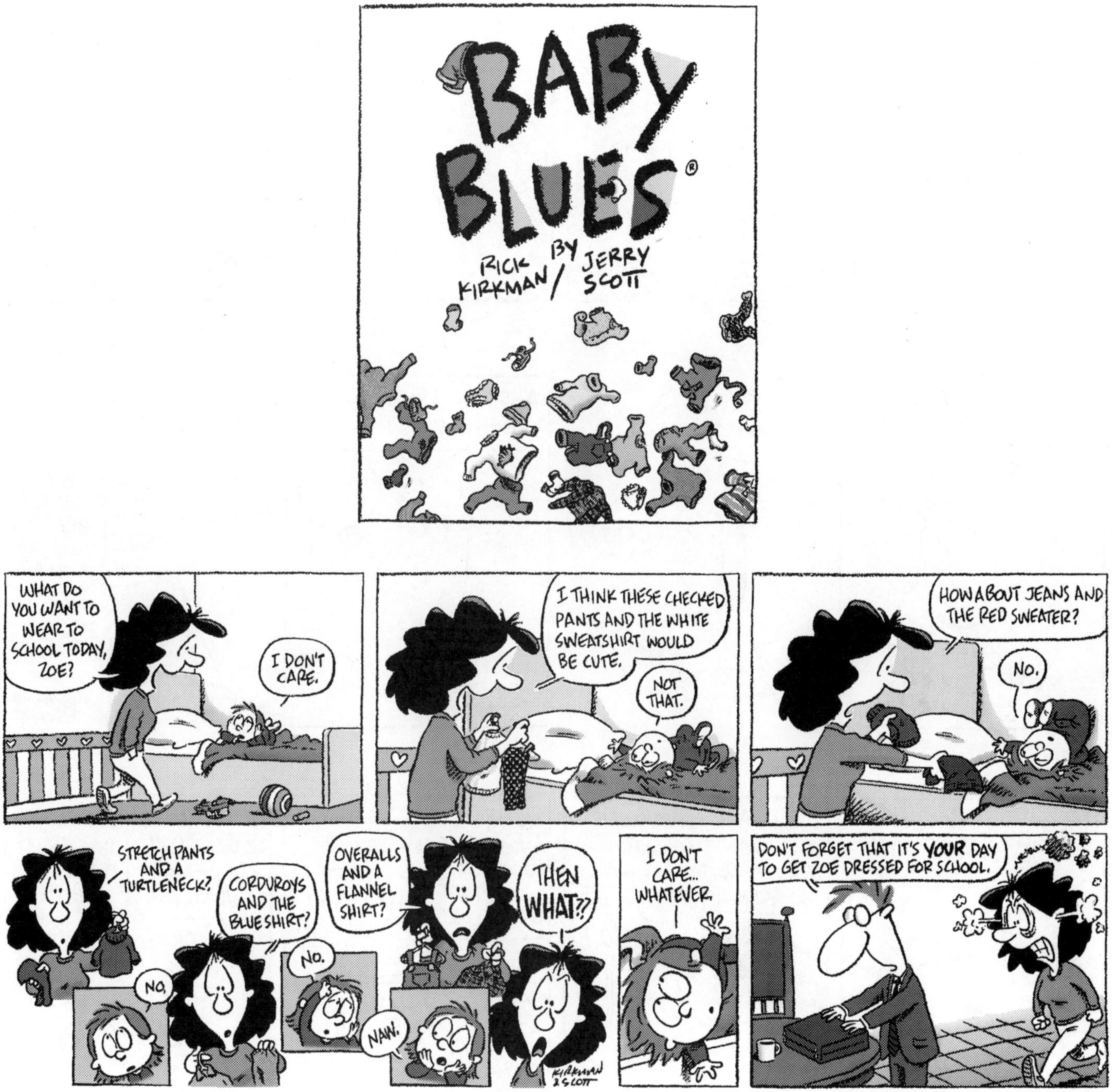
BABY BLUES®
BY RICK KIRKMAN / JERRY SCOTT
WHAT DO YOU WANT TO WEAR TO SCHOOL TODAY, ZOE?
I DON'T CARE.
I THINK THESE CHECKED PANTS AND THE WHITE SWEATSHIRT WOULD BE CUTE.
NOT THAT.
HOW ABOUT JEANS AND THE RED SWEATER?
NO.
STRETCH PANTS AND A TURTLENECK?
NO.
CORDUROYS AND THE BLUE SHIRT?
NO.
OVERALLS AND A FLANNEL SHIRT?
NAW.
THEN WHAT??
I DON'T CARE... WHATEVER.
DON'T FORGET THAT IT'S **YOUR** DAY TO GET ZOE DRESSED FOR SCHOOL.
KIRKMAN & SCOTT

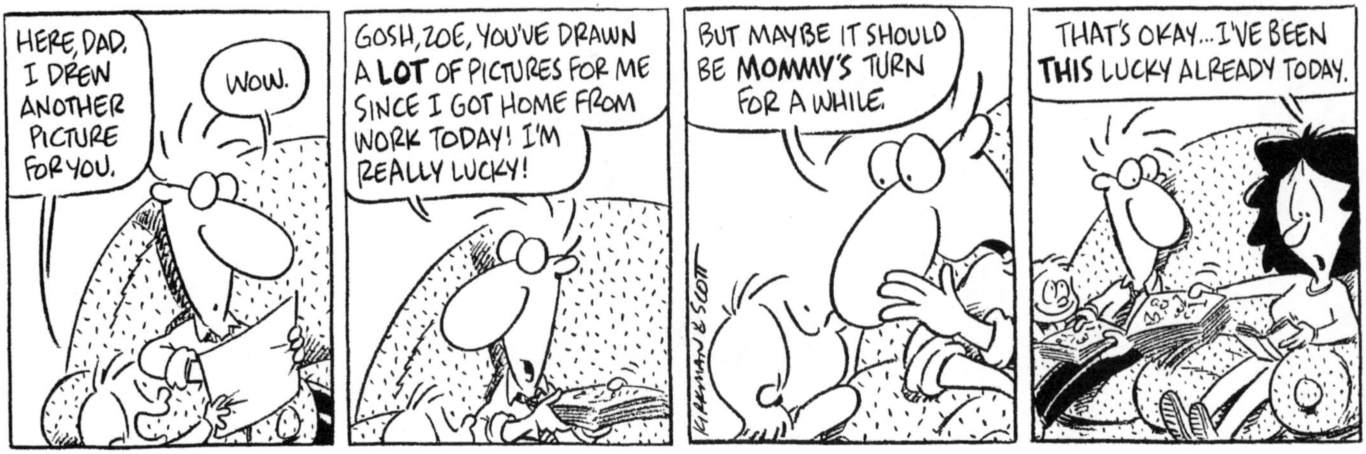
HERE, DAD. I DREW ANOTHER PICTURE FOR YOU.
WOW.
GOSH, ZOE, YOU'VE DRAWN A LOT OF PICTURES FOR ME SINCE I GOT HOME FROM WORK TODAY! I'M REALLY LUCKY!
BUT MAYBE IT SHOULD BE MOMMY'S TURN FOR A WHILE.
KIRKMAN & SCOTT
THAT'S OKAY... I'VE BEEN THIS LUCKY ALREADY TODAY.

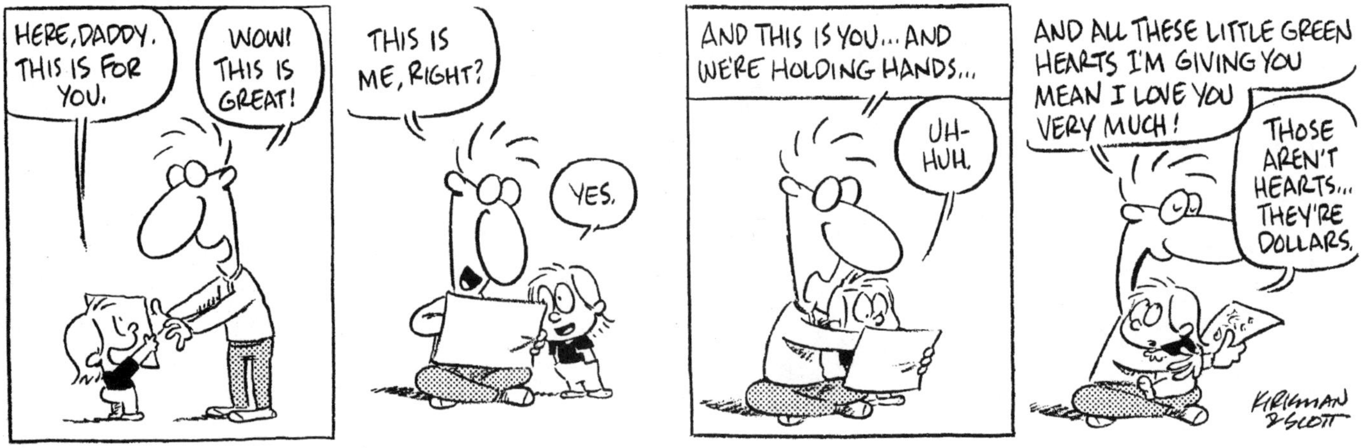
HERE, DADDY. THIS IS FOR YOU.
WOW! THIS IS GREAT!
THIS IS ME, RIGHT?
YES.
AND THIS IS YOU... AND WE'RE HOLDING HANDS...
UH-HUH.
AND ALL THESE LITTLE GREEN HEARTS I'M GIVING YOU MEAN I LOVE YOU VERY MUCH!
THOSE AREN'T HEARTS... THEY'RE DOLLARS.
KIRKMAN & SCOTT

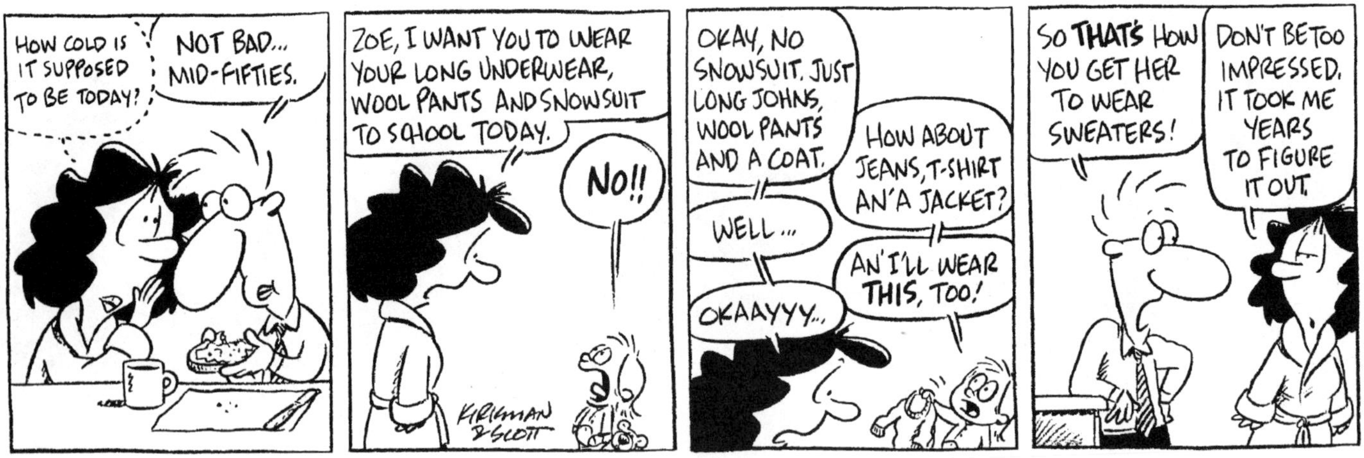
HOW COLD IS IT SUPPOSED TO BE TODAY?
NOT BAD... MID-FIFTIES.
ZOE, I WANT YOU TO WEAR YOUR LONG UNDERWEAR, WOOL PANTS AND SNOWSUIT TO SCHOOL TODAY.
NO!!
KIRKMAN & SCOTT
OKAY, NO SNOWSUIT. JUST LONG JOHNS, WOOL PANTS AND A COAT.
HOW ABOUT JEANS, T-SHIRT AN'A JACKET?
WELL...
AN' I'LL WEAR THIS, TOO!
OKAAYYY...
SO THAT'S HOW YOU GET HER TO WEAR SWEATERS!
DON'T BE TOO IMPRESSED. IT TOOK ME YEARS TO FIGURE IT OUT.

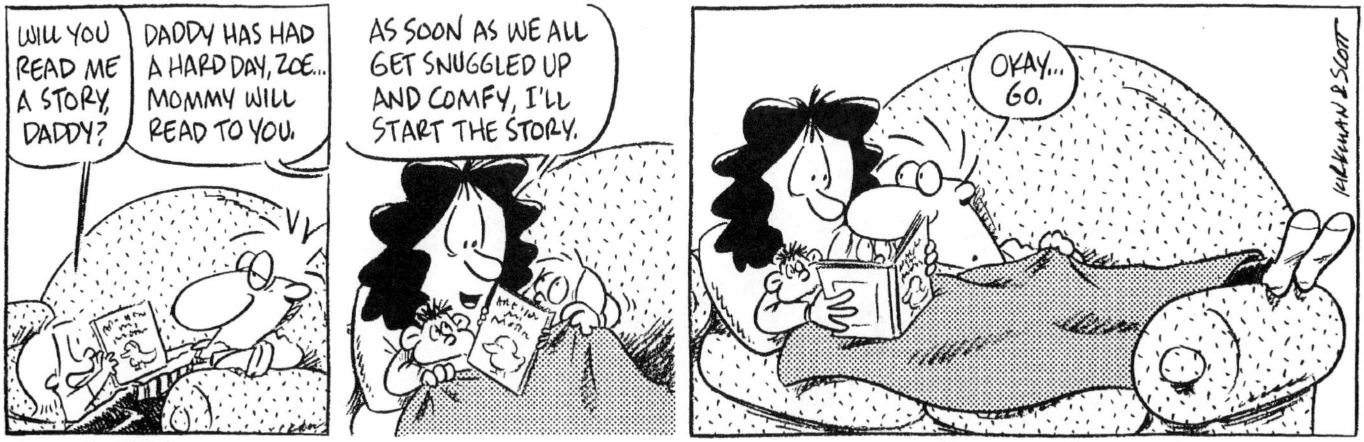
WILL YOU READ ME A STORY, DADDY?
DADDY HAS HAD A HARD DAY, ZOE... MOMMY WILL READ TO YOU.
AS SOON AS WE ALL GET SNUGGLED UP AND COMFY, I'LL START THE STORY.
OKAY... GO.
KIRKMAN & SCOTT

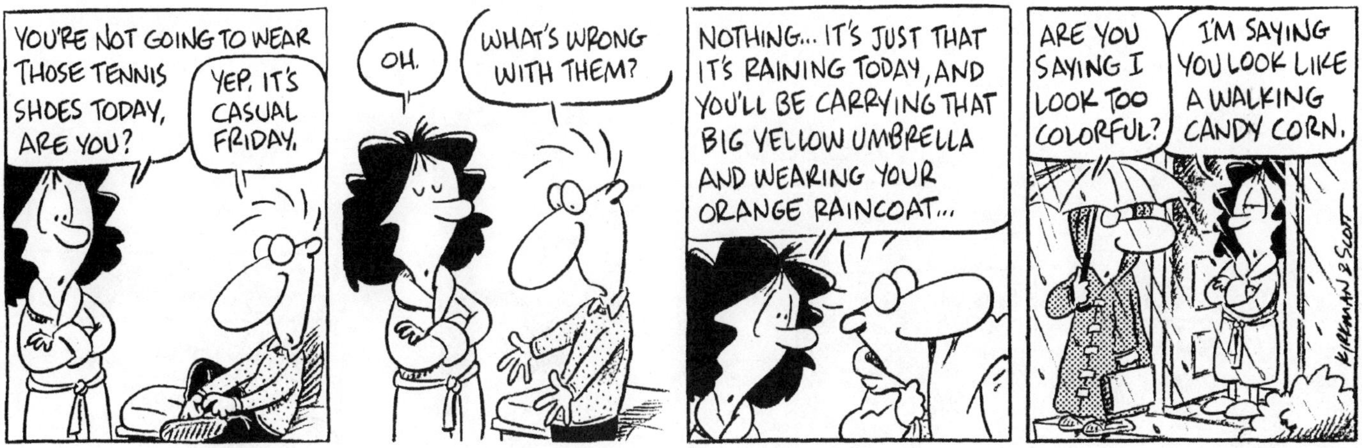
YOU'RE NOT GOING TO WEAR THOSE TENNIS SHOES TODAY, ARE YOU?
YEP. IT'S CASUAL FRIDAY.
OH.
WHAT'S WRONG WITH THEM?
NOTHING... IT'S JUST THAT IT'S RAINING TODAY, AND YOU'LL BE CARRYING THAT BIG YELLOW UMBRELLA AND WEARING YOUR ORANGE RAINCOAT...
ARE YOU SAYING I LOOK TOO COLORFUL?
I'M SAYING YOU LOOK LIKE A WALKING CANDY CORN.
KIRKMAN & SCOTT

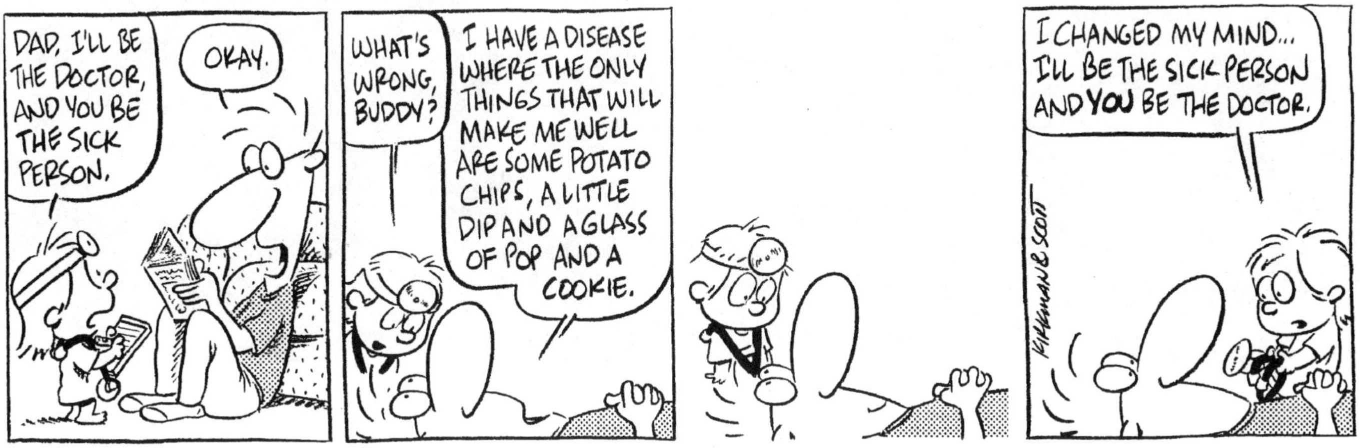
DAD, I'LL BE THE DOCTOR, AND YOU BE THE SICK PERSON.
OKAY.
WHAT'S WRONG, BUDDY?
I HAVE A DISEASE WHERE THE ONLY THINGS THAT WILL MAKE ME WELL ARE SOME POTATO CHIPS, A LITTLE DIP AND A GLASS OF POP AND A COOKIE.
KIRKMAN & SCOTT
I CHANGED MY MIND... I'LL BE THE SICK PERSON AND **YOU** BE THE DOCTOR.

BABY BLUES®
BY
RICK KIRKMAN / JERRY SCOTT

WAAAA!
WAA-AAA-AAAAA!
OW! OW! LET GO!
THAT'S IT. SEE? IT'S NOT SO BAD...
SNIF!
CHEEEEESE!
CLICK! CLICK! CLICK!
ISN'T THAT CUTE!
OKAY... THAT'S THE END OF THE FILM.
LET'S GO, KIDS!
WHIRRRR
WAAAAA!
WAA-AAA-AAAA!
SIGH!
OW! OW! LET GO!
KIRKMAN & SCOTT

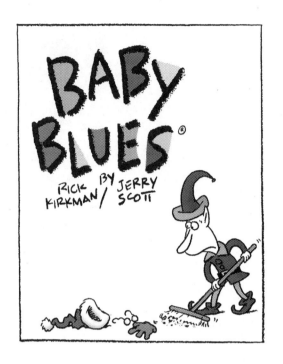

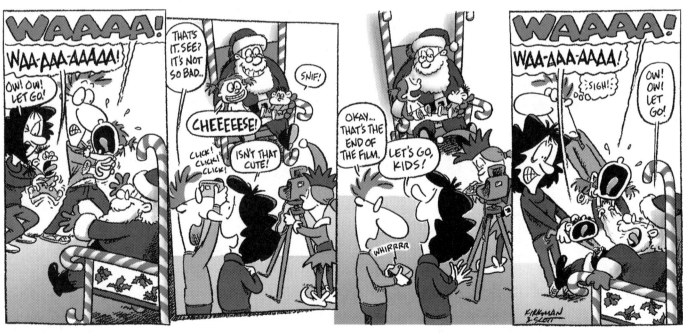

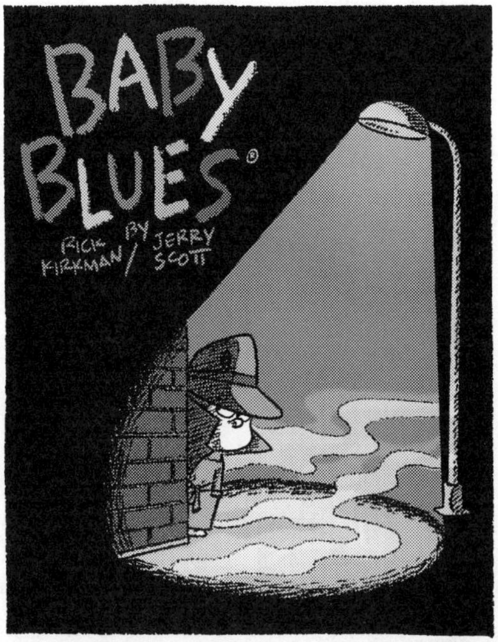
BABY BLUES®
BY
RICK KIRKMAN / JERRY SCOTT

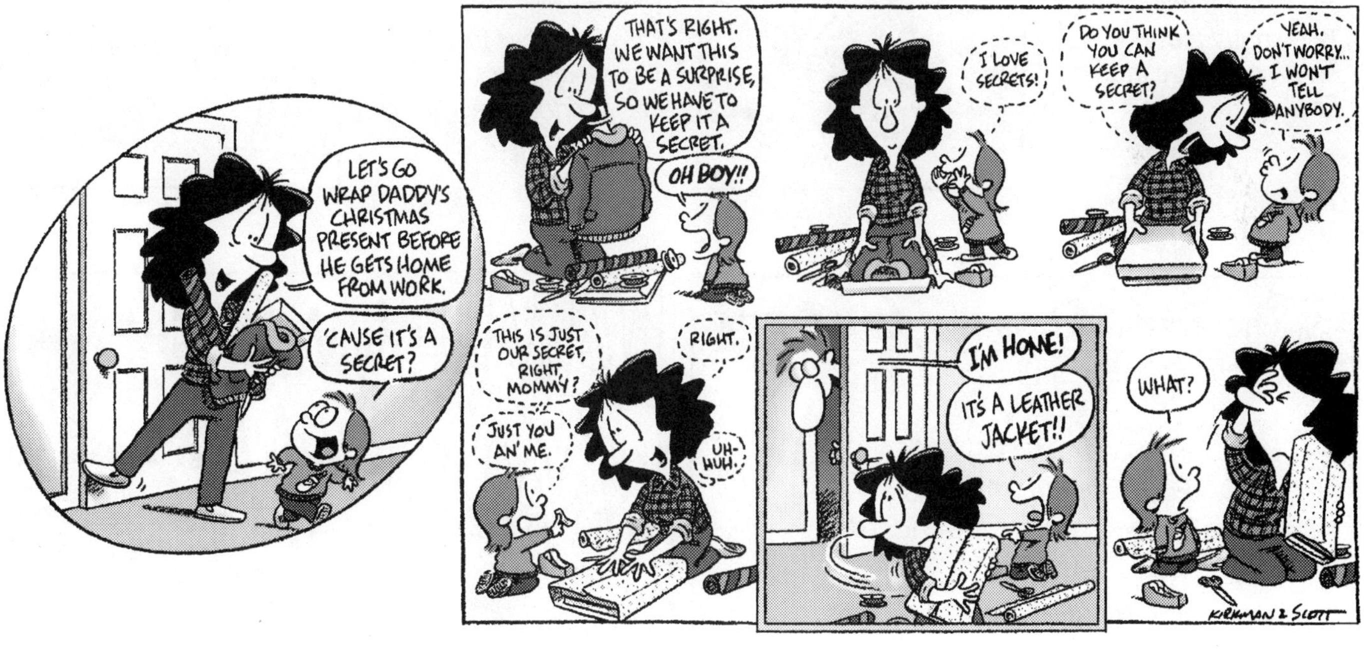
LET'S GO WRAP DADDY'S CHRISTMAS PRESENT BEFORE HE GETS HOME FROM WORK.
'CAUSE IT'S A SECRET?
THAT'S RIGHT. WE WANT THIS TO BE A SURPRISE, SO WE HAVE TO KEEP IT A SECRET.
OH BOY!!
I LOVE SECRETS!
DO YOU THINK YOU CAN KEEP A SECRET?
YEAH. DON'T WORRY... I WON'T TELL ANYBODY.
THIS IS JUST OUR SECRET, RIGHT, MOMMY?
RIGHT.
JUST YOU AN' ME.
UH-HUH.
I'M HOME!
IT'S A LEATHER JACKET!!
WHAT?
KIRKMAN & SCOTT

The Twelve Days of *Christmas*

On the first day of Christmas my children gave to me

A cartridge in a fir tree.

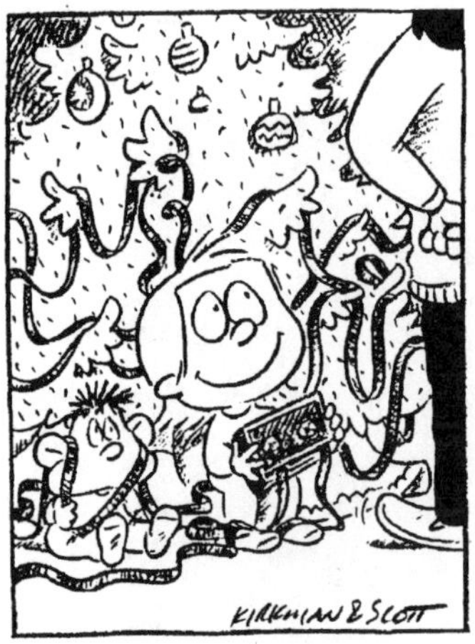

KIRKMAN & SCOTT

The Twelve Days of *Christmas*

On the second day of Christmas my children gave to me

Two snotty gloves,
And a cartridge in a fir tree.

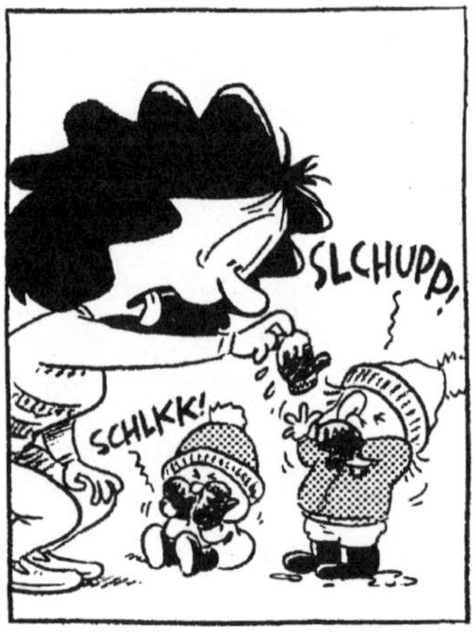

SLCHUPP!
SCHLKK!

The Twelve Days of *Christmas*

On the third day of Christmas my children gave to me

Three drenched friends,
Two snotty gloves,
And a cartridge in a fir tree.

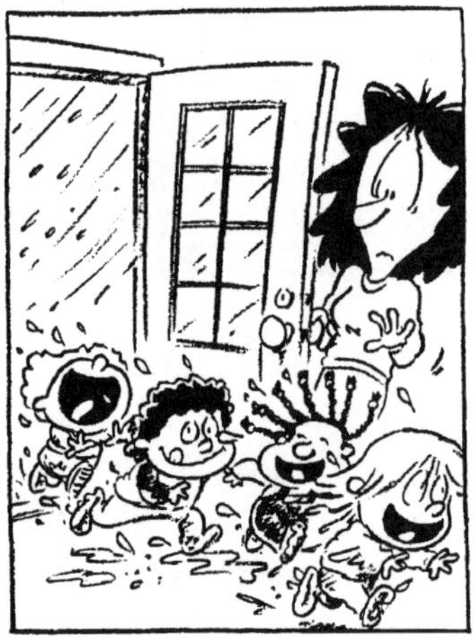

The Twelve Days of *Christmas*

On the fourth day of Christmas my children gave to me

Four appalling words,
Three drenched friends,
Two snotty gloves,
And a cartridge in a fir tree.

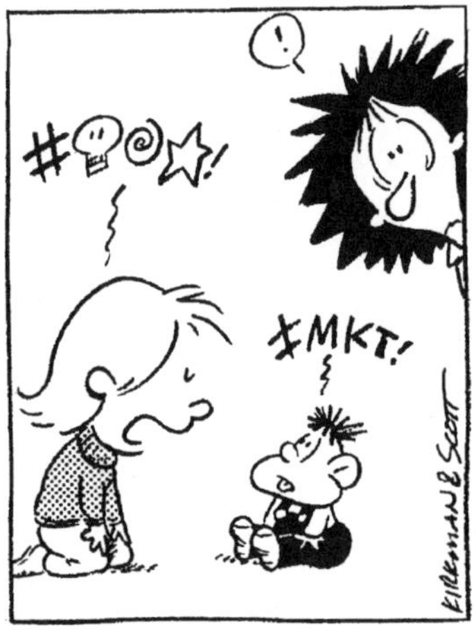

!
MKT!
KIRKMAN & SCOTT

The Twelve Days of *Christmas*

On the fifth day of Christmas my children gave to me

Five dozen **SCREAMS!**
Four appalling words,
Three drenched friends,
Two snotty gloves,
And a cartridge in a fir tree.

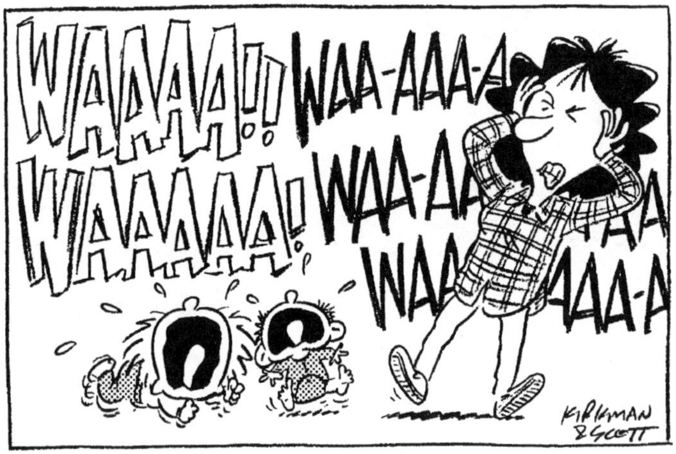

WAAAA!!
WAA-AAA-A
WAAAAAA!
KIRKMAN & SCOTT

The Twelve Days of Christmas

On the sixth day of Christmas my children gave to me

Six teeth decaying,
Five dozen **SCREAMS!**
Four appalling words,
Three drenched friends,
Two snotty gloves,
And a cartridge in a fir tree.

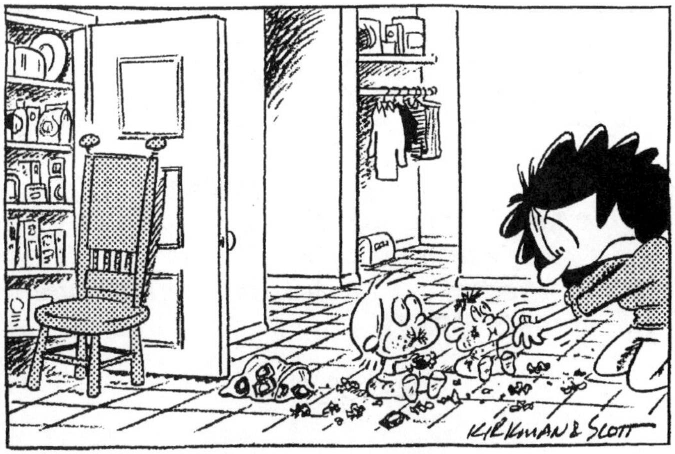
KIRKMAN & SCOTT

The Twelve Days of Christmas

On the seventh day of Christmas my children gave to me

Seven tons of washing,
Six teeth decaying,
Five dozen **SCREAMS!**
Four appalling words,
Three drenched friends,
Two snotty gloves,
And a cartridge in a fir tree.

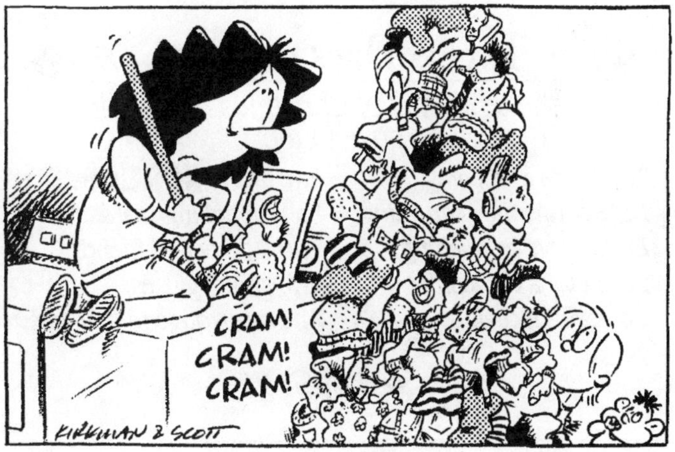
CRAM!
CRAM!
CRAM!
KIRKMAN & SCOTT

The Twelve Days of Christmas

On the eighth day of Christmas my children gave to me

Eight ways of belching,
Seven tons of washing,
Six teeth decaying,
Five dozen **SCREAMS!**
Four appalling words,
Three drenched friends,
Two snotty gloves,
And a cartridge in a fir tree.

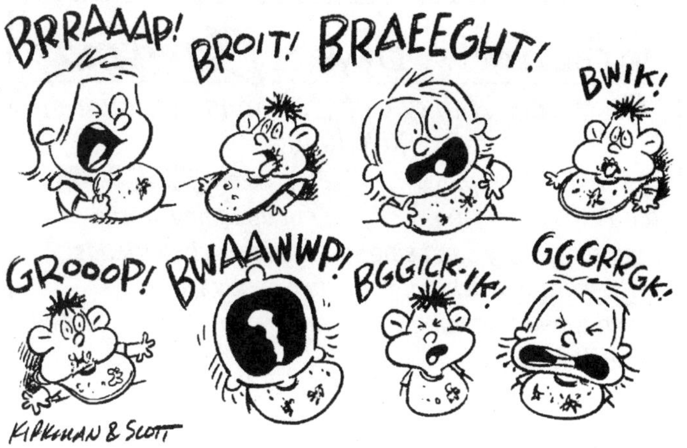
BRRAAAP!
BROIT!
BRAEEGHT!
BWIK!
GROOOP!
BWAAWWP!
BGGICK-IK!
GGGRRGK!
KIRKMAN & SCOTT

The Twelve Days of *Christmas*

On the ninth day of Christmas my children gave to me

Nine songs they can't sing,
Eight ways of belching,
Seven tons of washing,
Six teeth decaying,
Five dozen **SCREAMS!**
Four appalling words,
Three drenched friends,
Two snotty gloves,
And a cartridge in a fir tree.

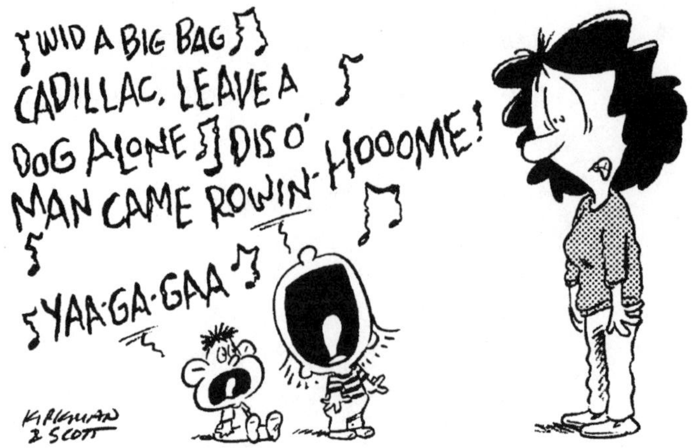
WID A BIG BAG
CADILLAC. LEAVE A DOG ALONE DIS O' MAN CAME ROWIN'-HOOOME!
YAA-GA-GAA
KIRKMAN & SCOTT

The Twelve Days of *Christmas*

On the tenth day of Christmas my children gave to me

Ten Fords a-beeping,
Nine songs they can't sing,
Eight ways of belching,
Seven tons of washing,
Six teeth decaying,
Five dozen **SCREAMS!**
Four appalling words,
Three drenched friends,
Two snotty gloves,
And a cartridge in a fir tree.

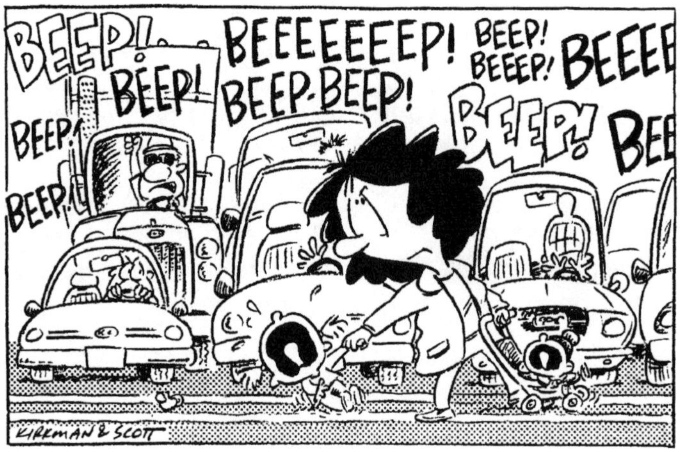
BEEP!
BEEP!
BEEP!
BEEP!
BEEEEEEEP!
BEEP-BEEP!
BEEP!
BEEEP!
BEEP!
KIRKMAN & SCOTT

The Twelve Days of *Christmas*

On the eleventh day of Christmas my children gave to me

Eleven diaper wipings,
Ten Fords a-beeping,
Nine songs they can't sing,
Eight ways of belching,
Seven tons of washing,
Six teeth decaying,
Five dozen **SCREAMS!**
Four appalling words,
Three drenched friends,
Two snotty gloves,
And a cartridge in a fir tree.

KIRKMAN & SCOTT

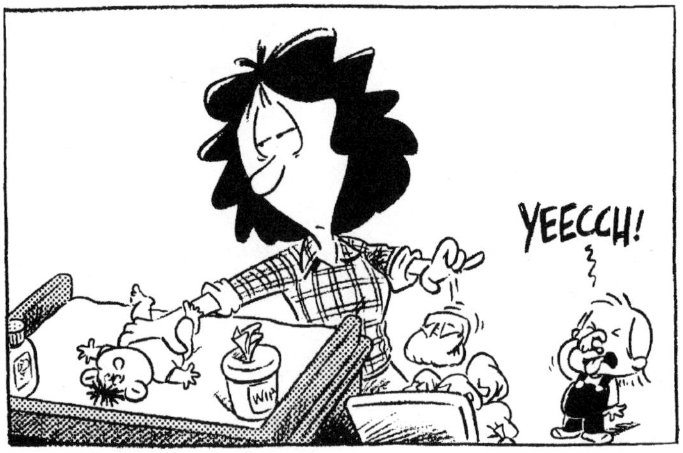
YEECCH!

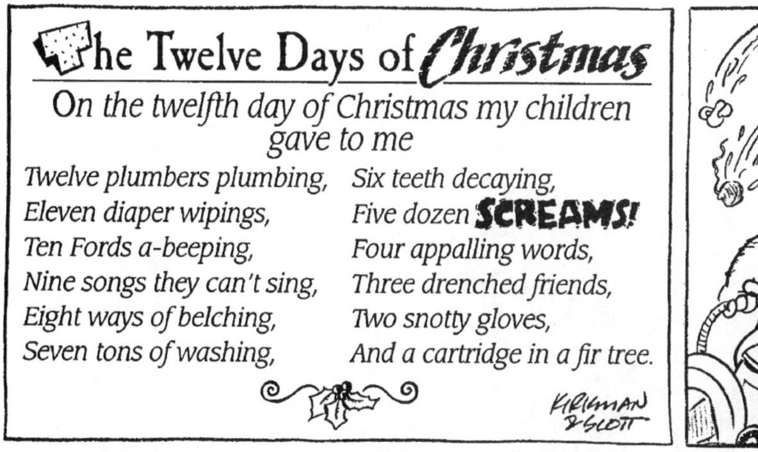
The Twelve Days of Christmas
On the twelfth day of Christmas my children gave to me
Twelve plumbers plumbing,
Eleven diaper wipings,
Ten Fords a-beeping,
Nine songs they can't sing,
Eight ways of belching,
Seven tons of washing,
Six teeth decaying,
Five dozen SCREAMS!
Four appalling words,
Three drenched friends,
Two snotty gloves,
And a cartridge in a fir tree.
KIRKMAN & SCOTT
PLUM CO
BIG AL'S PLUMBING
Mr. Root'em

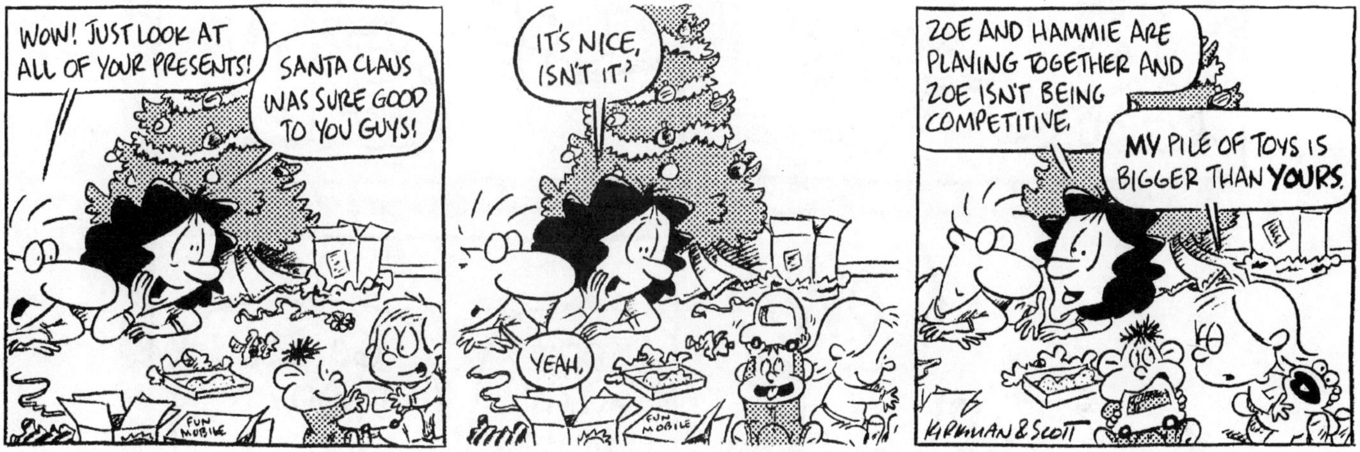
WOW! JUST LOOK AT ALL OF YOUR PRESENTS!
SANTA CLAUS WAS SURE GOOD TO YOU GUYS!
FUN MOBILE
IT'S NICE, ISN'T IT?
YEAH.
FUN MOBILE
ZOE AND HAMMIE ARE PLAYING TOGETHER AND ZOE ISN'T BEING COMPETITIVE.
MY PILE OF TOYS IS BIGGER THAN YOURS.
KIRKMAN & SCOTT

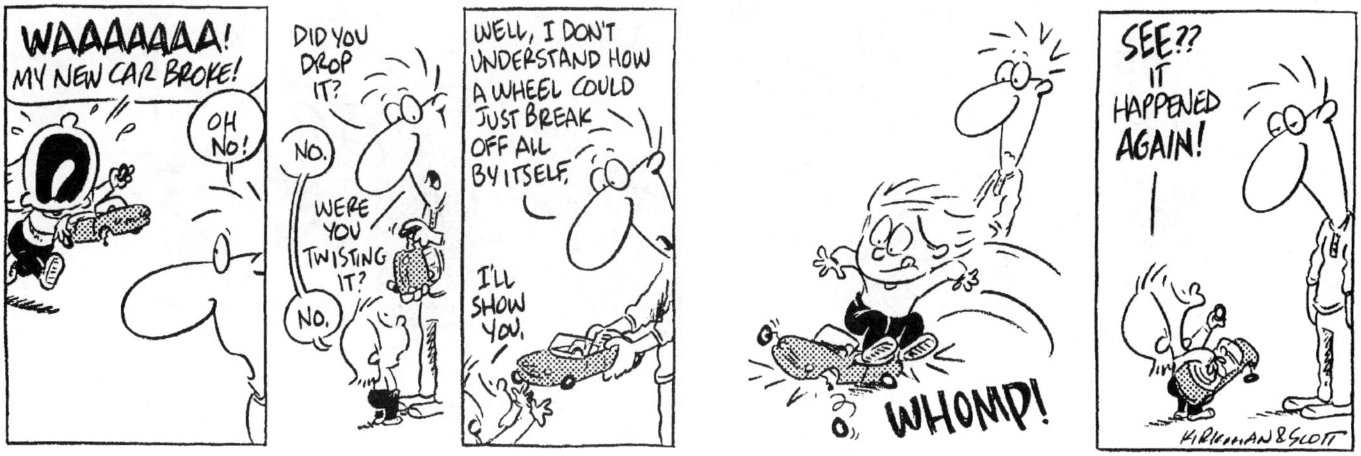
WAAAAAAA! MY NEW CAR BROKE!
OH NO!
DID YOU DROP IT?
NO.
WERE YOU TWISTING IT?
NO.
WELL, I DON'T UNDERSTAND HOW A WHEEL COULD JUST BREAK OFF ALL BY ITSELF.
I'LL SHOW YOU.
WHOMP!
SEE?? IT HAPPENED AGAIN!
KIRKMAN & SCOTT

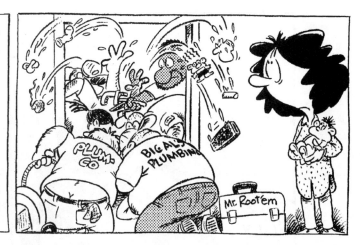

WHEEEEE!
OKAY, NOW ROLL IT BACK TO MOMMY! COME ON... YOU CAN DO IT!
OW!
THWAP!
WHIPP!
DADDY TAUGHT HAMMIE TO THROW.
GO TELL DADDY I WANT TO TALK TO HIM.
CLAP! CLAP! CLAP!
KIRKMAN & SCOTT

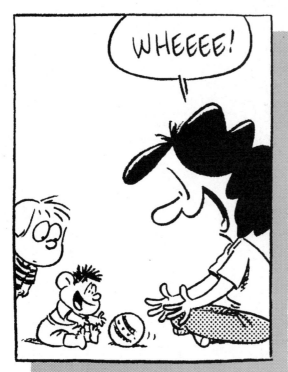

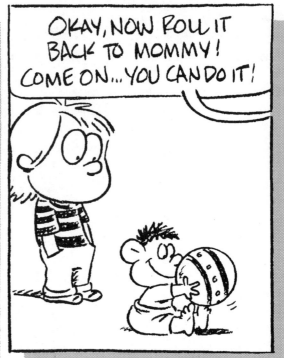

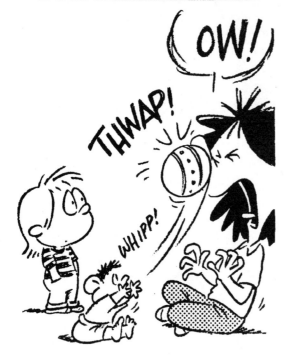

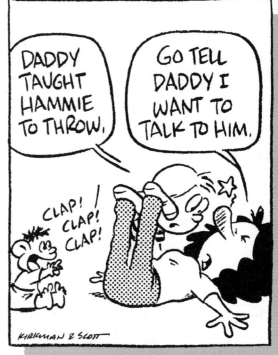

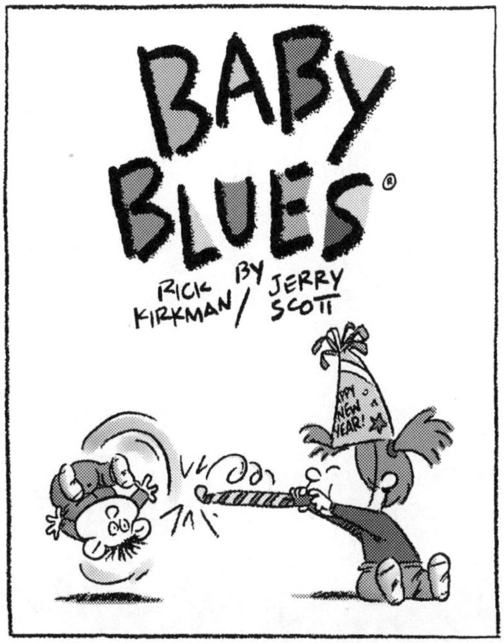
BABY BLUES®
BY RICK KIRKMAN / JERRY SCOTT
HAPPY NEW YEAR!

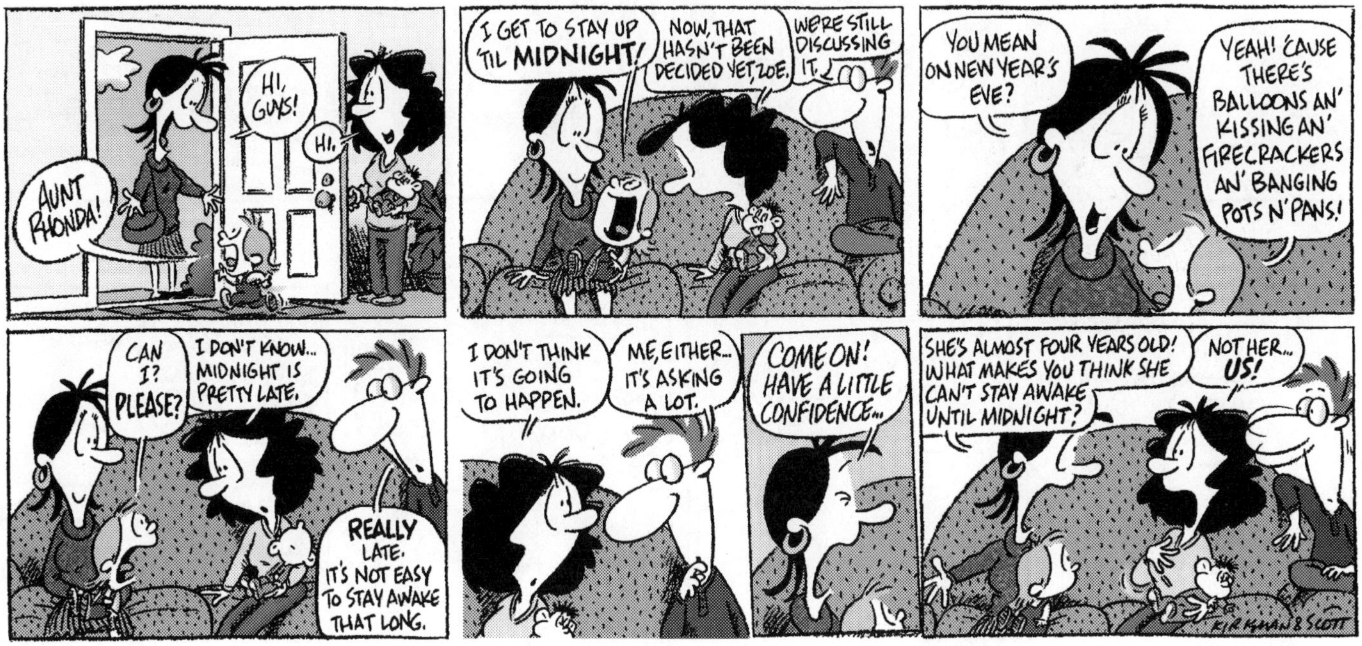
AUNT RHONDA!
HI, GUYS!
HI.
I GET TO STAY UP 'TIL MIDNIGHT!
NOW, THAT HASN'T BEEN DECIDED YET, ZOE.
WE'RE STILL DISCUSSING IT.
YOU MEAN ON NEW YEAR'S EVE?
YEAH! 'CAUSE THERE'S BALLOONS AN' KISSING AN' FIRECRACKERS AN' BANGING POTS N' PANS!
CAN I? PLEASE?
I DON'T KNOW... MIDNIGHT IS PRETTY LATE.
REALLY LATE. IT'S NOT EASY TO STAY AWAKE THAT LONG.
I DON'T THINK IT'S GOING TO HAPPEN.
ME, EITHER... IT'S ASKING A LOT.
COME ON! HAVE A LITTLE CONFIDENCE...
SHE'S ALMOST FOUR YEARS OLD! WHAT MAKES YOU THINK SHE CAN'T STAY AWAKE UNTIL MIDNIGHT?
NOT HER... US!
KIRKMAN & SCOTT

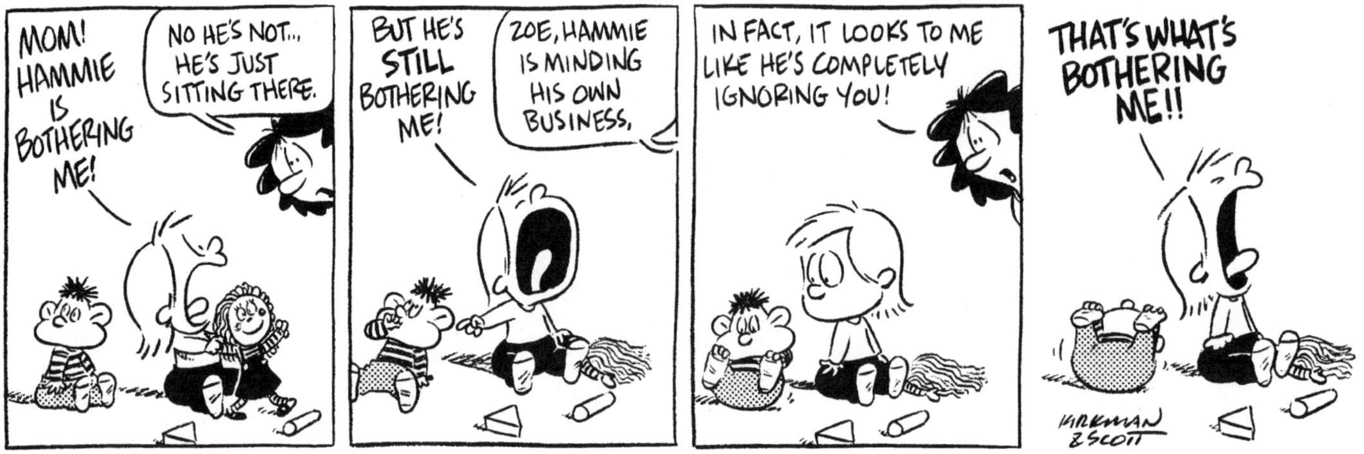
MOM! HAMMIE IS BOTHERING ME!
NO HE'S NOT... HE'S JUST SITTING THERE.
BUT HE'S STILL BOTHERING ME!
ZOE, HAMMIE IS MINDING HIS OWN BUSINESS.
IN FACT, IT LOOKS TO ME LIKE HE'S COMPLETELY IGNORING YOU!
THAT'S WHAT'S BOTHERING ME!!
KIRKMAN & SCOTT

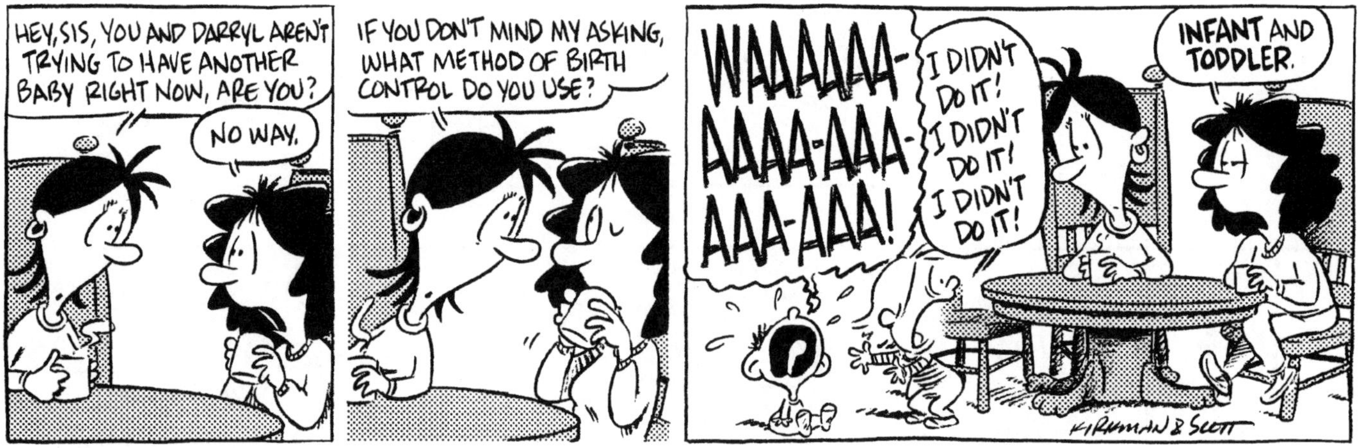
HEY, SIS, YOU AND DARRYL AREN'T TRYING TO HAVE ANOTHER BABY RIGHT NOW, ARE YOU?
NO WAY.
IF YOU DON'T MIND MY ASKING, WHAT METHOD OF BIRTH CONTROL DO YOU USE?
WAAAAAA-AAAA-AAA-AAA-AAA!
I DIDN'T DO IT! I DIDN'T DO IT! I DIDN'T DO IT!
INFANT AND TODDLER.
KIRKMAN & SCOTT

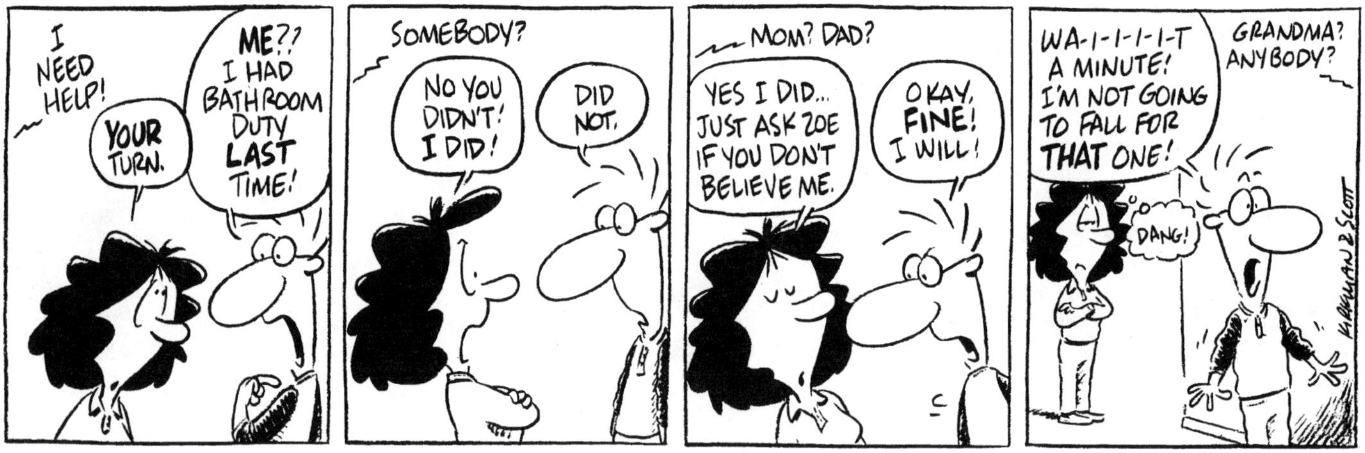
I NEED HELP!
YOUR TURN.
ME?? I HAD BATHROOM DUTY LAST TIME!
SOMEBODY?
NO YOU DIDN'T! I DID!
DID NOT.
MOM? DAD?
YES I DID... JUST ASK ZOE IF YOU DON'T BELIEVE ME.
OKAY, FINE! I WILL!
GRANDMA? ANYBODY?
WA-I-I-I-I-T A MINUTE! I'M NOT GOING TO FALL FOR THAT ONE!
DANG!
KIRKMAN & SCOTT

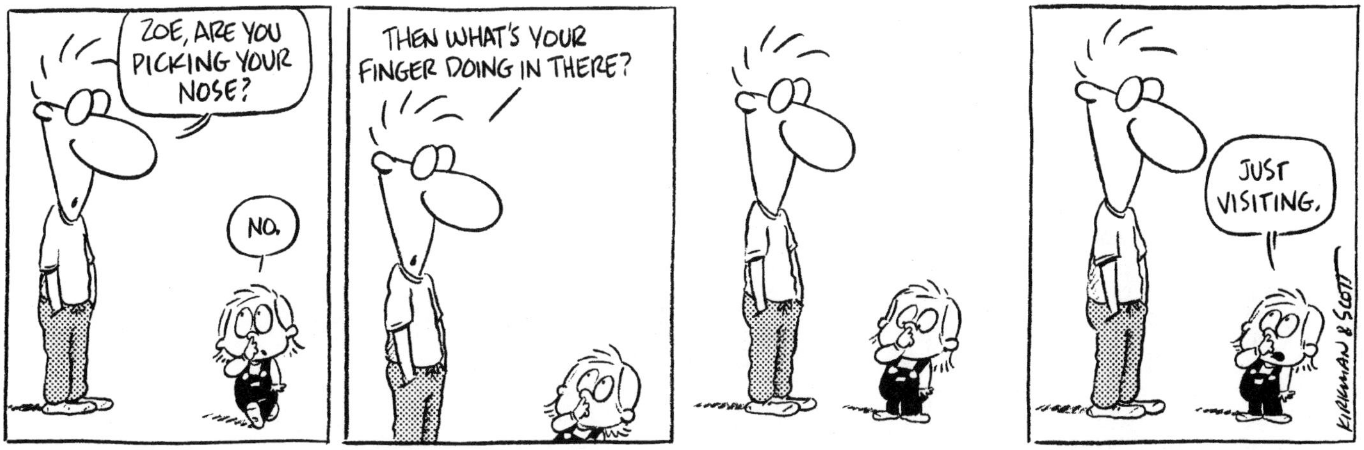
ZOE, ARE YOU PICKING YOUR NOSE?
NO.
THEN WHAT'S YOUR FINGER DOING IN THERE?
JUST VISITING.
KIRKMAN & SCOTT

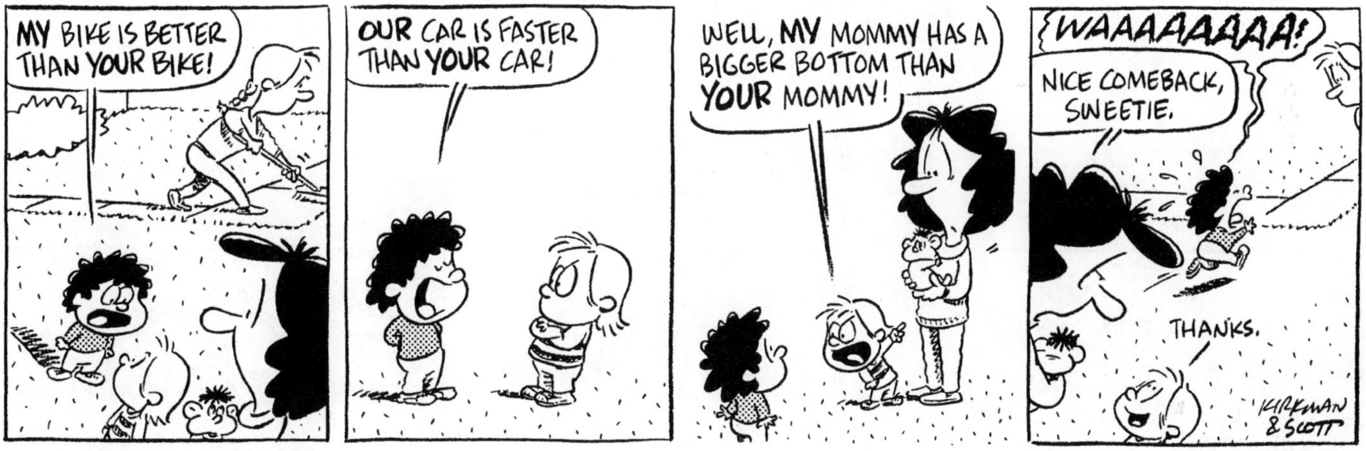
MY BIKE IS BETTER THAN YOUR BIKE!
OUR CAR IS FASTER THAN YOUR CAR!
WELL, MY MOMMY HAS A BIGGER BOTTOM THAN YOUR MOMMY!
WAAAAAAAA!
NICE COMEBACK, SWEETIE.
THANKS.
KIRKMAN & SCOTT

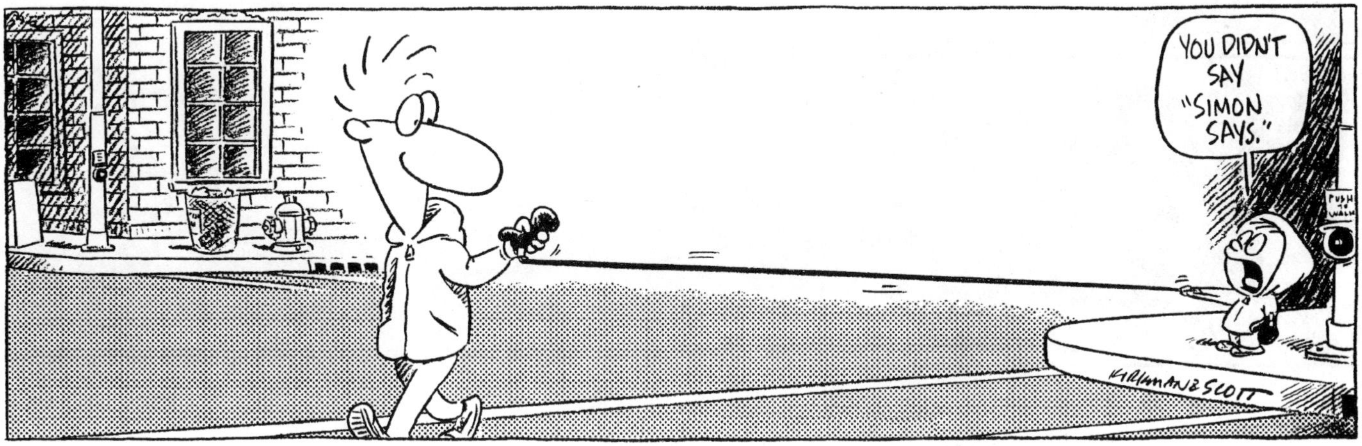
YOU DIDN'T SAY "SIMON SAYS."
KIRKMAN & SCOTT

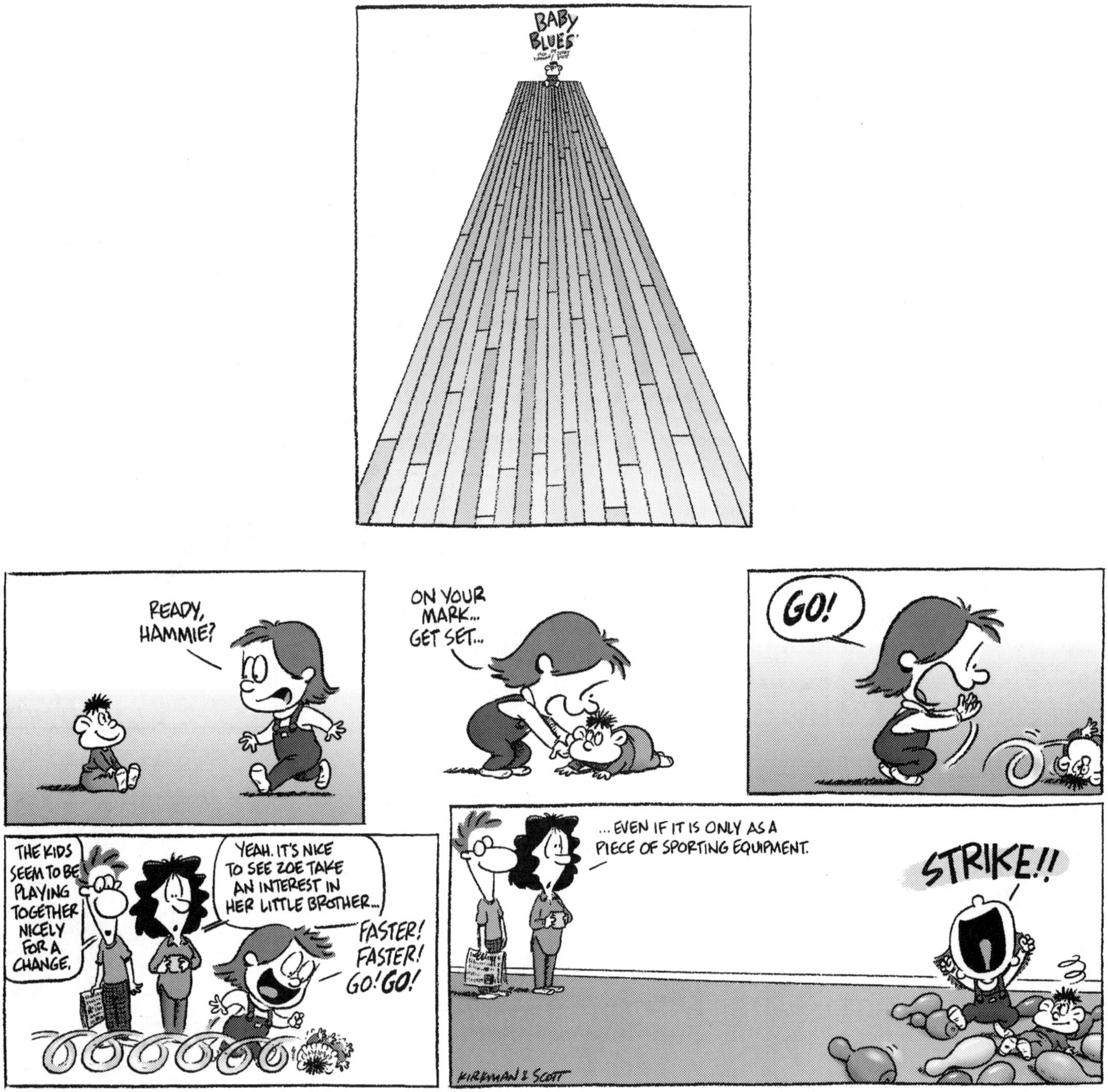

BABY BLUES
READY, HAMMIE?
ON YOUR MARK... GET SET...
GO!
THE KIDS SEEM TO BE PLAYING TOGETHER NICELY FOR A CHANGE.
YEAH. IT'S NICE TO SEE ZOE TAKE AN INTEREST IN HER LITTLE BROTHER...
FASTER! FASTER! GO! GO!
...EVEN IF IT IS ONLY AS A PIECE OF SPORTING EQUIPMENT.
STRIKE!!
KIRKMAN & SCOTT

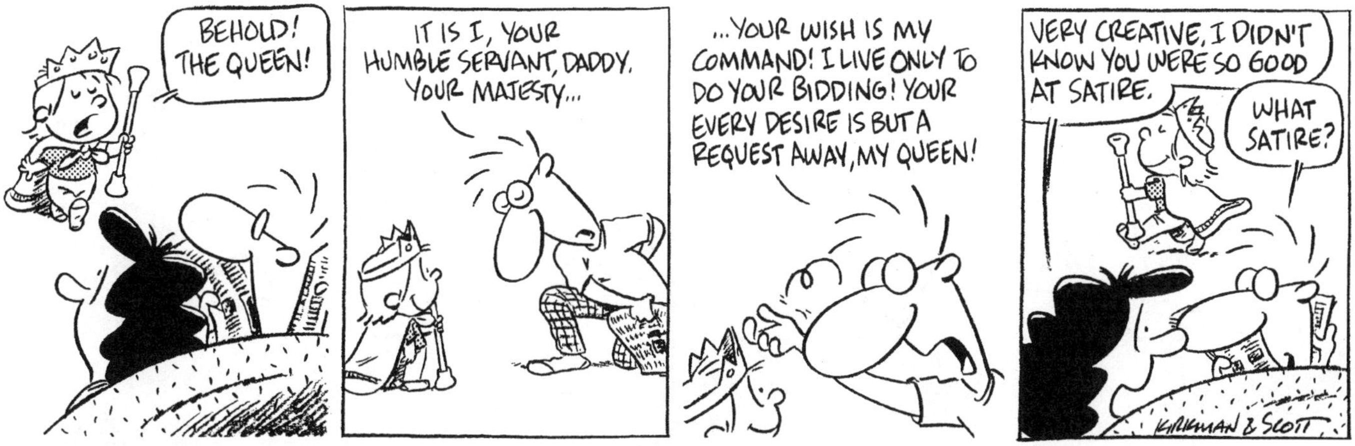
BEHOLD! THE QUEEN!
IT IS I, YOUR HUMBLE SERVANT, DADDY. YOUR MAJESTY...
...YOUR WISH IS MY COMMAND! I LIVE ONLY TO DO YOUR BIDDING! YOUR EVERY DESIRE IS BUT A REQUEST AWAY, MY QUEEN!
VERY CREATIVE, I DIDN'T KNOW YOU WERE SO GOOD AT SATIRE.
WHAT SATIRE?
KIRKMAN & SCOTT

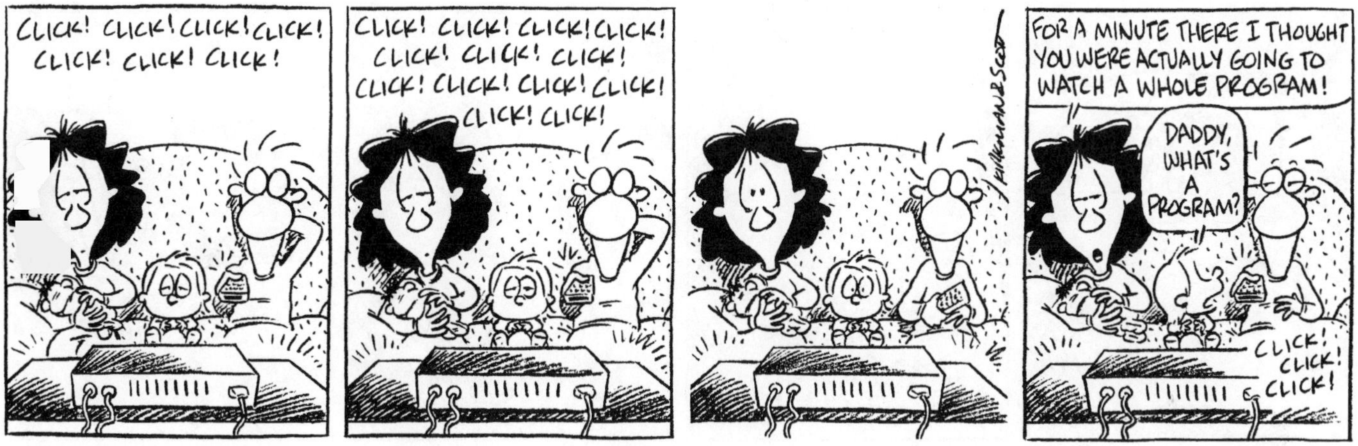
CLICK! CLICK! CLICK! CLICK! CLICK! CLICK! CLICK!
CLICK! CLICK! CLICK! CLICK! CLICK! CLICK! CLICK! CLICK! CLICK! CLICK! CLICK! CLICK! CLICK!
KIRKMAN & SCOTT
FOR A MINUTE THERE I THOUGHT YOU WERE ACTUALLY GOING TO WATCH A WHOLE PROGRAM!
DADDY, WHAT'S A PROGRAM?
CLICK! CLICK! CLICK!

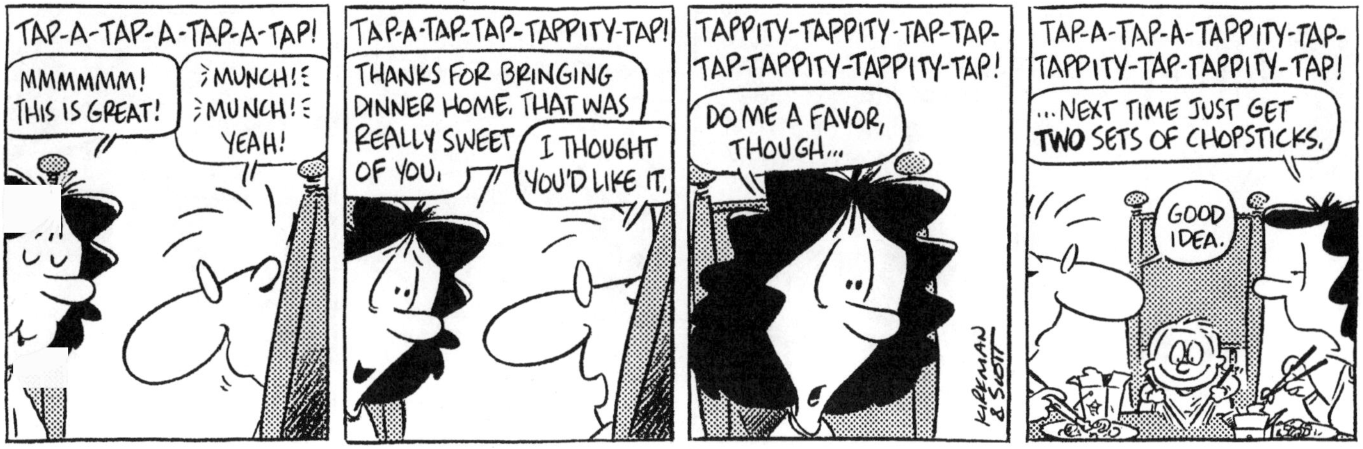
TAP-A-TAP-A-TAP-A-TAP!
MMMMMM! THIS IS GREAT!
MUNCH! MUNCH! YEAH!
TAP-A-TAP-TAP-TAPPITY-TAP!
THANKS FOR BRINGING DINNER HOME. THAT WAS REALLY SWEET OF YOU.
I THOUGHT YOU'D LIKE IT.
TAPPITY-TAPPITY-TAP-TAP-TAP-TAPPITY-TAPPITY-TAP!
DO ME A FAVOR, THOUGH...
KIRKMAN & SCOTT
TAP-A-TAP-A-TAPPITY-TAP-TAPPITY-TAP-TAPPITY-TAP!
...NEXT TIME JUST GET TWO SETS OF CHOPSTICKS.
GOOD IDEA.

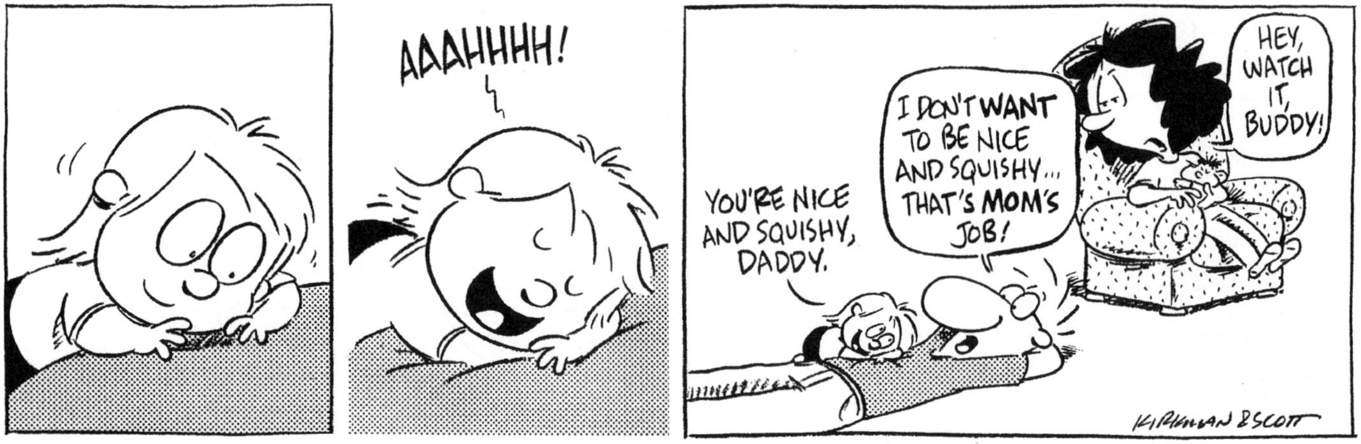
AAAHHHH!
YOU'RE NICE AND SQUISHY, DADDY.
I DON'T WANT TO BE NICE AND SQUISHY... THAT'S MOM'S JOB!
HEY, WATCH IT, BUDDY!
KIRKMAN & SCOTT

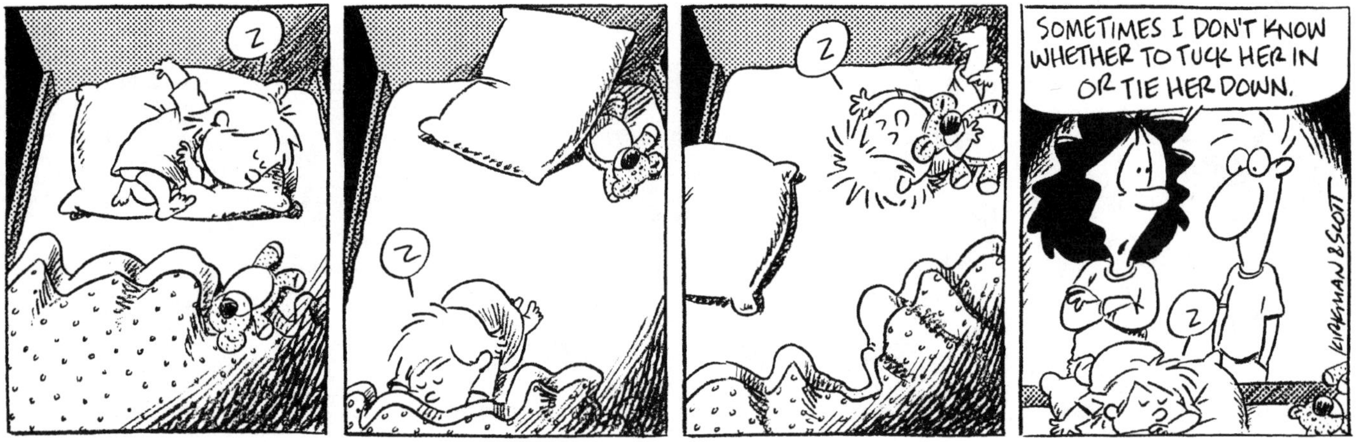
Z
Z
Z
SOMETIMES I DON'T KNOW WHETHER TO TUCK HER IN OR TIE HER DOWN.
Z
KIRKMAN & SCOTT

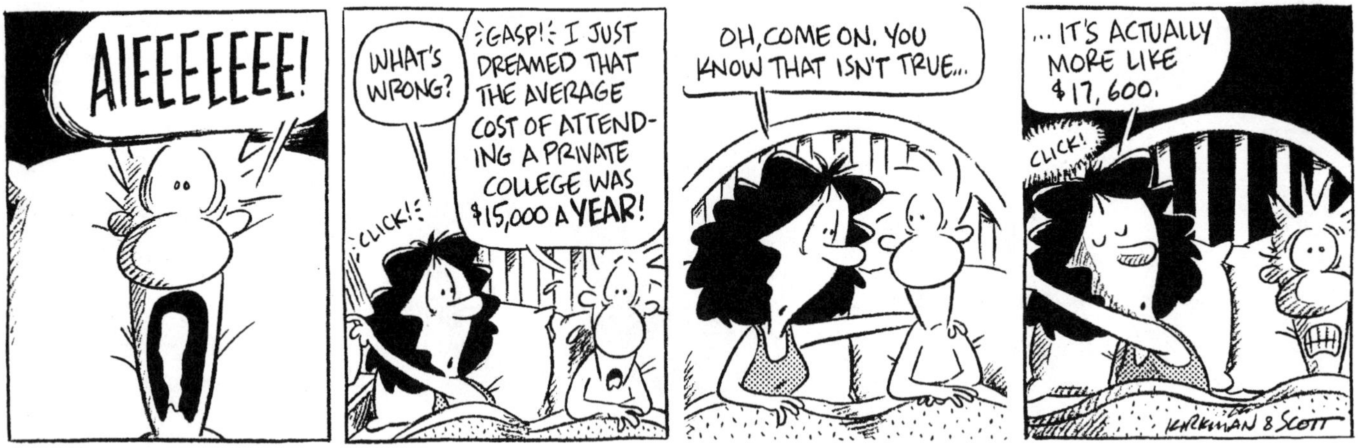
AIEEEEEEE!
WHAT'S WRONG?
CLICK!
GASP! I JUST DREAMED THAT THE AVERAGE COST OF ATTENDING A PRIVATE COLLEGE WAS $15,000 A YEAR!
OH, COME ON. YOU KNOW THAT ISN'T TRUE...
... IT'S ACTUALLY MORE LIKE $17,600.
CLICK!
KIRKMAN & SCOTT

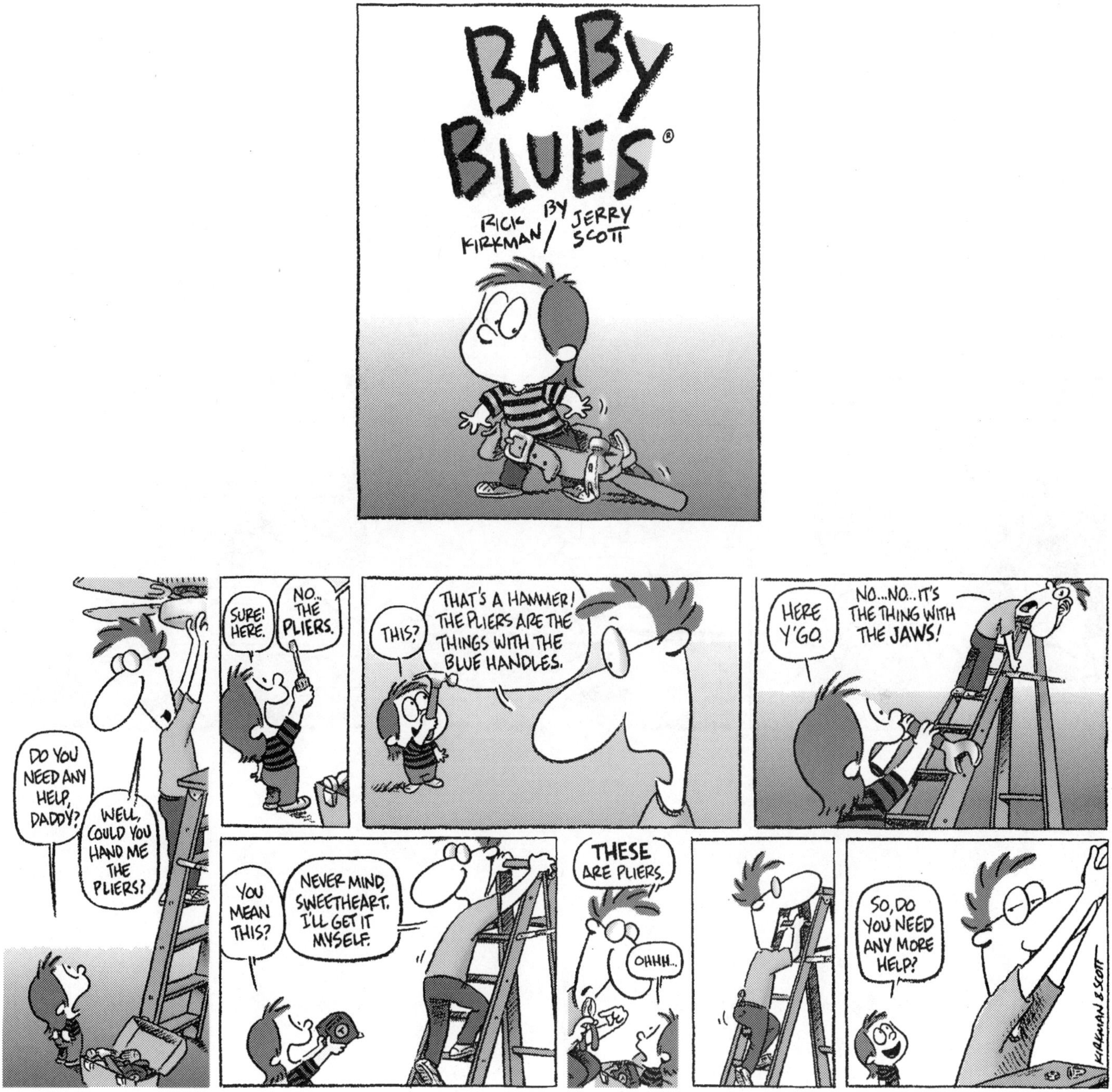
BABY BLUES®
BY RICK KIRKMAN / JERRY SCOTT
DO YOU NEED ANY HELP, DADDY?
WELL, COULD YOU HAND ME THE PLIERS?
SURE! HERE.
NO.. THE PLIERS.
THIS?
THAT'S A HAMMER! THE PLIERS ARE THE THINGS WITH THE BLUE HANDLES.
HERE Y'GO.
NO...NO...IT'S THE THING WITH THE JAWS!
YOU MEAN THIS?
NEVER MIND, SWEETHEART. I'LL GET IT MYSELF.
THESE ARE PLIERS.
OHHH..
SO, DO YOU NEED ANY MORE HELP?
KIRKMAN & SCOTT

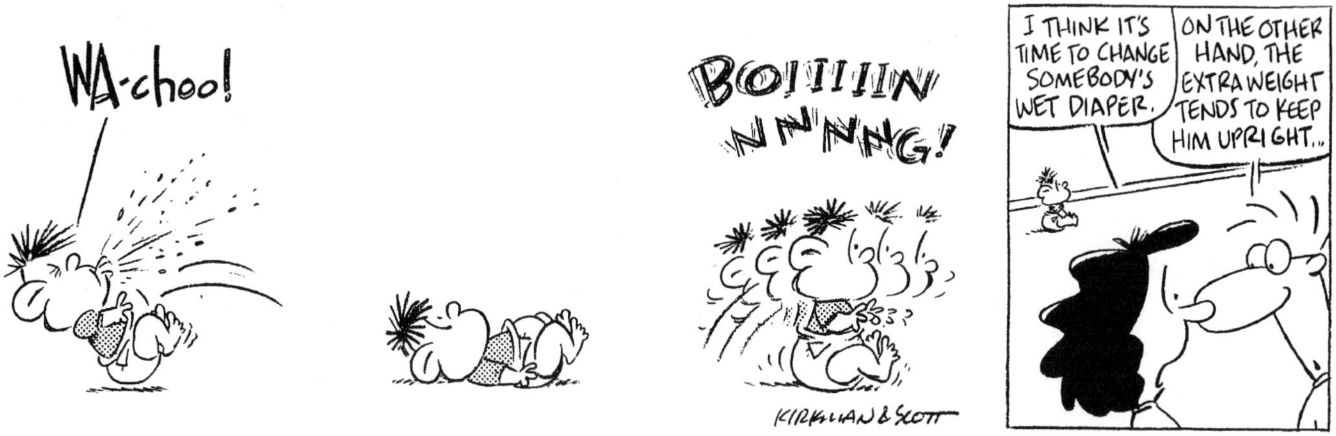
WA-choo!
BOIIIIIN NNNNG!
KIRKMAN & SCOTT
I THINK IT'S TIME TO CHANGE SOMEBODY'S WET DIAPER.
ON THE OTHER HAND, THE EXTRA WEIGHT TENDS TO KEEP HIM UPRIGHT...

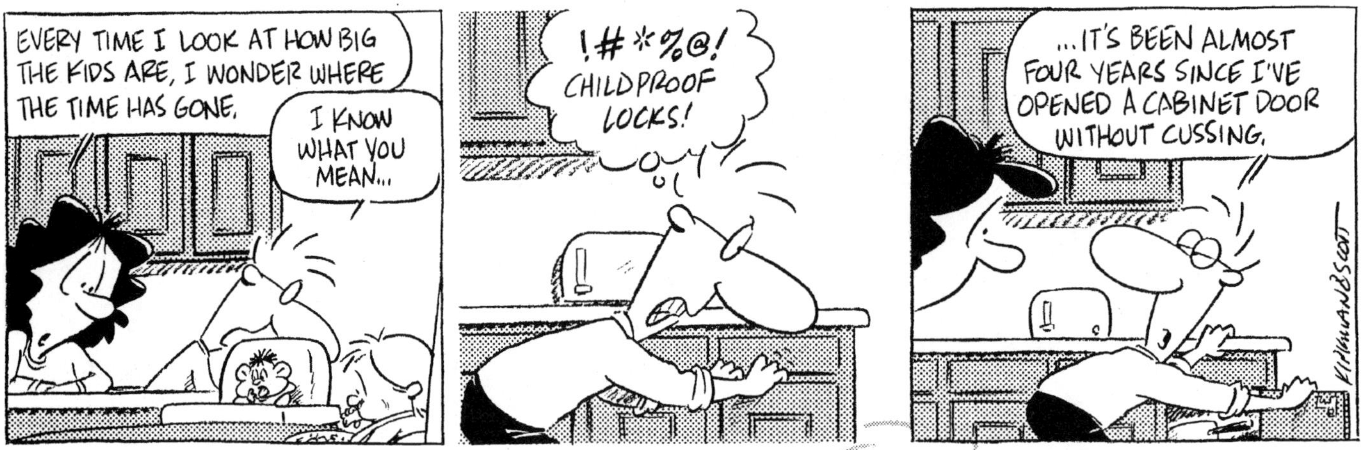
EVERY TIME I LOOK AT HOW BIG THE KIDS ARE, I WONDER WHERE THE TIME HAS GONE.
I KNOW WHAT YOU MEAN...
!#*%@! CHILDPROOF LOCKS!
...IT'S BEEN ALMOST FOUR YEARS SINCE I'VE OPENED A CABINET DOOR WITHOUT CUSSING.
KIRKMAN & SCOTT

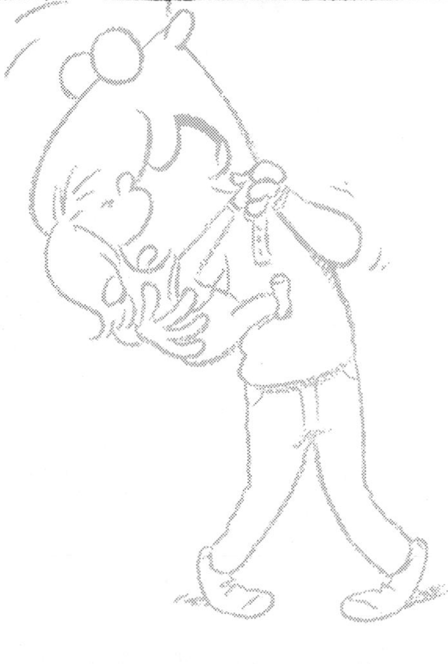

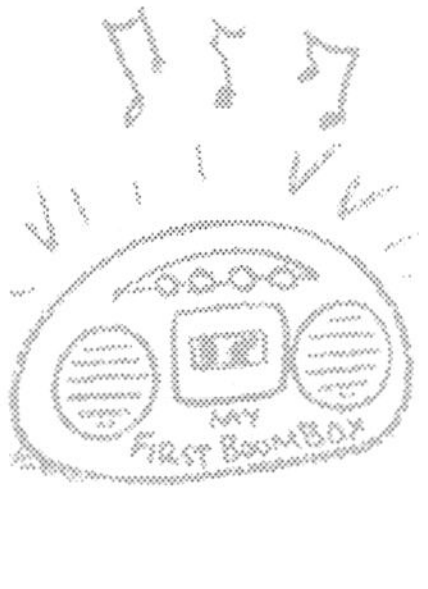
MY FIRST BOOMBOX

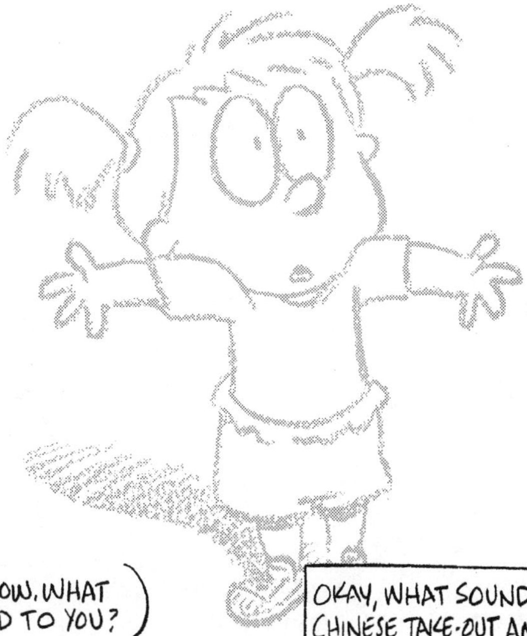

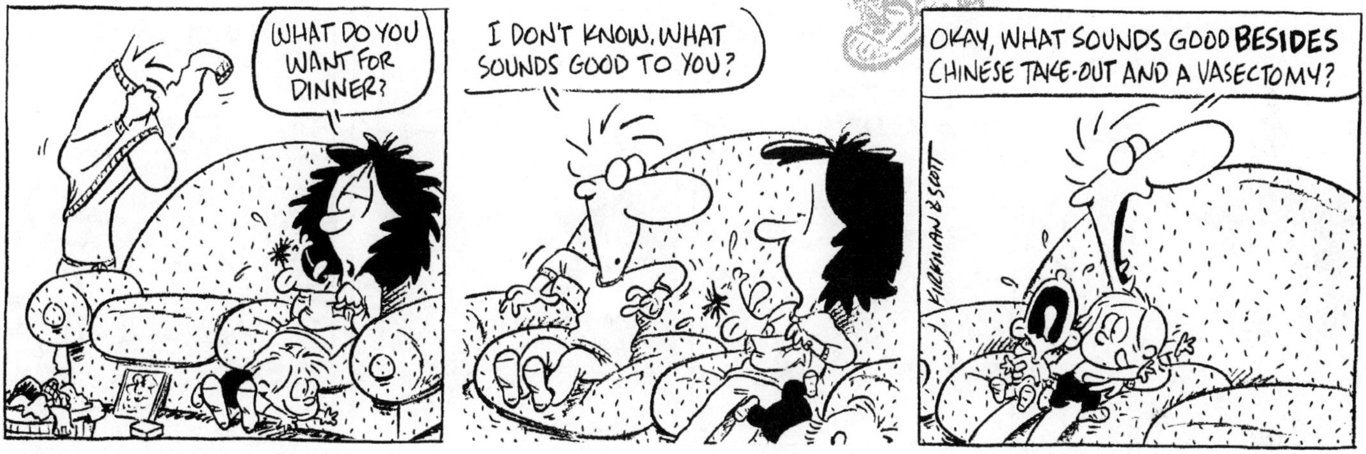

WHAT DO YOU WANT FOR DINNER?
I DON'T KNOW. WHAT SOUNDS GOOD TO YOU?
OKAY, WHAT SOUNDS GOOD **BESIDES** CHINESE TAKE-OUT AND A VASECTOMY?
KIRKMAN & SCOTT

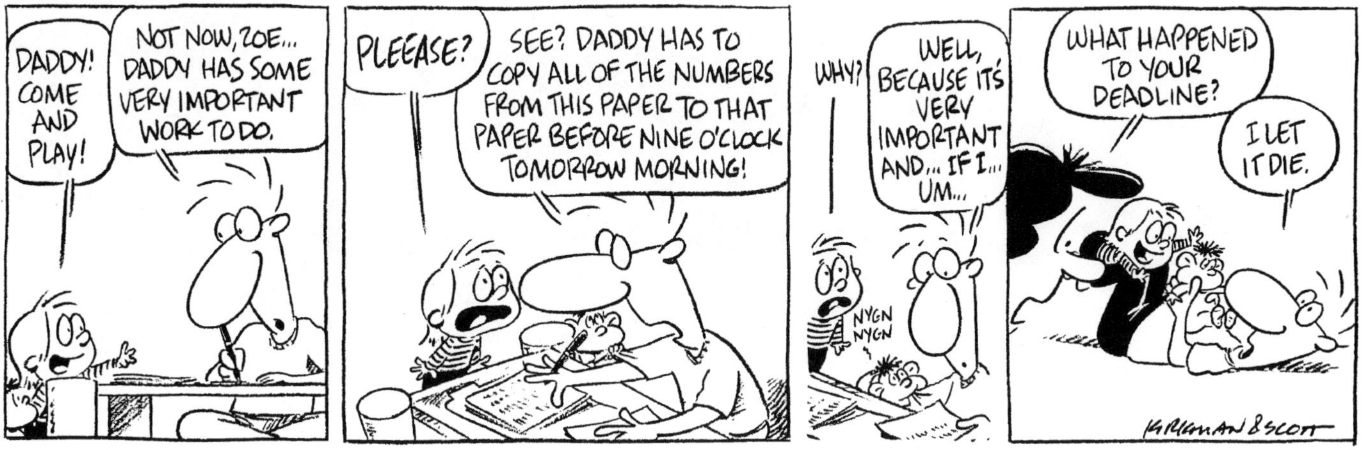

DADDY! COME AND PLAY!
NOT NOW, ZOE... DADDY HAS SOME VERY IMPORTANT WORK TO DO.
PLEEASE?
SEE? DADDY HAS TO COPY ALL OF THE NUMBERS FROM THIS PAPER TO THAT PAPER BEFORE NINE O'CLOCK TOMORROW MORNING!
WHY?
WELL, BECAUSE IT'S VERY IMPORTANT AND... IF I... UM...
NYGN NYGN
WHAT HAPPENED TO YOUR DEADLINE?
I LET IT DIE.
KIRKMAN & SCOTT

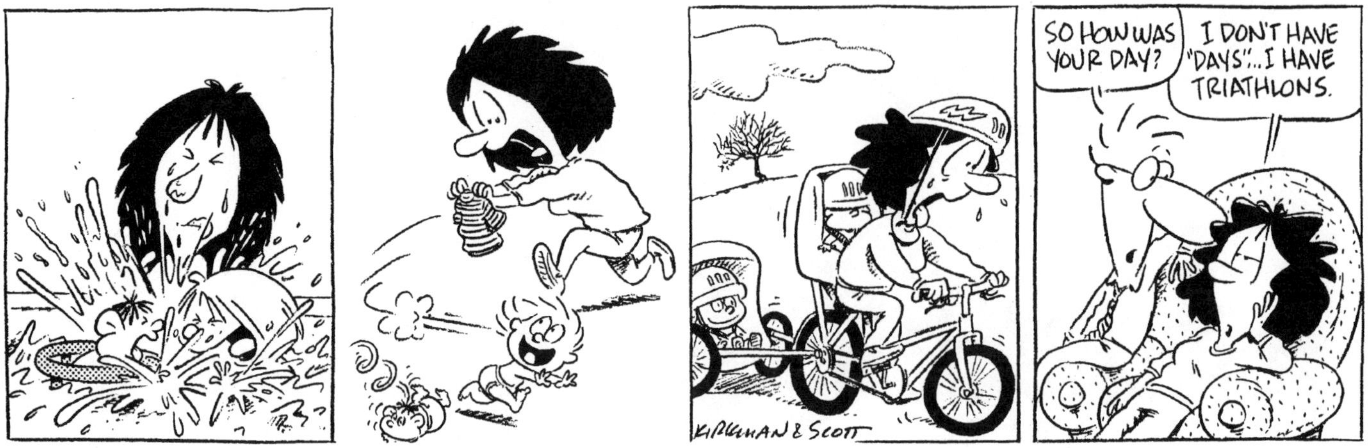
KIRKMAN & SCOTT
SO HOW WAS YOUR DAY?
I DON'T HAVE "DAYS"...I HAVE TRIATHLONS.

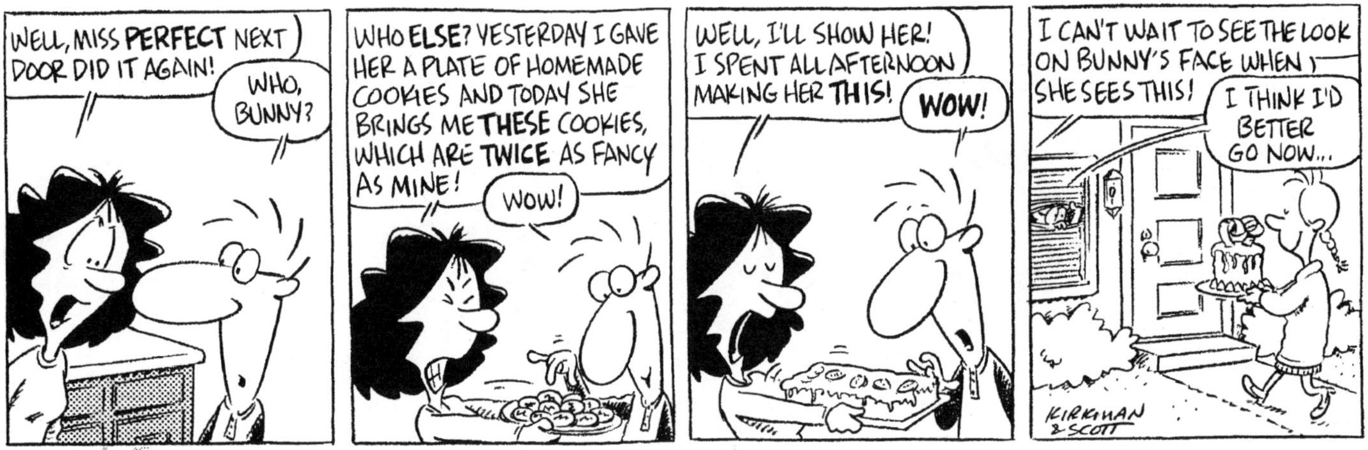
WELL, MISS PERFECT NEXT DOOR DID IT AGAIN!
WHO, BUNNY?
WHO ELSE? YESTERDAY I GAVE HER A PLATE OF HOMEMADE COOKIES AND TODAY SHE BRINGS ME THESE COOKIES, WHICH ARE TWICE AS FANCY AS MINE!
WOW!
WELL, I'LL SHOW HER! I SPENT ALL AFTERNOON MAKING HER THIS!
WOW!
I CAN'T WAIT TO SEE THE LOOK ON BUNNY'S FACE WHEN SHE SEES THIS!
I THINK I'D BETTER GO NOW...
KIRKMAN & SCOTT

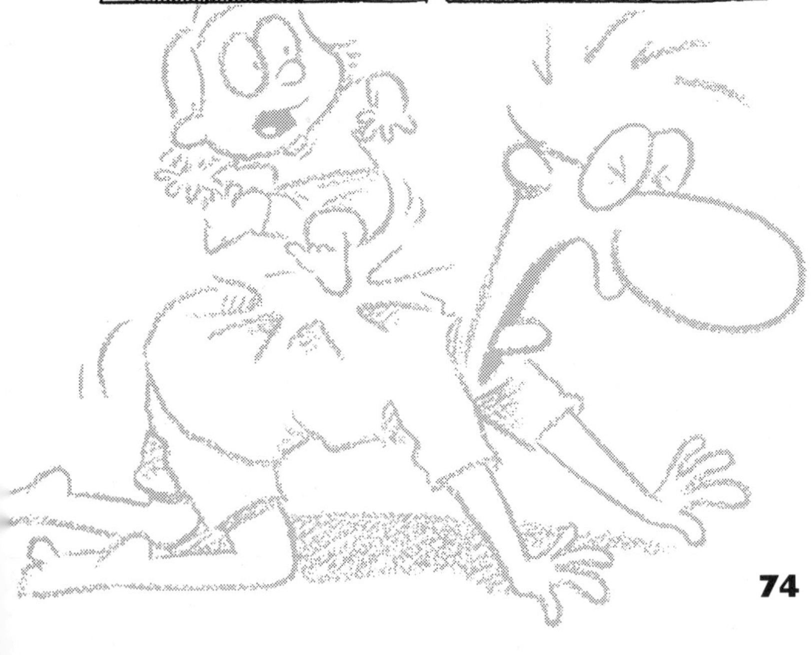

BABY BLUES®
BY RICK KIRKMAN / JERRY SCOTT

COME ON, ZOE... NO MORE STALLING. IT'S TIME FOR YOUR BATH.
NOOO! I DON'T WANNA TAKE A BAFF!
NO!!!...
NO BAFF! NO BAFF! NO BAFF!
IN YOU GO, SWEETHEART.
WAAAAAAAAAAA!
EEEEEE! NO SHAMPOO! NO SHAMPOO!
OKAY... ALL FINISHED!
NO! I DON'T WANNA GET OUT!
WAAAAAAAAAAA!
YOU'RE SO PATIENT WITH HER... HOW DO YOU KEEP YOUR COOL WHEN SHE'S BEING SUCH A TERROR?
KIRKMAN & SCOTT
WHAT?

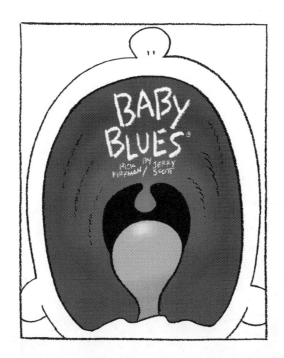

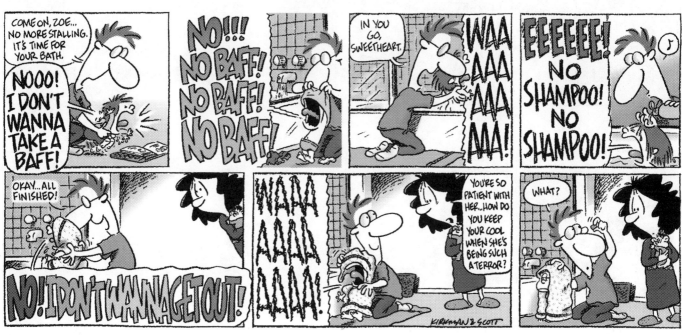

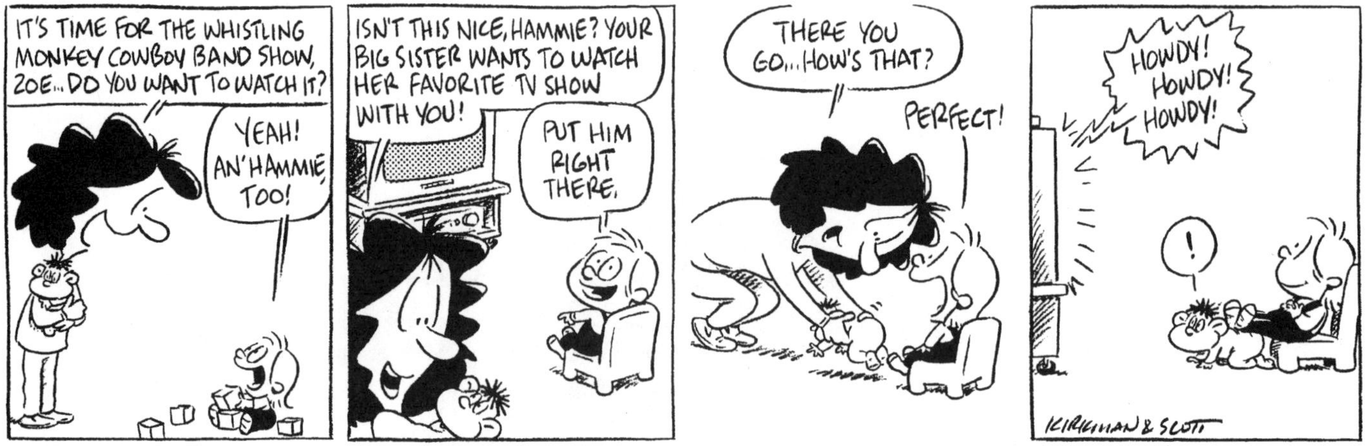
IT'S TIME FOR THE WHISTLING MONKEY COWBOY BAND SHOW, ZOE... DO YOU WANT TO WATCH IT?
YEAH! AN' HAMMIE, TOO!
ISN'T THIS NICE, HAMMIE? YOUR BIG SISTER WANTS TO WATCH HER FAVORITE TV SHOW WITH YOU!
PUT HIM RIGHT THERE.
THERE YOU GO... HOW'S THAT?
PERFECT!
HOWDY! HOWDY! HOWDY!
!
KIRKMAN & SCOTT

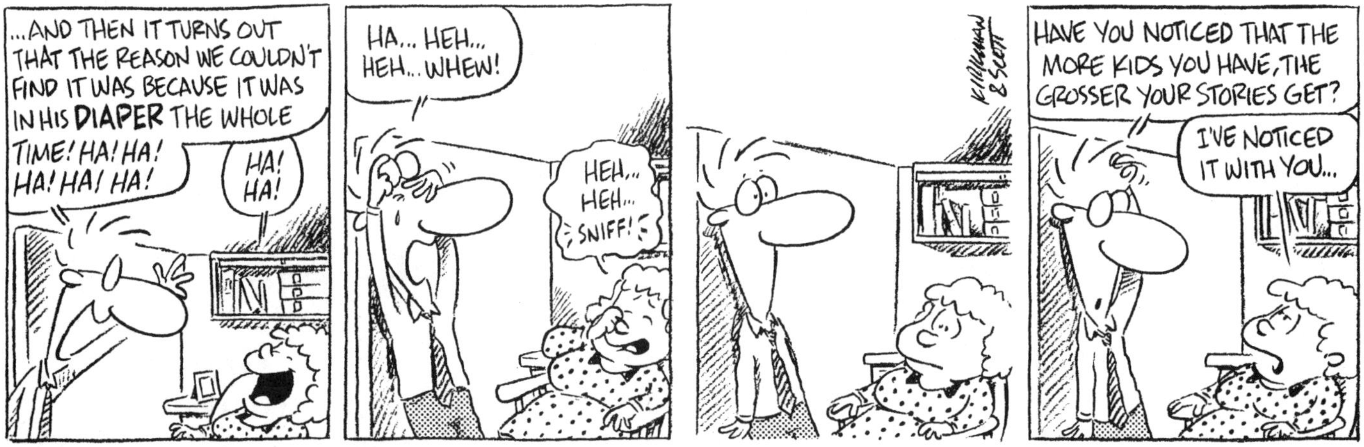
...AND THEN IT TURNS OUT THAT THE REASON WE COULDN'T FIND IT WAS BECAUSE IT WAS IN HIS DIAPER THE WHOLE TIME! HA! HA! HA! HA! HA!
HA! HA!
HA... HEH... HEH... WHEW!
HEH... HEH... SNIFF!
KIRKMAN & SCOTT
HAVE YOU NOTICED THAT THE MORE KIDS YOU HAVE, THE GROSSER YOUR STORIES GET?
I'VE NOTICED IT WITH YOU...

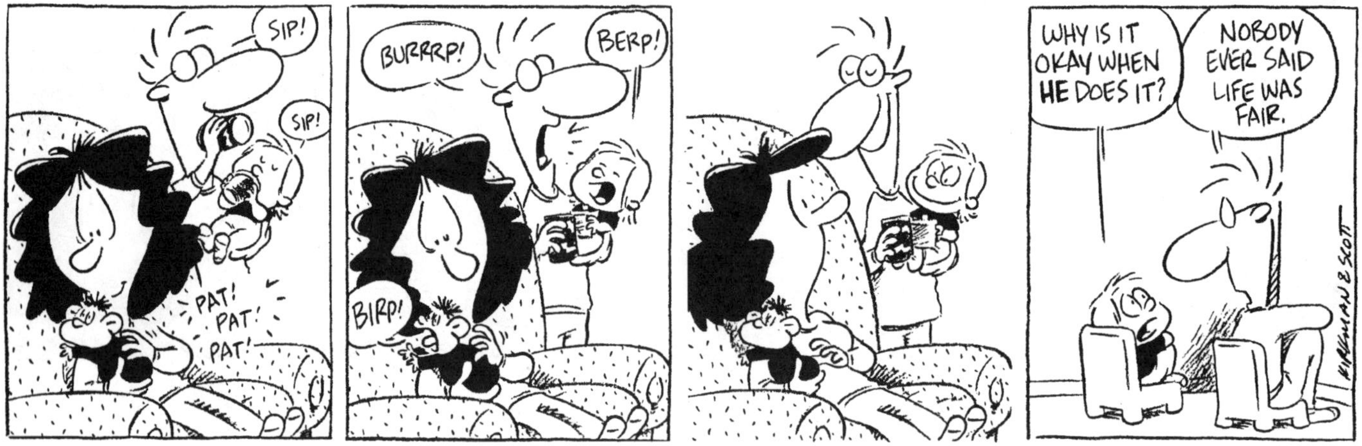
SIP!
SIP!
PAT! PAT! PAT!
BURRRP!
BERP!
BIRP!
WHY IS IT OKAY WHEN HE DOES IT?
NOBODY EVER SAID LIFE WAS FAIR.
KIRKMAN & SCOTT

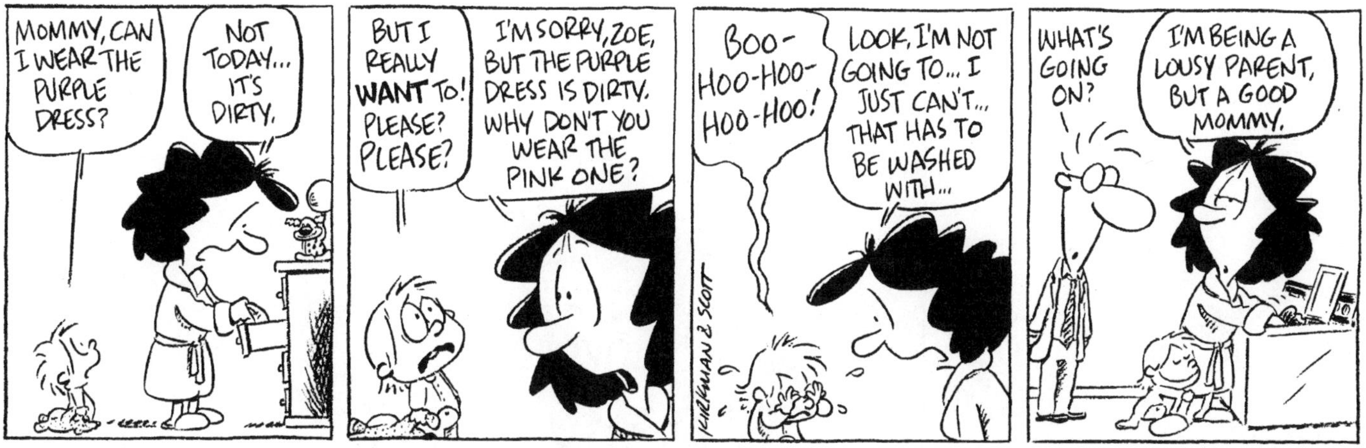
MOMMY, CAN I WEAR THE PURPLE DRESS?
NOT TODAY... IT'S DIRTY.
BUT I REALLY WANT TO! PLEASE? PLEASE?
I'M SORRY, ZOE, BUT THE PURPLE DRESS IS DIRTY. WHY DON'T YOU WEAR THE PINK ONE?
BOO-HOO-HOO-HOO-HOO!
LOOK, I'M NOT GOING TO... I JUST CAN'T... THAT HAS TO BE WASHED WITH...
KIRKMAN & SCOTT
WHAT'S GOING ON?
I'M BEING A LOUSY PARENT, BUT A GOOD MOMMY.

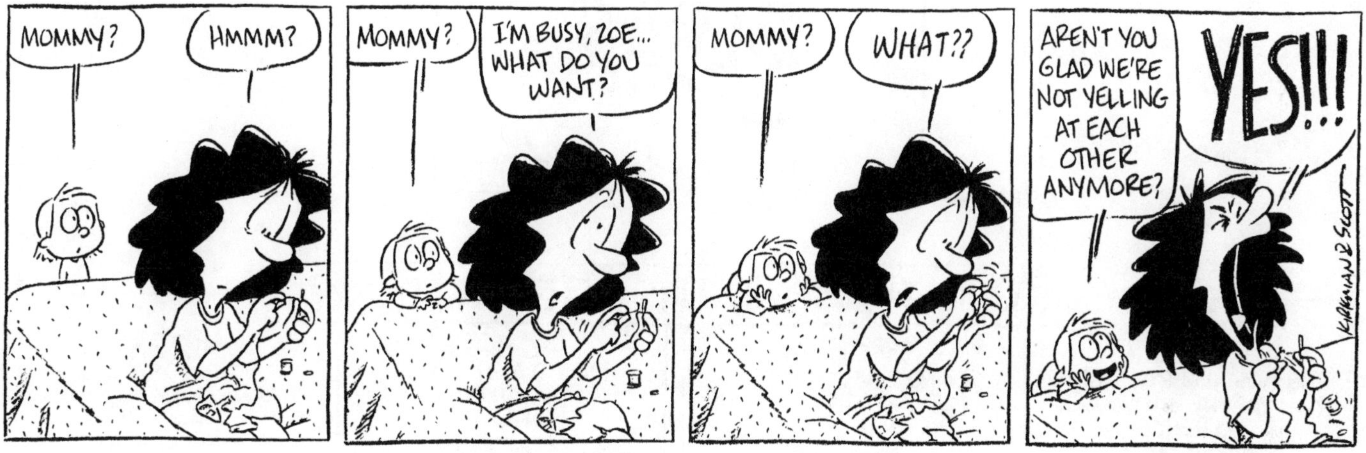
MOMMY?
HMMM?
MOMMY?
I'M BUSY, ZOE... WHAT DO YOU WANT?
MOMMY?
WHAT??
AREN'T YOU GLAD WE'RE NOT YELLING AT EACH OTHER ANYMORE?
YES!!!
KIRKMAN & SCOTT

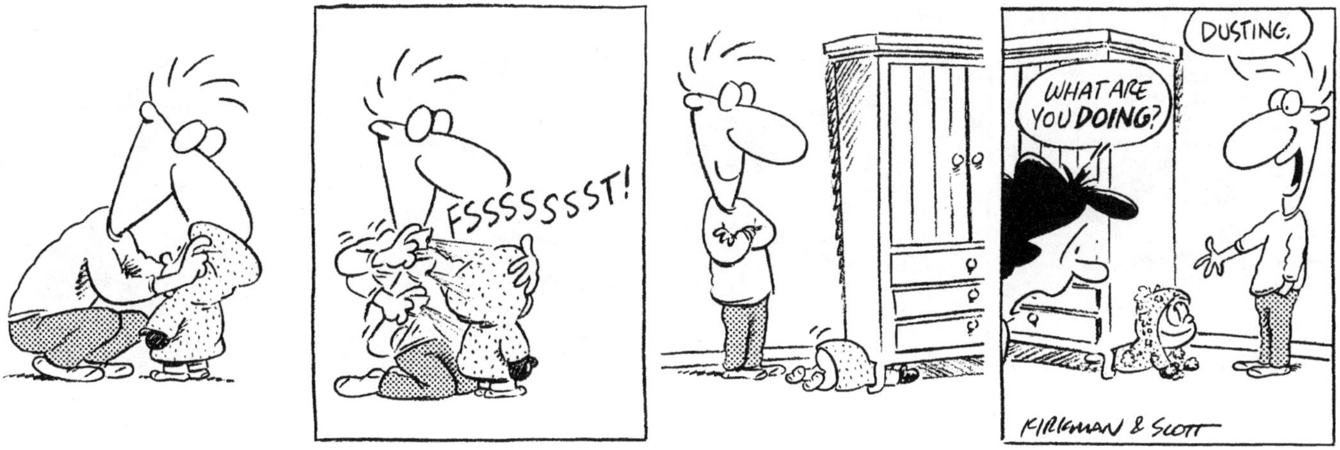
FSSSSSSST!
WHAT ARE YOU DOING?
DUSTING.
KIRKMAN & SCOTT

BABY BLUES®

RICK KIRKMAN / BY JERRY SCOTT

FOUR GREAT MYTHS OF PARENTING

MYTH 1
THE MOST IMPORTANT THING FOR A PARENT TO POSSESS IS PATIENCE.

REALITY

THE MOST IMPORTANT THING FOR A PARENT TO POSSESS IS AN EXTRA SET OF CAR KEYS!

JUST TRY TO REMEMBER WHERE YOU PUT THEM, OKAY? PLEEEEEASE?

MYTH 2
TAKING LOTS OF PICTURES OF YOUR BABY WILL FILL YOUR LIVES WITH MEMORIES.

REALITY

TAKING LOTS OF PICTURES OF YOUR BABY WILL FILL YOUR **CLOSETS** WITH MEMORIES!

JUST A LITTLE HARDER...WE ALMOST HAD IT!

MAYBE WE SHOULD GET SOME PHOTO ALBUMS.

MYTH 3
A GOOD BABY SITTER IS WORTH HER WEIGHT IN GOLD.

REALITY

A GOOD BABY SITTER **CHARGES** HER WEIGHT IN GOLD!

THAT'S OKAY... I TAKE MASTERCARD, VISA AND AMERICAN EXPRESS...

KIRKMAN & SCOTT

MYTH 4
TWO CHILDREN AREN'T REALLY MUCH MORE WORK THAN ONE.

REALITY

YEAH. RIGHT.

HA! HA! HAAAAAA! :SNORT!: **WA**-HAA-HAAA! HAHAHAHA!

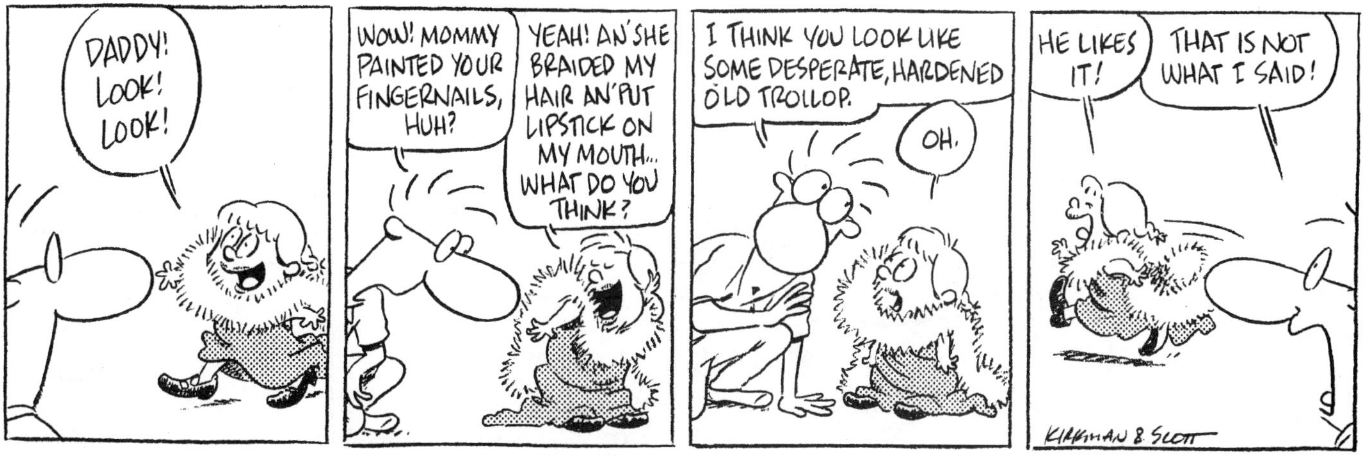
DADDY! LOOK! LOOK!
WOW! MOMMY PAINTED YOUR FINGERNAILS, HUH?
YEAH! AN' SHE BRAIDED MY HAIR AN' PUT LIPSTICK ON MY MOUTH... WHAT DO YOU THINK?
I THINK YOU LOOK LIKE SOME DESPERATE, HARDENED OLD TROLLOP.
OH.
HE LIKES IT!
THAT IS NOT WHAT I SAID!
KIRKMAN & SCOTT

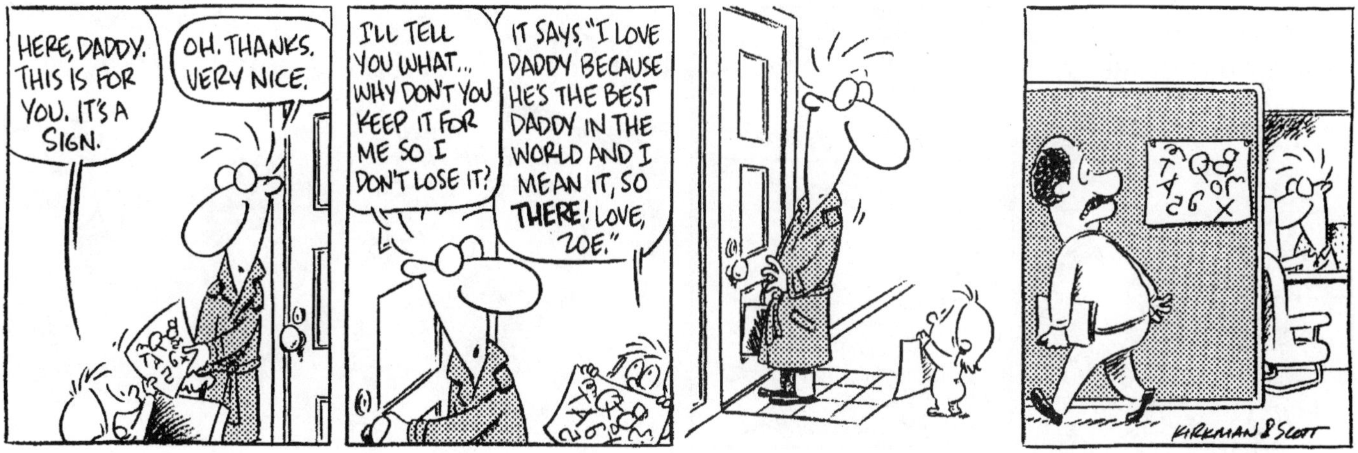
HERE, DADDY. THIS IS FOR YOU. IT'S A SIGN.
OH. THANKS. VERY NICE.
I'LL TELL YOU WHAT... WHY DON'T YOU KEEP IT FOR ME SO I DON'T LOSE IT?
IT SAYS, "I LOVE DADDY BECAUSE HE'S THE BEST DADDY IN THE WORLD AND I MEAN IT, SO **THERE**! LOVE, ZOE."
KIRKMAN & SCOTT

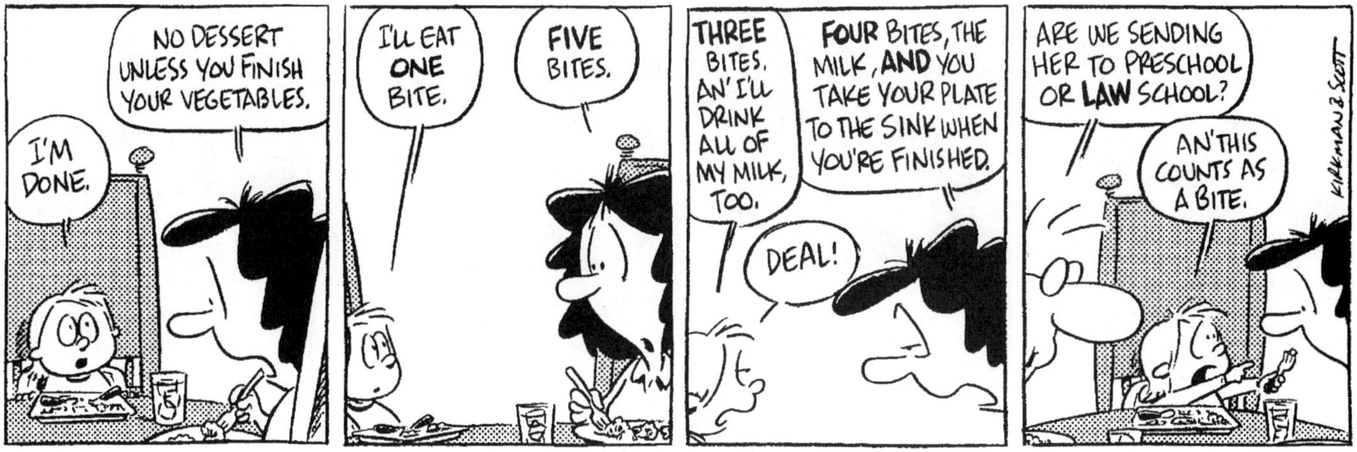
NO DESSERT UNLESS YOU FINISH YOUR VEGETABLES.
I'M DONE.
I'LL EAT **ONE** BITE.
FIVE BITES.
THREE BITES. AN' I'LL DRINK ALL OF MY MILK, TOO.
FOUR BITES, THE MILK, **AND** YOU TAKE YOUR PLATE TO THE SINK WHEN YOU'RE FINISHED.
DEAL!
ARE WE SENDING HER TO PRESCHOOL OR **LAW** SCHOOL?
AN' THIS COUNTS AS A BITE.
KIRKMAN & SCOTT

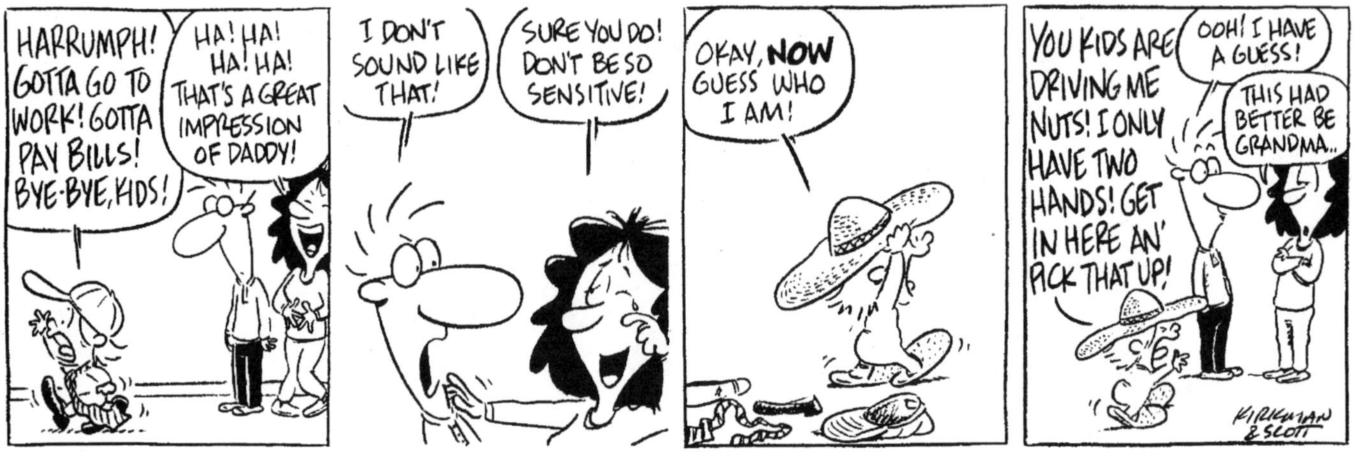
HARRUMPH! GOTTA GO TO WORK! GOTTA PAY BILLS! BYE-BYE, KIDS!
HA! HA! HA! HA! THAT'S A GREAT IMPRESSION OF DADDY!
I DON'T SOUND LIKE THAT!
SURE YOU DO! DON'T BE SO SENSITIVE!
OKAY, **NOW** GUESS WHO I AM!
YOU KIDS ARE DRIVING ME NUTS! I ONLY HAVE TWO HANDS! GET IN HERE AN' PICK THAT UP!
OOH! I HAVE A GUESS!
THIS HAD BETTER BE GRANDMA...
KIRKMAN & SCOTT

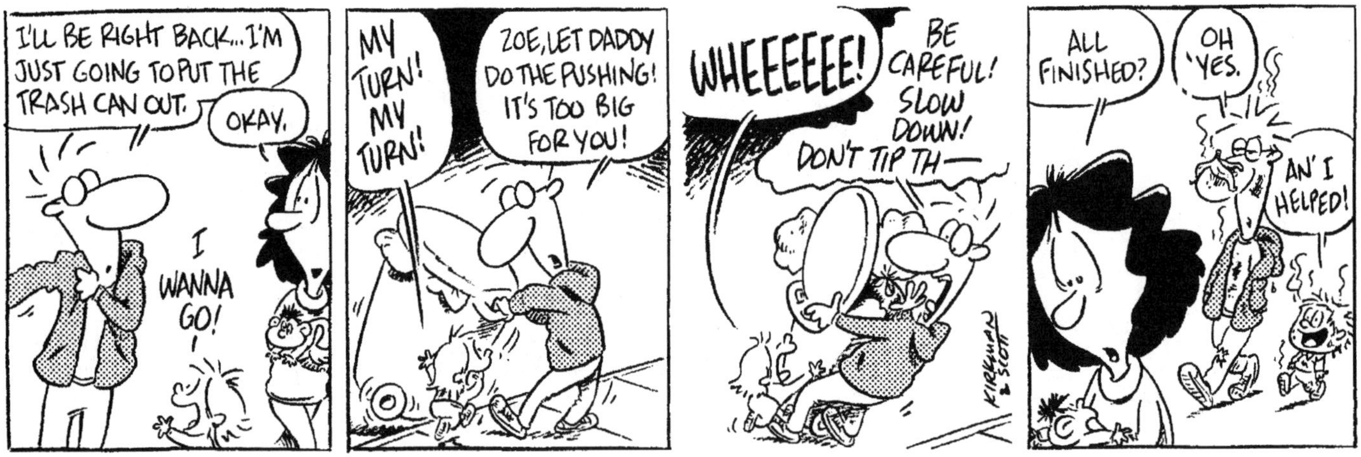
I'LL BE RIGHT BACK... I'M JUST GOING TO PUT THE TRASH CAN OUT.
OKAY.
I WANNA GO!
MY TURN! MY TURN!
ZOE, LET DADDY DO THE PUSHING! IT'S TOO BIG FOR YOU!
WHEEEEEEE!
BE CAREFUL! SLOW DOWN!
DON'T TIP TH—
KIRKMAN & SCOTT
ALL FINISHED?
OH YES.
AN' I HELPED!

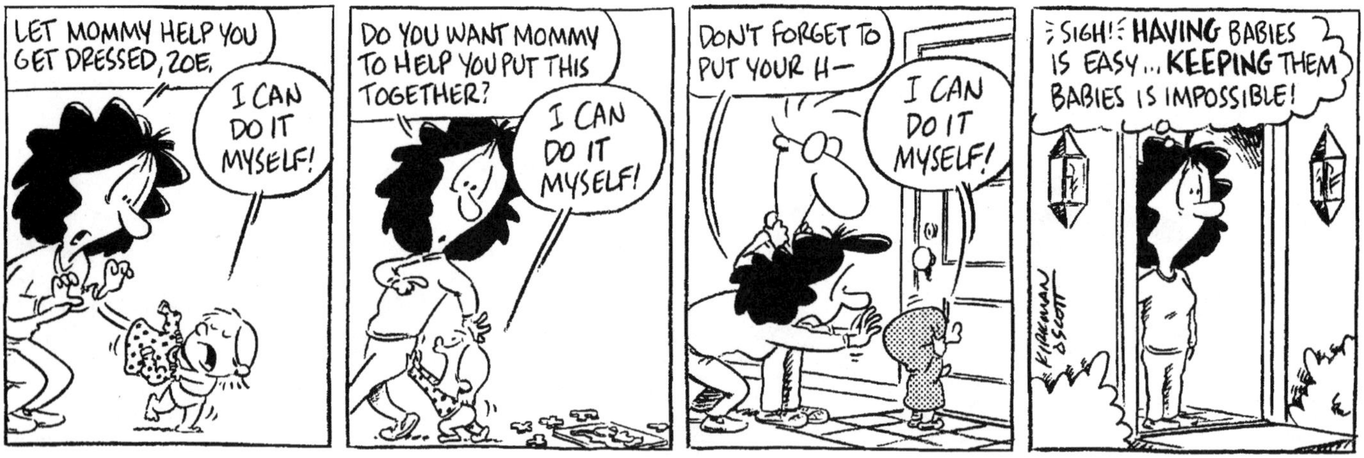
LET MOMMY HELP YOU GET DRESSED, ZOE.
I CAN DO IT MYSELF!
DO YOU WANT MOMMY TO HELP YOU PUT THIS TOGETHER?
I CAN DO IT MYSELF!
DON'T FORGET TO PUT YOUR H—
I CAN DO IT MYSELF!
KIRKMAN & SCOTT
SIGH! **HAVING** BABIES IS EASY... **KEEPING** THEM BABIES IS IMPOSSIBLE!

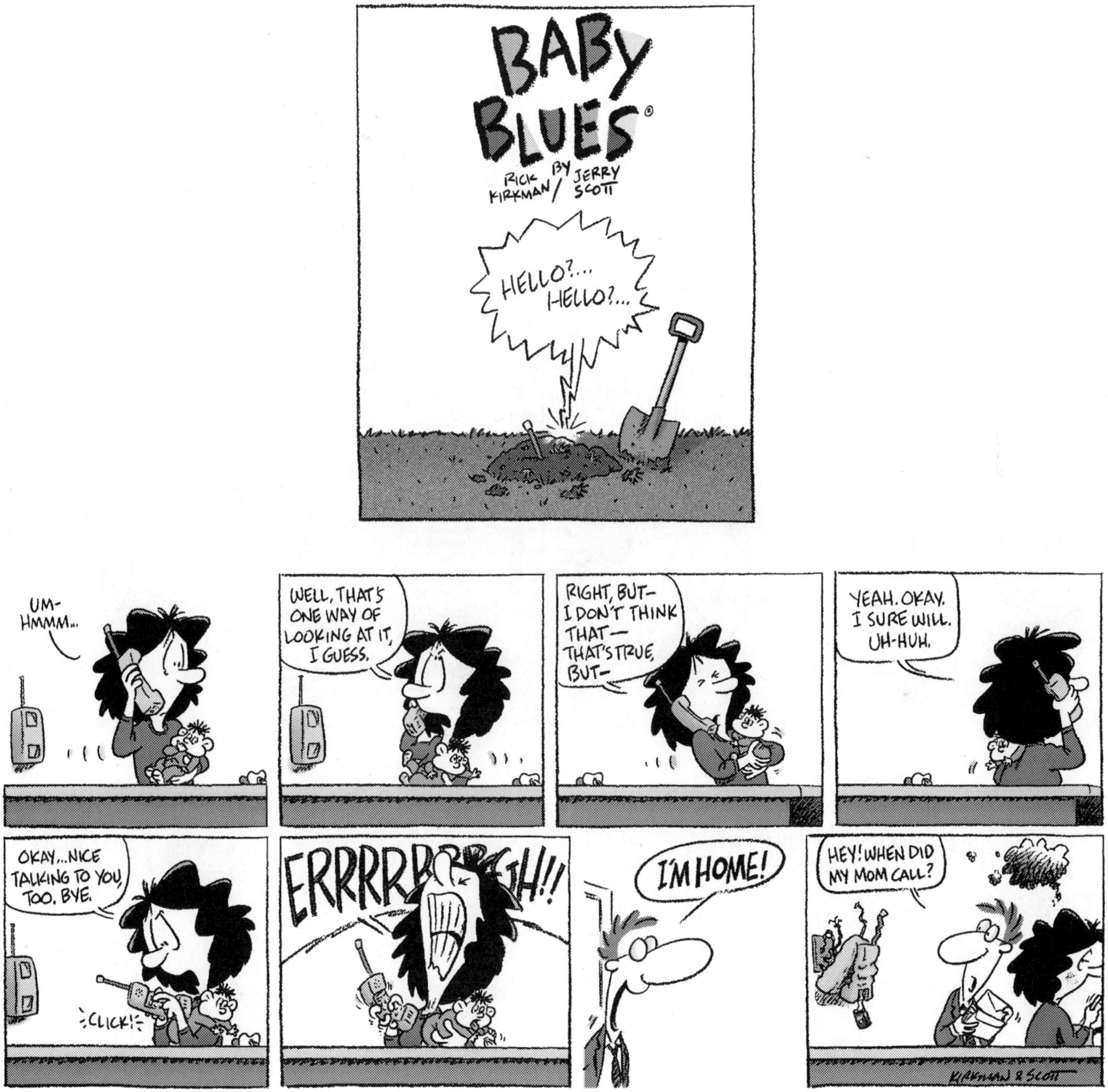
BABY BLUES®
RICK KIRKMAN / BY JERRY SCOTT
HELLO?... HELLO?...
UM-HMMM...
WELL, THAT'S ONE WAY OF LOOKING AT IT, I GUESS.
RIGHT, BUT- I DON'T THINK THAT— THAT'S TRUE, BUT-
YEAH. OKAY. I SURE WILL. UH-HUH.
OKAY... NICE TALKING TO YOU, TOO. BYE.
CLICK!
ERRRRBBBGH!!
I'M HOME!
HEY! WHEN DID MY MOM CALL?
KIRKMAN & SCOTT

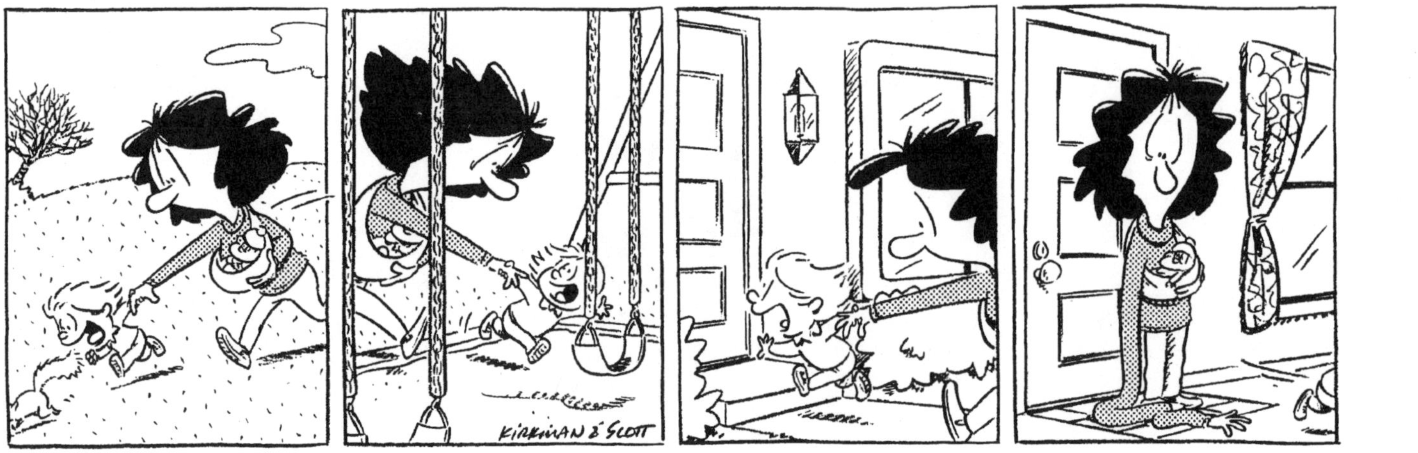
KIRKMAN & SCOTT

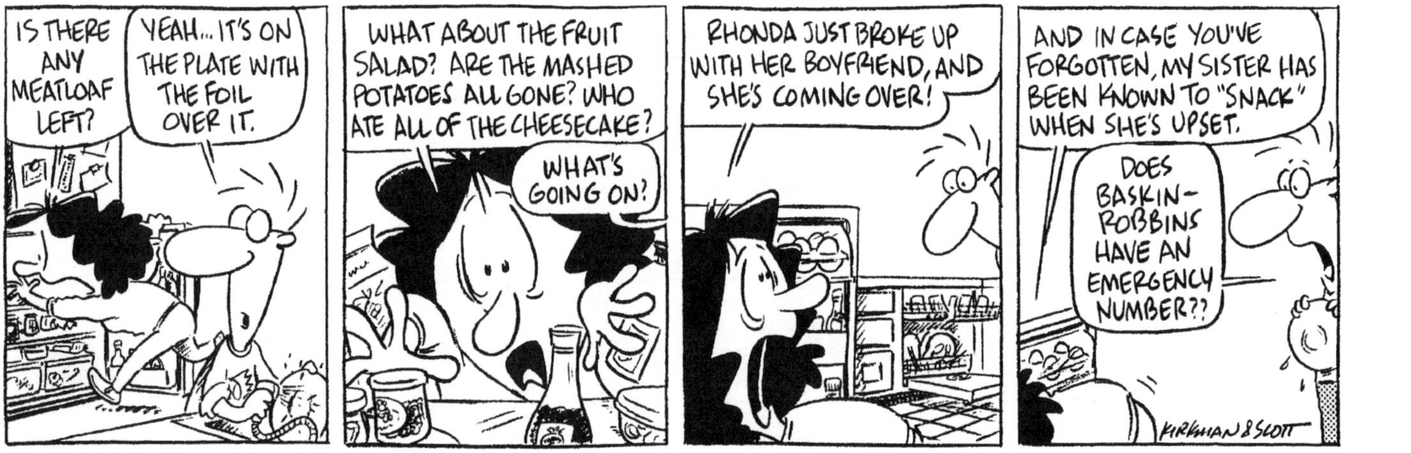
IS THERE ANY MEATLOAF LEFT?
YEAH... IT'S ON THE PLATE WITH THE FOIL OVER IT.
WHAT ABOUT THE FRUIT SALAD? ARE THE MASHED POTATOES ALL GONE? WHO ATE ALL OF THE CHEESECAKE?
WHAT'S GOING ON?
RHONDA JUST BROKE UP WITH HER BOYFRIEND, AND SHE'S COMING OVER!
AND IN CASE YOU'VE FORGOTTEN, MY SISTER HAS BEEN KNOWN TO "SNACK" WHEN SHE'S UPSET.
DOES BASKIN-ROBBINS HAVE AN EMERGENCY NUMBER??
KIRKMAN & SCOTT

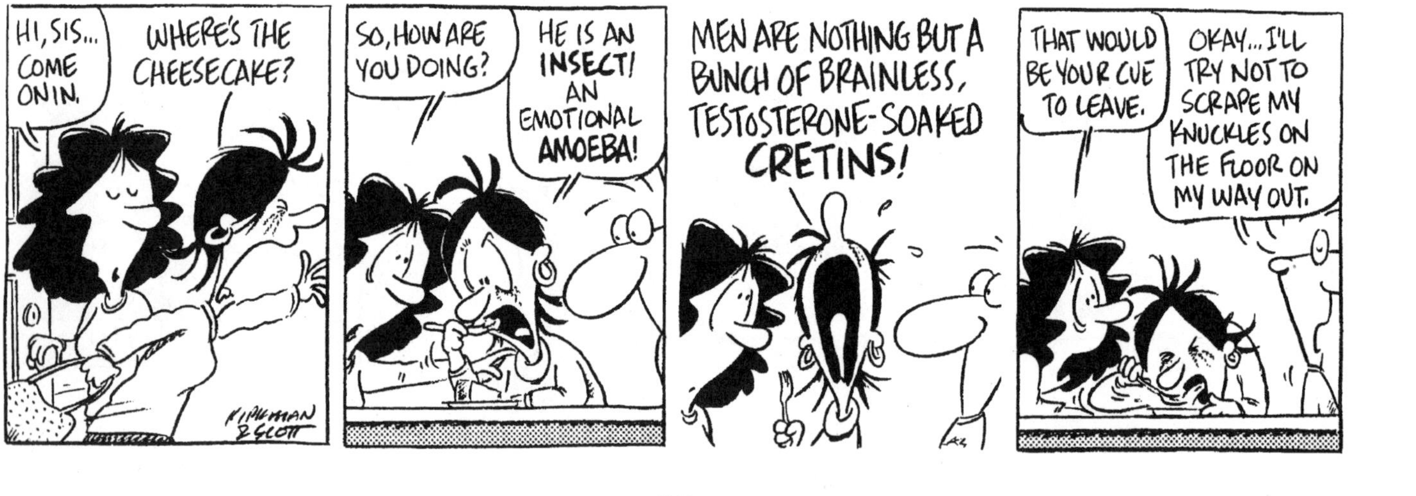
HI, SIS... COME ON IN.
WHERE'S THE CHEESECAKE?
KIRKMAN & SCOTT
SO, HOW ARE YOU DOING?
HE IS AN INSECT! AN EMOTIONAL AMOEBA!
MEN ARE NOTHING BUT A BUNCH OF BRAINLESS, TESTOSTERONE-SOAKED CRETINS!
THAT WOULD BE YOUR CUE TO LEAVE.
OKAY... I'LL TRY NOT TO SCRAPE MY KNUCKLES ON THE FLOOR ON MY WAY OUT.

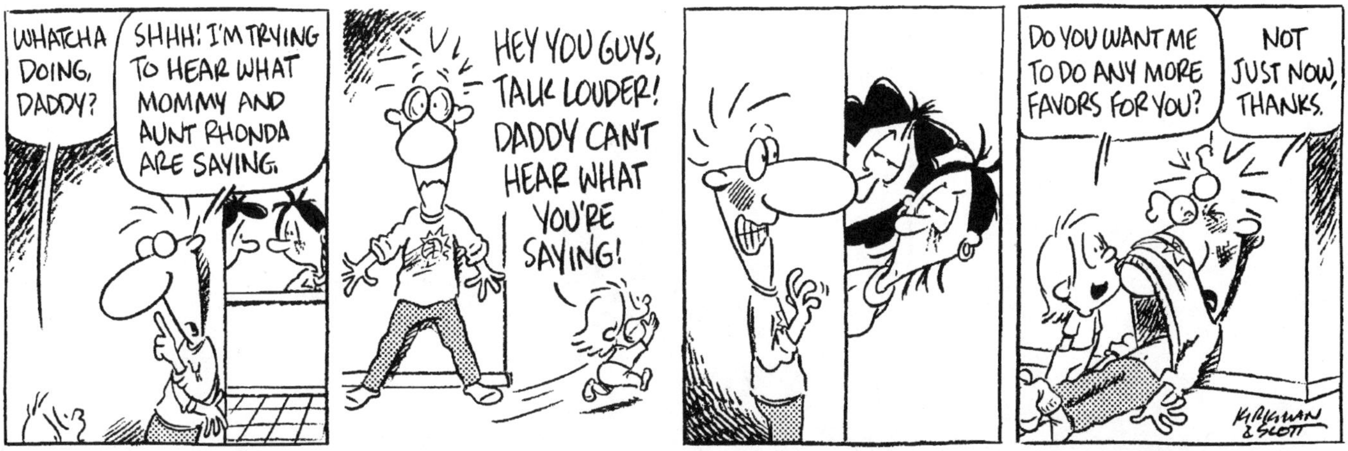
WHATCHA DOING, DADDY?
SHHH! I'M TRYING TO HEAR WHAT MOMMY AND AUNT RHONDA ARE SAYING.
HEY YOU GUYS, TALK LOUDER! DADDY CAN'T HEAR WHAT YOU'RE SAYING!
DO YOU WANT ME TO DO ANY MORE FAVORS FOR YOU?
NOT JUST NOW, THANKS.
KIRKMAN & SCOTT

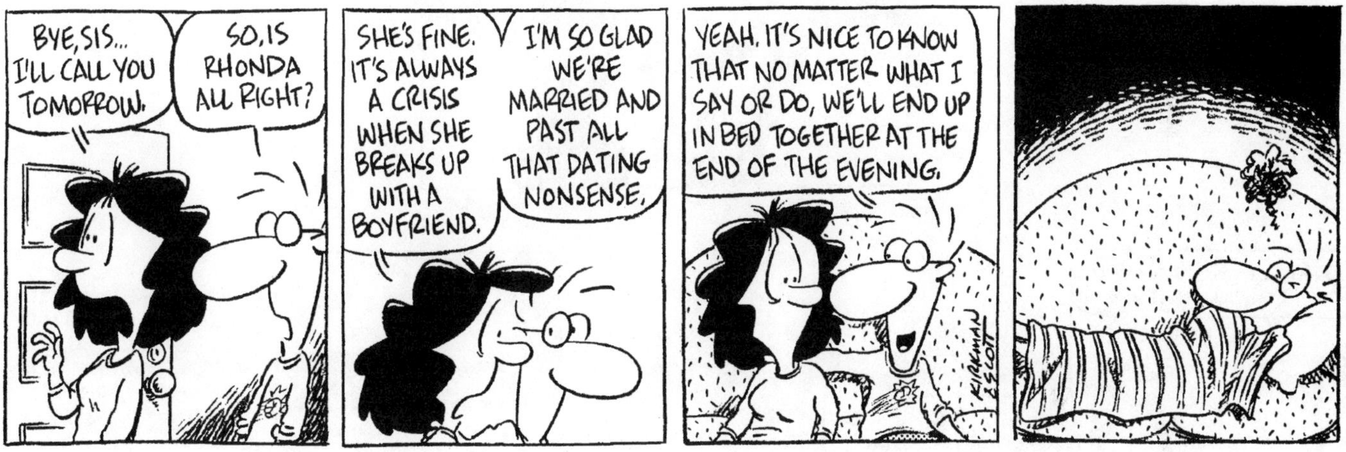
BYE, SIS... I'LL CALL YOU TOMORROW.
SO, IS RHONDA ALL RIGHT?
SHE'S FINE. IT'S ALWAYS A CRISIS WHEN SHE BREAKS UP WITH A BOYFRIEND.
I'M SO GLAD WE'RE MARRIED AND PAST ALL THAT DATING NONSENSE.
YEAH. IT'S NICE TO KNOW THAT NO MATTER WHAT I SAY OR DO, WE'LL END UP IN BED TOGETHER AT THE END OF THE EVENING.
KIRKMAN & SCOTT

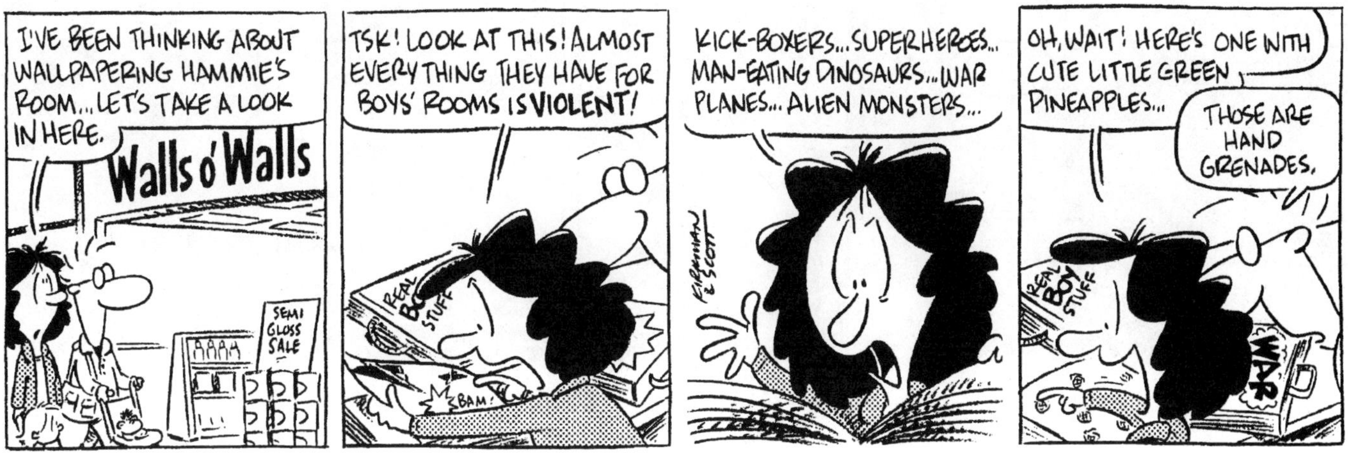
I'VE BEEN THINKING ABOUT WALLPAPERING HAMMIE'S ROOM... LET'S TAKE A LOOK IN HERE.
Walls o' Walls
SEMI GLOSS SALE
TSK! LOOK AT THIS! ALMOST EVERYTHING THEY HAVE FOR BOYS' ROOMS IS **VIOLENT**!
REAL BOY STUFF
BAM!
KIRKMAN & SCOTT
KICK-BOXERS... SUPERHEROES... MAN-EATING DINOSAURS... WAR PLANES... ALIEN MONSTERS...
OH, WAIT! HERE'S ONE WITH CUTE LITTLE GREEN PINEAPPLES...
THOSE ARE HAND GRENADES.
REAL BOY STUFF
WAR

BABY BLUES®
BY
RICK KIRKMAN / JERRY SCOTT
*APOLOGIES TO JAY WARD

OKAY, LET'S SEE...HOW ABOUT A PAIR OF NAIL CLIPPERS?
FINGER OR TOE?
A FLASHLIGHT?
RIGHT HERE... INCLUDING SPARE BATTERIES.
DENTAL FLOSS?
WAXED OR UNWAXED? COME ON... CHALLENGE ME!
KIRKMAN & SCOTT
SOY SAUCE?
FIVE PACKETS!
TIRE REPAIR KIT.
YEP. HERE.
PLIERS?
REGULAR OR NEEDLE-NOSE
BIRDSEED!
OF COURSE!
I'VE GOTTA ADMIT, WANDA... NOBODY PACKS LIKE YOU DO.
LIKE I ALWAYS SAY, "IF IT'S NOT IN MY DIAPER BAG, YOU PROBABLY DON'T NEED IT.

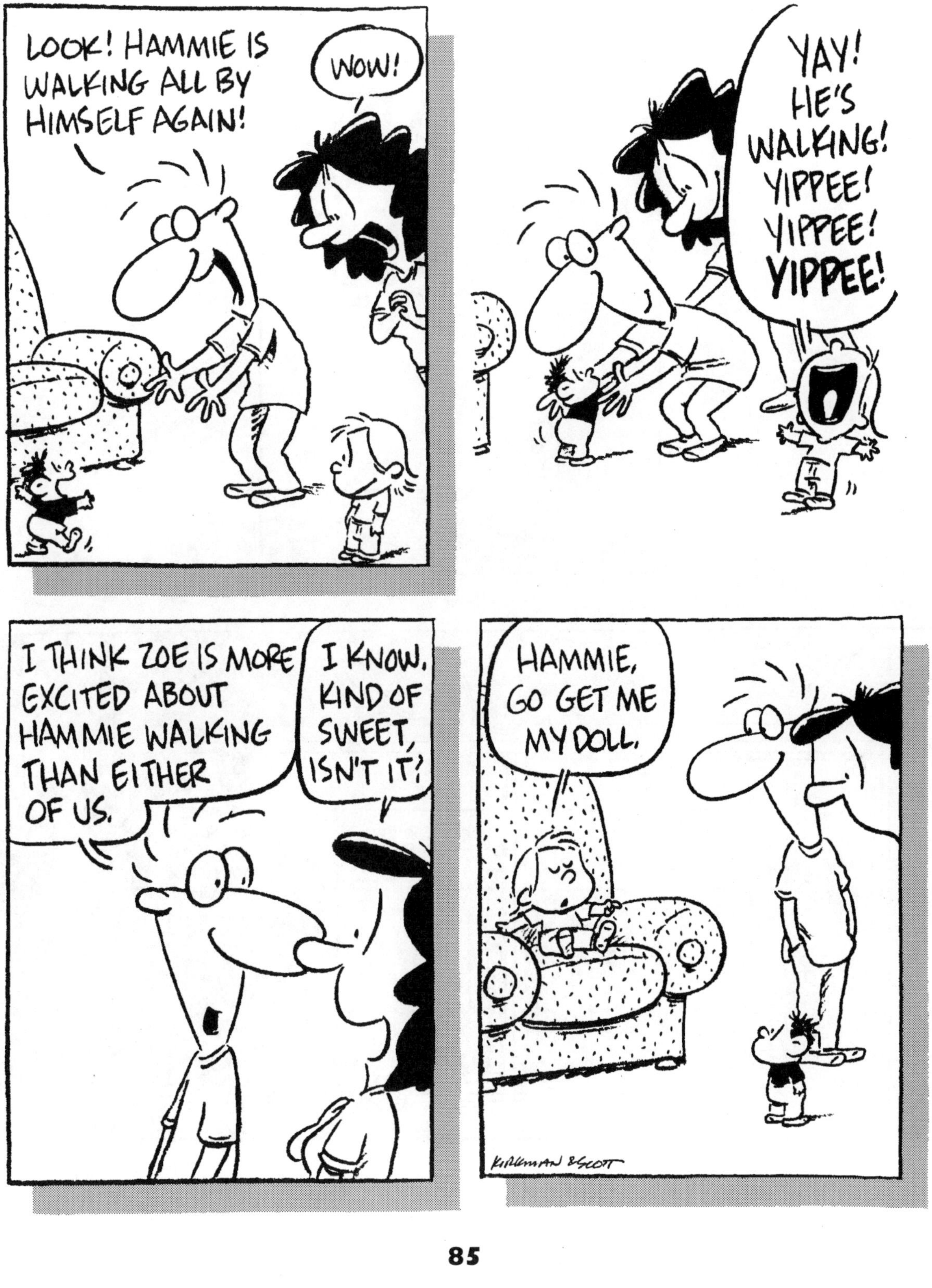
LOOK! HAMMIE IS WALKING ALL BY HIMSELF AGAIN!
WOW!
YAY! HE'S WALKING! YIPPEE! YIPPEE! YIPPEE!
I THINK ZOE IS MORE EXCITED ABOUT HAMMIE WALKING THAN EITHER OF US.
I KNOW. KIND OF SWEET, ISN'T IT?
HAMMIE, GO GET ME MY DOLL.
KIRKMAN & SCOTT

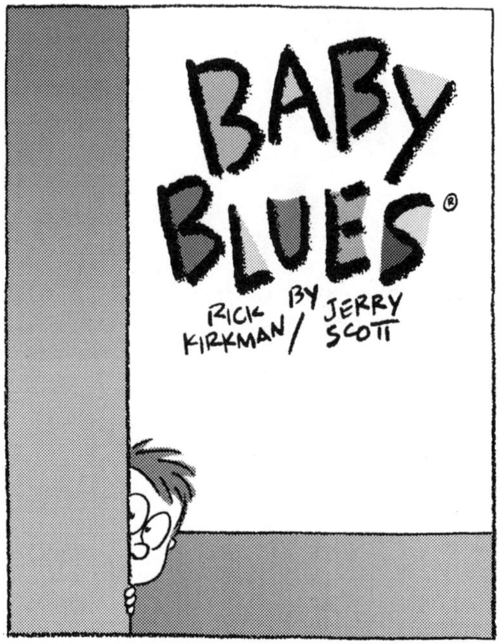
BABY BLUES®
BY
RICK KIRKMAN / JERRY SCOTT

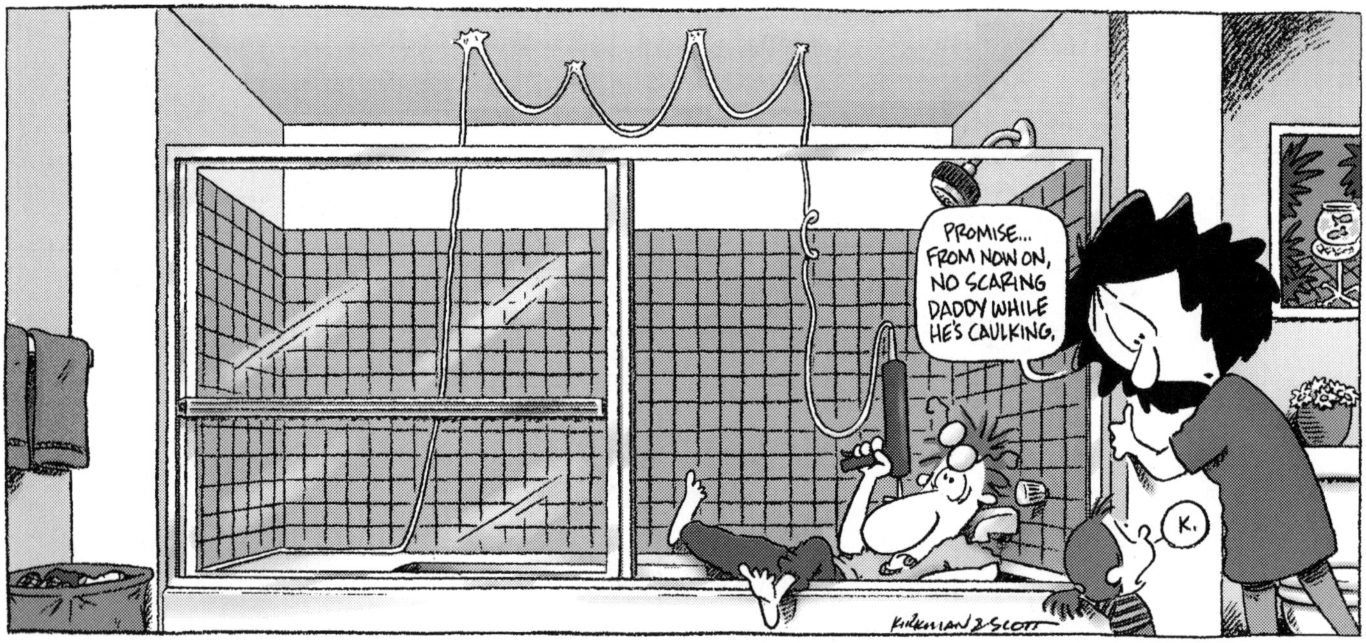
PROMISE... FROM NOW ON, NO SCARING DADDY WHILE HE'S CAULKING.
K.
KIRKMAN & SCOTT

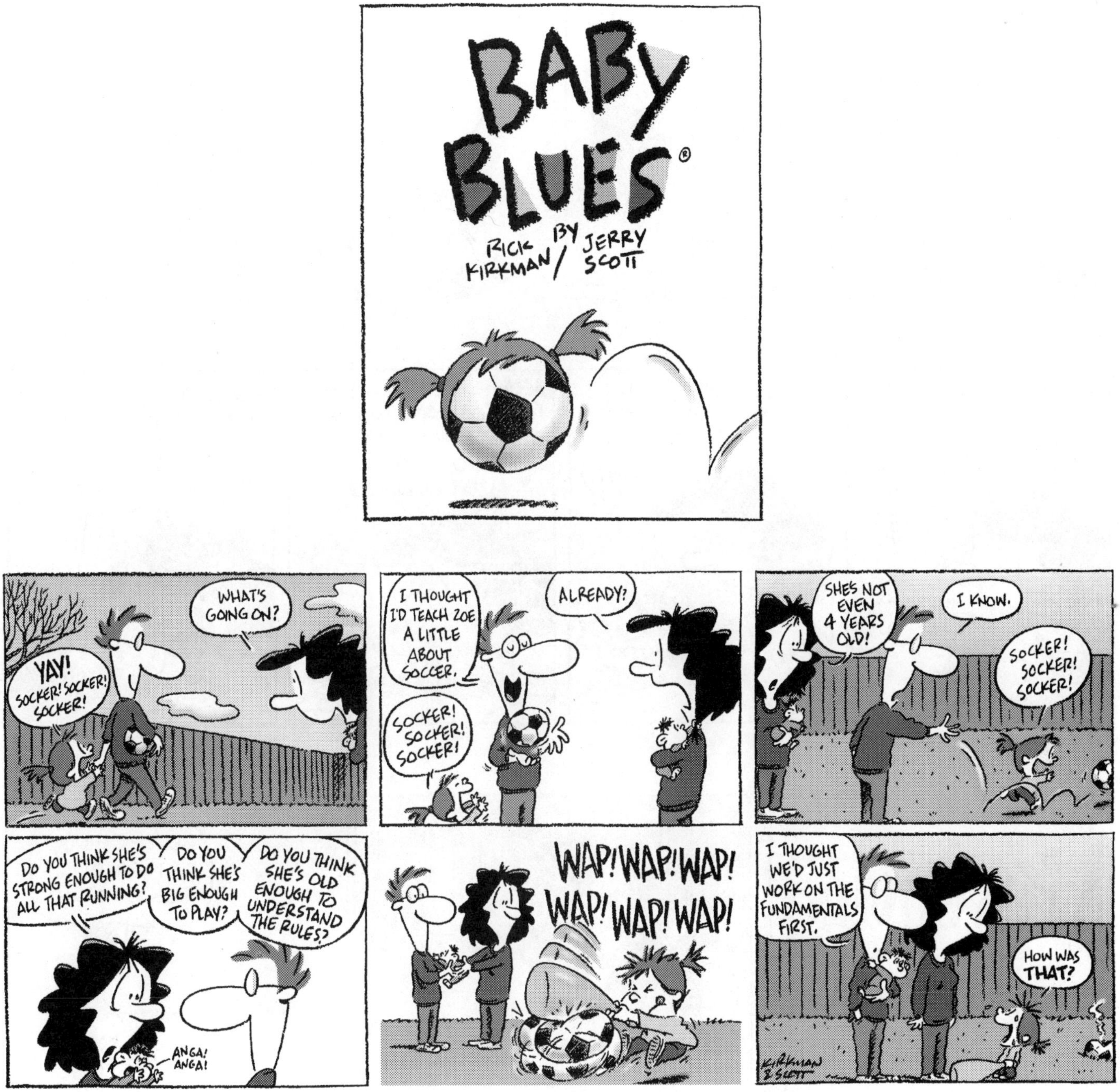
BABY BLUES®
BY RICK KIRKMAN / JERRY SCOTT
WHAT'S GOING ON?
YAY! SOCKER! SOCKER! SOCKER!
I THOUGHT I'D TEACH ZOE A LITTLE ABOUT SOCCER.
ALREADY?
SOCKER! SOCKER! SOCKER!
SHE'S NOT EVEN 4 YEARS OLD!
I KNOW.
SOCKER! SOCKER! SOCKER!
DO YOU THINK SHE'S STRONG ENOUGH TO DO ALL THAT RUNNING?
DO YOU THINK SHE'S BIG ENOUGH TO PLAY?
DO YOU THINK SHE'S OLD ENOUGH TO UNDERSTAND THE RULES?
ANGA! ANGA!
WAP! WAP! WAP! WAP! WAP! WAP!
I THOUGHT WE'D JUST WORK ON THE FUNDAMENTALS FIRST.
HOW WAS THAT?
KIRKMAN & SCOTT

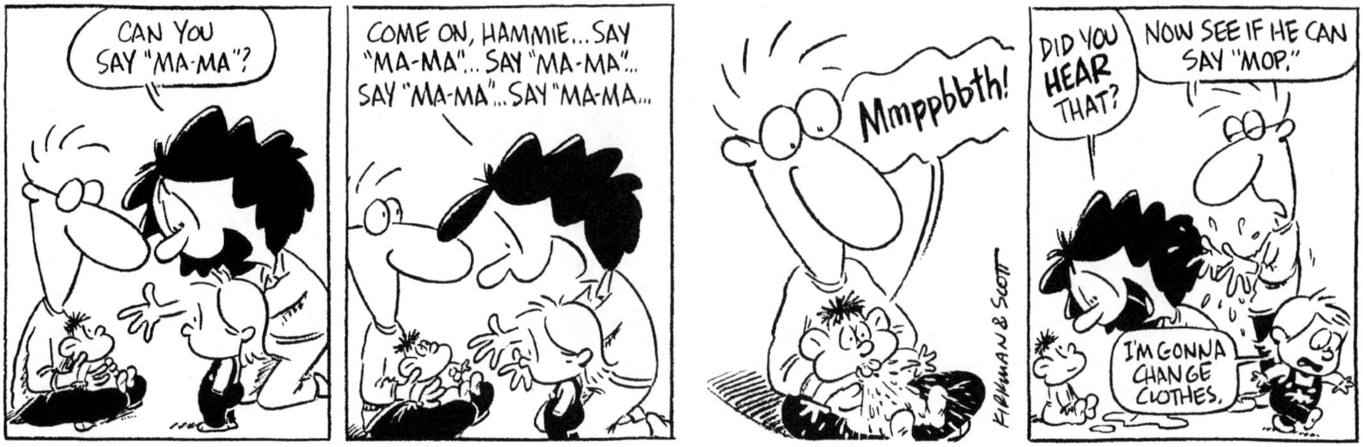
CAN YOU SAY "MA-MA"?
COME ON, HAMMIE... SAY "MA-MA"... SAY "MA-MA"... SAY "MA-MA"... SAY "MA-MA...
Mmppbbth!
KIRKMAN & SCOTT
DID YOU HEAR THAT?
NOW SEE IF HE CAN SAY "MOP."
I'M GONNA CHANGE CLOTHES.

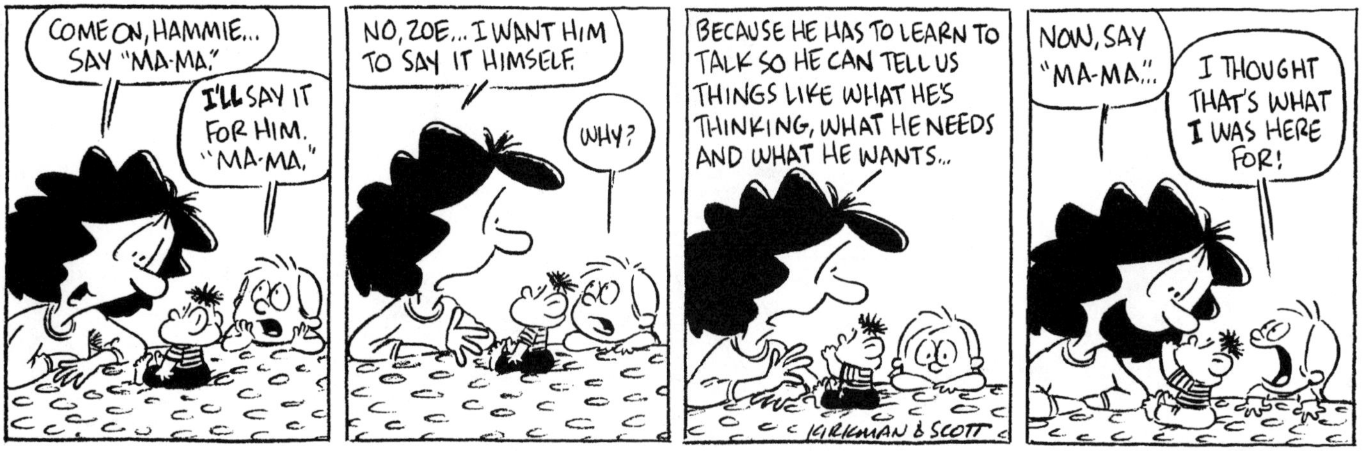
COME ON, HAMMIE... SAY "MA-MA."
I'LL SAY IT FOR HIM. "MA-MA."
NO, ZOE... I WANT HIM TO SAY IT HIMSELF.
WHY?
BECAUSE HE HAS TO LEARN TO TALK SO HE CAN TELL US THINGS LIKE WHAT HE'S THINKING, WHAT HE NEEDS AND WHAT HE WANTS...
KIRKMAN & SCOTT
NOW, SAY "MA-MA."
I THOUGHT THAT'S WHAT I WAS HERE FOR!

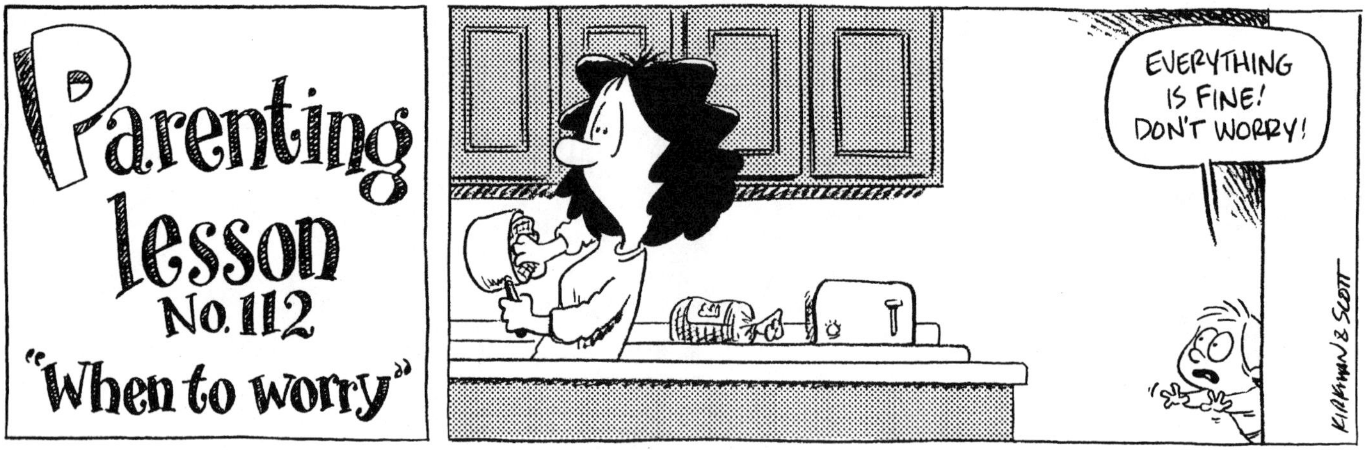
Parenting lesson
No. 112
"When to worry"
EVERYTHING IS FINE! DON'T WORRY!
KIRKMAN & SCOTT

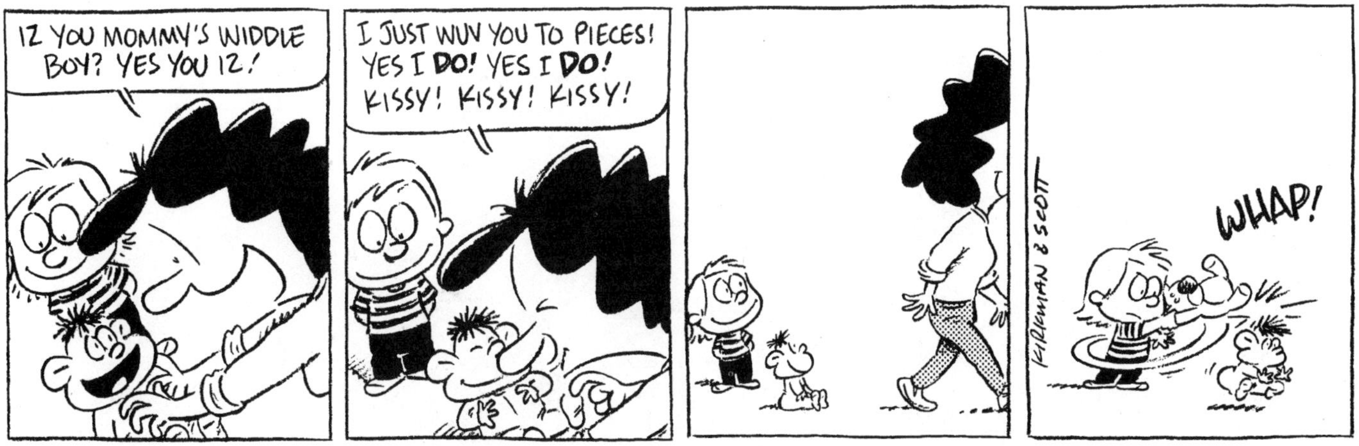
IZ YOU MOMMY'S WIDDLE BOY? YES YOU IZ!
I JUST WUV YOU TO PIECES! YES I **DO!** YES I **DO!** KISSY! KISSY! KISSY!
KIRKMAN & SCOTT
WHAP!

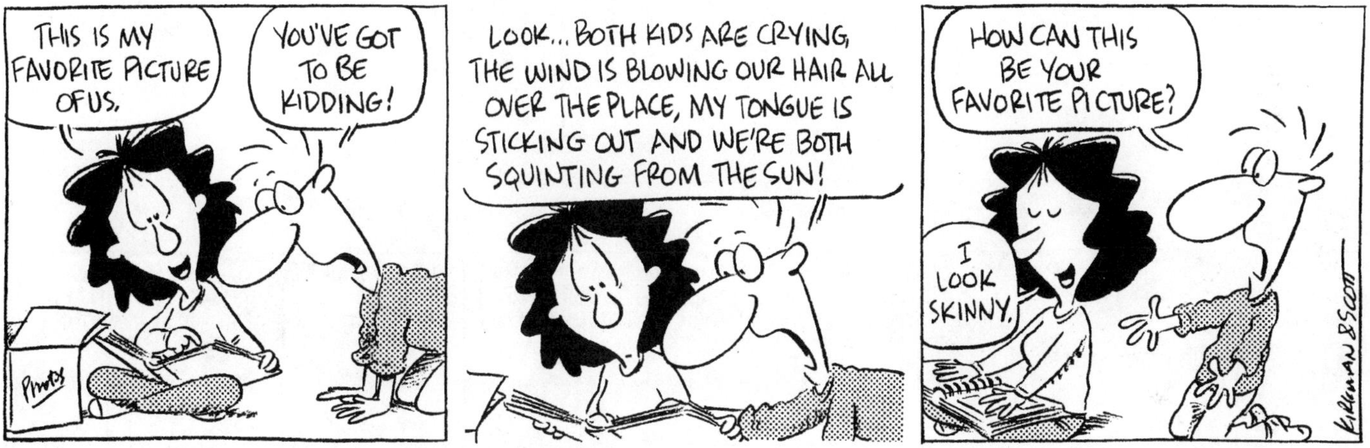
THIS IS MY FAVORITE PICTURE OF US.
YOU'VE GOT TO BE KIDDING!
Photos
LOOK... BOTH KIDS ARE CRYING, THE WIND IS BLOWING OUR HAIR ALL OVER THE PLACE, MY TONGUE IS STICKING OUT AND WE'RE BOTH SQUINTING FROM THE SUN!
HOW CAN THIS BE YOUR FAVORITE PICTURE?
I LOOK SKINNY.
KIRKMAN & SCOTT

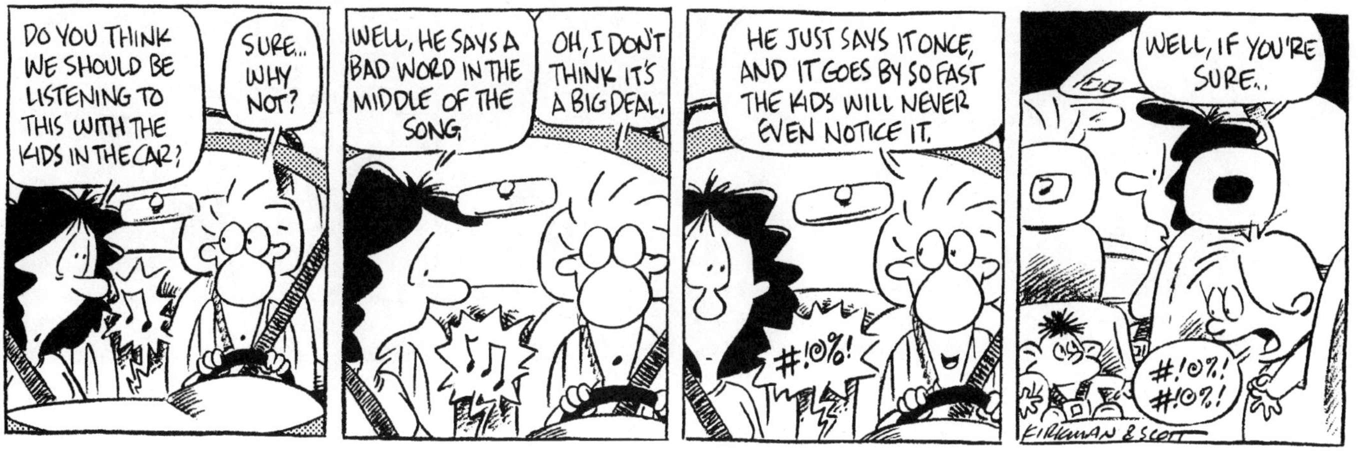
DO YOU THINK WE SHOULD BE LISTENING TO THIS WITH THE KIDS IN THE CAR?
SURE... WHY NOT?
WELL, HE SAYS A BAD WORD IN THE MIDDLE OF THE SONG.
OH, I DON'T THINK IT'S A BIG DEAL.
HE JUST SAYS IT ONCE, AND IT GOES BY SO FAST THE KIDS WILL NEVER EVEN NOTICE IT.
#!@%!
WELL, IF YOU'RE SURE..
#!@%! #!@%!
KIRKMAN & SCOTT

BABY BLUES®
BY RICK KIRKMAN / JERRY SCOTT
7
6
5
4
3
2
1

HI, MIKE. THANKS FOR COMING OVER.
NO PROBLEM.
IT'S THE CEILING FAN IN ZOE'S ROOM...THE THING IS HUMMING PRETTY LOUD.
THAT HAPPENED TO OURS, TOO. I THINK I CAN FIX IT.
WATCH YOUR STEP.
WOW! LOOK AT ALL THIS STUFF!
IS IT ALWAYS LIKE THIS IN HERE?
YEAH... PRETTY MUCH.
WE GAVE UP ON THE IDEA OF ORGANIZING ZOE'S TOYS A LONG TIME AGO...
KIRKMAN & SCOTT
...NOW WE JUST WORK ON CONTROLLING THE DEPTH.

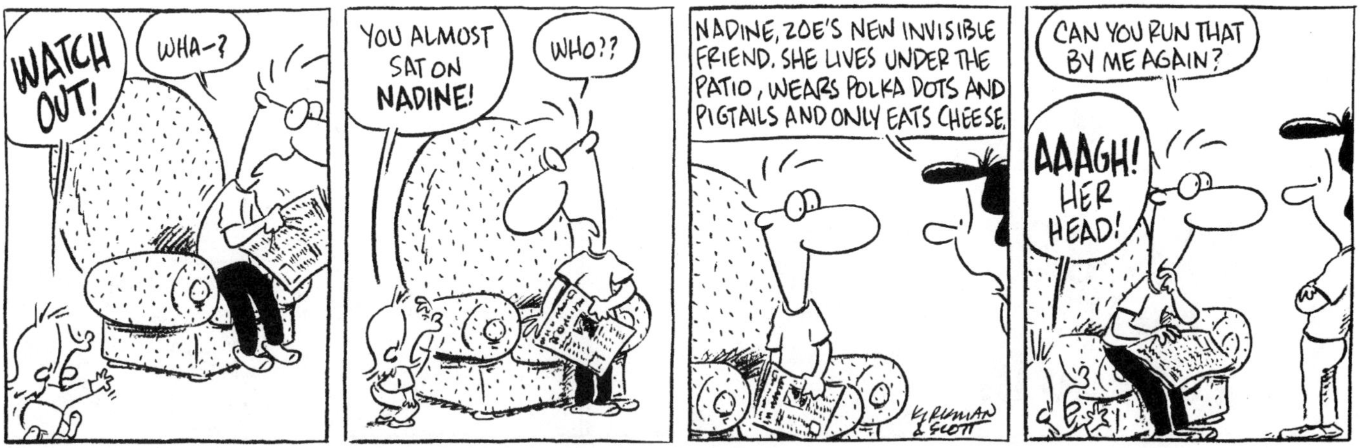
WATCH OUT!
WHA-?
YOU ALMOST SAT ON NADINE!
WHO??
NADINE, ZOE'S NEW INVISIBLE FRIEND. SHE LIVES UNDER THE PATIO, WEARS POLKA DOTS AND PIGTAILS AND ONLY EATS CHEESE.
KIRKMAN & SCOTT
CAN YOU RUN THAT BY ME AGAIN?
AAAGH! HER HEAD!

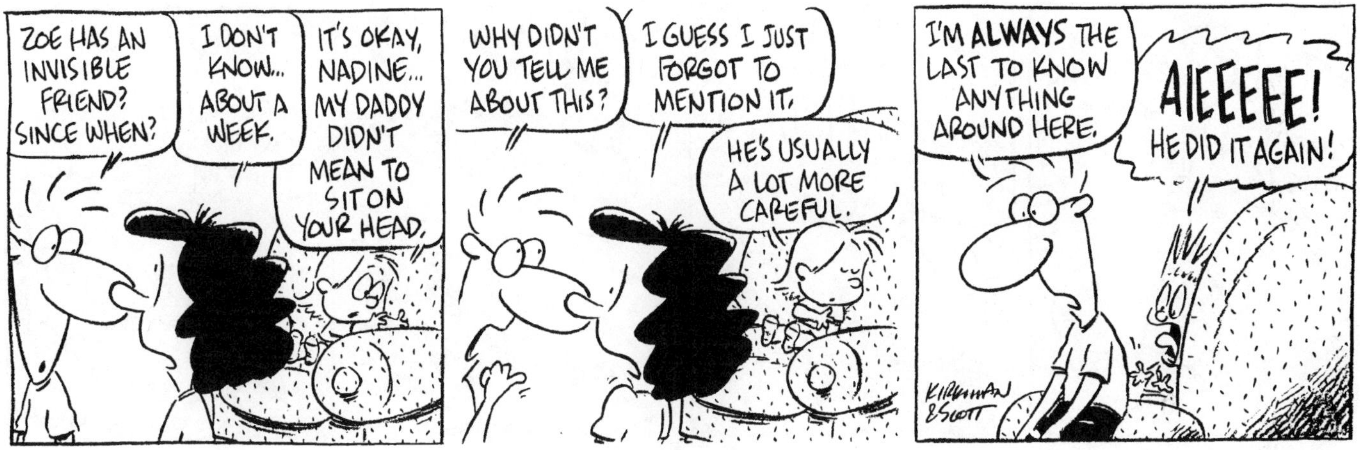
ZOE HAS AN INVISIBLE FRIEND? SINCE WHEN?
I DON'T KNOW... ABOUT A WEEK.
IT'S OKAY, NADINE... MY DADDY DIDN'T MEAN TO SIT ON YOUR HEAD.
WHY DIDN'T YOU TELL ME ABOUT THIS?
I GUESS I JUST FORGOT TO MENTION IT.
HE'S USUALLY A LOT MORE CAREFUL.
I'M ALWAYS THE LAST TO KNOW ANYTHING AROUND HERE.
AIEEEEE! HE DID IT AGAIN!
KIRKMAN & SCOTT

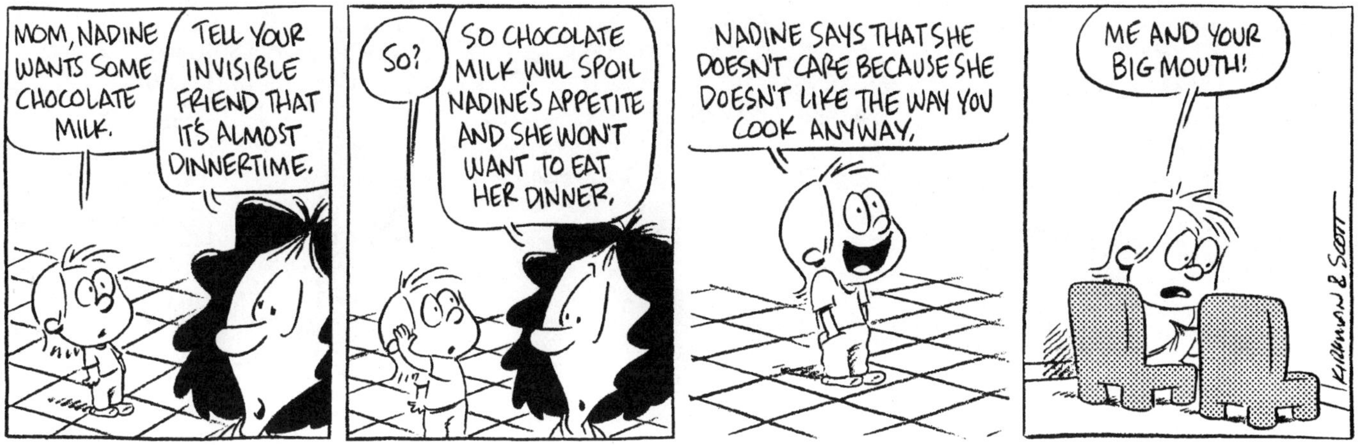
MOM, NADINE WANTS SOME CHOCOLATE MILK.
TELL YOUR INVISIBLE FRIEND THAT IT'S ALMOST DINNERTIME.
SO?
SO CHOCOLATE MILK WILL SPOIL NADINE'S APPETITE AND SHE WON'T WANT TO EAT HER DINNER.
NADINE SAYS THAT SHE DOESN'T CARE BECAUSE SHE DOESN'T LIKE THE WAY YOU COOK ANYWAY.
ME AND YOUR BIG MOUTH!
KIRKMAN & SCOTT

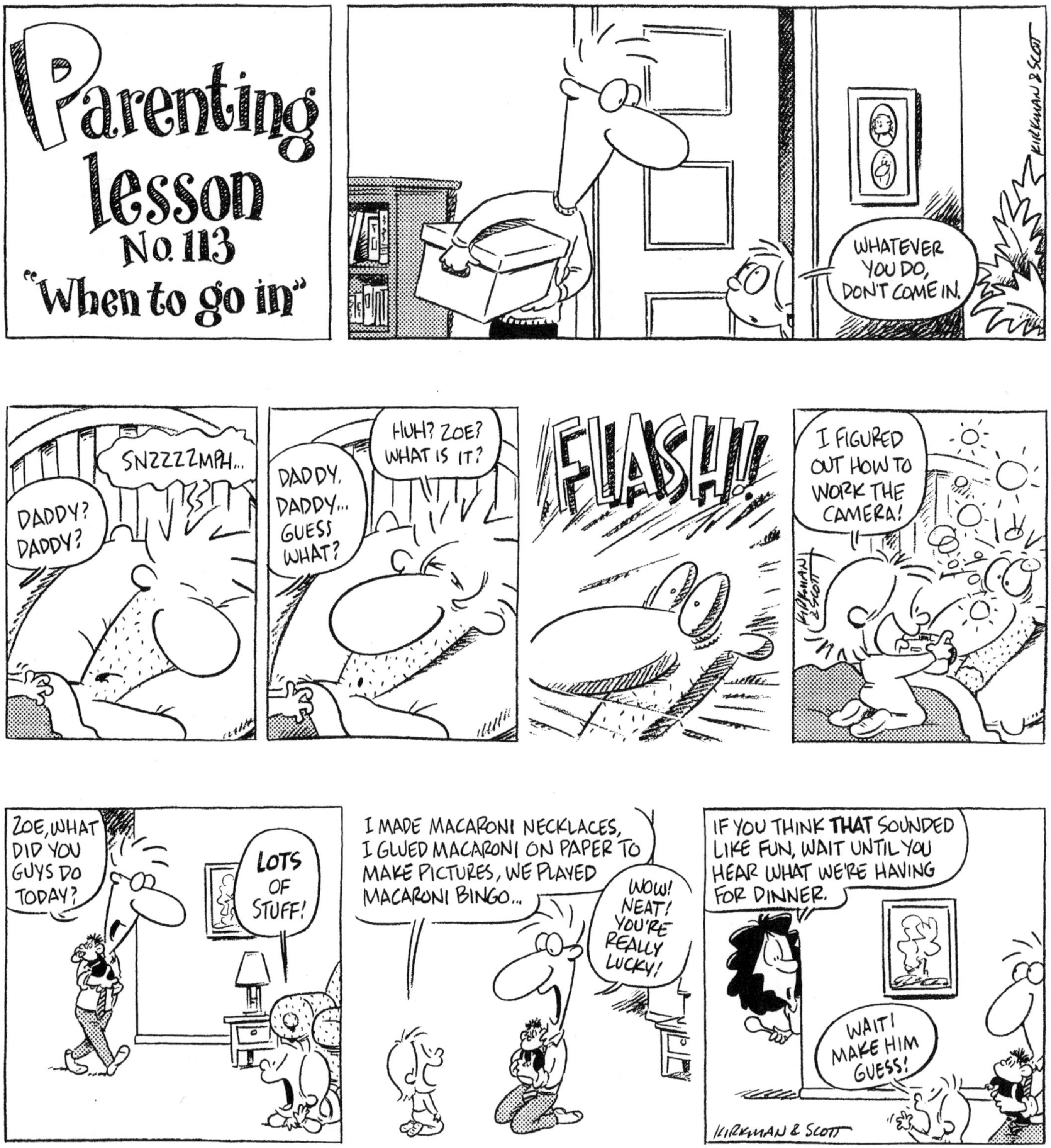
Parenting lesson
No. 113
"When to go in"
KIRKMAN & SCOTT
WHATEVER YOU DO, DON'T COME IN.
SNZZZZMPH...
DADDY? DADDY?
DADDY. DADDY... GUESS WHAT?
HUH? ZOE? WHAT IS IT?
FLASH!!
I FIGURED OUT HOW TO WORK THE CAMERA!
KIRKMAN & SCOTT
ZOE, WHAT DID YOU GUYS DO TODAY?
LOTS OF STUFF!
I MADE MACARONI NECKLACES, I GLUED MACARONI ON PAPER TO MAKE PICTURES, WE PLAYED MACARONI BINGO...
WOW! NEAT! YOU'RE REALLY LUCKY!
IF YOU THINK THAT SOUNDED LIKE FUN, WAIT UNTIL YOU HEAR WHAT WE'RE HAVING FOR DINNER.
WAIT! MAKE HIM GUESS!
KIRKMAN & SCOTT

BABY BLUES®
RICK KIRKMAN / BY JERRY SCOTT
I'VE GOT AN IDEA... LET'S WALLPAPER IT!

4 THINGS MEN WILL DO WITH THEIR DAUGHTERS, BUT NOT WITH THEIR WIVES...
WHAT?
DANCE
HEE! HEE! THIS IS FUN!
SIGH!
MY FIRST BOOMBOX
SHOP
ZOE WANTS TO GO TO THE MALL AND SHOW ME SOMETHING... WE'LL BE BACK IN A COUPLE OF HOURS.
HUH?
TALK
SO, LET ME TELL YOU ABOUT MY DAY AT THE OFFICE...
GRRRRR.
LISTEN
NOW, TELL ME ALL ABOUT YOUR DAY...
KIRKMAN & SCOTT

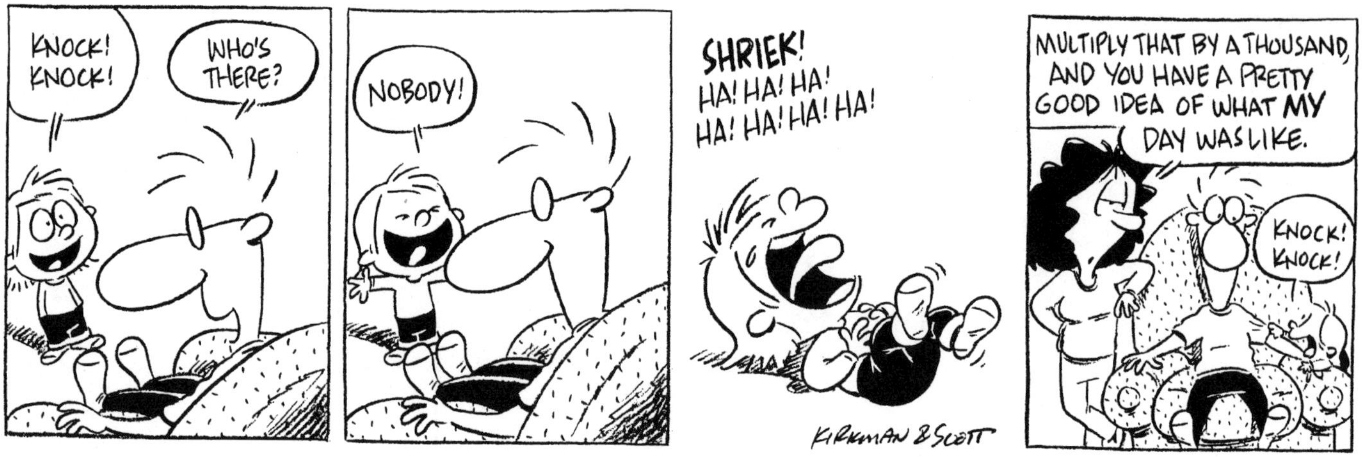
KNOCK! KNOCK!
WHO'S THERE?
NOBODY!
SHRIEK! HA! HA! HA! HA! HA! HA! HA!
MULTIPLY THAT BY A THOUSAND, AND YOU HAVE A PRETTY GOOD IDEA OF WHAT MY DAY WAS LIKE.
KNOCK! KNOCK!
KIRKMAN & SCOTT

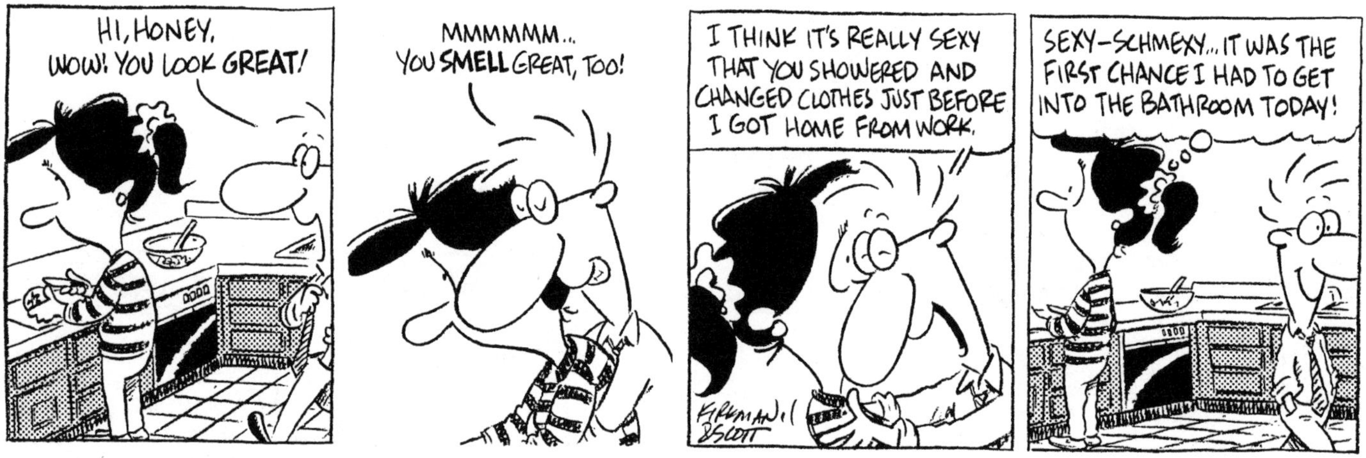
HI, HONEY. WOW! YOU LOOK GREAT!
MMMMMM... YOU SMELL GREAT, TOO!
I THINK IT'S REALLY SEXY THAT YOU SHOWERED AND CHANGED CLOTHES JUST BEFORE I GOT HOME FROM WORK.
KIRKMAN & SCOTT
SEXY-SCHMEXY... IT WAS THE FIRST CHANCE I HAD TO GET INTO THE BATHROOM TODAY!

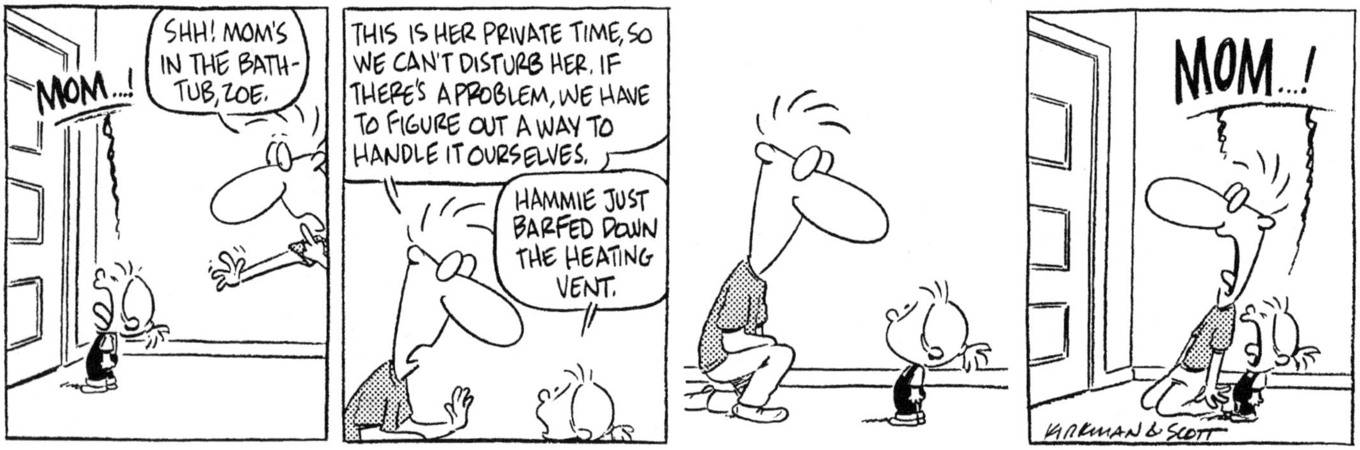
MOM...!
SHH! MOM'S IN THE BATH-TUB, ZOE.
THIS IS HER PRIVATE TIME, SO WE CAN'T DISTURB HER. IF THERE'S A PROBLEM, WE HAVE TO FIGURE OUT A WAY TO HANDLE IT OURSELVES.
HAMMIE JUST BARFED DOWN THE HEATING VENT.
MOM...!
KIRKMAN & SCOTT

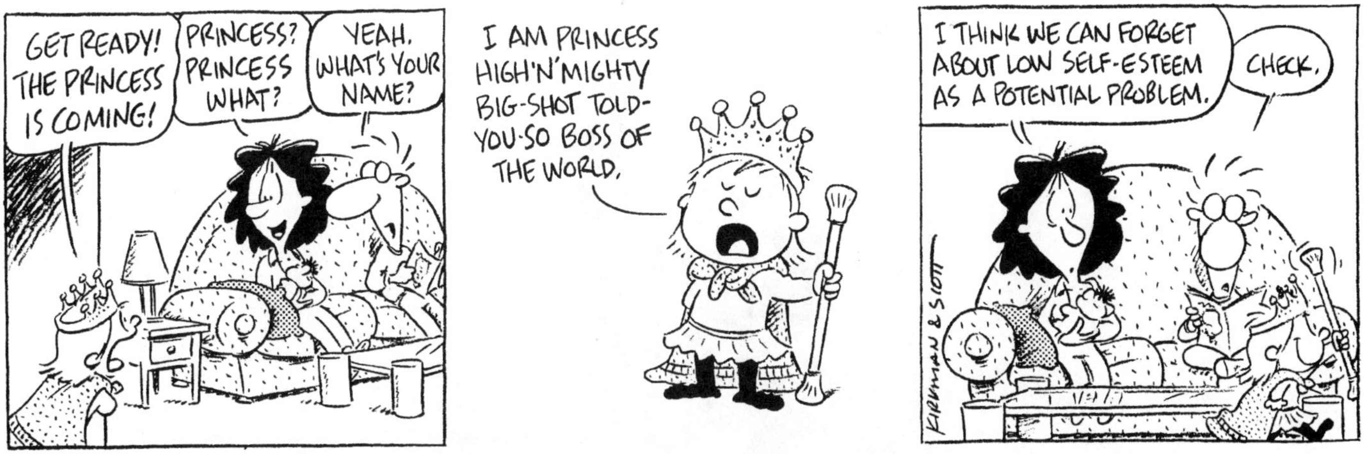
GET READY! THE PRINCESS IS COMING!
PRINCESS? PRINCESS WHAT?
YEAH. WHAT'S YOUR NAME?
I AM PRINCESS HIGH'N'MIGHTY BIG-SHOT TOLD-YOU-SO BOSS OF THE WORLD.
I THINK WE CAN FORGET ABOUT LOW SELF-ESTEEM AS A POTENTIAL PROBLEM.
CHECK.
KIRKMAN & SCOTT

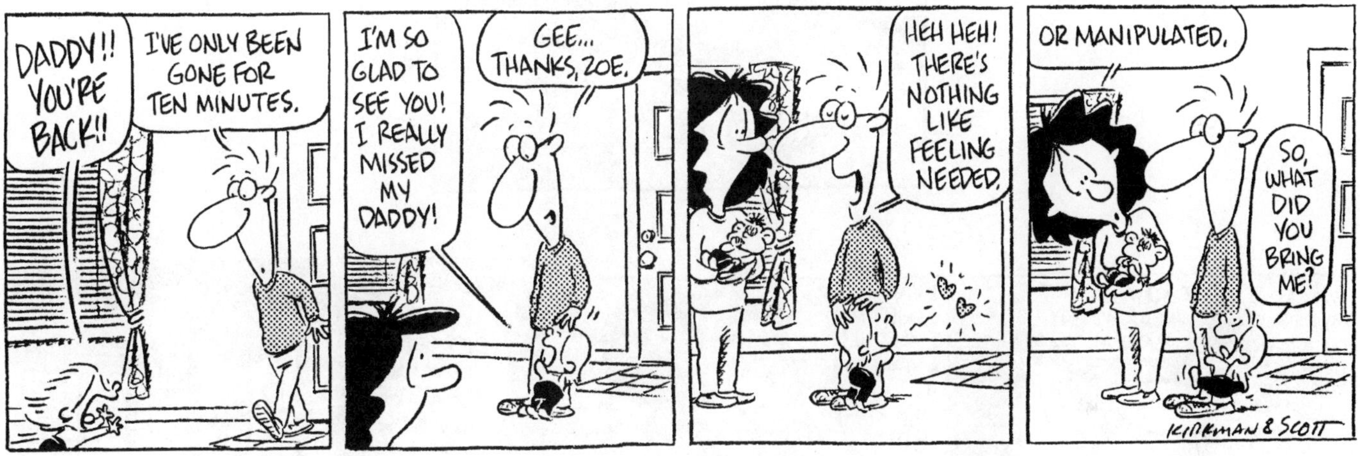
DADDY!! YOU'RE BACK!!
I'VE ONLY BEEN GONE FOR TEN MINUTES.
I'M SO GLAD TO SEE YOU! I REALLY MISSED MY DADDY!
GEE... THANKS, ZOE.
HEH HEH! THERE'S NOTHING LIKE FEELING NEEDED.
OR MANIPULATED.
SO, WHAT DID YOU BRING ME?
KIRKMAN & SCOTT

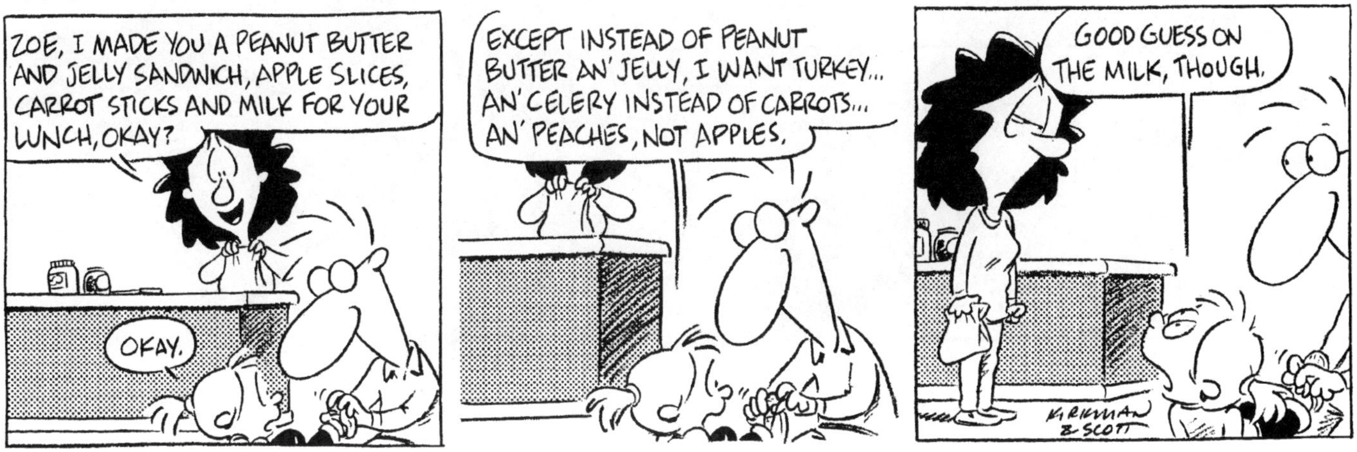
ZOE, I MADE YOU A PEANUT BUTTER AND JELLY SANDWICH, APPLE SLICES, CARROT STICKS AND MILK FOR YOUR LUNCH, OKAY?
OKAY.
EXCEPT INSTEAD OF PEANUT BUTTER AN' JELLY, I WANT TURKEY... AN' CELERY INSTEAD OF CARROTS... AN' PEACHES, NOT APPLES.
GOOD GUESS ON THE MILK, THOUGH.
KIRKMAN & SCOTT

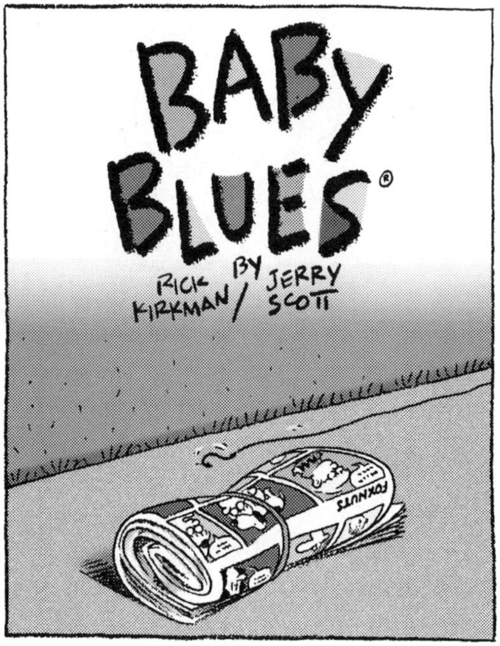
BABY BLUES®
BY RICK KIRKMAN / JERRY SCOTT
FOXNUTS

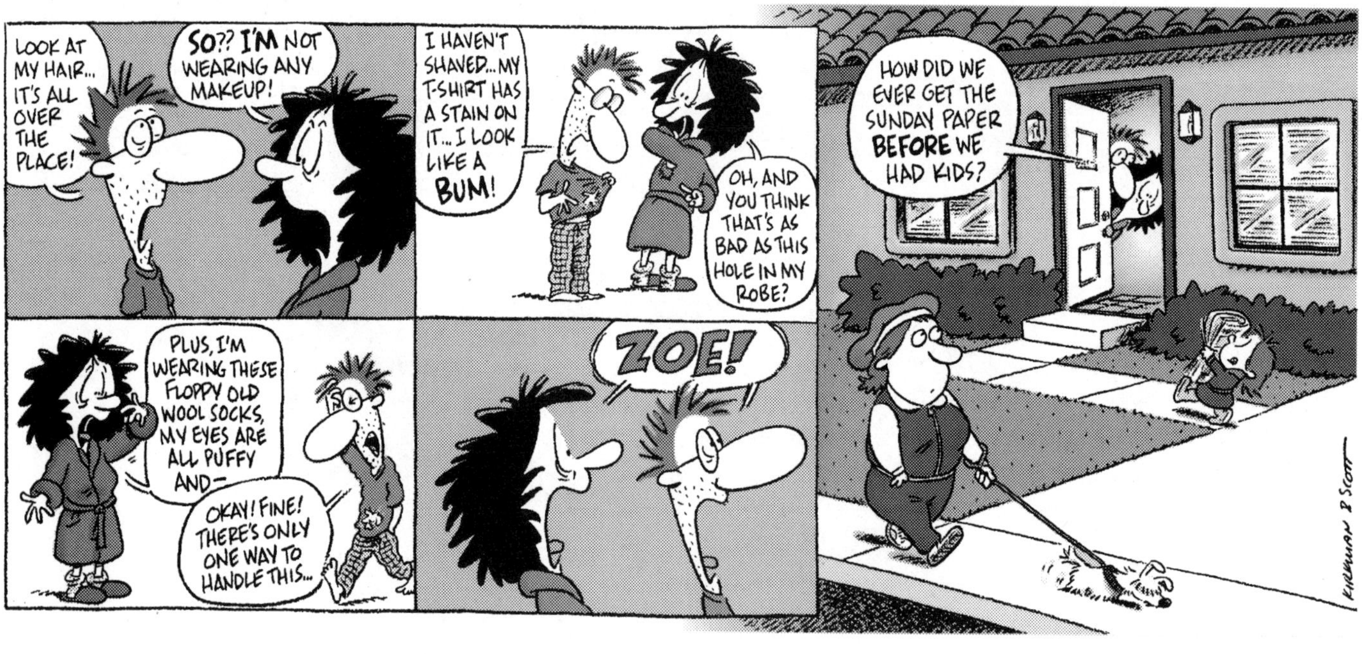
LOOK AT MY HAIR... IT'S ALL OVER THE PLACE!
SO?? I'M NOT WEARING ANY MAKEUP!
I HAVEN'T SHAVED... MY T-SHIRT HAS A STAIN ON IT... I LOOK LIKE A BUM!
OH, AND YOU THINK THAT'S AS BAD AS THIS HOLE IN MY ROBE?
PLUS, I'M WEARING THESE FLOPPY OLD WOOL SOCKS, MY EYES ARE ALL PUFFY AND—
OKAY! FINE! THERE'S ONLY ONE WAY TO HANDLE THIS...
ZOE!
HOW DID WE EVER GET THE SUNDAY PAPER BEFORE WE HAD KIDS?
KIRKMAN & SCOTT

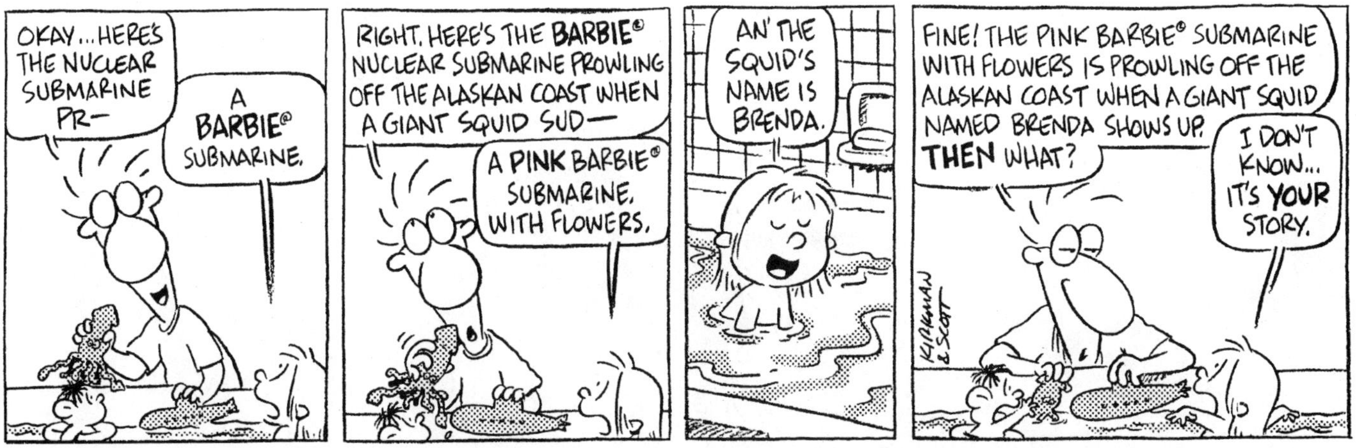
OKAY... HERE'S THE NUCLEAR SUBMARINE PR—
A BARBIE® SUBMARINE.
RIGHT. HERE'S THE BARBIE® NUCLEAR SUBMARINE PROWLING OFF THE ALASKAN COAST WHEN A GIANT SQUID SUD—
A PINK BARBIE® SUBMARINE. WITH FLOWERS.
AN' THE SQUID'S NAME IS BRENDA.
KIRKMAN & SCOTT
FINE! THE PINK BARBIE® SUBMARINE WITH FLOWERS IS PROWLING OFF THE ALASKAN COAST WHEN A GIANT SQUID NAMED BRENDA SHOWS UP. THEN WHAT?
I DON'T KNOW... IT'S YOUR STORY.

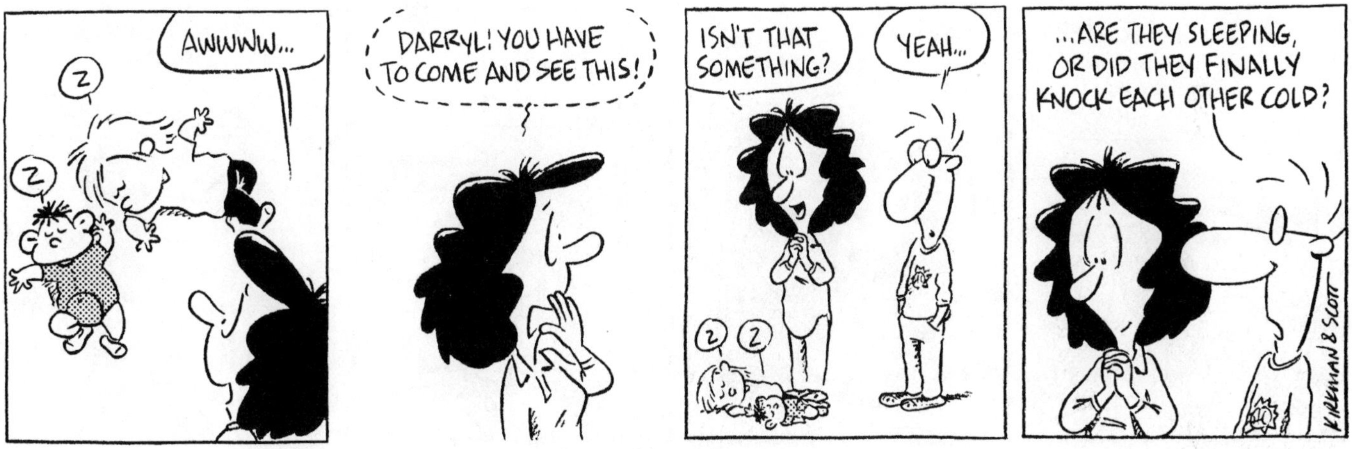
Z
Z
AWWWW...
DARRYL! YOU HAVE TO COME AND SEE THIS!
ISN'T THAT SOMETHING?
YEAH...
Z
Z
...ARE THEY SLEEPING, OR DID THEY FINALLY KNOCK EACH OTHER COLD?
KIRKMAN & SCOTT

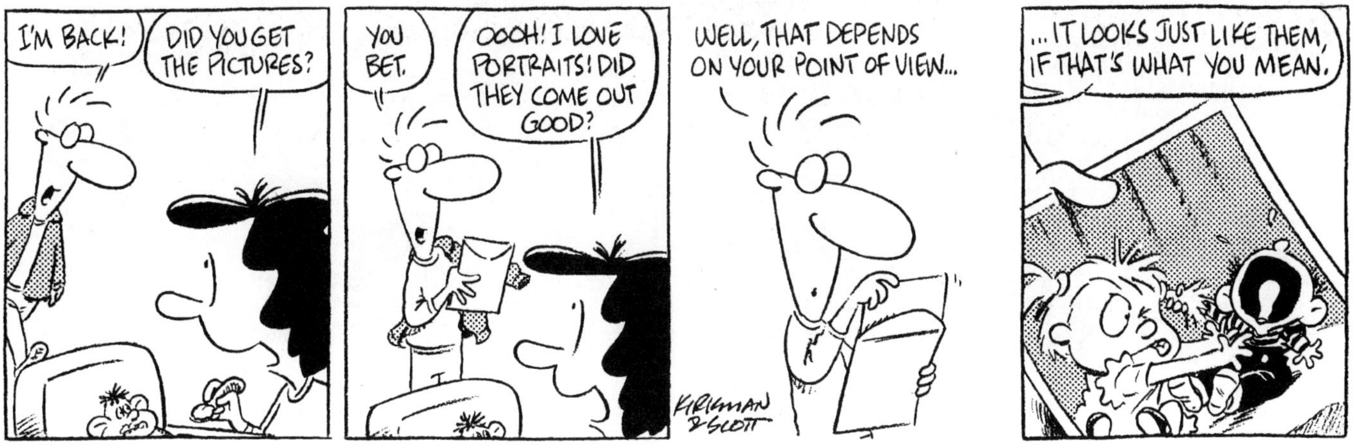
I'M BACK!
DID YOU GET THE PICTURES?
YOU BET.
OOOH! I LOVE PORTRAITS! DID THEY COME OUT GOOD?
WELL, THAT DEPENDS ON YOUR POINT OF VIEW...
KIRKMAN & SCOTT
...IT LOOKS JUST LIKE THEM, IF THAT'S WHAT YOU MEAN.

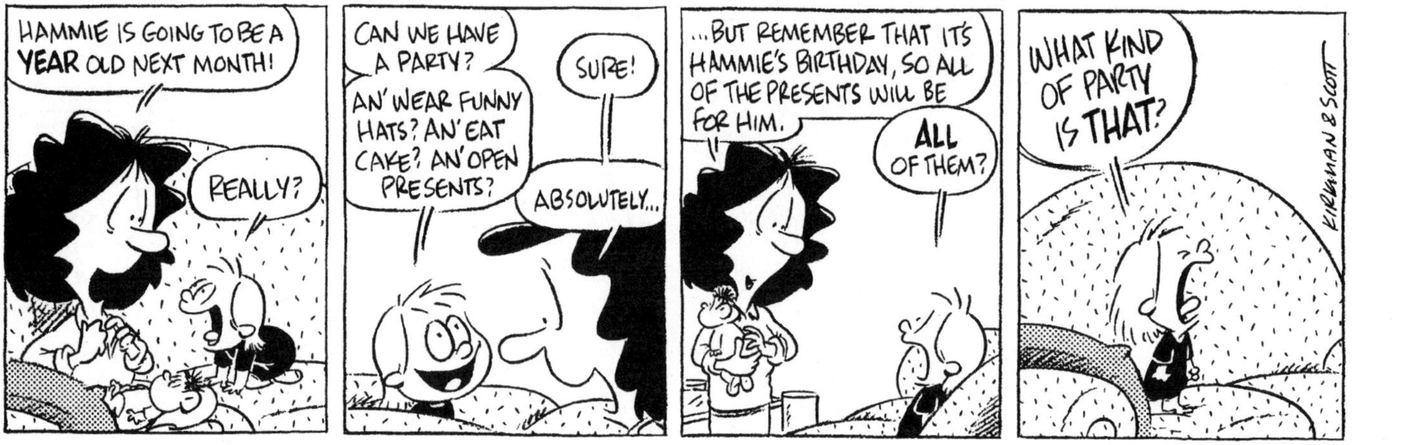
HAMMIE IS GOING TO BE A YEAR OLD NEXT MONTH!
REALLY?
CAN WE HAVE A PARTY?
AN' WEAR FUNNY HATS? AN' EAT CAKE? AN' OPEN PRESENTS?
SURE!
ABSOLUTELY...
...BUT REMEMBER THAT IT'S HAMMIE'S BIRTHDAY, SO ALL OF THE PRESENTS WILL BE FOR HIM.
ALL OF THEM?
WHAT KIND OF PARTY IS THAT?
KIRKMAN & SCOTT

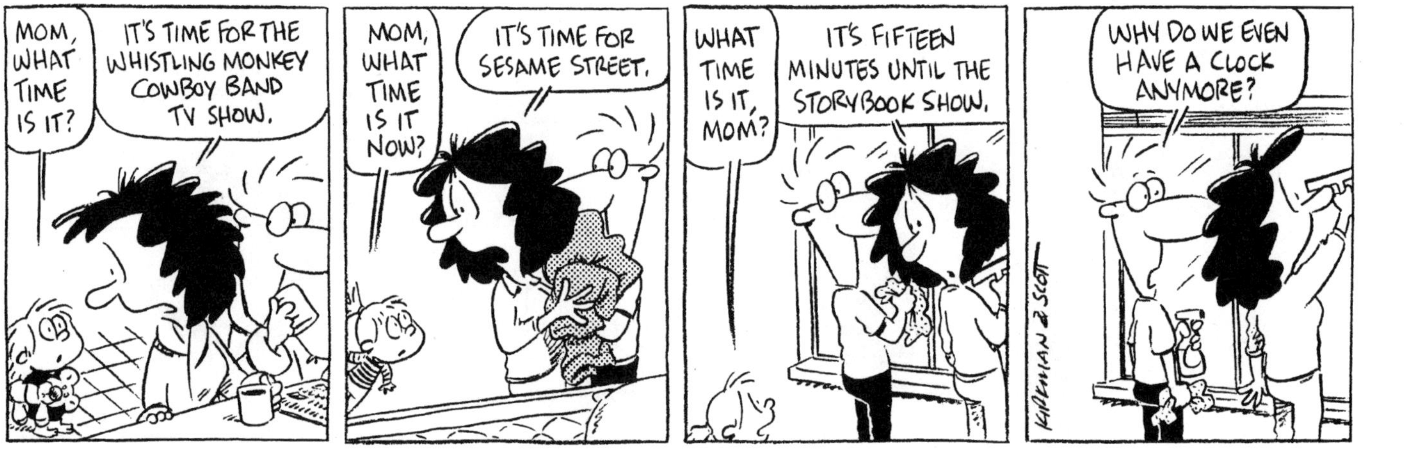
MOM, WHAT TIME IS IT?
IT'S TIME FOR THE WHISTLING MONKEY COWBOY BAND TV SHOW.
MOM, WHAT TIME IS IT NOW?
IT'S TIME FOR SESAME STREET.
WHAT TIME IS IT, MOM?
IT'S FIFTEEN MINUTES UNTIL THE STORYBOOK SHOW.
KIRKMAN & SCOTT
WHY DO WE EVEN HAVE A CLOCK ANYMORE?

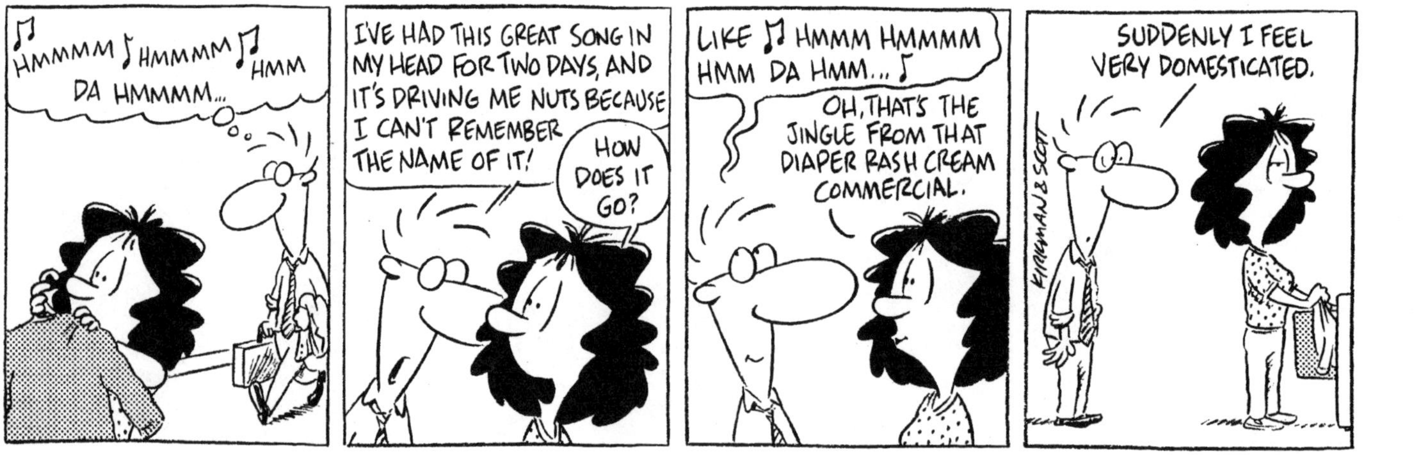
♫ HMMMM ♪ HMMMM ♫ HMM DA HMMMM...
I'VE HAD THIS GREAT SONG IN MY HEAD FOR TWO DAYS, AND IT'S DRIVING ME NUTS BECAUSE I CAN'T REMEMBER THE NAME OF IT!
HOW DOES IT GO?
LIKE ♫ HMMM HMMMM HMM DA HMM... ♪
OH, THAT'S THE JINGLE FROM THAT DIAPER RASH CREAM COMMERCIAL.
KIRKMAN & SCOTT
SUDDENLY I FEEL VERY DOMESTICATED.

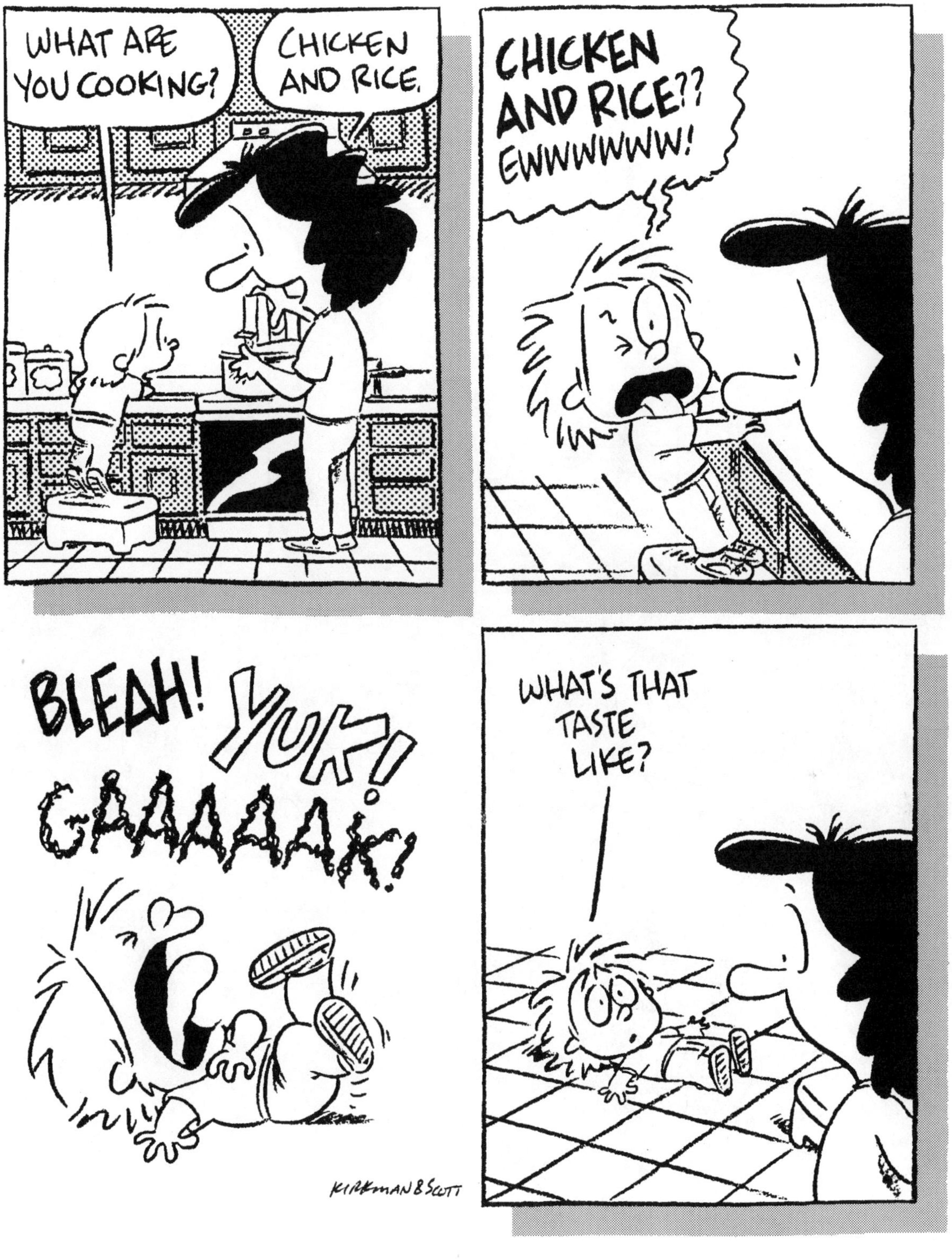
WHAT ARE YOU COOKING?
CHICKEN AND RICE.
CHICKEN AND RICE?? EWWWWWW!
BLEAH!
YUK!
GAAAAK!
KIRKMAN & SCOTT
WHAT'S THAT TASTE LIKE?

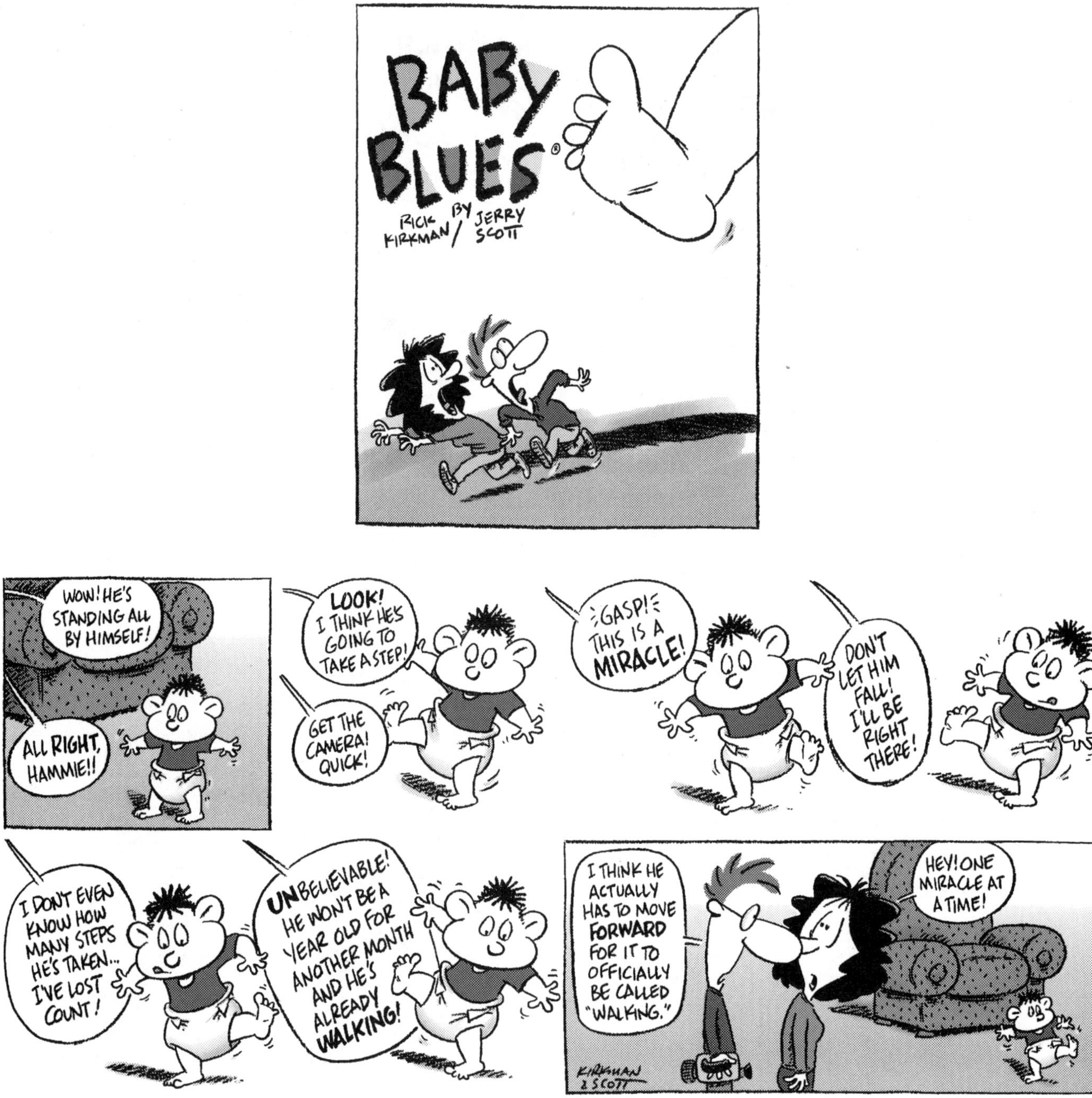
BABY BLUES®
BY RICK KIRKMAN / JERRY SCOTT
WOW! HE'S STANDING ALL BY HIMSELF!
ALL RIGHT, HAMMIE!!
LOOK! I THINK HE'S GOING TO TAKE A STEP!
GET THE CAMERA! QUICK!
GASP! THIS IS A MIRACLE!
DON'T LET HIM FALL! I'LL BE RIGHT THERE!
I DON'T EVEN KNOW HOW MANY STEPS HE'S TAKEN... I'VE LOST COUNT!
UNBELIEVABLE! HE WON'T BE A YEAR OLD FOR ANOTHER MONTH AND HE'S ALREADY WALKING!
I THINK HE ACTUALLY HAS TO MOVE FORWARD FOR IT TO OFFICIALLY BE CALLED "WALKING."
HEY! ONE MIRACLE AT A TIME!
KIRKMAN & SCOTT

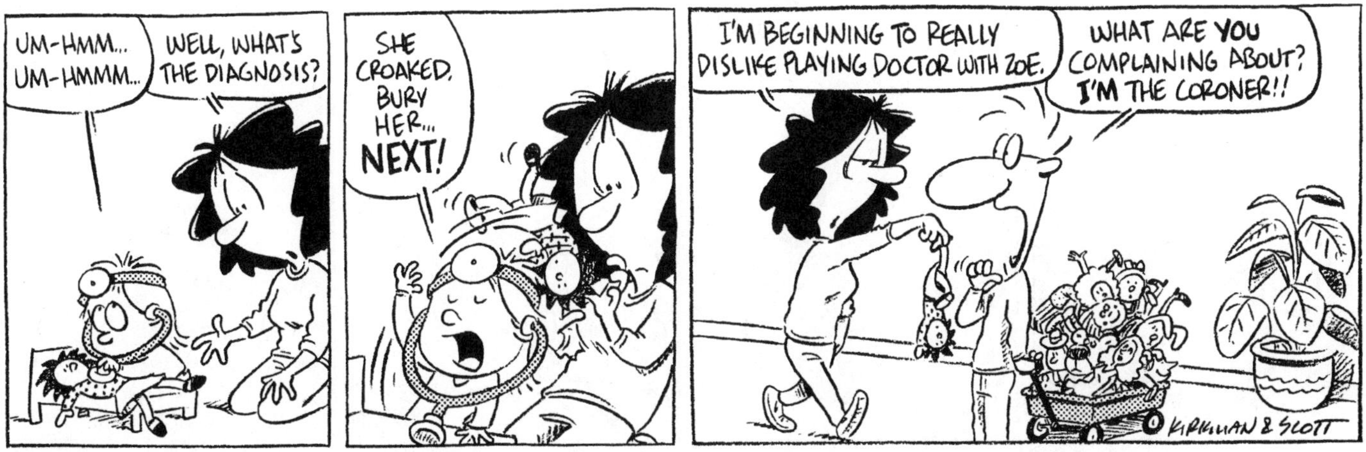
UM-HMM... UM-HMMM...
WELL, WHAT'S THE DIAGNOSIS?
SHE CROAKED. BURY HER... NEXT!
I'M BEGINNING TO REALLY DISLIKE PLAYING DOCTOR WITH ZOE.
WHAT ARE YOU COMPLAINING ABOUT? I'M THE CORONER!!
KIRKMAN & SCOTT

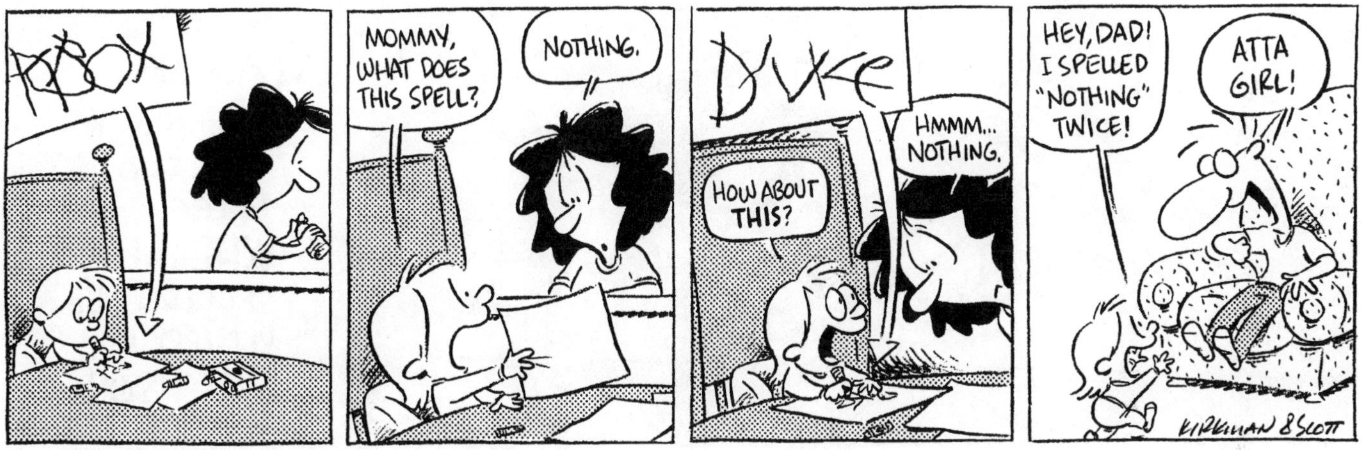
MOMMY, WHAT DOES THIS SPELL?
NOTHING.
HOW ABOUT THIS?
HMMM... NOTHING.
HEY, DAD! I SPELLED "NOTHING" TWICE!
ATTA GIRL!
KIRKMAN & SCOTT

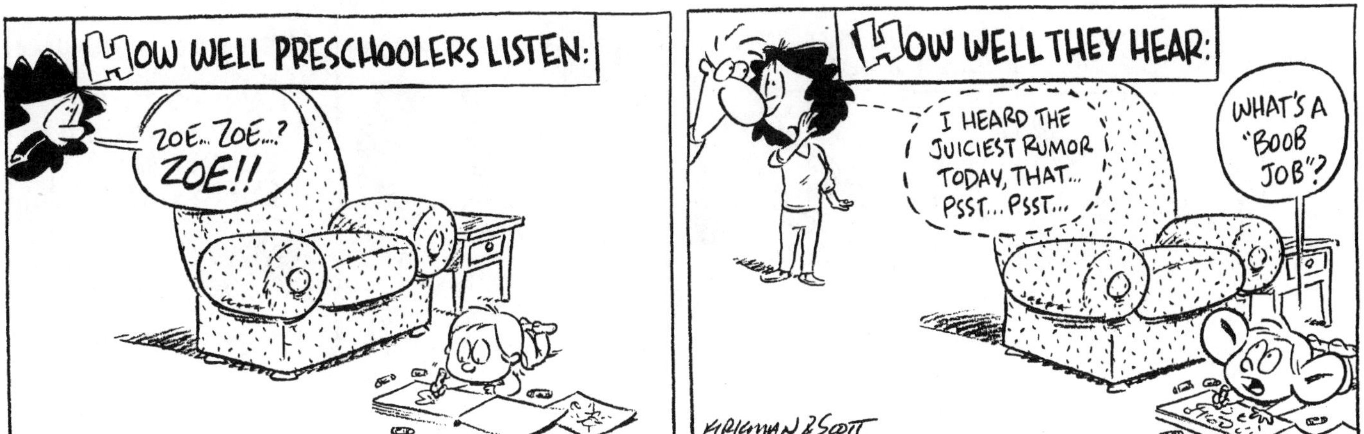
HOW WELL PRESCHOOLERS LISTEN:
ZOE... ZOE...? ZOE!!
HOW WELL THEY HEAR:
I HEARD THE JUICIEST RUMOR TODAY, THAT... PSST... PSST...
WHAT'S A "BOOB JOB"?
KIRKMAN & SCOTT

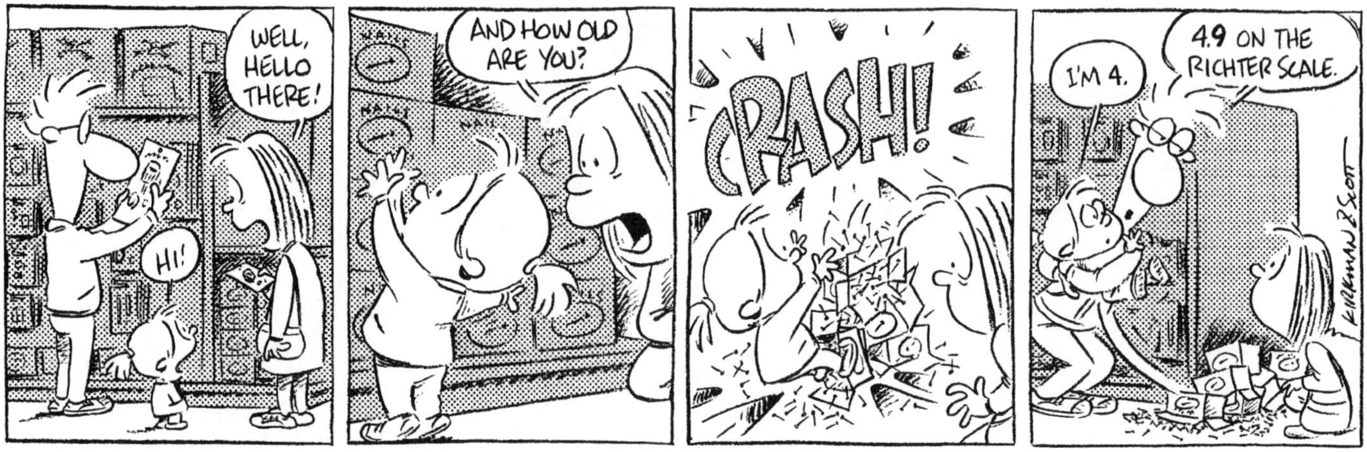
WELL, HELLO THERE!
HI!
AND HOW OLD ARE YOU?
CRASH!
I'M 4.
4.9 ON THE RICHTER SCALE.

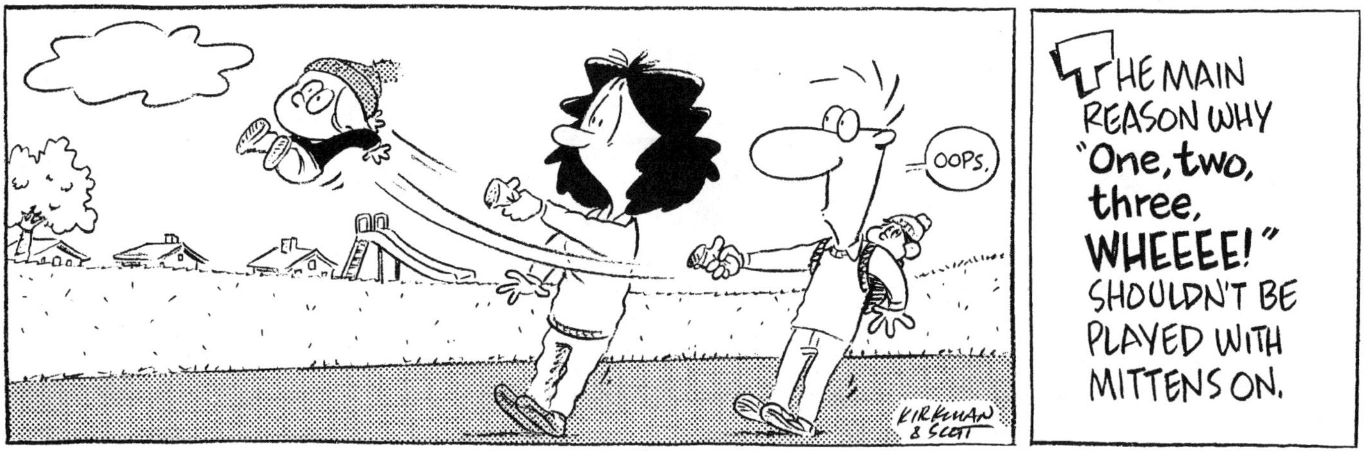
OOPS.
THE MAIN REASON WHY "One, two, three, WHEEEE!" SHOULDN'T BE PLAYED WITH MITTENS ON.

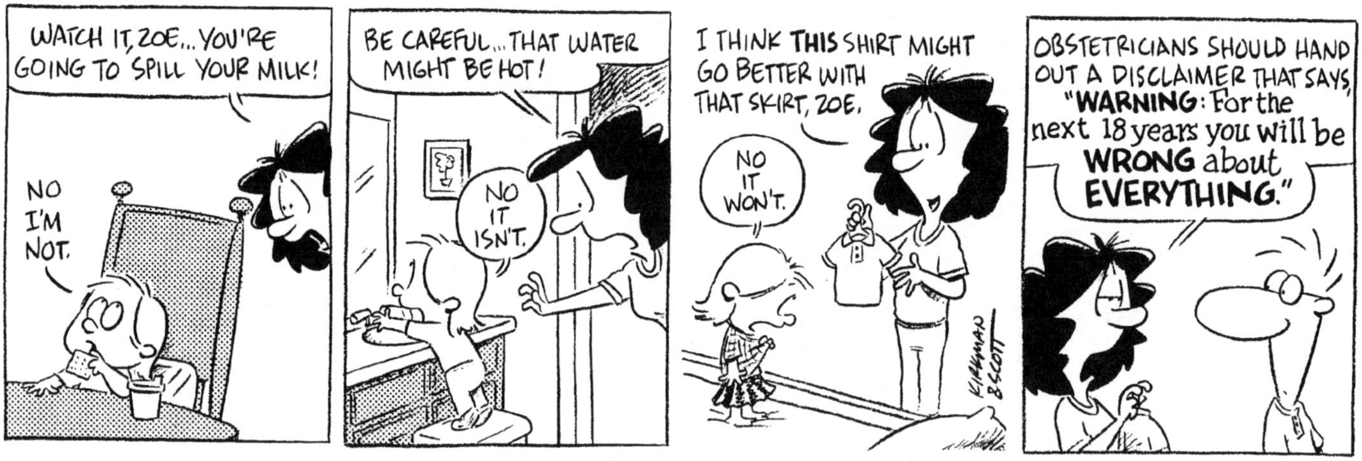
WATCH IT, ZOE... YOU'RE GOING TO SPILL YOUR MILK!
NO I'M NOT.
BE CAREFUL... THAT WATER MIGHT BE HOT!
NO IT ISN'T.
I THINK THIS SHIRT MIGHT GO BETTER WITH THAT SKIRT, ZOE.
NO IT WON'T.
OBSTETRICIANS SHOULD HAND OUT A DISCLAIMER THAT SAYS, "WARNING: For the next 18 years you will be WRONG about EVERYTHING."

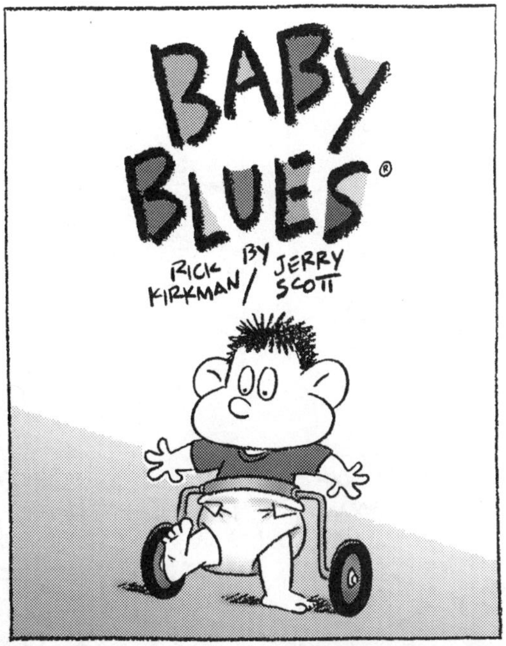
BABY BLUES®
RICK KIRKMAN / BY JERRY SCOTT

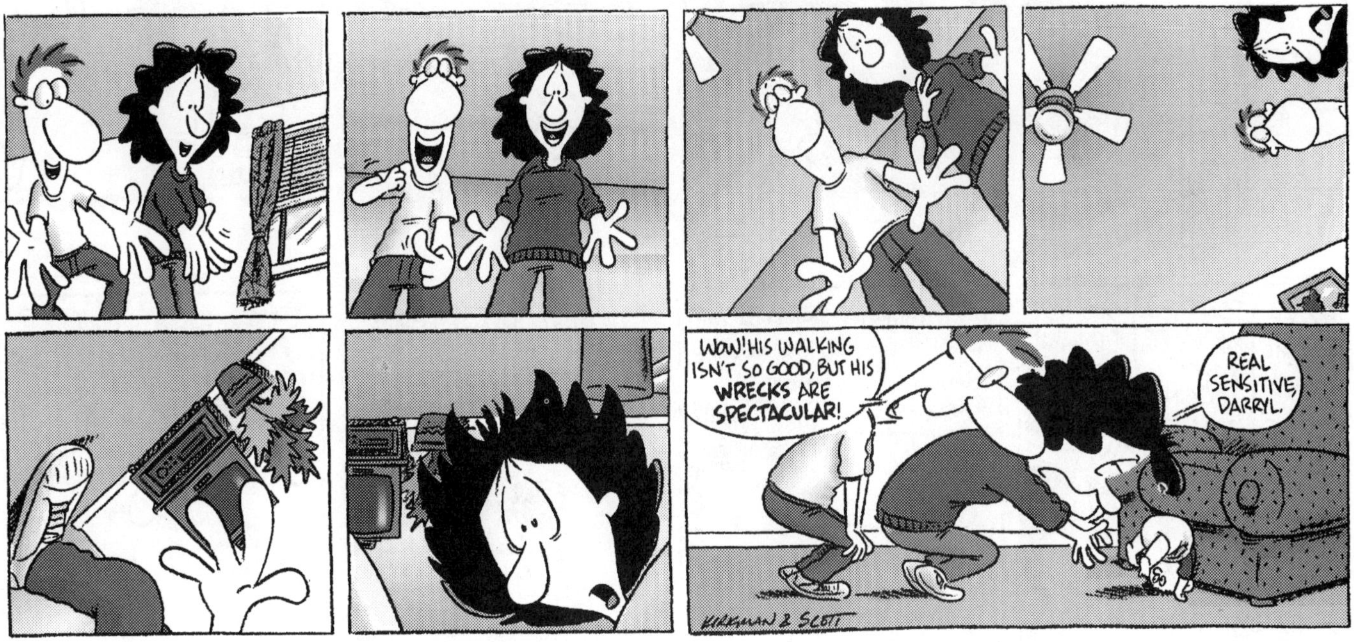
WOW! HIS WALKING ISN'T SO GOOD, BUT HIS WRECKS ARE SPECTACULAR!
REAL SENSITIVE, DARRYL.
KIRKMAN & SCOTT

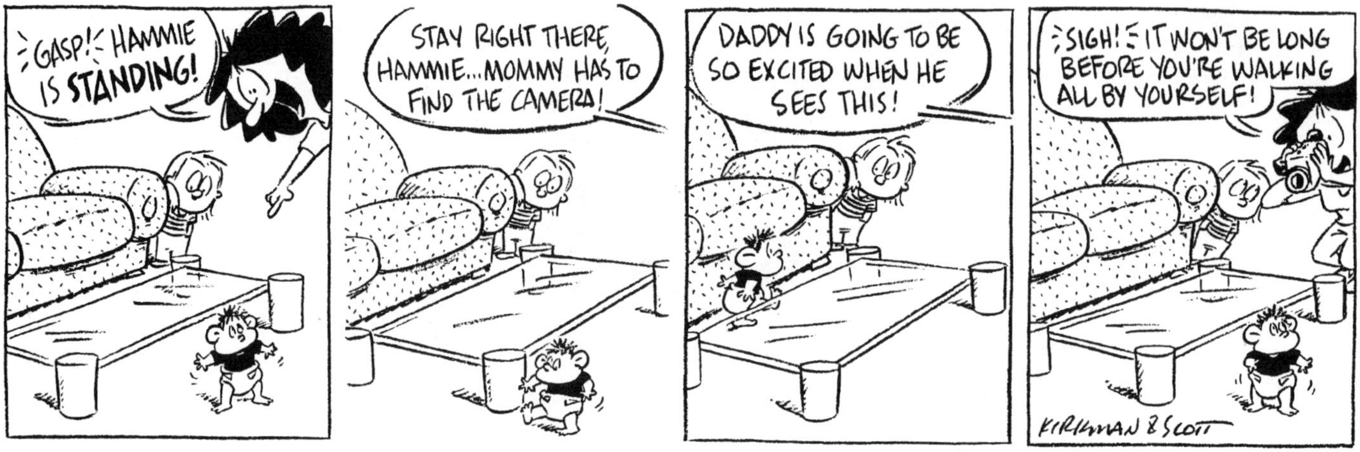
GASP! HAMMIE IS STANDING!
STAY RIGHT THERE, HAMMIE... MOMMY HAS TO FIND THE CAMERA!
DADDY IS GOING TO BE SO EXCITED WHEN HE SEES THIS!
SIGH! IT WON'T BE LONG BEFORE YOU'RE WALKING ALL BY YOURSELF!
KIRKMAN & SCOTT

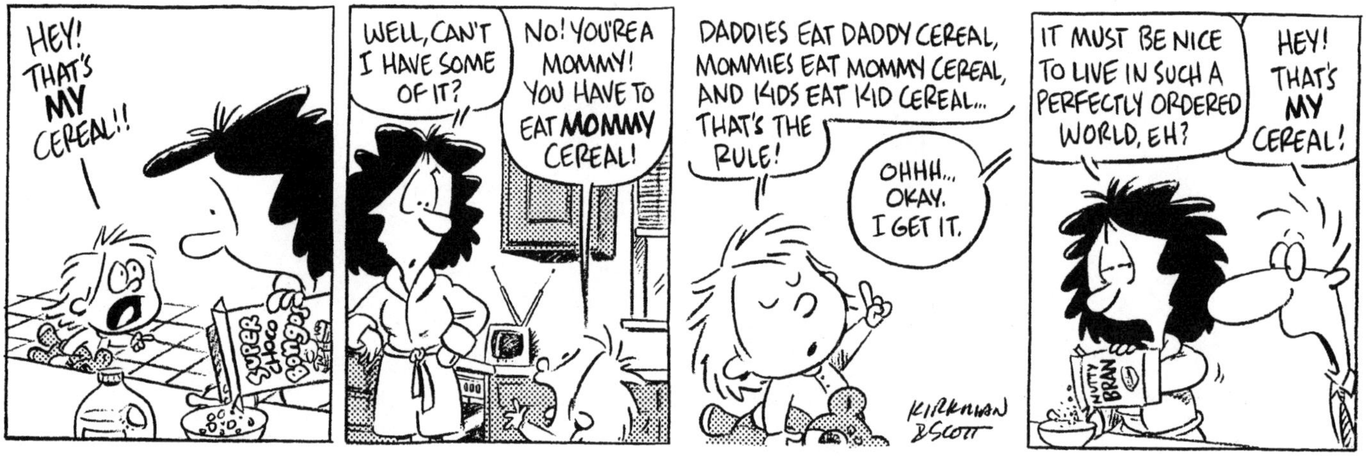
HEY! THAT'S MY CEREAL!!
SUPER CHOCO BONGOS
WELL, CAN'T I HAVE SOME OF IT?
NO! YOU'RE A MOMMY! YOU HAVE TO EAT MOMMY CEREAL!
DADDIES EAT DADDY CEREAL, MOMMIES EAT MOMMY CEREAL, AND KIDS EAT KID CEREAL... THAT'S THE RULE!
OHHH... OKAY. I GET IT.
KIRKMAN & SCOTT
IT MUST BE NICE TO LIVE IN SUCH A PERFECTLY ORDERED WORLD, EH?
HEY! THAT'S MY CEREAL!
NUTTY BRAN

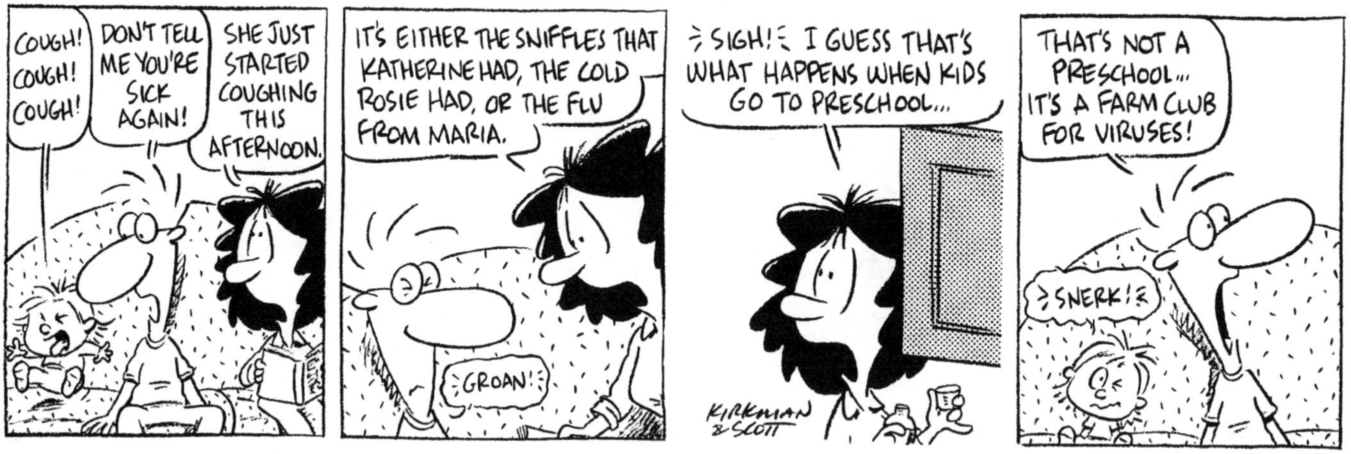
COUGH! COUGH! COUGH!
DON'T TELL ME YOU'RE SICK AGAIN!
SHE JUST STARTED COUGHING THIS AFTERNOON.
IT'S EITHER THE SNIFFLES THAT KATHERINE HAD, THE COLD ROSIE HAD, OR THE FLU FROM MARIA.
GROAN!
SIGH! I GUESS THAT'S WHAT HAPPENS WHEN KIDS GO TO PRESCHOOL...
KIRKMAN & SCOTT
THAT'S NOT A PRESCHOOL... IT'S A FARM CLUB FOR VIRUSES!
SNERK!

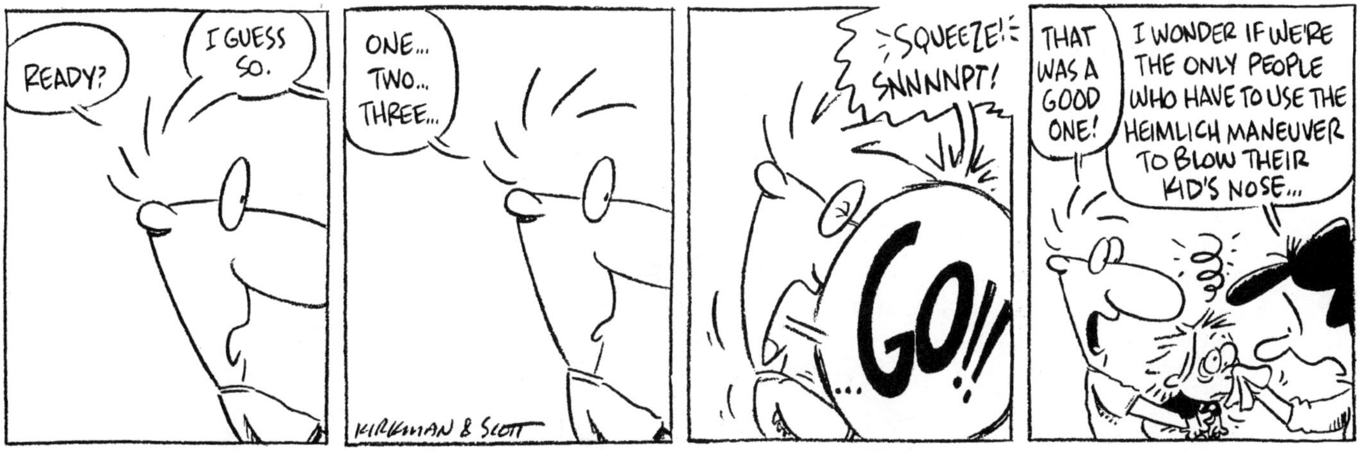
READY?
I GUESS SO.
ONE... TWO... THREE...
KIRKMAN & SCOTT
SQUEEZE!
SNNNNPT!
GO!!
THAT WAS A GOOD ONE!
I WONDER IF WE'RE THE ONLY PEOPLE WHO HAVE TO USE THE HEIMLICH MANEUVER TO BLOW THEIR KID'S NOSE...

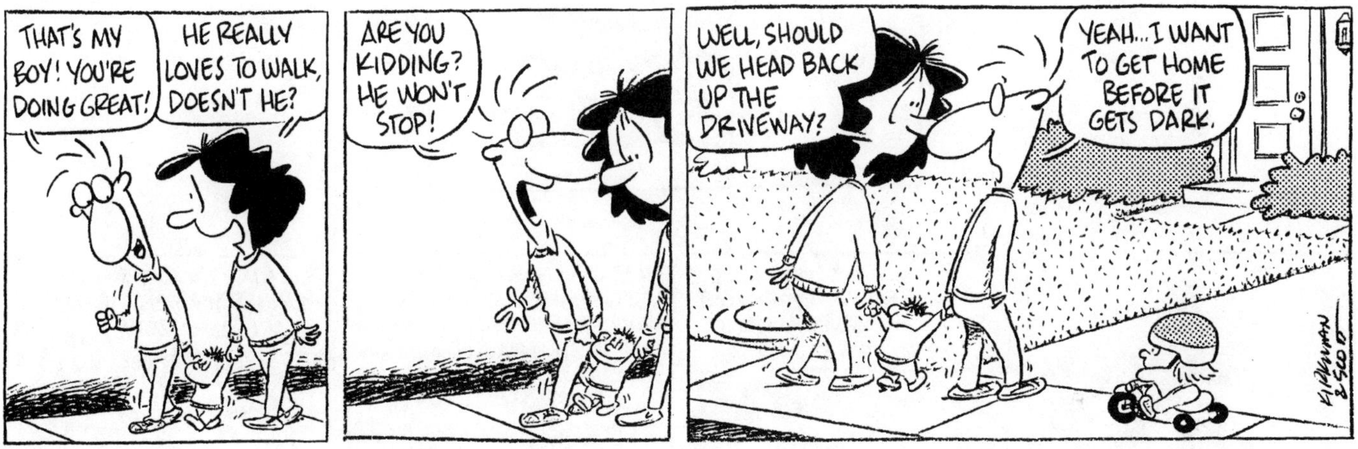
THAT'S MY BOY! YOU'RE DOING GREAT!
HE REALLY LOVES TO WALK, DOESN'T HE?
ARE YOU KIDDING? HE WON'T STOP!
WELL, SHOULD WE HEAD BACK UP THE DRIVEWAY?
YEAH... I WANT TO GET HOME BEFORE IT GETS DARK.
KIRKMAN & SCOTT

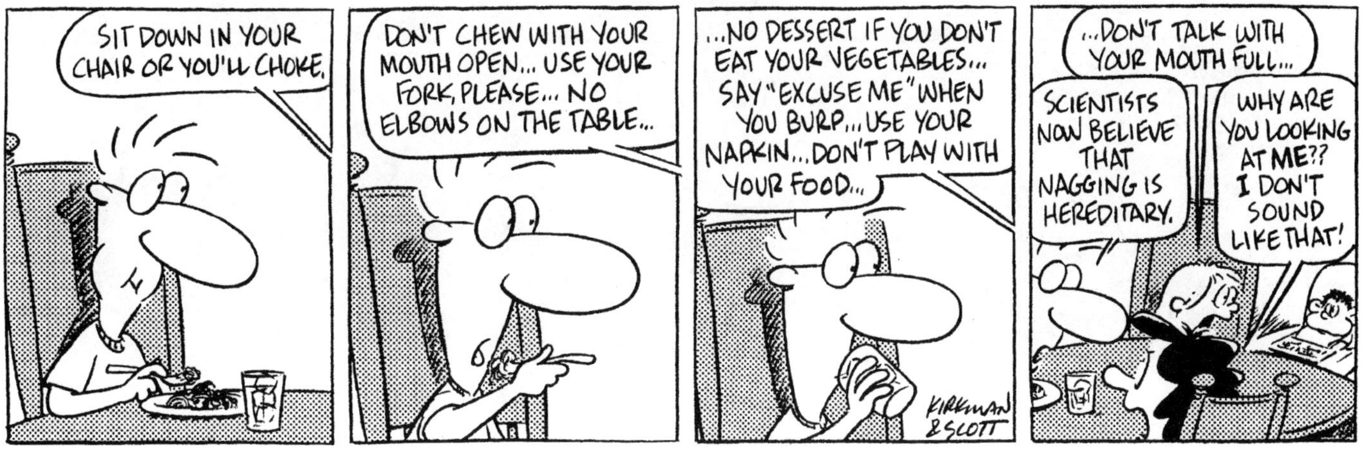
SIT DOWN IN YOUR CHAIR OR YOU'LL CHOKE.
DON'T CHEW WITH YOUR MOUTH OPEN... USE YOUR FORK, PLEASE... NO ELBOWS ON THE TABLE...
...NO DESSERT IF YOU DON'T EAT YOUR VEGETABLES... SAY "EXCUSE ME" WHEN YOU BURP... USE YOUR NAPKIN... DON'T PLAY WITH YOUR FOOD...
KIRKMAN & SCOTT
...DON'T TALK WITH YOUR MOUTH FULL...
SCIENTISTS NOW BELIEVE THAT NAGGING IS HEREDITARY.
WHY ARE YOU LOOKING AT ME?? I DON'T SOUND LIKE THAT!

BABY BLUES

RICK KIRKMAN / JERRY SCOTT BY

YOU LOOK TIRED, SWEETIE.

DO I?

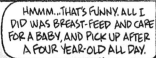

HMMM...THAT'S FUNNY. ALL I DID WAS BREAST-FEED AND CARE FOR A BABY, AND PICK UP AFTER A FOUR YEAR-OLD ALL DAY.

AND I ONLY WASHED SIX LOADS OF LAUNDRY, PREPARED BREAKFAST, LUNCH AND DINNER, MADE 25 FUND-RAISING CALLS FOR THE PRE-SCHOOL AND WENT GROCERY SHOP-PING WITH TWO SCREAMING KIDS.

SILLY ME! I'LL TRY TO LOOK **PERKIER** FOR YOU AT THE END OF THE DAY **TOMORROW!**

TIRED? DID I SAY "TIRED"?

I MEANT **CONTENT!** AND **ACCOMPLISHED!** YES SIR! CONTENT, ACCOMPLISHED AND TOTALLY TOGETHER. THAT'S YOU!

REALLY?

ABSOLUTELY! YOU BET!

THAT'S BETTER.

PLUS, YOUR VARICOSE VEINS AREN'T LOOKING TOO BAD TODAY, EITHER!

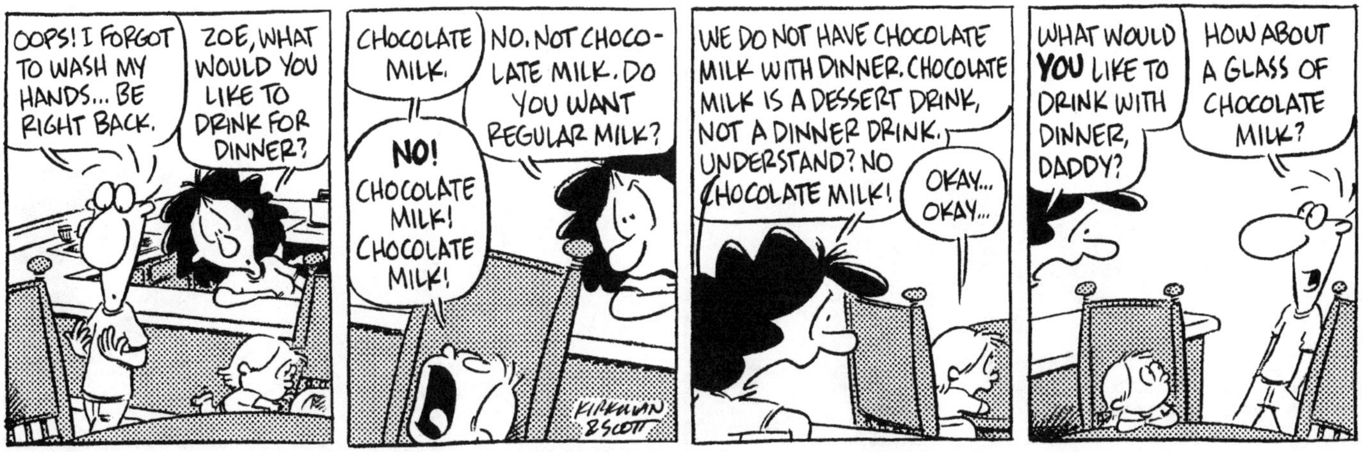
OOPS! I FORGOT TO WASH MY HANDS... BE RIGHT BACK.
ZOE, WHAT WOULD YOU LIKE TO DRINK FOR DINNER?
CHOCOLATE MILK.
NO. NOT CHOCOLATE MILK. DO YOU WANT REGULAR MILK?
NO! CHOCOLATE MILK! CHOCOLATE MILK!
KIRKMAN & SCOTT
WE DO NOT HAVE CHOCOLATE MILK WITH DINNER. CHOCOLATE MILK IS A DESSERT DRINK, NOT A DINNER DRINK. UNDERSTAND? NO CHOCOLATE MILK!
OKAY... OKAY...
WHAT WOULD YOU LIKE TO DRINK WITH DINNER, DADDY?
HOW ABOUT A GLASS OF CHOCOLATE MILK?

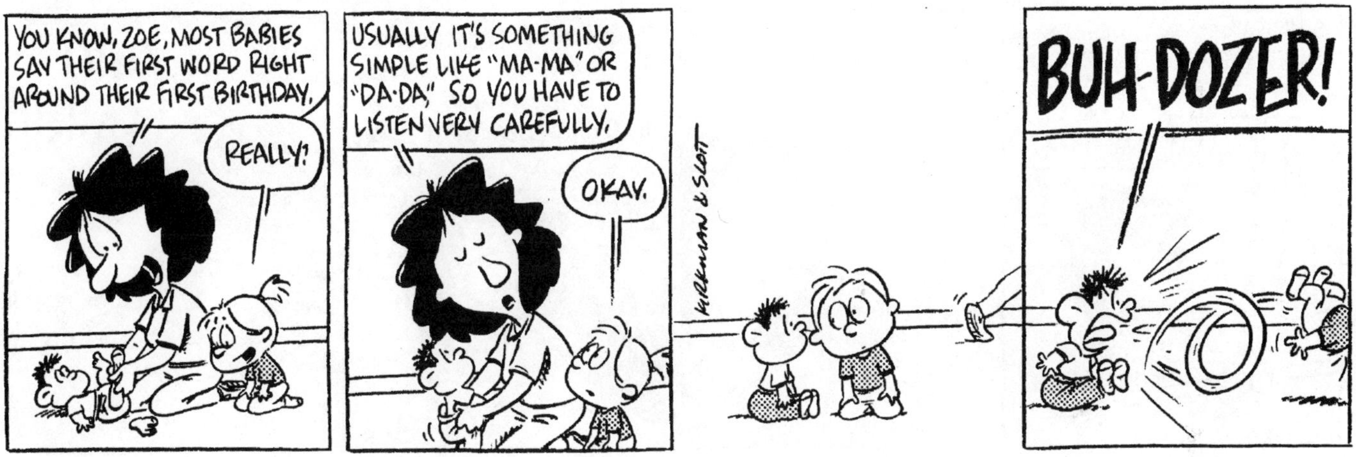
YOU KNOW, ZOE, MOST BABIES SAY THEIR FIRST WORD RIGHT AROUND THEIR FIRST BIRTHDAY.
REALLY?
USUALLY IT'S SOMETHING SIMPLE LIKE "MA-MA" OR "DA-DA," SO YOU HAVE TO LISTEN VERY CAREFULLY.
OKAY.
KIRKMAN & SCOTT
BUH-DOZER!

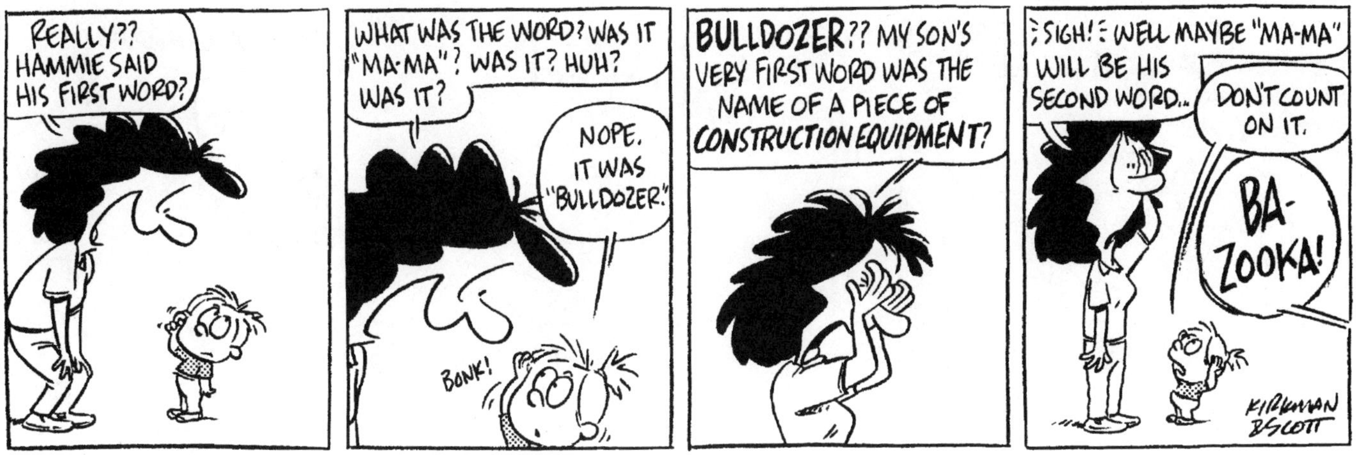
REALLY?? HAMMIE SAID HIS FIRST WORD?
WHAT WAS THE WORD? WAS IT "MA-MA"? WAS IT? HUH? WAS IT?
NOPE. IT WAS "BULLDOZER."
BONK!
BULLDOZER?? MY SON'S VERY FIRST WORD WAS THE NAME OF A PIECE OF CONSTRUCTION EQUIPMENT?
SIGH! WELL MAYBE "MA-MA" WILL BE HIS SECOND WORD...
DON'T COUNT ON IT.
BA-ZOOKA!
KIRKMAN & SCOTT

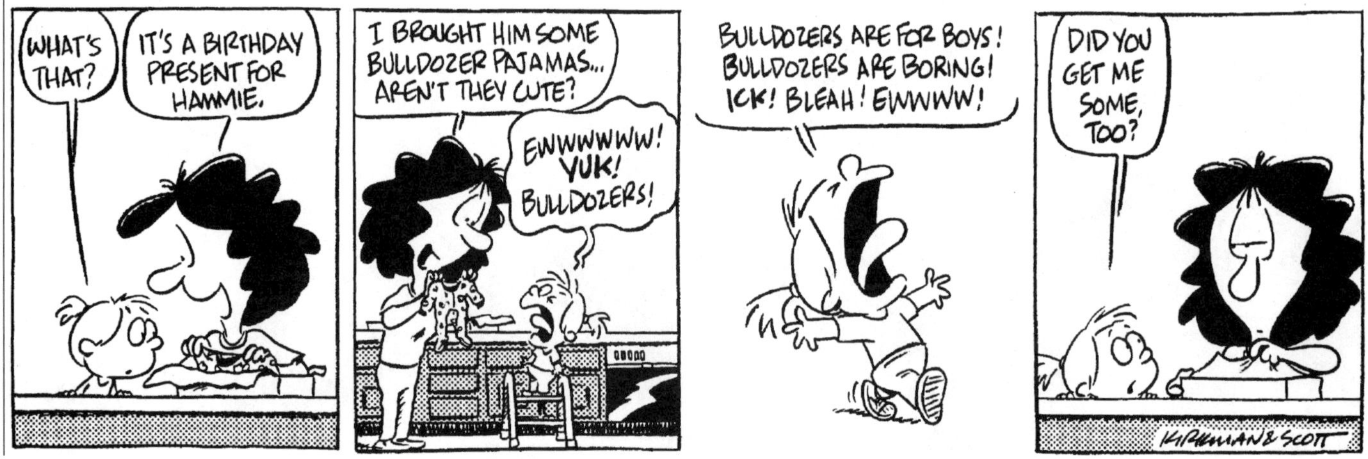
WHAT'S THAT?
IT'S A BIRTHDAY PRESENT FOR HAMMIE.
I BROUGHT HIM SOME BULLDOZER PAJAMAS... AREN'T THEY CUTE?
EWWWWWW! YUK! BULLDOZERS!
BULLDOZERS ARE FOR BOYS! BULLDOZERS ARE BORING! ICK! BLEAH! EWWWW!
DID YOU GET ME SOME, TOO?
KIRKMAN & SCOTT

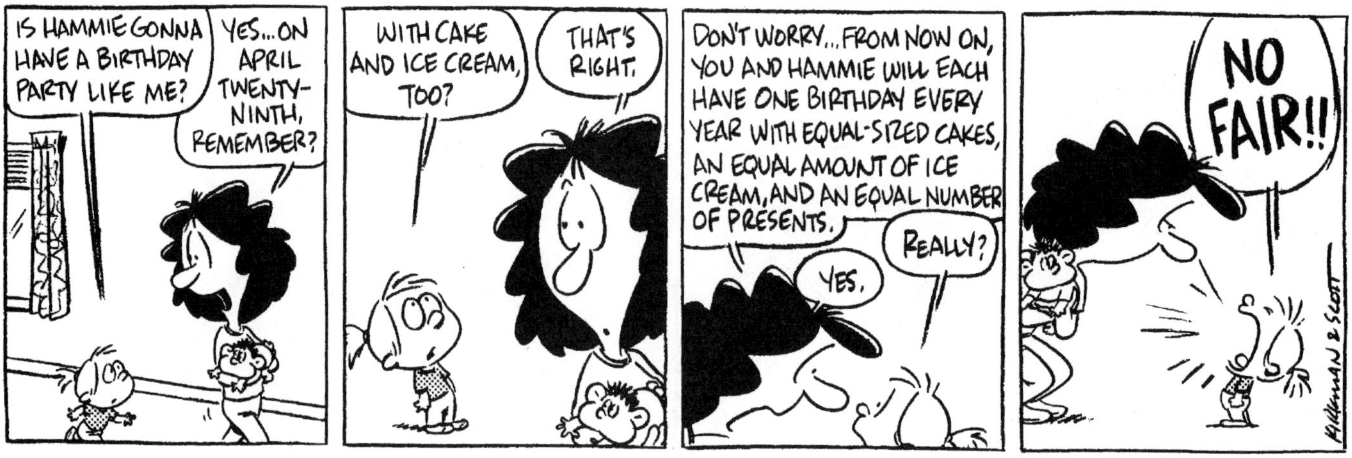
IS HAMMIE GONNA HAVE A BIRTHDAY PARTY LIKE ME?
YES...ON APRIL TWENTY-NINTH, REMEMBER?
WITH CAKE AND ICE CREAM, TOO?
THAT'S RIGHT.
DON'T WORRY...FROM NOW ON, YOU AND HAMMIE WILL EACH HAVE ONE BIRTHDAY EVERY YEAR WITH EQUAL-SIZED CAKES, AN EQUAL AMOUNT OF ICE CREAM, AND AN EQUAL NUMBER OF PRESENTS.
REALLY?
YES.
NO FAIR!!
KIRKMAN & SCOTT

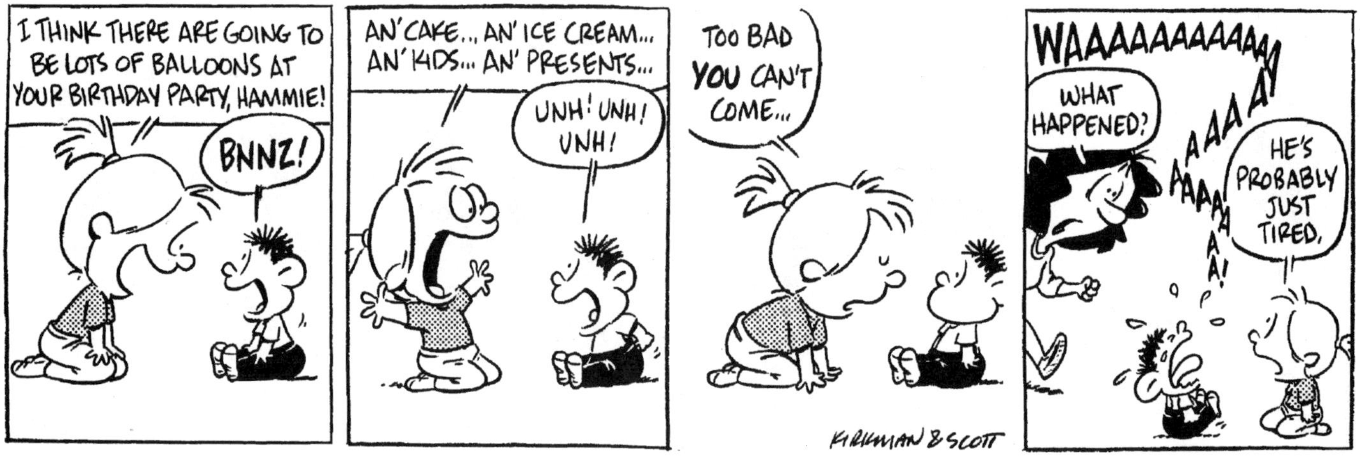
I THINK THERE ARE GOING TO BE LOTS OF BALLOONS AT YOUR BIRTHDAY PARTY, HAMMIE!
BNNZ!
AN' CAKE... AN' ICE CREAM... AN' KIDS... AN' PRESENTS...
UNH! UNH! UNH!
TOO BAD YOU CAN'T COME...
KIRKMAN & SCOTT
WAAAAAAAAAAAAAAAAAAAAAA!
WHAT HAPPENED?
HE'S PROBABLY JUST TIRED.

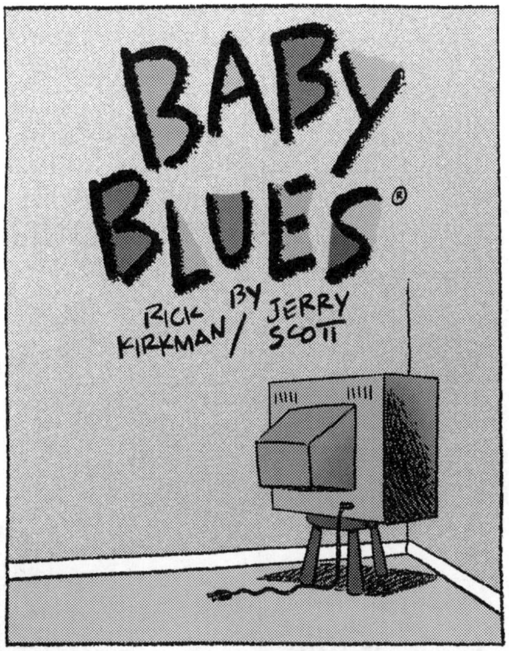
BABY BLUES®
BY RICK KIRKMAN / JERRY SCOTT

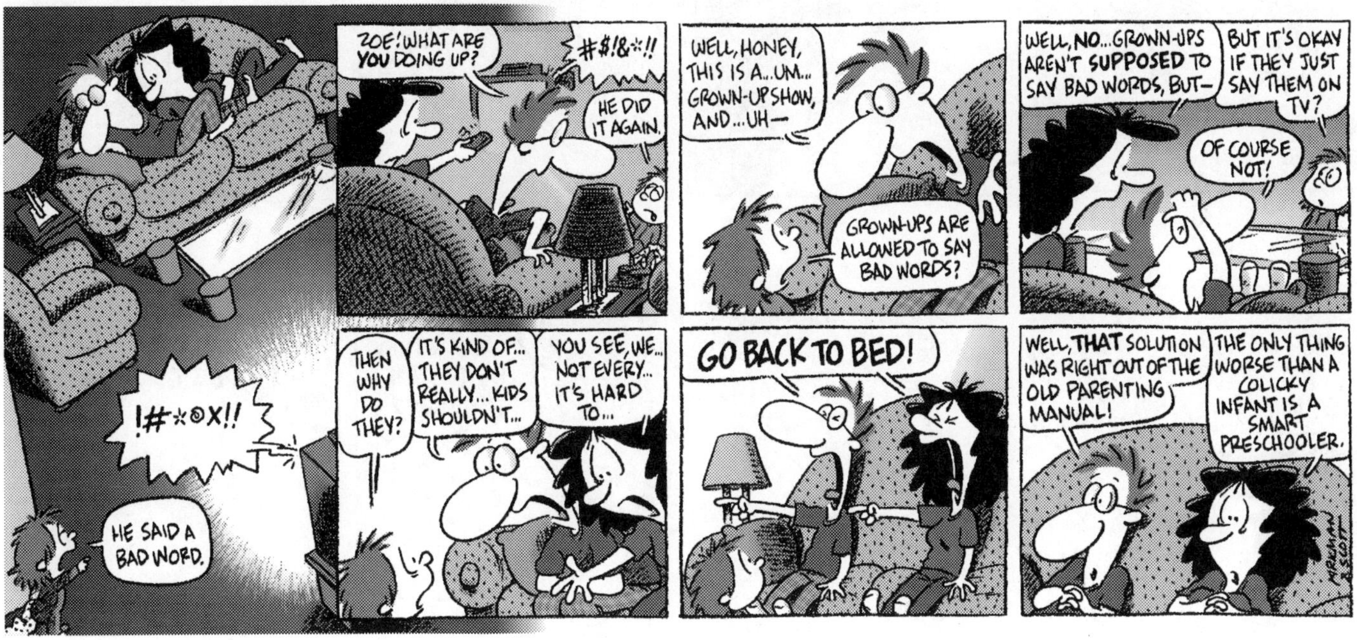
!#*©X!!
HE SAID A BAD WORD.
ZOE! WHAT ARE YOU DOING UP?
#$!&*!!
HE DID IT AGAIN.
WELL, HONEY, THIS IS A...UM... GROWN-UP SHOW, AND...UH—
GROWN-UPS ARE ALLOWED TO SAY BAD WORDS?
WELL, NO...GROWN-UPS AREN'T SUPPOSED TO SAY BAD WORDS, BUT—
BUT IT'S OKAY IF THEY JUST SAY THEM ON TV?
OF COURSE NOT!
THEN WHY DO THEY?
IT'S KIND OF... THEY DON'T REALLY...KIDS SHOULDN'T...
YOU SEE, WE... NOT EVERY... IT'S HARD TO...
GO BACK TO BED!
WELL, THAT SOLUTION WAS RIGHT OUT OF THE OLD PARENTING MANUAL!
THE ONLY THING WORSE THAN A COLICKY INFANT IS A SMART PRESCHOOLER.

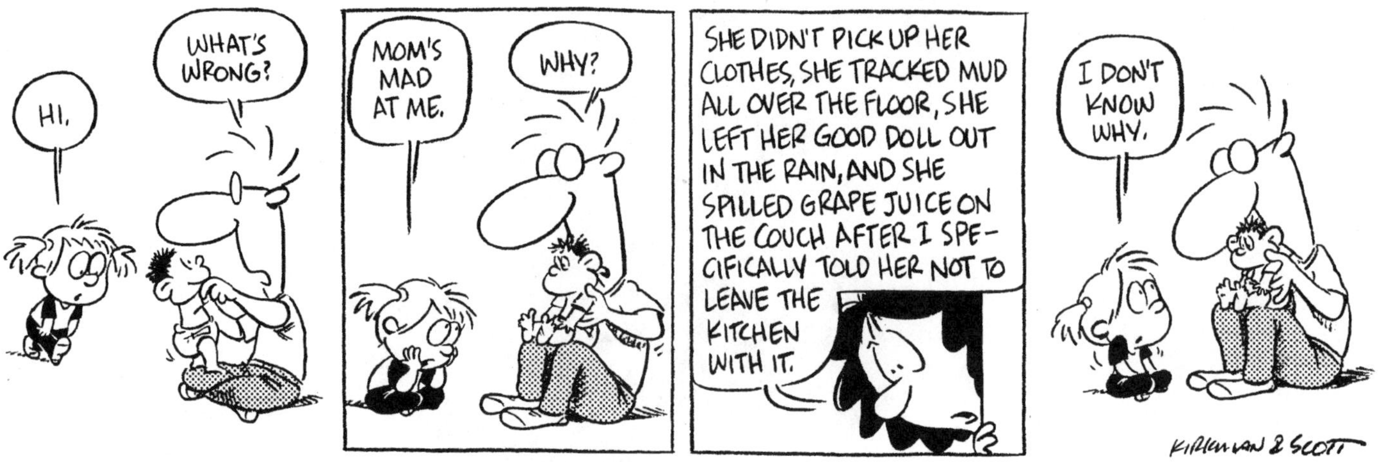
HI.
WHAT'S WRONG?
MOM'S MAD AT ME.
WHY?
SHE DIDN'T PICK UP HER CLOTHES, SHE TRACKED MUD ALL OVER THE FLOOR, SHE LEFT HER GOOD DOLL OUT IN THE RAIN, AND SHE SPILLED GRAPE JUICE ON THE COUCH AFTER I SPE-CIFICALLY TOLD HER NOT TO LEAVE THE KITCHEN WITH IT.
I DON'T KNOW WHY.
KIRKMAN & SCOTT

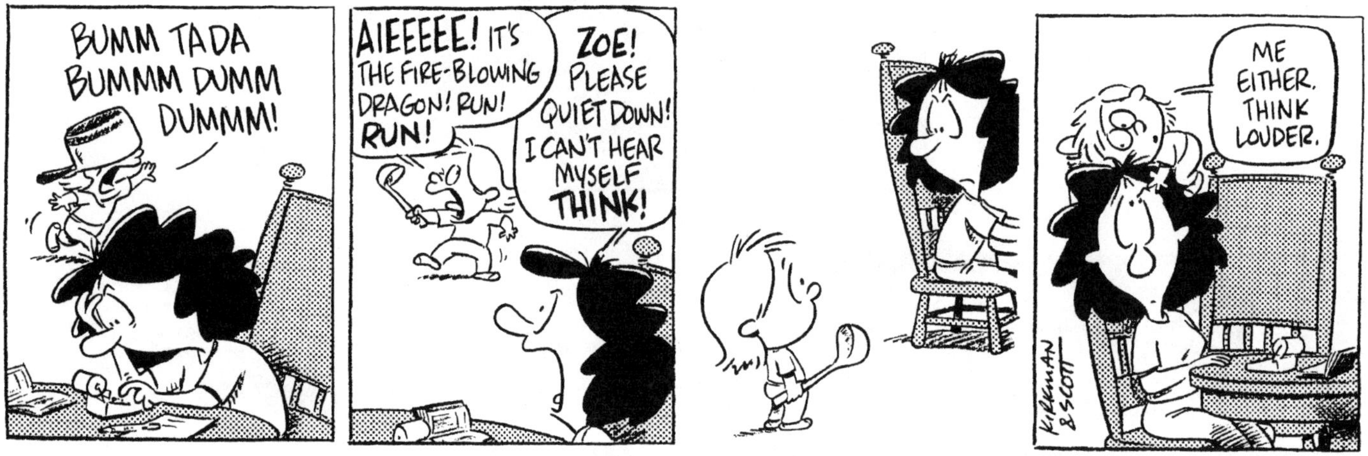
BUMM TADA BUMMM DUMM DUMMM!
AIEEEEE! IT'S THE FIRE-BLOWING DRAGON! RUN! RUN!
ZOE! PLEASE QUIET DOWN! I CAN'T HEAR MYSELF THINK!
ME EITHER. THINK LOUDER.
KIRKMAN & SCOTT

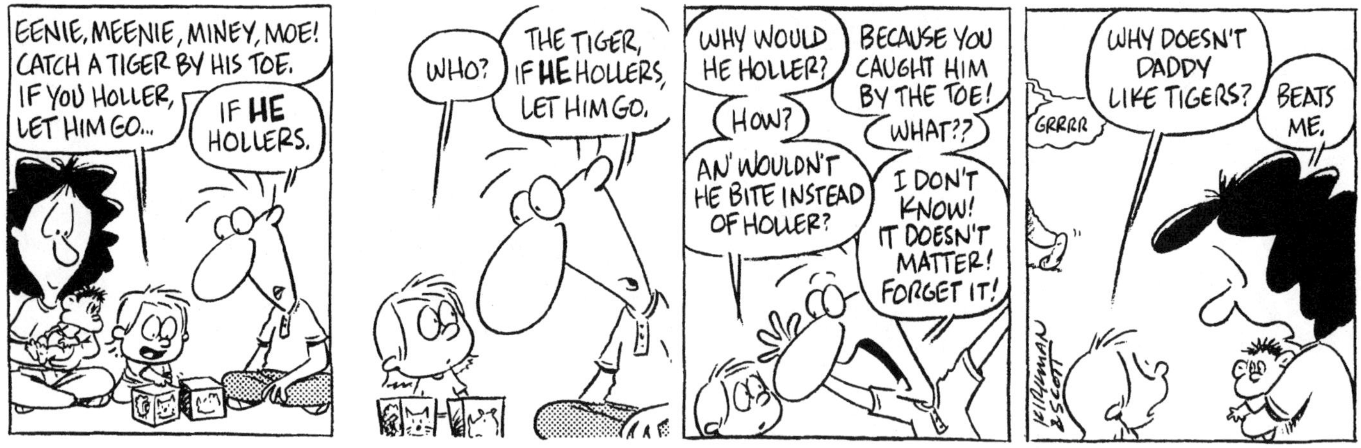
EENIE, MEENIE, MINEY, MOE! CATCH A TIGER BY HIS TOE. IF YOU HOLLER, LET HIM GO...
IF HE HOLLERS.
WHO?
THE TIGER, IF HE HOLLERS, LET HIM GO.
WHY WOULD HE HOLLER?
BECAUSE YOU CAUGHT HIM BY THE TOE!
HOW?
WHAT??
AN' WOULDN'T HE BITE INSTEAD OF HOLLER?
I DON'T KNOW! IT DOESN'T MATTER! FORGET IT!
GRRRR
WHY DOESN'T DADDY LIKE TIGERS?
BEATS ME.
KIRKMAN & SCOTT

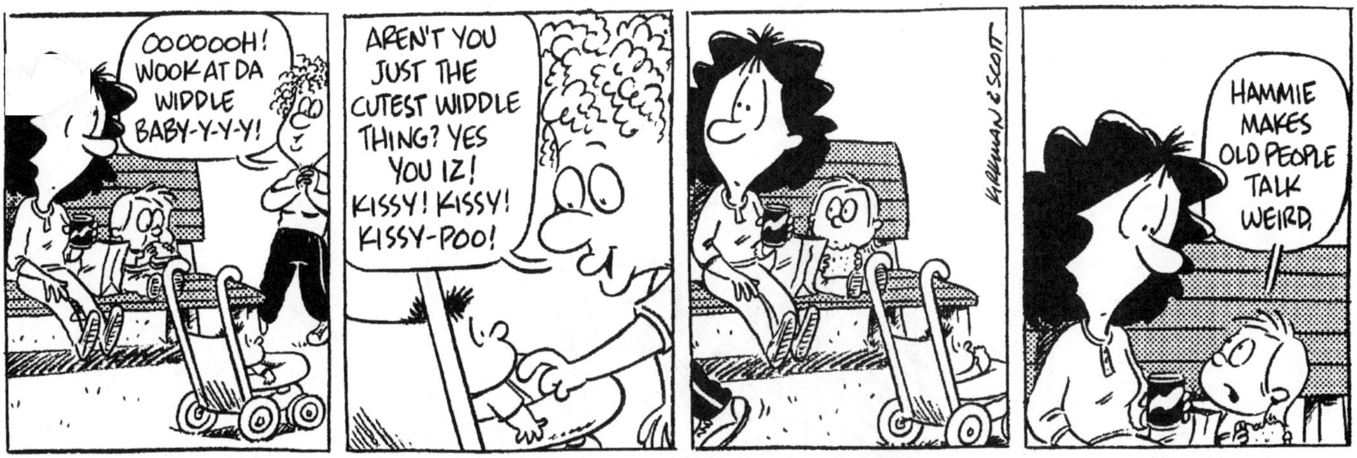
OOOOOOH! WOOK AT DA WIDDLE BABY-Y-Y-Y!
AREN'T YOU JUST THE CUTEST WIDDLE THING? YES YOU IZ! KISSY! KISSY! KISSY-POO!
KIRKMAN & SCOTT
HAMMIE MAKES OLD PEOPLE TALK WEIRD.

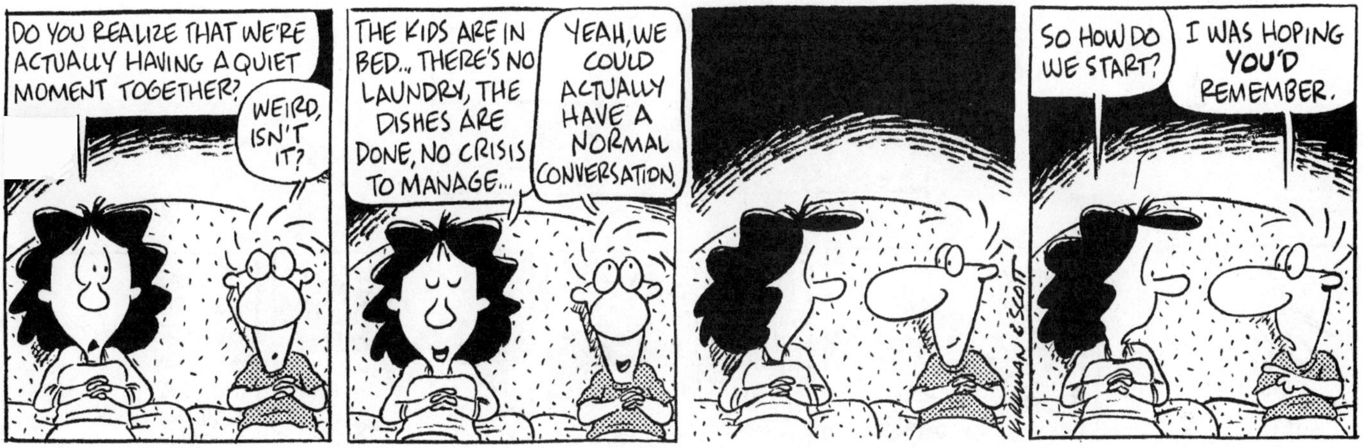
DO YOU REALIZE THAT WE'RE ACTUALLY HAVING A QUIET MOMENT TOGETHER?
WEIRD, ISN'T IT?
THE KIDS ARE IN BED... THERE'S NO LAUNDRY, THE DISHES ARE DONE, NO CRISIS TO MANAGE...
YEAH, WE COULD ACTUALLY HAVE A NORMAL CONVERSATION.
KIRKMAN & SCOTT
SO HOW DO WE START?
I WAS HOPING YOU'D REMEMBER.

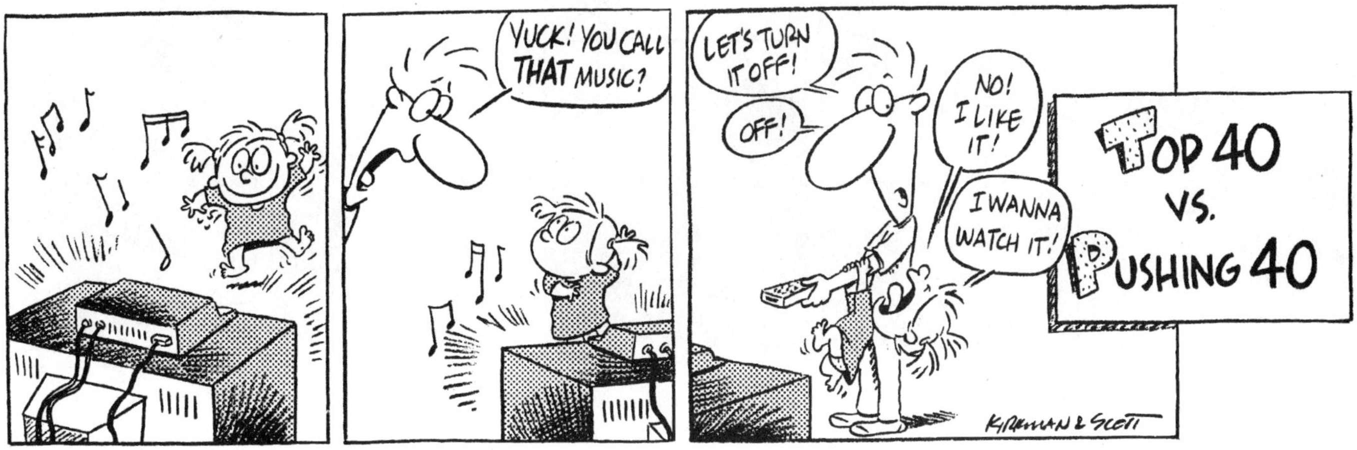
YUCK! YOU CALL THAT MUSIC?
LET'S TURN IT OFF!
OFF!
NO! I LIKE IT!
I WANNA WATCH IT!
KIRKMAN & SCOTT
TOP 40 VS. PUSHING 40

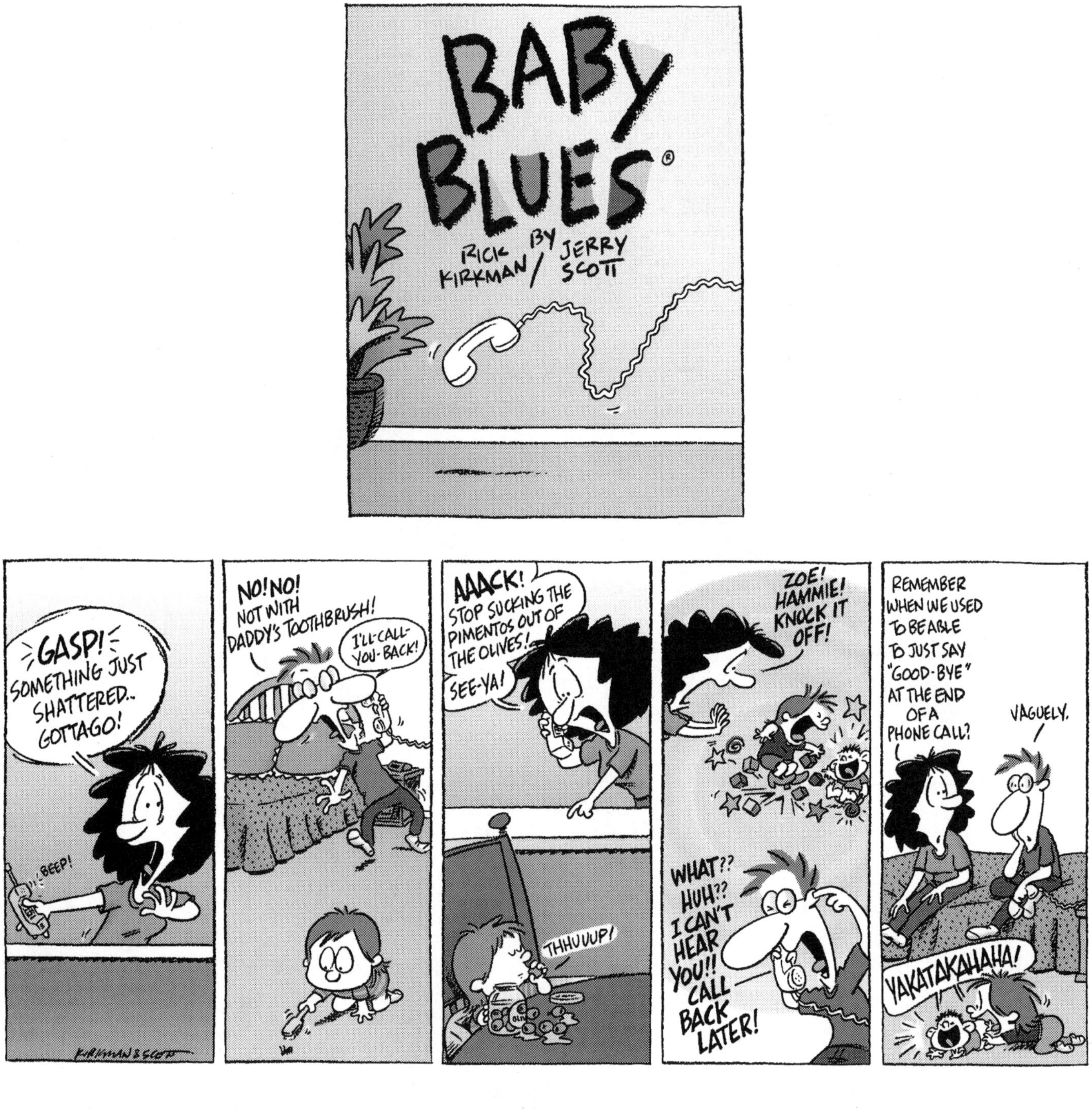
BABY BLUES®
BY RICK KIRKMAN / JERRY SCOTT
GASP! SOMETHING JUST SHATTERED.. GOTTAGO!
BEEP!
NO! NO! NOT WITH DADDY'S TOOTHBRUSH!
I'LL-CALL-YOU-BACK!
AAACK! STOP SUCKING THE PIMENTOS OUT OF THE OLIVES!
SEE-YA!
THHUUUP!
ZOE! HAMMIE! KNOCK IT OFF!
WHAT?? HUH?? I CAN'T HEAR YOU!! CALL BACK LATER!
REMEMBER WHEN WE USED TO BE ABLE TO JUST SAY "GOOD-BYE" AT THE END OF A PHONE CALL?
VAGUELY.
YAKATAKAHAHA!

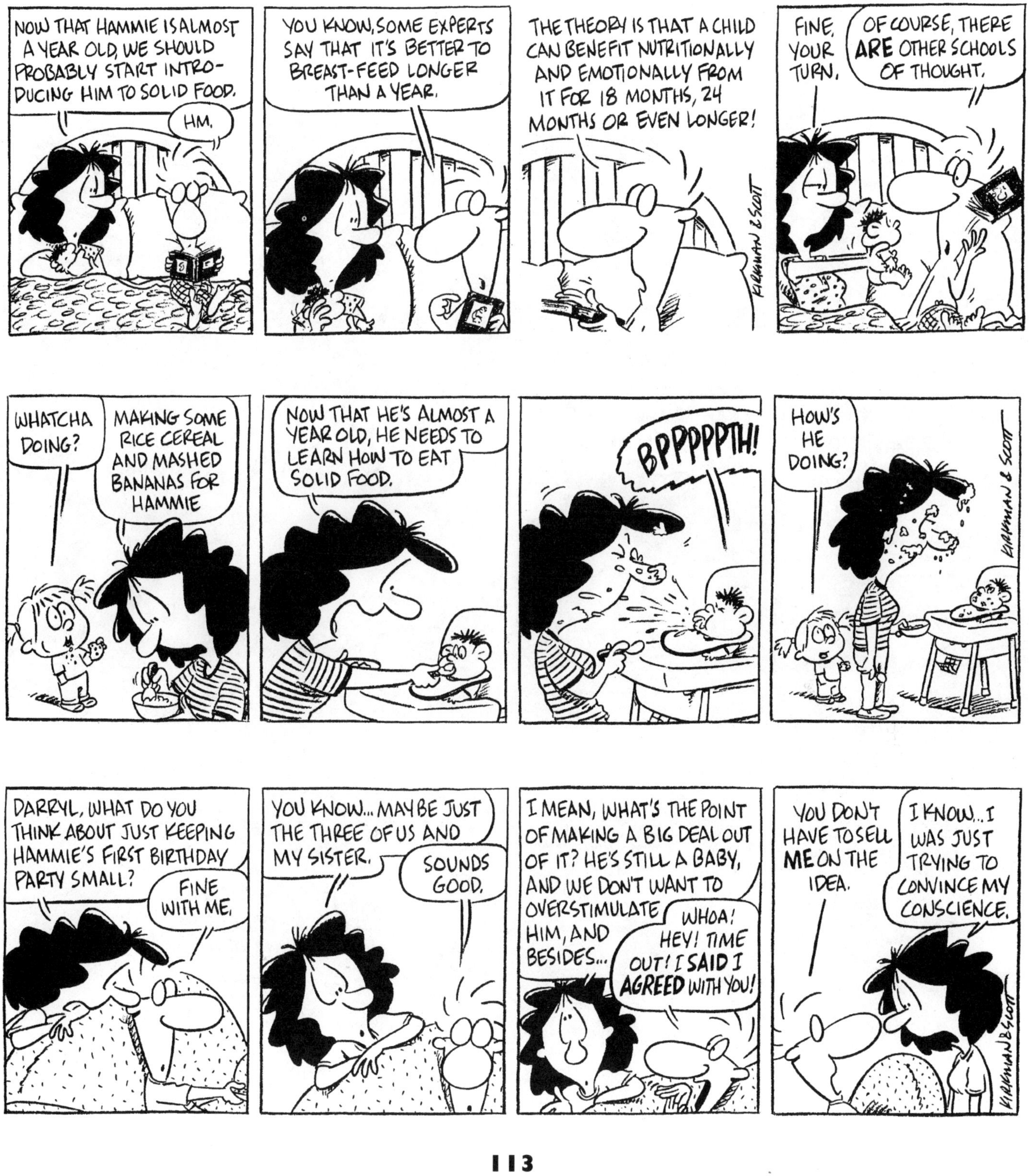
NOW THAT HAMMIE IS ALMOST A YEAR OLD, WE SHOULD PROBABLY START INTRODUCING HIM TO SOLID FOOD.
HM.
YOU KNOW, SOME EXPERTS SAY THAT IT'S BETTER TO BREAST-FEED LONGER THAN A YEAR.
THE THEORY IS THAT A CHILD CAN BENEFIT NUTRITIONALLY AND EMOTIONALLY FROM IT FOR 18 MONTHS, 24 MONTHS OR EVEN LONGER!
KIRKMAN & SCOTT
FINE, YOUR TURN.
OF COURSE, THERE **ARE** OTHER SCHOOLS OF THOUGHT.
WHATCHA DOING?
MAKING SOME RICE CEREAL AND MASHED BANANAS FOR HAMMIE
NOW THAT HE'S ALMOST A YEAR OLD, HE NEEDS TO LEARN HOW TO EAT SOLID FOOD.
BPPPPPTH!
HOW'S HE DOING?
KIRKMAN & SCOTT
DARRYL, WHAT DO YOU THINK ABOUT JUST KEEPING HAMMIE'S FIRST BIRTHDAY PARTY SMALL?
FINE WITH ME.
YOU KNOW... MAYBE JUST THE THREE OF US AND MY SISTER.
SOUNDS GOOD.
I MEAN, WHAT'S THE POINT OF MAKING A BIG DEAL OUT OF IT? HE'S STILL A BABY, AND WE DON'T WANT TO OVERSTIMULATE HIM, AND BESIDES...
WHOA! HEY! TIME OUT! I **SAID** I **AGREED** WITH YOU!
YOU DON'T HAVE TO SELL **ME** ON THE IDEA.
I KNOW... I WAS JUST TRYING TO CONVINCE MY CONSCIENCE.
KIRKMAN & SCOTT

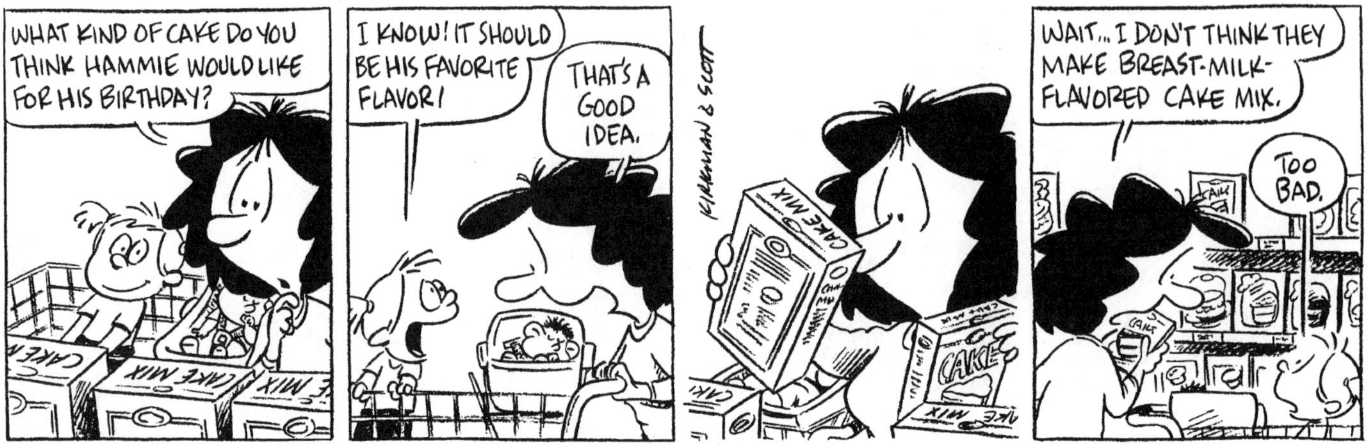
WHAT KIND OF CAKE DO YOU THINK HAMMIE WOULD LIKE FOR HIS BIRTHDAY?
I KNOW! IT SHOULD BE HIS FAVORITE FLAVOR!
THAT'S A GOOD IDEA.
KIRKMAN & SCOTT
WAIT... I DON'T THINK THEY MAKE BREAST-MILK-FLAVORED CAKE MIX.
TOO BAD.

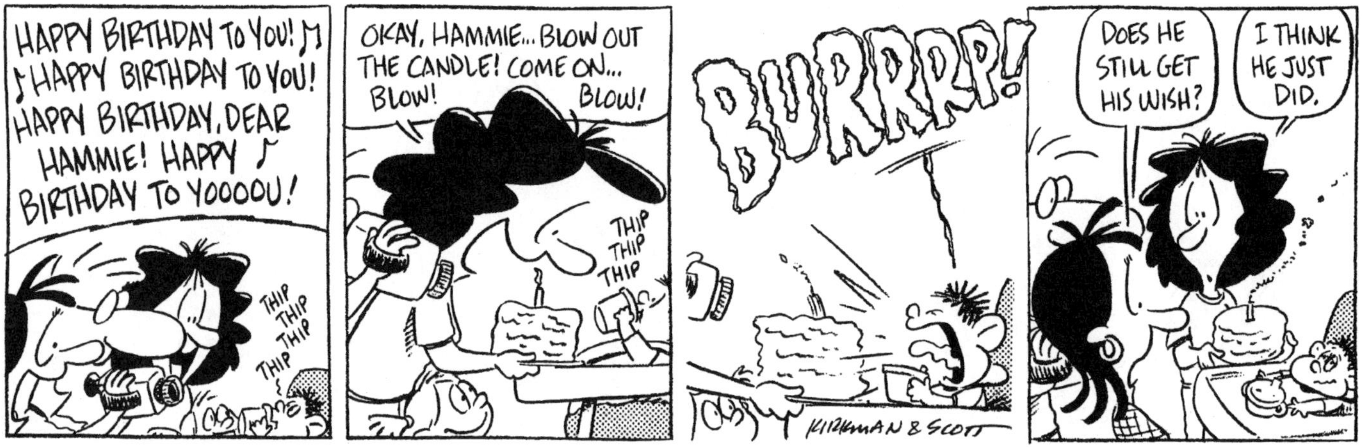
HAPPY BIRTHDAY TO YOU! HAPPY BIRTHDAY TO YOU! HAPPY BIRTHDAY, DEAR HAMMIE! HAPPY BIRTHDAY TO YOOOOU!
THIP THIP THIP THIP
OKAY, HAMMIE... BLOW OUT THE CANDLE! COME ON... BLOW! BLOW!
THIP THIP THIP
BURRRP!
KIRKMAN & SCOTT
DOES HE STILL GET HIS WISH?
I THINK HE JUST DID.

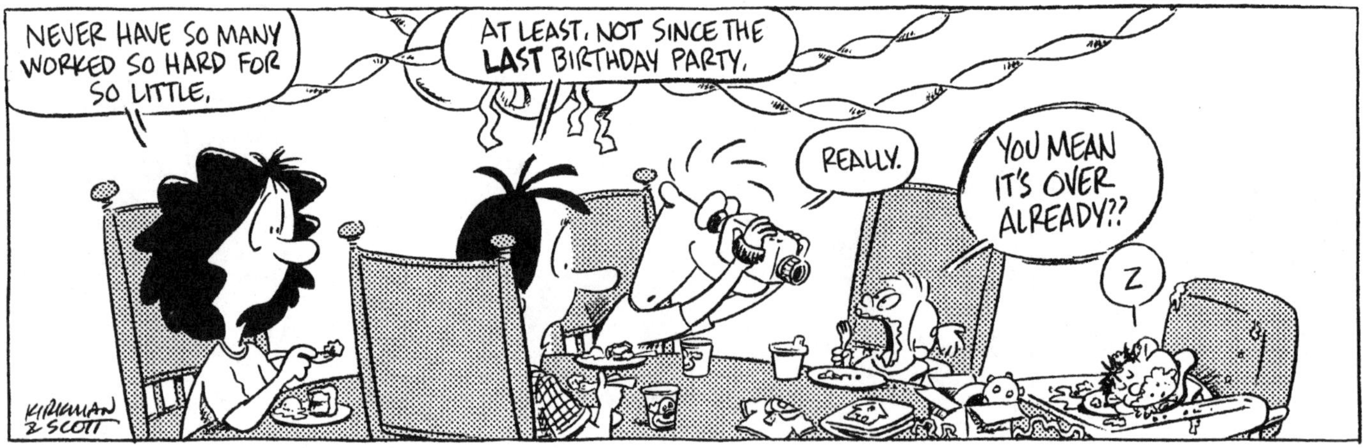
NEVER HAVE SO MANY WORKED SO HARD FOR SO LITTLE.
AT LEAST, NOT SINCE THE LAST BIRTHDAY PARTY.
REALLY.
YOU MEAN IT'S OVER ALREADY??
Z
KIRKMAN & SCOTT

BABY BLUES®

BY RICK KIRKMAN / JERRY SCOTT

...SO THEN I FOLLOW THIS TRAIL OF LITTLE ORANGE HAIRS DOWN THE HALL AND INTO THE BATHROOM.

OH, NO...

YEP! AND THERE'S ZOE UP ON THE VANITY HOLDING MY GOOD SCISSORS ADMIRING THE "HAIRCUT" SHE'D JUST GIVEN HERSELF.

I DIDN'T SEE ANYTHING.

BY THE WAY, HAVE YOU SEEN MY PAPER PUNCH?

KA-POINK! KA-POINK! KA-POINK! KAPOINK! KA-POINK! KAPOINK!

IT COULD HAVE BEEN WORSE. SHE CUT A HUNK OF THE SIDE RIGHT HERE, BUT I WAS ABLE TO BLEND IT IN.

WHEW!

ANYWAY, I SAT HER DOWN AND WE HAD A LONG TALK ABOUT HOW SCISSORS ARE NOT FOR CUTTING HAIR UNLESS YOU WORK IN A BEAUTY SHOP AND SHE PROMISED ME THAT SHE'D NEVER DO IT AGAIN.

THAT'S GREAT.

IT SOUNDS LIKE LIKE YOU GOT YOUR MESSAGE ACROSS LOUD AND CLEAR.

KIRKMAN & SCOTT

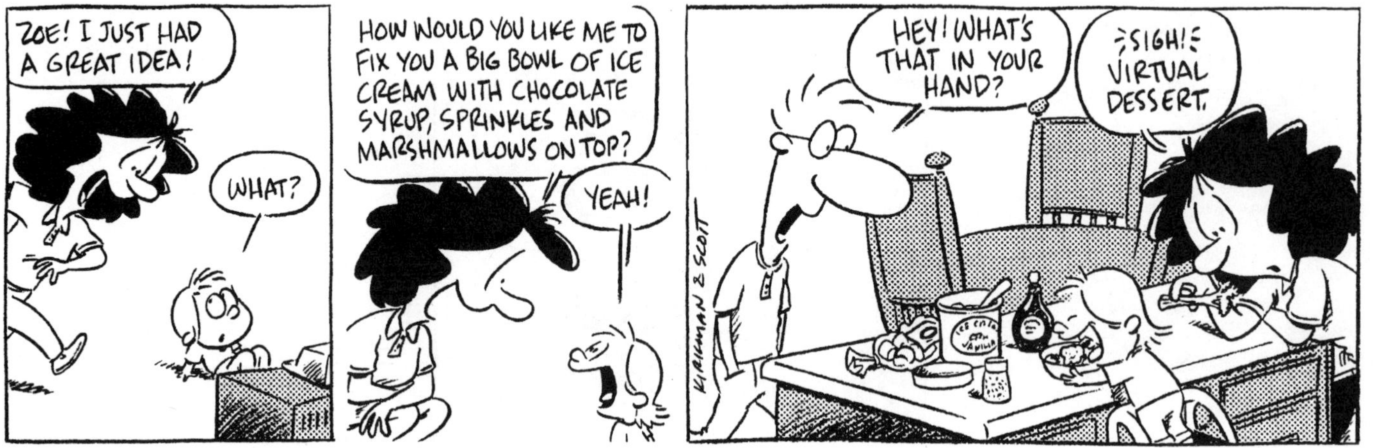
ZOE! I JUST HAD A GREAT IDEA!
WHAT?
HOW WOULD YOU LIKE ME TO FIX YOU A BIG BOWL OF ICE CREAM WITH CHOCOLATE SYRUP, SPRINKLES AND MARSHMALLOWS ON TOP?
YEAH!
KIRKMAN & SCOTT
HEY! WHAT'S THAT IN YOUR HAND?
SIGH! VIRTUAL DESSERT.

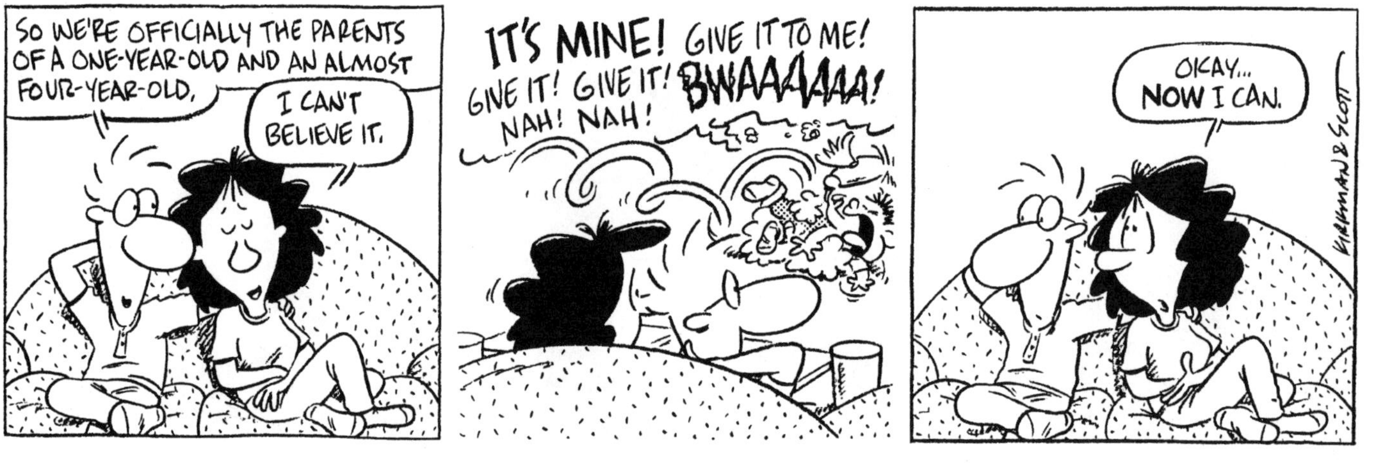
SO WE'RE OFFICIALLY THE PARENTS OF A ONE-YEAR-OLD AND AN ALMOST FOUR-YEAR-OLD.
I CAN'T BELIEVE IT.
IT'S MINE!
GIVE IT TO ME!
GIVE IT! GIVE IT!
NAH! NAH!
BWAAAAAAA!
OKAY... NOW I CAN.
KIRKMAN & SCOTT

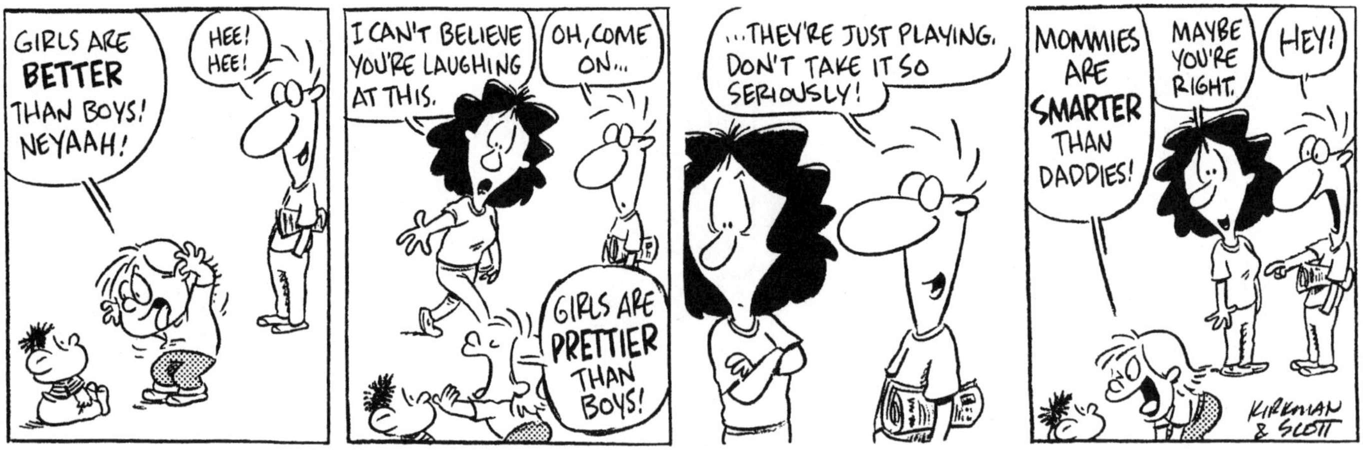
GIRLS ARE BETTER THAN BOYS! NEYAAH!
HEE! HEE!
I CAN'T BELIEVE YOU'RE LAUGHING AT THIS.
OH, COME ON...
GIRLS ARE PRETTIER THAN BOYS!
...THEY'RE JUST PLAYING. DON'T TAKE IT SO SERIOUSLY!
MOMMIES ARE SMARTER THAN DADDIES!
MAYBE YOU'RE RIGHT.
HEY!
KIRKMAN & SCOTT

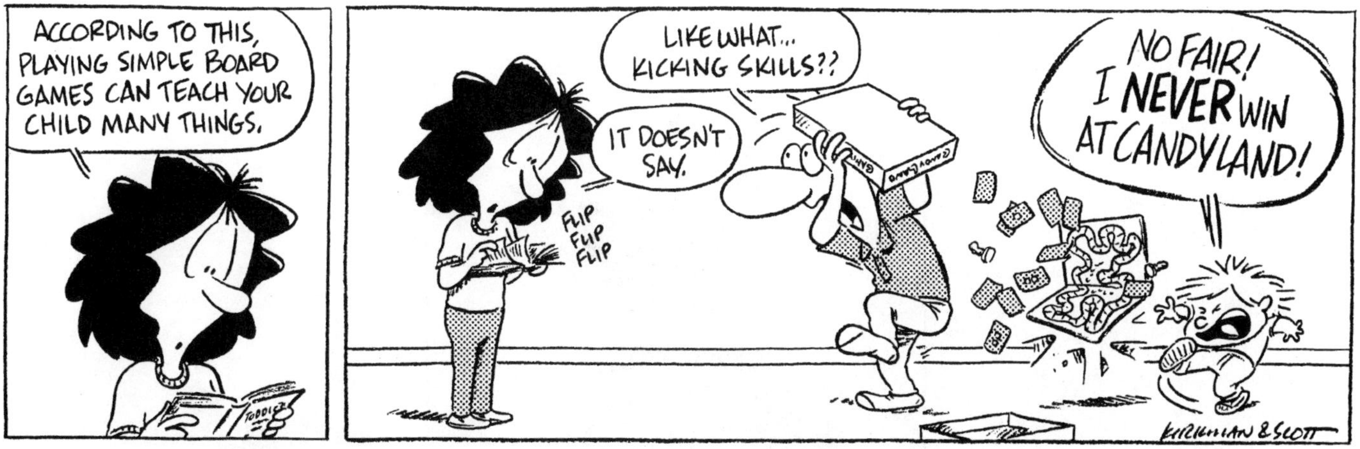
ACCORDING TO THIS, PLAYING SIMPLE BOARD GAMES CAN TEACH YOUR CHILD MANY THINGS.
LIKE WHAT... KICKING SKILLS??
IT DOESN'T SAY.
FLIP FLIP FLIP
NO FAIR! I NEVER WIN AT CANDYLAND!
KIRKMAN & SCOTT

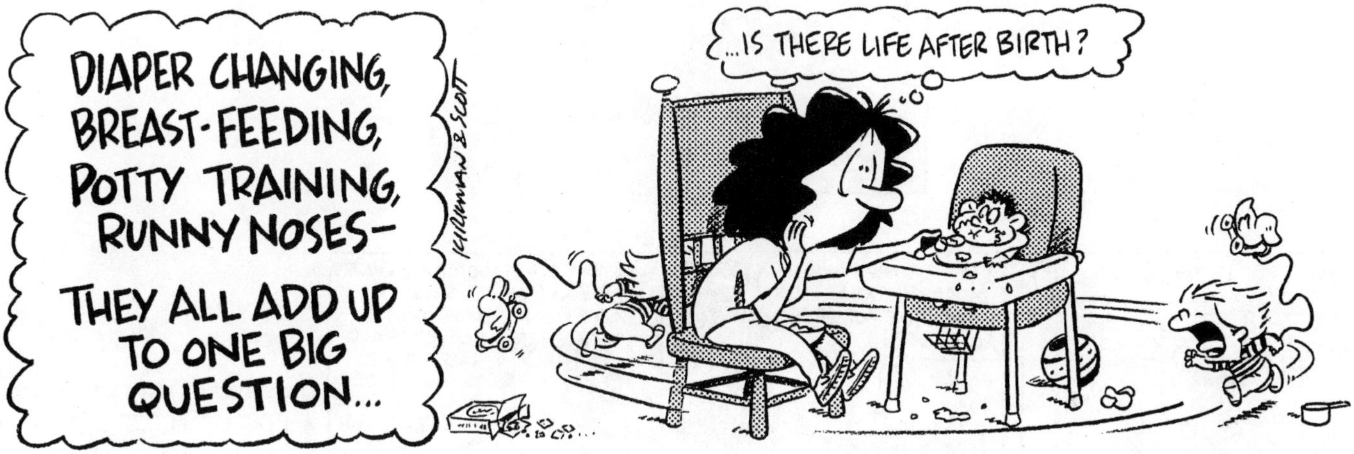
DIAPER CHANGING, BREAST-FEEDING, POTTY TRAINING, RUNNY NOSES- THEY ALL ADD UP TO ONE BIG QUESTION...
KIRKMAN & SCOTT
...IS THERE LIFE AFTER BIRTH?

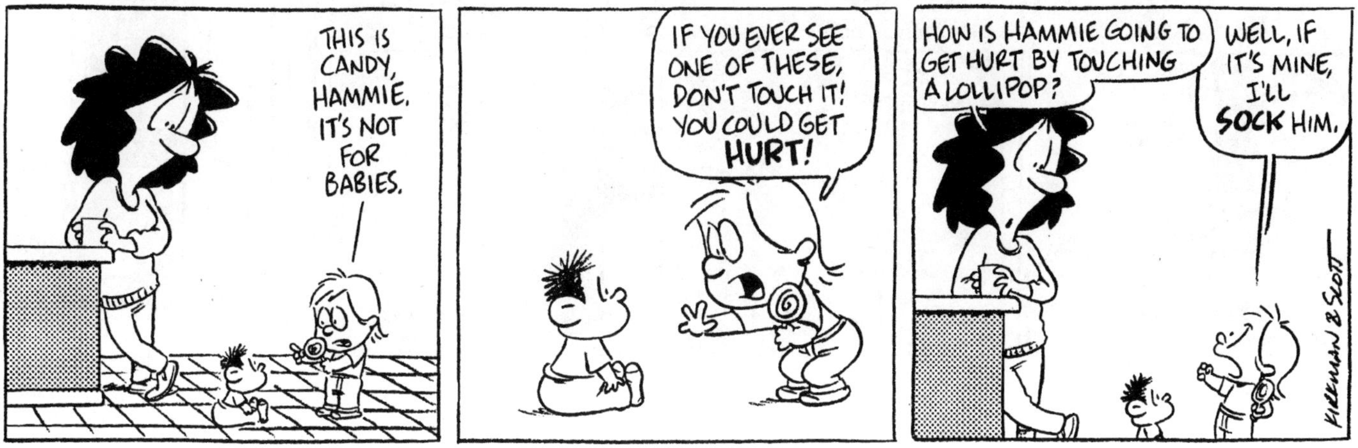
THIS IS CANDY, HAMMIE. IT'S NOT FOR BABIES.
IF YOU EVER SEE ONE OF THESE, DON'T TOUCH IT! YOU COULD GET HURT!
HOW IS HAMMIE GOING TO GET HURT BY TOUCHING A LOLLIPOP?
WELL, IF IT'S MINE, I'LL SOCK HIM.
KIRKMAN & SCOTT

BABY BLUES®
BY RICK KIRKMAN / JERRY SCOTT
GUILT

WHEW! WE DID IT!
WHAT A DIFFERENCE!
I DIDN'T THINK IT WAS POSSIBLE, BUT WE ACTUALLY CLEANED THE MOTHER OF ALL CLOSETS!
YESSS!
REMEMBER HOW IT LOOKED A FEW HOURS AGO? PAPERS FROM PRESCHOOL ALL OVER THE FLOOR... STACKS OF OLD SCRIBBLES AND HALF-FINISHED COLORING BOOK PAGES... YOU COULD HARDLY GET THE DOOR CLOSED!
YEAH... I CAN'T BELIEVE WE LIVED WITH THAT MESS FOR SO LONG!
BUT I DREW THESE FOR YOU.
KIRKMAN & SCOTT

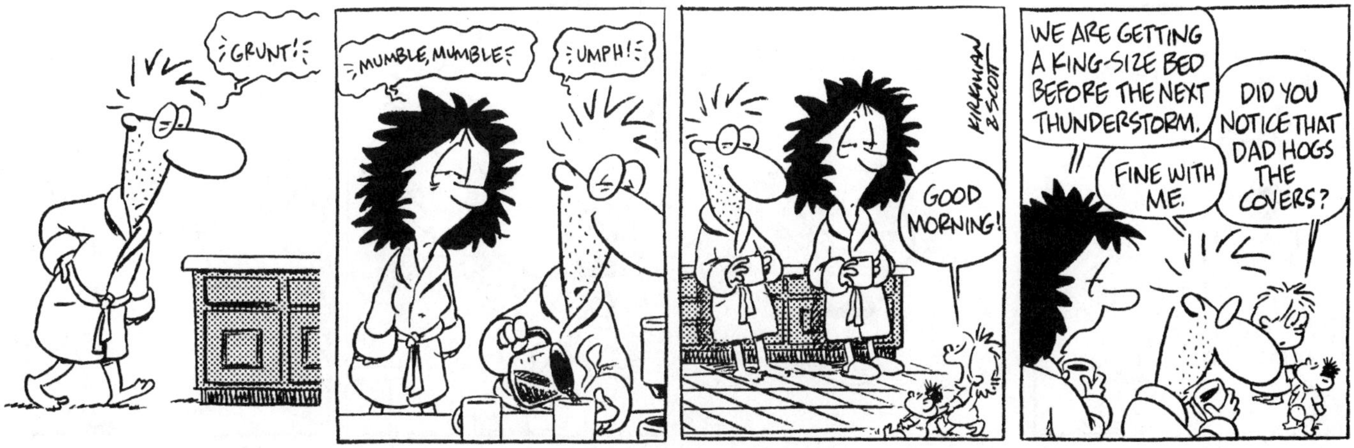
GRUNT!
MUMBLE, MUMBLE
UMPH!
KIRKMAN & SCOTT
GOOD MORNING!
WE ARE GETTING A KING-SIZE BED BEFORE THE NEXT THUNDERSTORM.
FINE WITH ME.
DID YOU NOTICE THAT DAD HOGS THE COVERS?

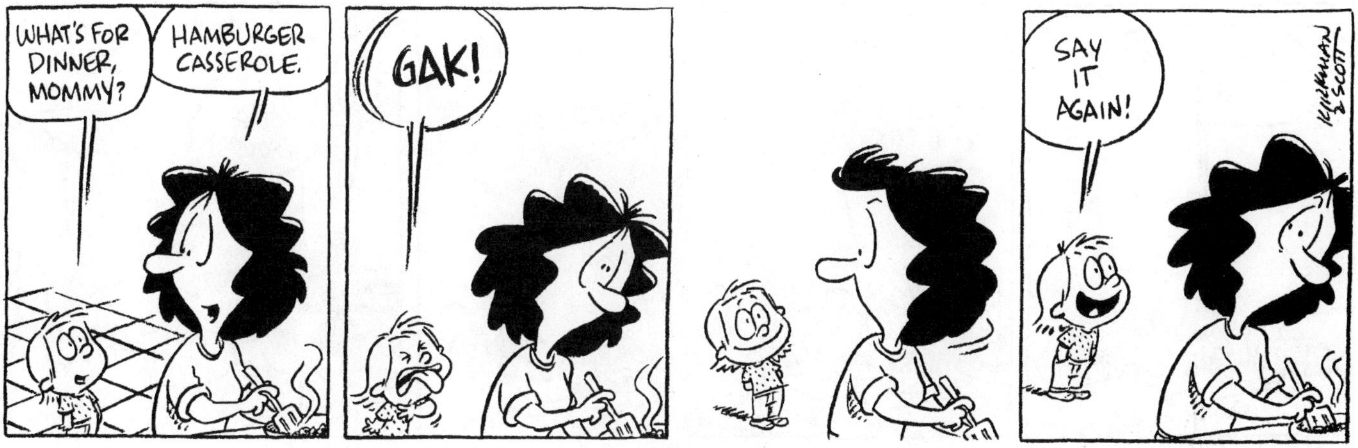
WHAT'S FOR DINNER, MOMMY?
HAMBURGER CASSEROLE.
GAK!
SAY IT AGAIN!
KIRKMAN & SCOTT

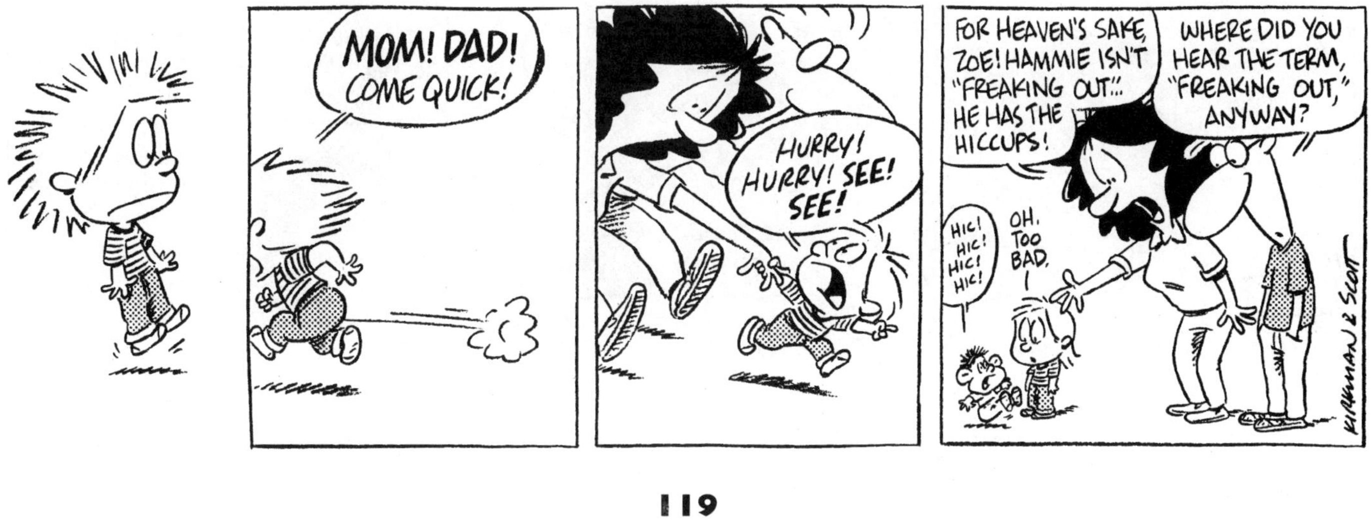
MOM! DAD! COME QUICK!
HURRY! HURRY! SEE! SEE!
FOR HEAVEN'S SAKE, ZOE! HAMMIE ISN'T "FREAKING OUT"... HE HAS THE HICCUPS!
WHERE DID YOU HEAR THE TERM, "FREAKING OUT," ANYWAY?
HIC! HIC! HIC! HIC!
OH. TOO BAD.
KIRKMAN & SCOTT

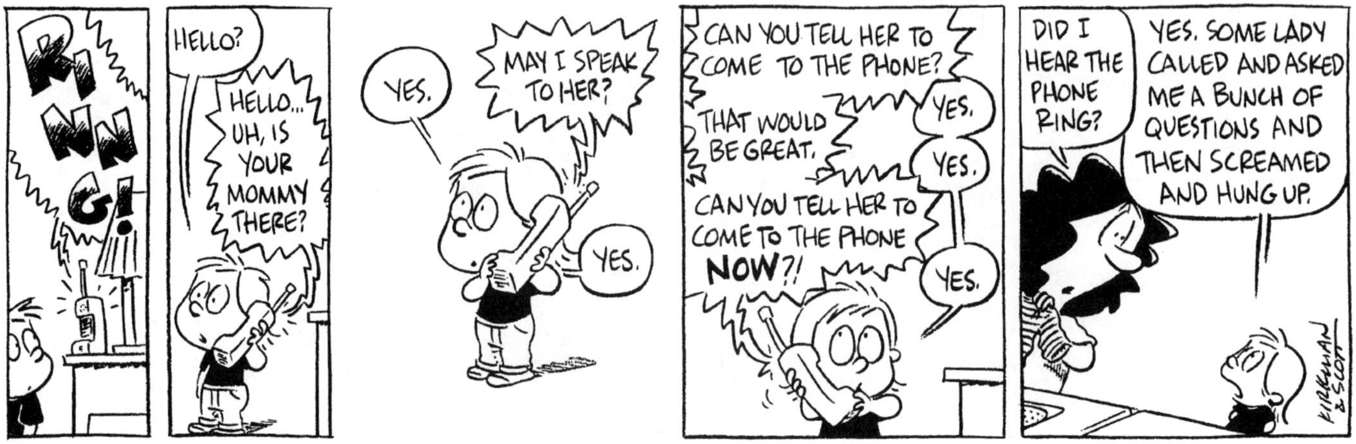
RIIINNG!
HELLO?
HELLO... UH, IS YOUR MOMMY THERE?
YES.
MAY I SPEAK TO HER?
YES.
CAN YOU TELL HER TO COME TO THE PHONE?
YES.
THAT WOULD BE GREAT.
YES.
CAN YOU TELL HER TO COME TO THE PHONE **NOW**?!
YES.
DID I HEAR THE PHONE RING?
YES. SOME LADY CALLED AND ASKED ME A BUNCH OF QUESTIONS AND THEN SCREAMED AND HUNG UP.
KIRKMAN & SCOTT

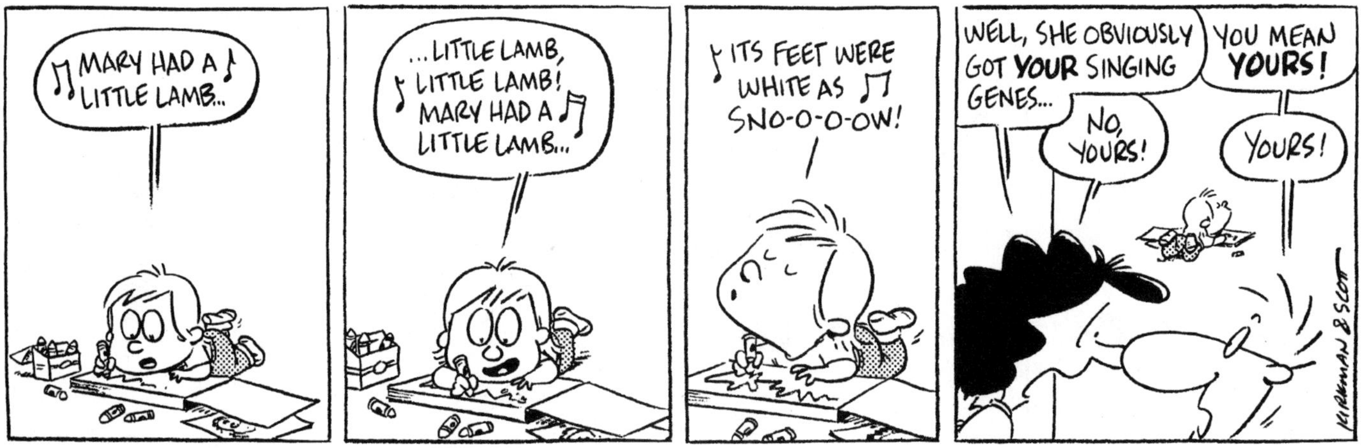
♫ MARY HAD A ♪ LITTLE LAMB...
...LITTLE LAMB, ♪ LITTLE LAMB! MARY HAD A ♫ LITTLE LAMB...
♪ ITS FEET WERE WHITE AS ♫ SNO-O-O-OW!
WELL, SHE OBVIOUSLY GOT **YOUR** SINGING GENES...
YOU MEAN **YOURS**!
NO, YOURS!
YOURS!
KIRKMAN & SCOTT

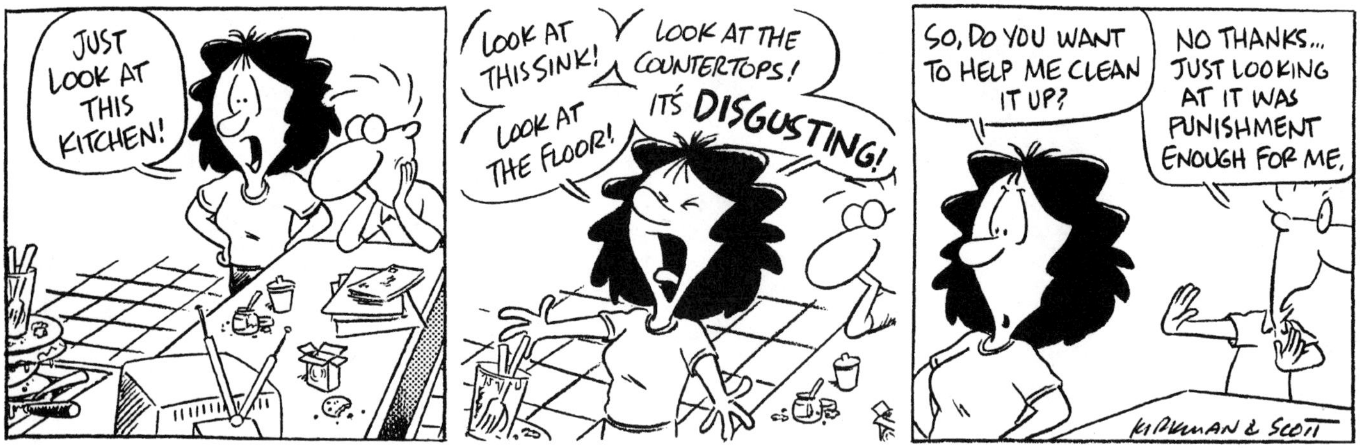
JUST LOOK AT THIS KITCHEN!
LOOK AT THIS SINK!
LOOK AT THE COUNTERTOPS!
LOOK AT THE FLOOR!
IT'S **DISGUSTING**!
SO, DO YOU WANT TO HELP ME CLEAN IT UP?
NO THANKS... JUST LOOKING AT IT WAS PUNISHMENT ENOUGH FOR ME.
KIRKMAN & SCOTT

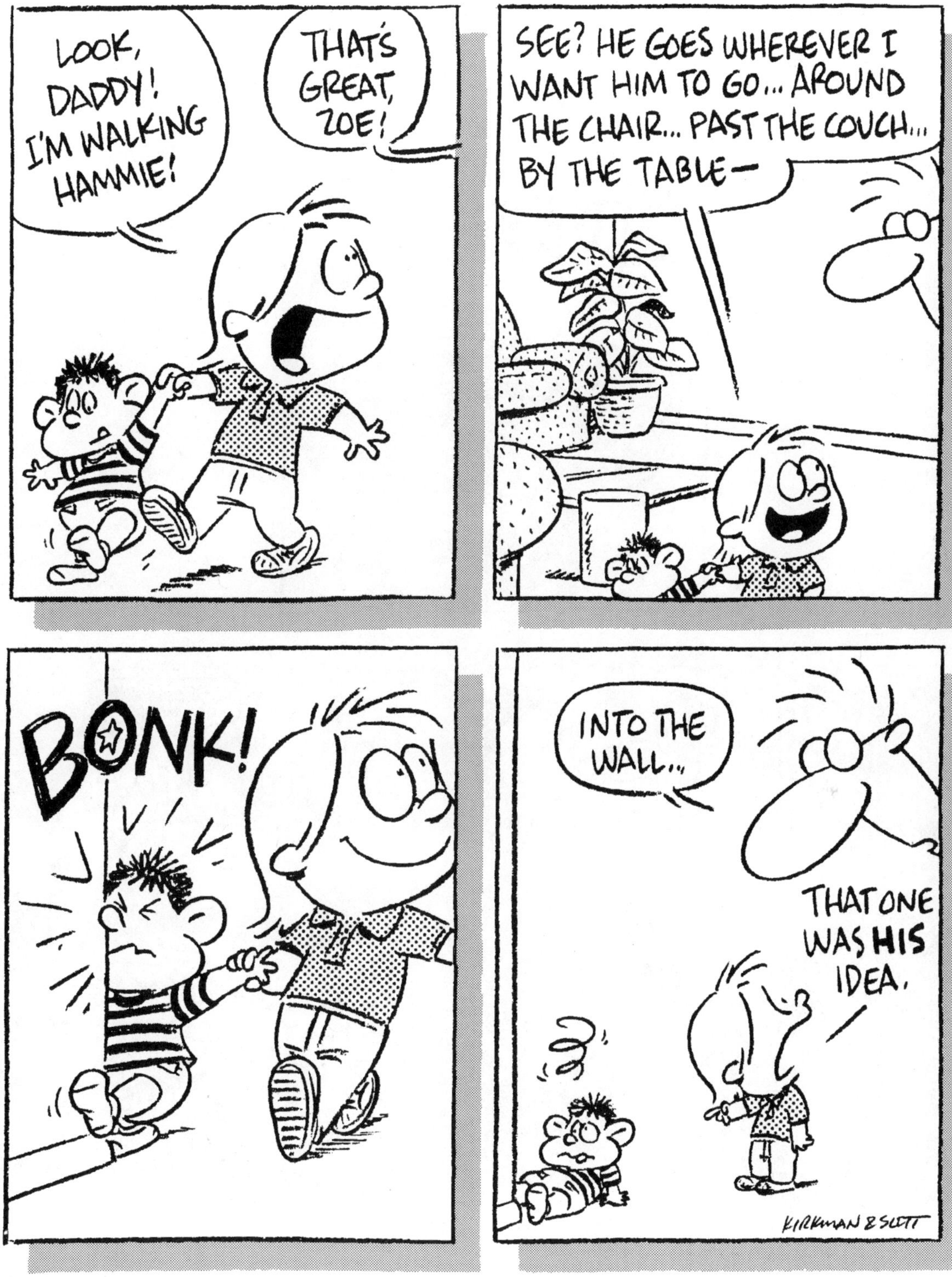

LOOK, DADDY! I'M WALKING HAMMIE!
THAT'S GREAT, ZOE!
SEE? HE GOES WHEREVER I WANT HIM TO GO... AROUND THE CHAIR... PAST THE COUCH... BY THE TABLE—
BONK!
INTO THE WALL...
THAT ONE WAS **HIS** IDEA.
KIRKMAN & SCOTT

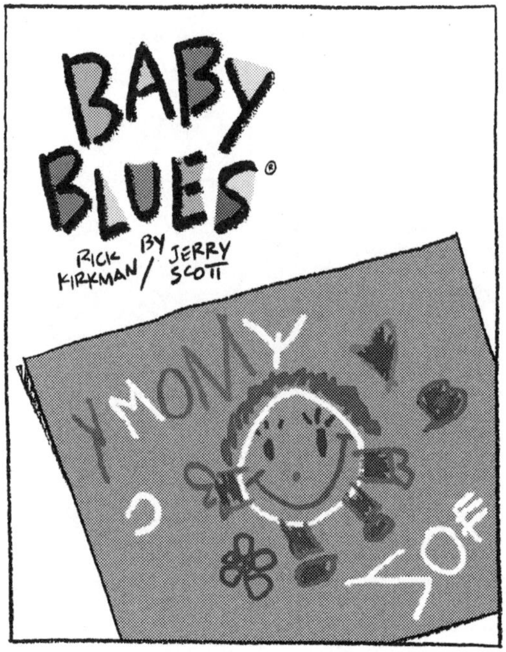
BABY BLUES®
RICK KIRKMAN / BY JERRY SCOTT

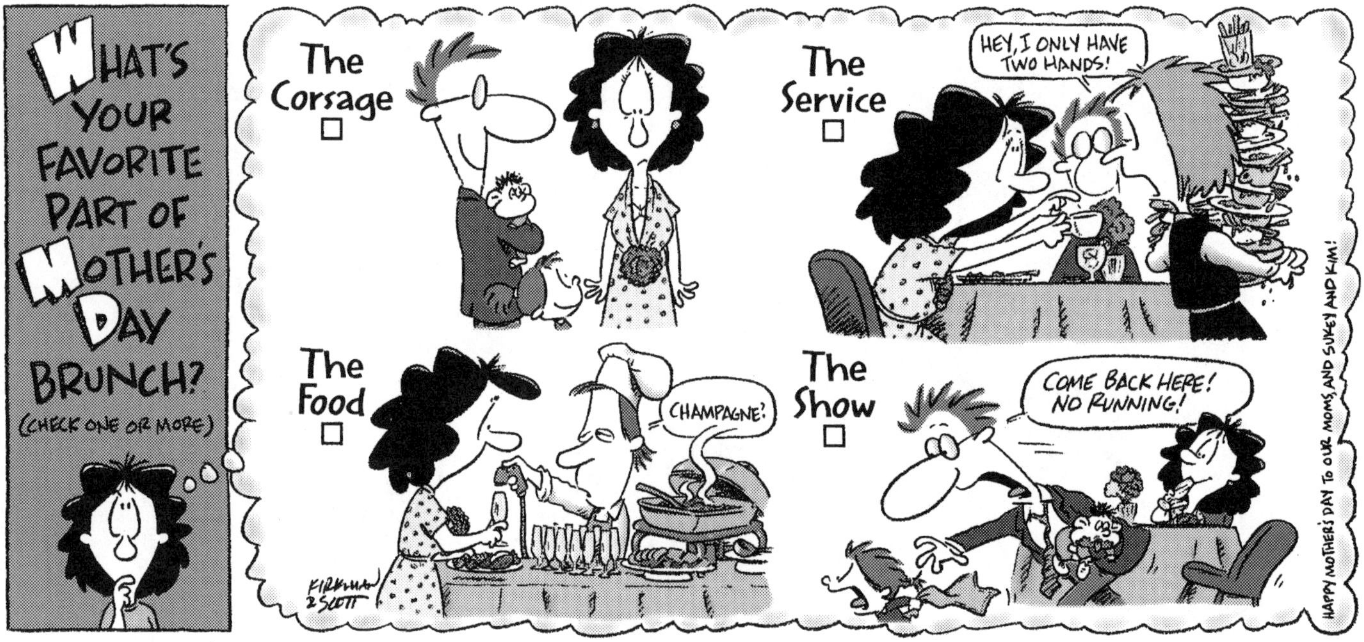
WHAT'S YOUR FAVORITE PART OF MOTHER'S DAY BRUNCH?
(CHECK ONE OR MORE)
The Corsage
The Service
HEY, I ONLY HAVE TWO HANDS!
The Food
CHAMPAGNE?
The Show
COME BACK HERE! NO RUNNING!
KIRKMAN & SCOTT
HAPPY MOTHER'S DAY TO OUR MOMS, AND SUKEY AND KIM!

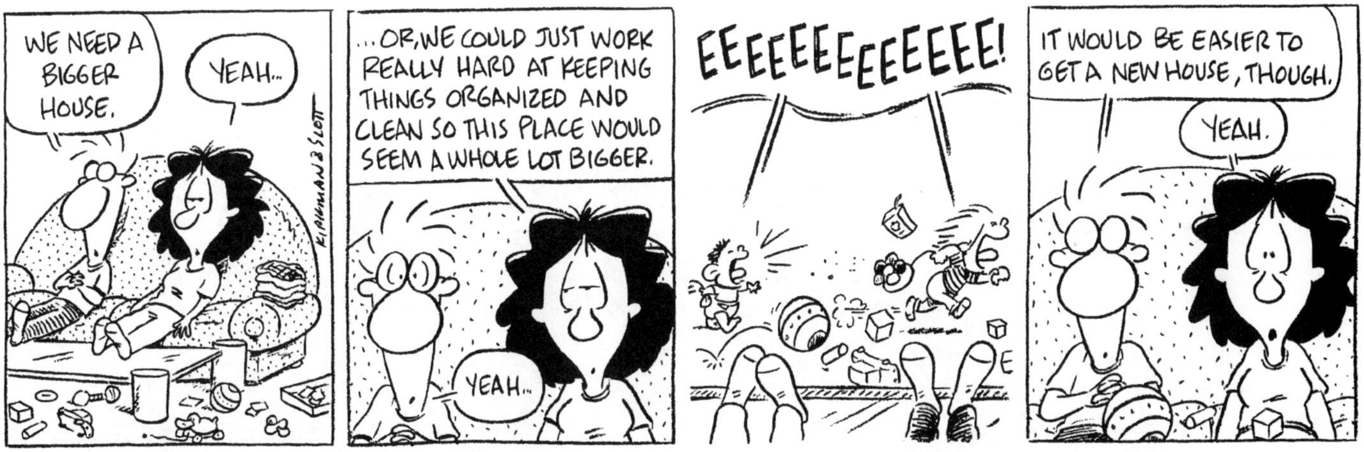
WE NEED A BIGGER HOUSE.
YEAH...
KIRKMAN & SCOTT
...OR, WE COULD JUST WORK REALLY HARD AT KEEPING THINGS ORGANIZED AND CLEAN SO THIS PLACE WOULD SEEM A WHOLE LOT BIGGER.
YEAH...
EEEEEEEEEEEEE!
IT WOULD BE EASIER TO GET A NEW HOUSE, THOUGH.
YEAH.

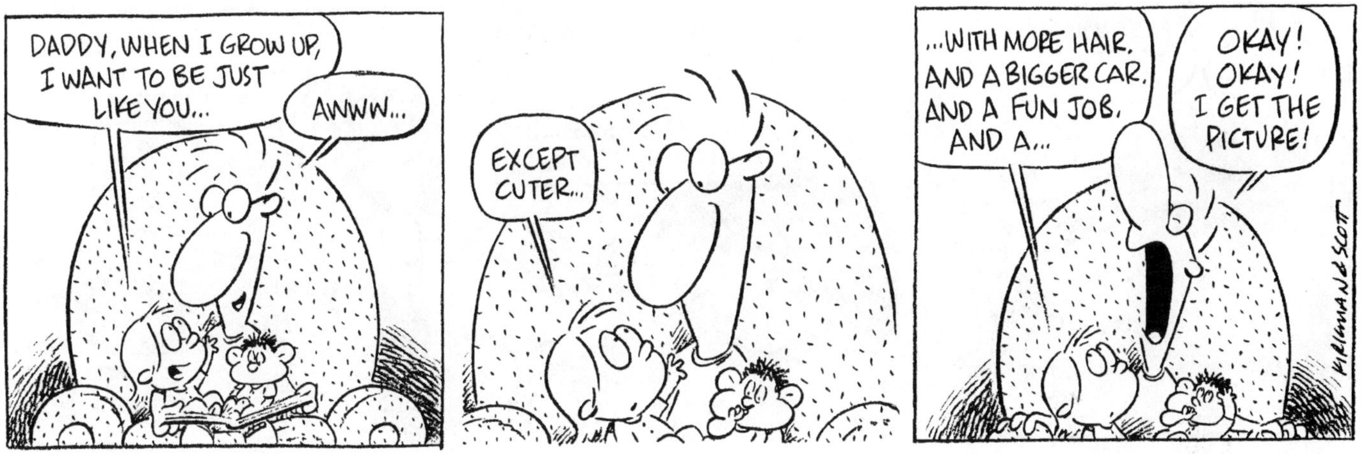
DADDY, WHEN I GROW UP, I WANT TO BE JUST LIKE YOU...
AWWW...
EXCEPT CUTER...
...WITH MORE HAIR. AND A BIGGER CAR. AND A FUN JOB. AND A...
OKAY! OKAY! I GET THE PICTURE!
KIRKMAN & SCOTT

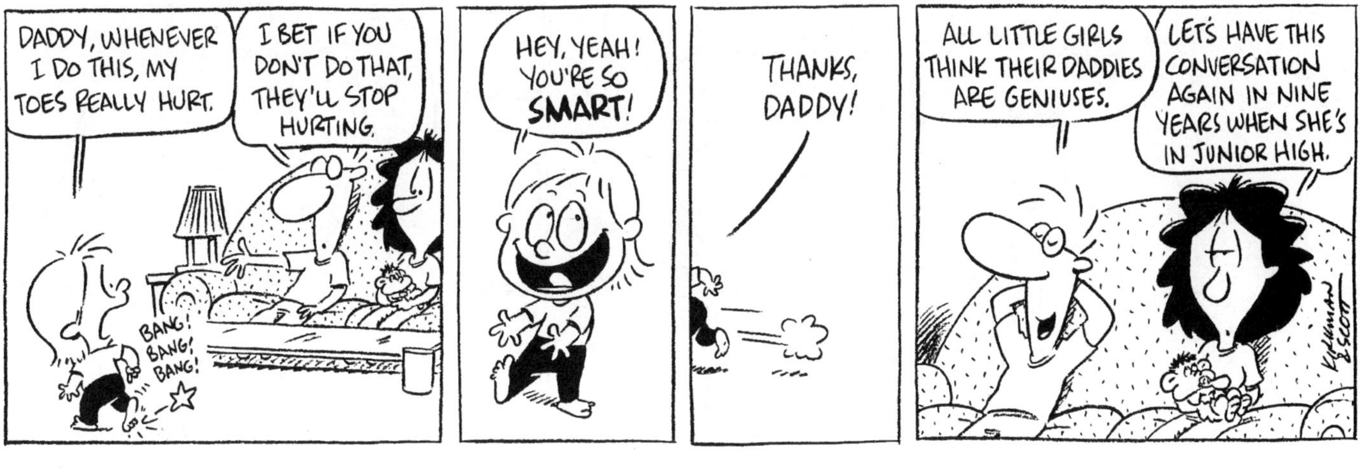
DADDY, WHENEVER I DO THIS, MY TOES REALLY HURT.
I BET IF YOU DON'T DO THAT, THEY'LL STOP HURTING.
BANG! BANG! BANG!
HEY, YEAH! YOU'RE SO SMART!
THANKS, DADDY!
ALL LITTLE GIRLS THINK THEIR DADDIES ARE GENIUSES.
LET'S HAVE THIS CONVERSATION AGAIN IN NINE YEARS WHEN SHE'S IN JUNIOR HIGH.
KIRKMAN & SCOTT

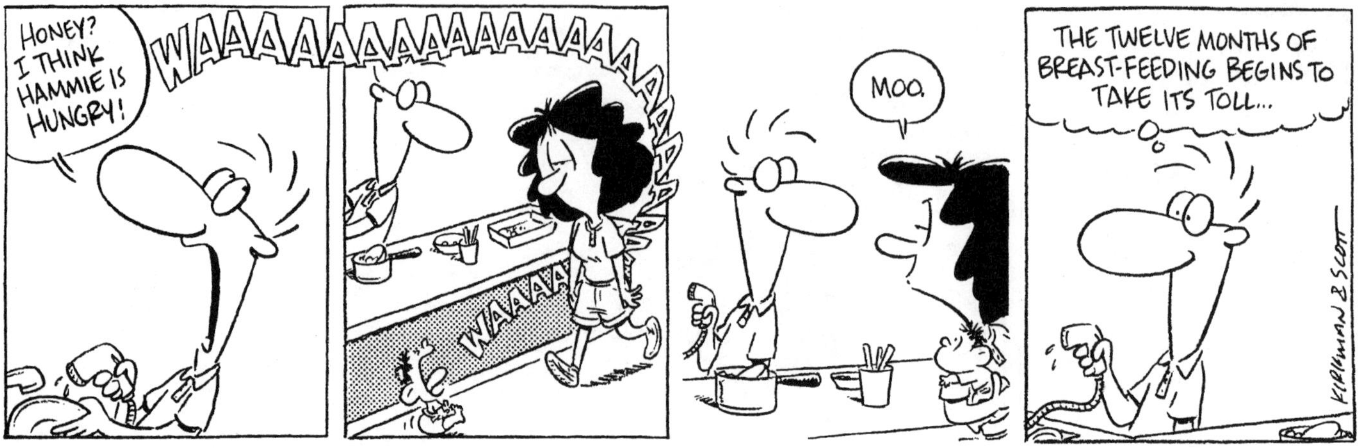
HONEY? I THINK HAMMIE IS HUNGRY!
WAAAAAAAAAAAAAAAAAAAA
WAAAA
MOO.
THE TWELVE MONTHS OF BREAST-FEEDING BEGINS TO TAKE ITS TOLL...
KIRKMAN & SCOTT

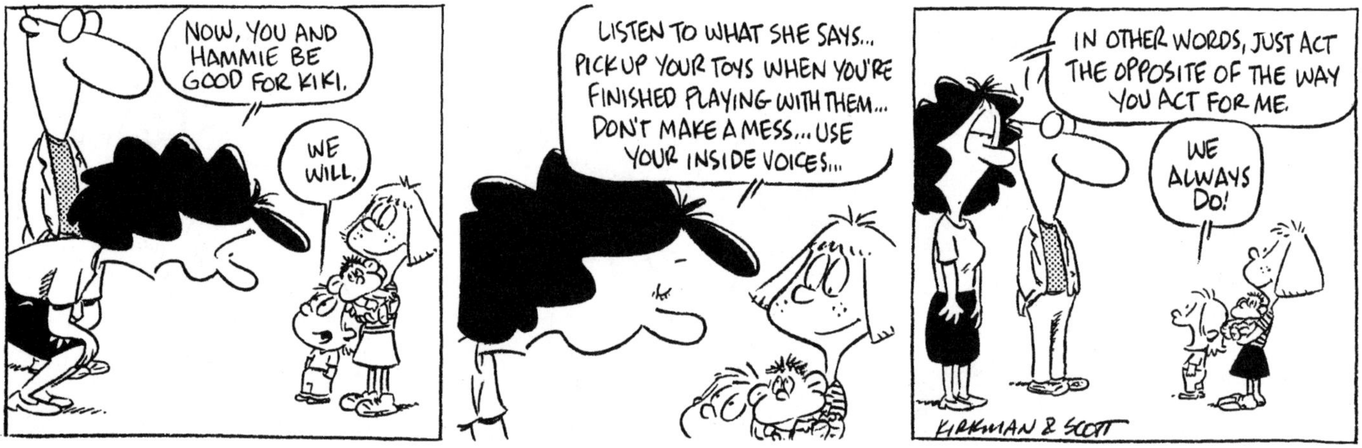
NOW, YOU AND HAMMIE BE GOOD FOR KIKI.
WE WILL.
LISTEN TO WHAT SHE SAYS... PICK UP YOUR TOYS WHEN YOU'RE FINISHED PLAYING WITH THEM... DON'T MAKE A MESS... USE YOUR INSIDE VOICES...
IN OTHER WORDS, JUST ACT THE OPPOSITE OF THE WAY YOU ACT FOR ME.
WE ALWAYS DO!
KIRKMAN & SCOTT

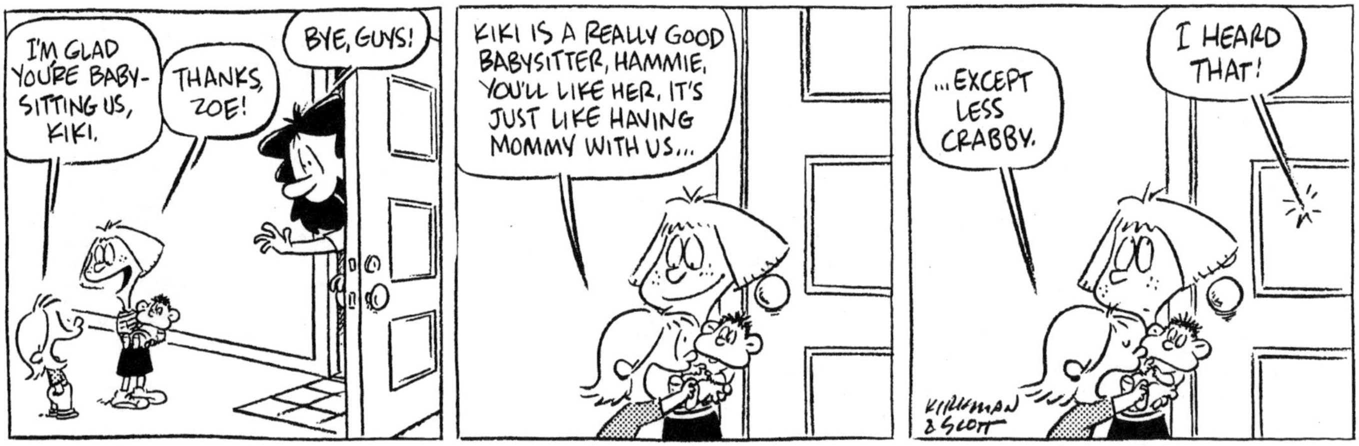
I'M GLAD YOU'RE BABY-SITTING US, KIKI.
THANKS, ZOE!
BYE, GUYS!
KIKI IS A REALLY GOOD BABYSITTER, HAMMIE. YOU'LL LIKE HER. IT'S JUST LIKE HAVING MOMMY WITH US...
...EXCEPT LESS CRABBY.
I HEARD THAT!
KIRKMAN & SCOTT

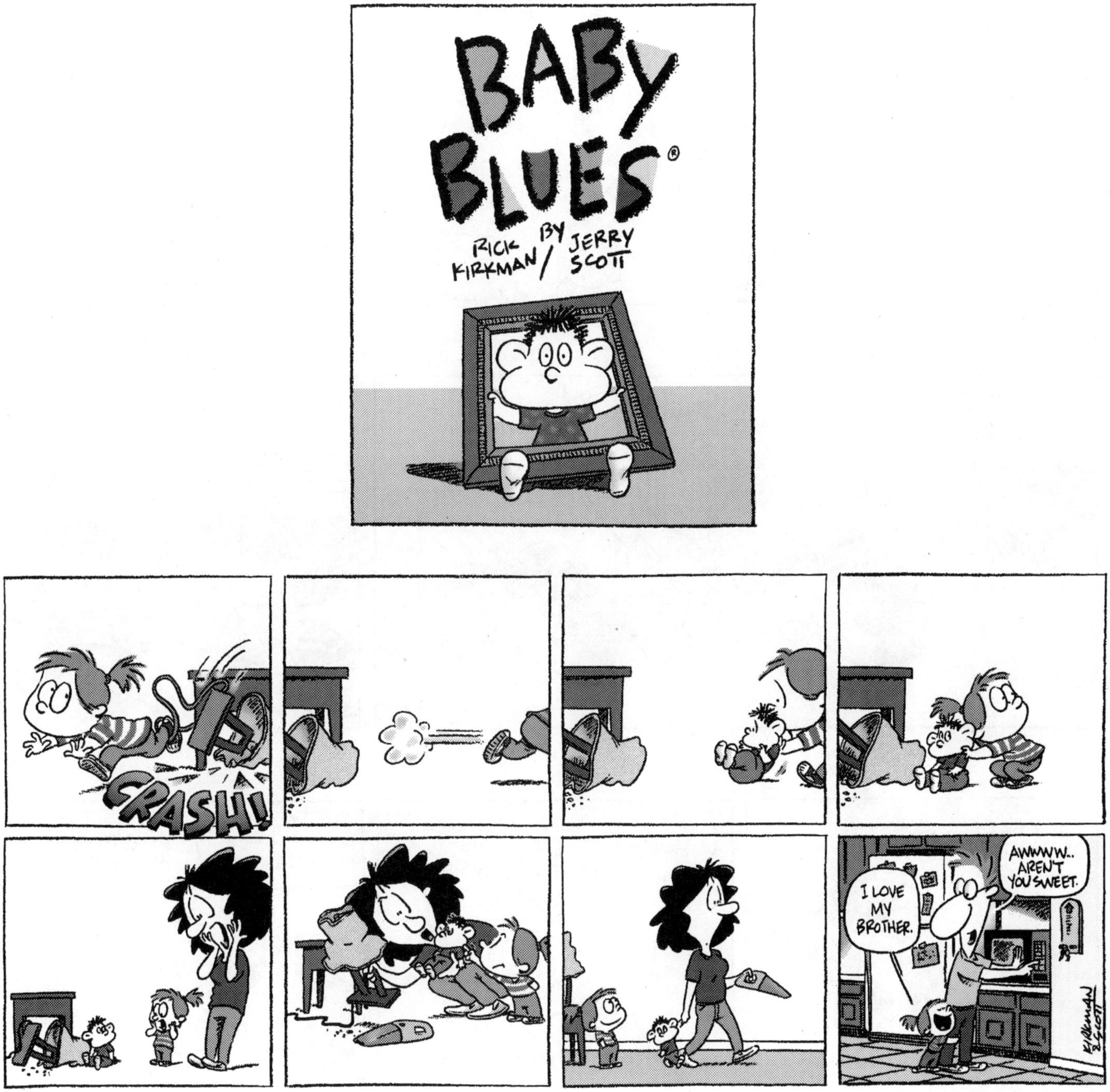
BABY BLUES®
BY RICK KIRKMAN / JERRY SCOTT
CRASH!
I LOVE MY BROTHER.
AWWWW.. AREN'T YOU SWEET.
KIRKMAN & SCOTT

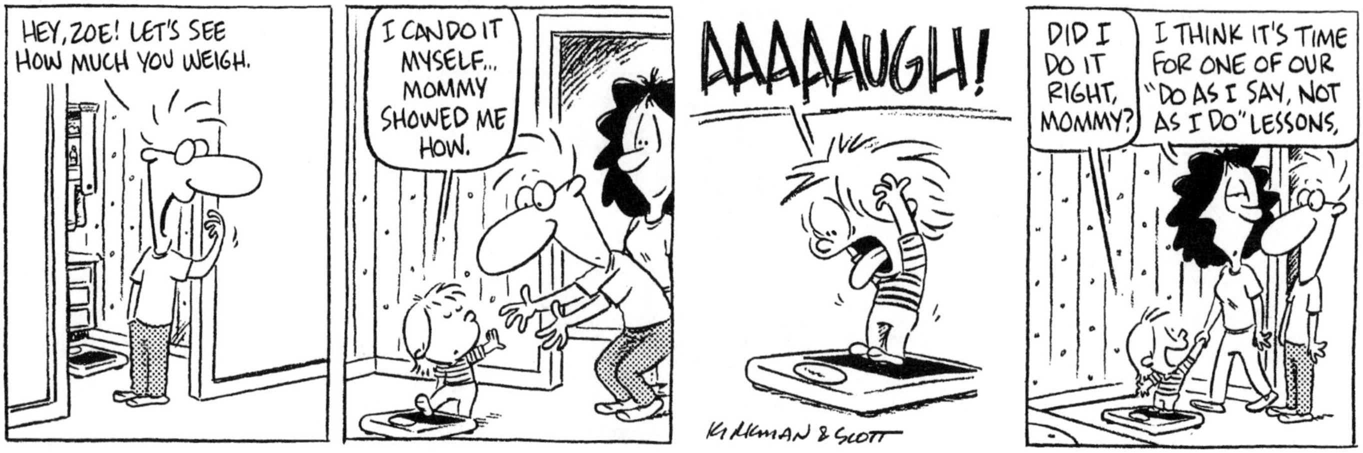
HEY, ZOE! LET'S SEE HOW MUCH YOU WEIGH.
I CAN DO IT MYSELF... MOMMY SHOWED ME HOW.
AAAAAUGH!
DID I DO IT RIGHT, MOMMY?
I THINK IT'S TIME FOR ONE OF OUR "DO AS I SAY, NOT AS I DO" LESSONS.
KIRKMAN & SCOTT

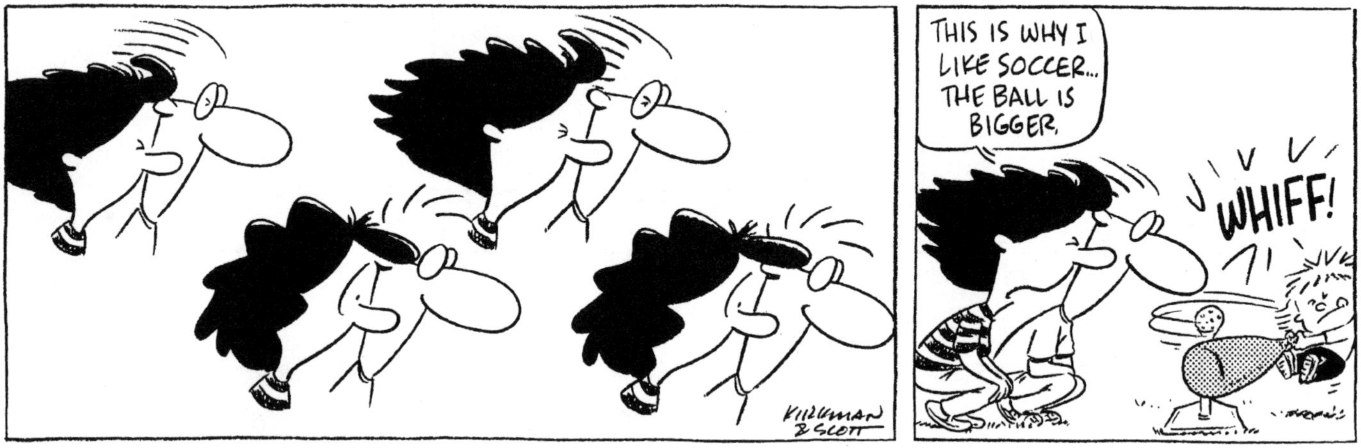
KIRKMAN & SCOTT
THIS IS WHY I LIKE SOCCER... THE BALL IS BIGGER.
WHIFF!

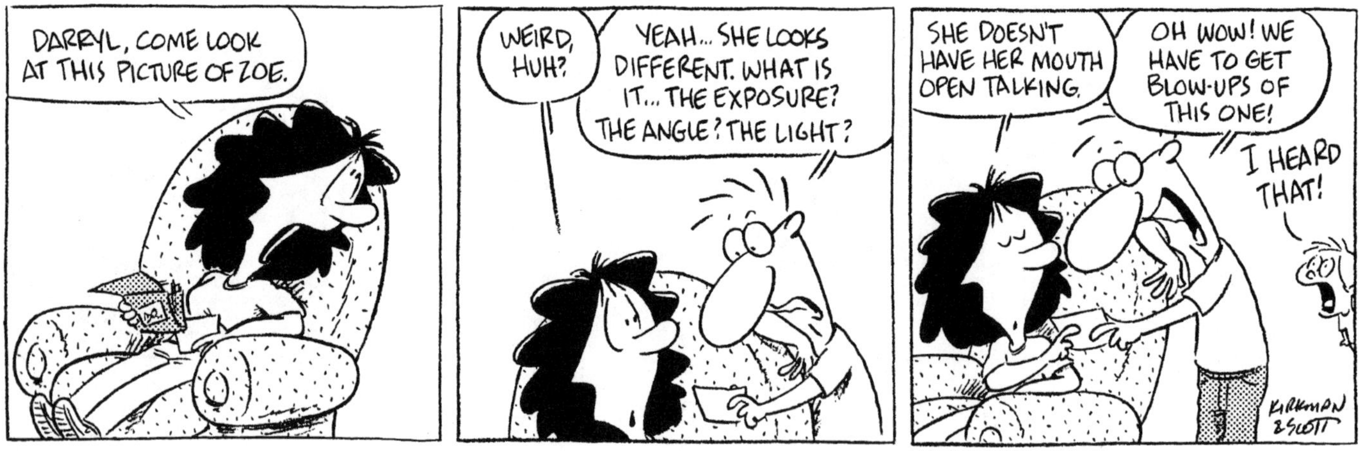
DARRYL, COME LOOK AT THIS PICTURE OF ZOE.
WEIRD, HUH?
YEAH... SHE LOOKS DIFFERENT. WHAT IS IT... THE EXPOSURE? THE ANGLE? THE LIGHT?
SHE DOESN'T HAVE HER MOUTH OPEN TALKING.
OH WOW! WE HAVE TO GET BLOW-UPS OF THIS ONE!
I HEARD THAT!
KIRKMAN & SCOTT

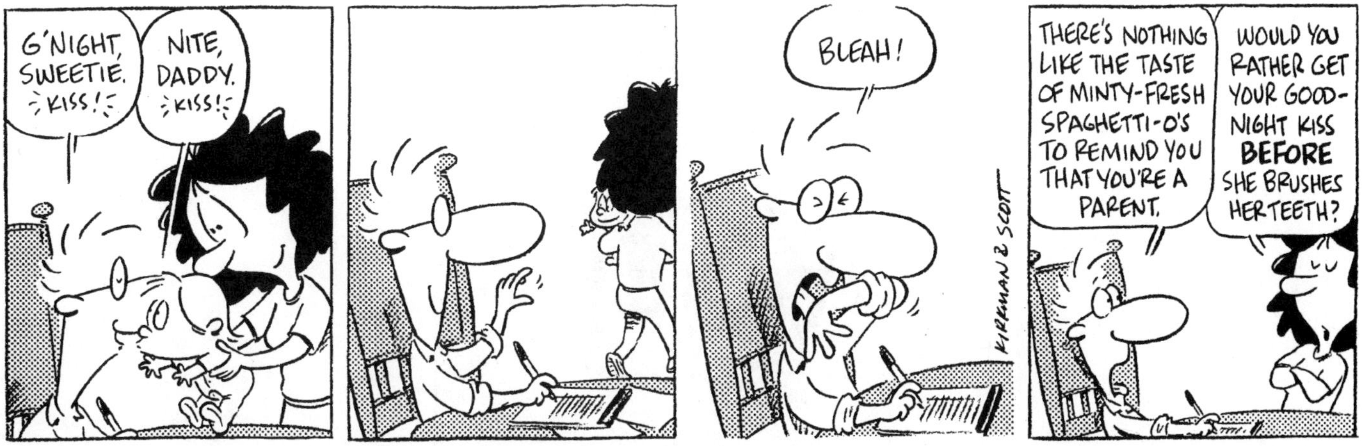
G'NIGHT, SWEETIE. KISS!
NITE, DADDY. KISS!
BLEAH!
KIRKMAN & SCOTT
THERE'S NOTHING LIKE THE TASTE OF MINTY-FRESH SPAGHETTI-O'S TO REMIND YOU THAT YOU'RE A PARENT.
WOULD YOU RATHER GET YOUR GOOD-NIGHT KISS **BEFORE** SHE BRUSHES HER TEETH?

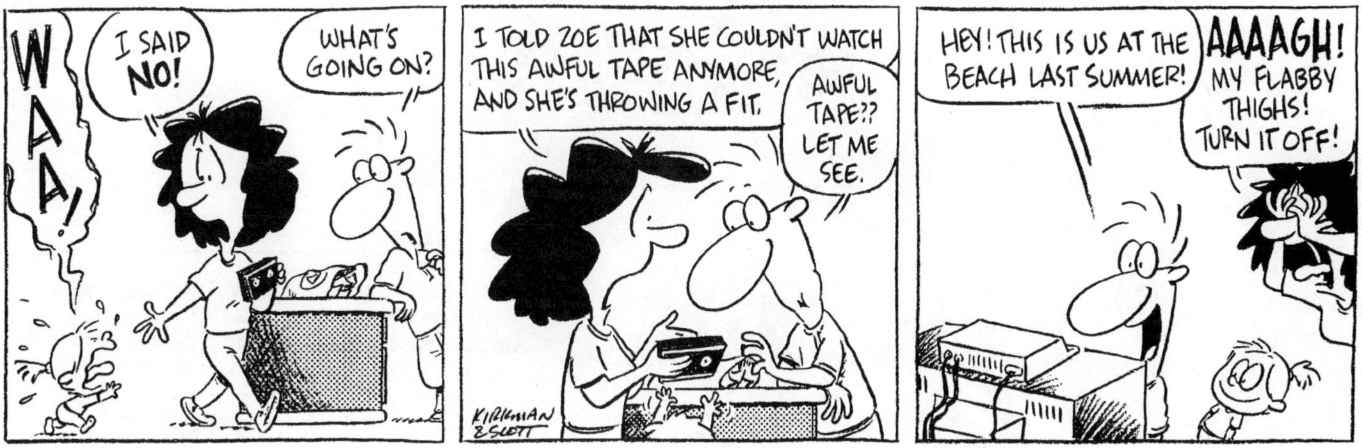
WAAA!
I SAID **NO!**
WHAT'S GOING ON?
KIRKMAN & SCOTT
I TOLD ZOE THAT SHE COULDN'T WATCH THIS AWFUL TAPE ANYMORE, AND SHE'S THROWING A FIT.
AWFUL TAPE?? LET ME SEE.
HEY! THIS IS US AT THE BEACH LAST SUMMER!
AAAAGH! MY FLABBY THIGHS! TURN IT OFF!

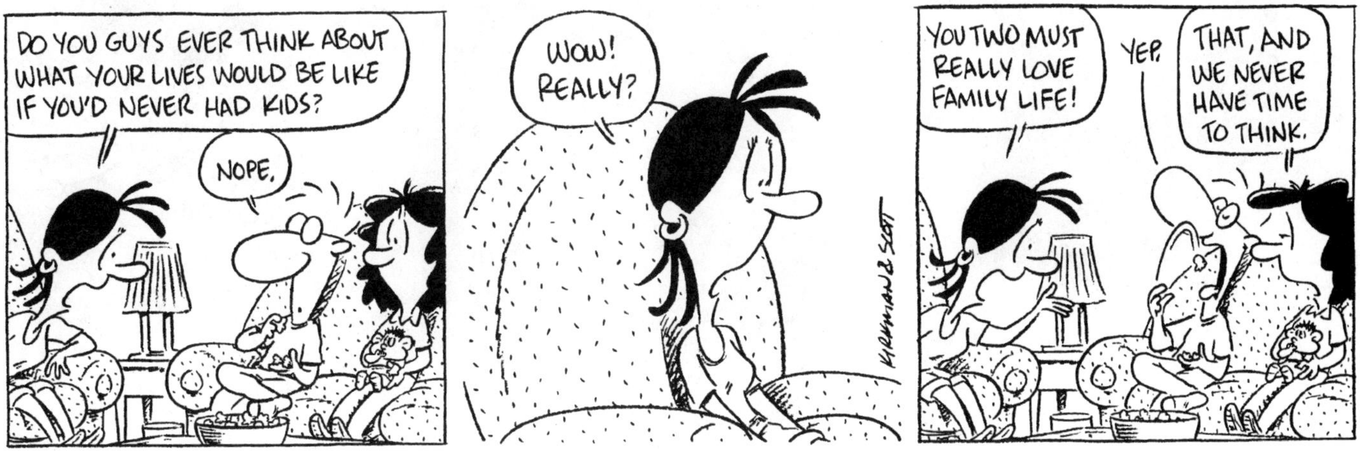
DO YOU GUYS EVER THINK ABOUT WHAT YOUR LIVES WOULD BE LIKE IF YOU'D NEVER HAD KIDS?
NOPE.
WOW! REALLY?
KIRKMAN & SCOTT
YOU TWO MUST REALLY LOVE FAMILY LIFE!
YEP.
THAT, AND WE NEVER HAVE TIME TO THINK.

BABY BLUES®
RICK KIRKMAN / BY / JERRY SCOTT

♪
HEY-Y-Y-Y!
WOW! HAVE YOU BEEN SHOPPING TODAY?
THOSE COLORS LOOK **GOOD** ON YOU! NICE! TRÉS CHIC. VER-R-Y HIP.
I DIDN'T EVEN KNOW THEY **MADE** MOTHER-DAUGHTER CAMOUFLAGE SUN DRESSES.
VERY FUNNY. NEXT TIME, **YOU'RE** FEEDING HIM THE STRAINED BEEF AND VEGETABLES.
INCOMING!
KIRKMAN&SCOTT